NETWORK RESPONSIBILITY

The contemporary landscape of transnational political economy is dominated by networks. Public and private networks, and networks that combine public and private actors, cross borders, they exert regulatory power, and their activities often harm third parties. However, tort law as a traditional source of remediation for third-party harms appears impotent when faced with the problem of regulating the 'society of networks'. This book, using a systems theory framework, retraces the emergence of tort law in modernity and highlights how two models of normative ascription – personal responsibility and organisational liability – have come to shape existing tort law's ambivalence towards network phenomena. This book breaks new ground by leaving behind the national-law 'frame of reference', drawing on the conceptual promise of EU law to develop a concept of 'network responsibility' for a network society, and lays the foundations of a tort law for the twenty-first century.

Rónán Condon is Assistant Professor in Private Law at Dublin City University, where he teaches contract, torts and commercial law. Previously, he was a researcher at the European Union Institute, and a visiting researcher at King's College London. His main research interests include sociological jurisprudence, contract and tort law, and their Europeanisation and transnationalisation.

Network Responsibility

EUROPEAN TORT LAW AND THE SOCIETY OF NETWORKS

RÓNÁN CONDON
Dublin City University

CAMBRIDGE
UNIVERSITY PRESS

CAMBRIDGE
UNIVERSITY PRESS

Shaftesbury Road, Cambridge CB2 8EA, United Kingdom

One Liberty Plaza, 20th Floor, New York, NY 10006, USA

477 Williamstown Road, Port Melbourne, VIC 3207, Australia

314–321, 3rd Floor, Plot 3, Splendor Forum, Jasola District Centre, New Delhi – 110025, India

103 Penang Road, #05–06/07, Visioncrest Commercial, Singapore 238467

Cambridge University Press is part of Cambridge University Press & Assessment, a department of the University of Cambridge.

We share the University's mission to contribute to society through the pursuit of education, learning and research at the highest international levels of excellence.

www.cambridge.org
Information on this title: www.cambridge.org/9781009054898

DOI: 10.1017/9781009051972

First published 2022

A catalogue record for this publication is available from the British Library

ISBN 978-1-316-51200-5 Hardback
ISBN 978-1-009-05489-8 Paperback

Contents

Acknowledgments *page* viii

Introduction 1

A Thinking in Networks 1

B Breaking Academic Frames of Reference 5

C Understanding Systems Theory as an Analytical 'Frame of Reference' rather than a Grand Theory 9

1 Tort Law from Individuals to Systems: Ladeur's Debt to Luhmann 9

2 Ladeur's Models of Modernity: Programmes and Paradigms 14

1 **Tort Law and the Society of Individuals** 29

A Introduction 29

B Re-programming the Law: The Contribution of Legal Science to an Acentric Legal Architecture 36

1 The Emergence of a Distinct and Subsidiary Tort Law: The Radiating Effect of the Will of the Parties and *Winterbottom v Wright* 41

2 Secondary Remodelling of Distributed 'Experience' through the Tort Standard of Care 45

C How Individualised Ascription Became a Normative Model for a General Law of Tort 51

1 Private Bureaucracy: The Doctrine of Vicarious Liability 51

2 Public Bureaucracy: A Public Law of Tort 54

D Conclusion 59

2 **Tort Law and the Society of Organisations** 61
A Introduction 61
B Cognitive Rupture and Organisational Responsibility 64
1 Materialised Social Responsibility: *Donoghue v Stevenson* 74
C The Eclipse of the Individual: Illustrations of the Turn to Organisational Liability 87
1 Product Liability *qua* Organisational Liability 88
2 The Slow Emergence of 'Enterprise Risk' Liability in the Common Law: Vicarious Liability 91
3 Direct Action against the State via Negligence: The Rise of the State *qua* Organisation 98
D Conclusion 114

3 **Currents and Counter-Currents in Contemporary Law** 116
A Introduction 116
B Cognitivisation in EU Law: De-differentiation in Legal Discourse 129
C Constitutions and Collisions: Against 'Hegemonic Programmes' or a Common Law for Europe 138
D Rights Balancing before the Court: Thinking through Non-commensurable Discourses 148
E Conclusion 154

4 **Re-norming Tort Law: From Network Rights to Network Remedies** 155
A Introduction 155
B The New Approach: The Emergence of Network Governance 158
1 A History of the New Approach: Building Network Governance 158
2 The *PIP* Imbroglio and *Schmitt*: Tort Law in the Spotlight 161
3 Of Bits and Pieces: The Emergence of the *Cupola* of Responsibility and Its Theoretical Consequences 174
4 Re-imagining *Francovich* State Liability 180
5 The Three-Track Liability Schemata: From Network Liability to Network Responsibility 192

C Beyond a Reconstruction of EU 'State Liability'? A Model for the Value Chain? 197
1 Between Individual and Organisational Liability in Tort 197
2 Beyond Individual and Organisational Responsibility in the Value Chain: Network Governance of the Supply Chain 208
D Conclusion 216

Conclusion 217

Index 223

Acknowledgments

This book is largely based on my PhD thesis submitted at the European University Institute, Florence, in 2017. Researching at the EUI was a formative experience both academically and socially, and it introduced me to new ways of seeing the world. I owe a particular debt of gratitude to Professor Hans Micklitz, who guided me through the process of writing the PhD, and beyond, and who cajoled and inspired me to think ambitiously and open-mindedly about tort law and much more besides. Professor Micklitz is a remarkable mentor and scholar, and has supported me, and many of my friends and colleagues, through his constant help and encouragement.

I would also like to thank my thesis defence panel – Professors Stefan Grundmann, Simon Deakin and Karl-Heinz Ladeur – for their insights and criticisms. The list of colleagues from whom I learned is very long, but thanks go to Yane Svetiev, Guido Comparato and Barend van Leeuven, in particular for their company and comradeship. Both Professors Roger Brownsword and Takis Tridimas have been generous and warm mentors.

Having left the EUI, I took up the position of Assistant Professor in Law at the School of Law and Government at Dublin City University. DCU is a young university and the School of Law and Government is lively and dynamic. I would like to thank my colleagues for their ongoing support, encouragement and assistance through the process of bringing this book to completion, especially Professors Gary Murphy, Iain McMenamin, Federico Fabbrini and Dr Aisling de Paor.

I am grateful to my parents, John and Angela, friends and family who have supported me throughout my researches. At Florence, Mihalis Dekastros and Colm Booth were a source of solace and support. At home, my partner Gréta has been the most wonderful and constant companion.

I am sure there are many mis-steps, and these belong to me. I hope this book has something genuinely distinct to offer. It is my attempt to move beyond the preoccupations of twentieth-century tort law.

Introduction

A THINKING IN NETWORKS

> But remember that words are signals, counters. They are not immortal. And it can happen . . . that a civilisation can be imprisoned in a linguistic contour which no longer matches the landscape of . . . fact.[1]

The new century is already twenty years old, but the old debates of the twentieth century still cast a long shadow over tort theory. This book in many ways is an attempt to go beyond the current academic debate in tort law by widening our vista in theoretical, methodological and conceptual terms. *Theoretically*, it breaks with mainstream tort law scholarship as it is neither a contribution to the philosophy of tort law nor the economic analysis of law. Instead, it opens a new theoretical line of enquiry by adopting insights from systems theory as its 'analytical frame of reference' to advance a theory of tort law beyond the state.[2] *Methodologically*, it engages in comparative theoretical investigations examining, first, the law France, the United Kingdom and the United States, before, secondly, moving from a comparative to a transnational orientation when confronting the role of tort law in the twenty-first century. The story that it tells is, I hope, a compelling and insightful one. The internal evolution of tort law from models of individual responsibility to organisational responsibility cannot be understood without reference to the broader social epistemologies in which tort law is embedded. The story is one of mutual

1 This phrase is taken from B Friel, *Translations: Selected Plays* (Washington, DC: Catholic University of America Press, 1984), 418, 419.

2 The book draws on both the path-breaking work of Niklas Luhmann and Karl-Heinz Ladeur; in particular, KH Ladeur, 'The Evolution of General Administrative Law and the Emergence of Postmodern Administrative Law', Osgoode CLPE Research Paper 16/2011; N Luhmann, *Law as a Social System* (Oxford: Oxford University Press, 2004).

feedback between law and society in which different knowledge paradigms – ways of seeing the world – have contributed, and also been influenced by, different models of responsibility.[3] Today, the society of networks forms the social epistemology of law and, it will be argued, tort law is, in bits and pieces, re-pivoting towards the society of networks. The final and *conceptual* contribution the book will make is to show how a new and distinctive form of responsibility – 'network responsibility' – is the best and most persuasive way to coherently braid these 'bits and pieces' into a new model of tort law for a new regime of liability beyond the state.

Making the case for network responsibility as an overall architecture for a new approach to tort law requires a reconstruction of tort law and its relationship with its wider social epistemologies. Therefore, once the theoretical 'frame of reference' has been established our attention turns to reconstructing the tort law of the nineteenth and twentieth centuries as giving rise to two models of responsibility – individual and organisational responsibility. The first two chapters are devoted to retracing and in some ways retelling the *evolution*[4] of modern tort law from its classical foundations through the twentieth century to the challenges facing tort law today.[5] In broad terms, they retrace the evolution of twentieth-century tort law from a paradigm of individual responsibility to a paradigm of *vertical* vicarious liability or organisational liability.[6] These models of responsibility, it will argued, cannot be divorced from broader transformations in the knowledge base of society. The common threads in this analysis will be drawn out through a sustained focus on product

3 This is not based on what systems theory characterises as an input–output model, but rather on autopoiesis of the legal system where the law reacts reflexively to changes in its environment. See Ladeur (n 2) .

4 *Compare* A Brudner, *The Unity of the Common Law* (Oxford: Oxford University Press, 2013). Unlike Brudner, I do not argue in Hegelian terms that the law renders itself pure by unfolding its internal contradictions dialectically towards an ideal of freedom. A systems theory account distinguishes system and environment, and contingency rather than progression is the driver of evolution.

5 See G Teubner, '"And if I by Beelzebub cast out Devils, . . .": An Essay on the Diabolics of Network Failure' (2009) 10(4) *German Law Journal* 397, referring to the problem of reticular or network irresponsibility.

6 G Teubner, 'The Invisible Cupola: From Causal to Collective Attribution in Ecological Liability' in G Teubner, L Farmer & Declan Murphy (eds), *Environmental Law and Ecological Responsibility: The Concept and Practice of Ecological Self-Organization* (Chichester: Wiley, 1994), 17. 'With "vertical" vicarious liability in hierarchical organizations, employers are made responsible for the actions of their employees. Here the law, by imputing causation where no causal link can actually be proven, makes one individual vicariously responsible "horizontally", for wrongs that have been committed by some other members of a group of actors.' For the term organisational liability, see G Brüggemeier, *Common Principles of Tort Law: A Pre-Statement of Law* (London: BIICL, 2004).

liability and state liability considered as illustrative of broader reorientations within tort law.[7] The first two chapters recount the rise of individual responsibility as a form of liability appropriate to a 'society of individuals' and how it was supplemented by secondary remodelling of tort law in the course of the twentieth century by organisational responsibility as a second and self-standing model of legal responsibility. This evolution will be retraced by examining public bureaucracy (the state) and private bureaucracy (the firm), in which it will be argued that whatever the precise doctrinal designation, organisational responsibility is the most plausible account of the tort liability regime that developed. On the public side, I will examine English and French law in particular,[8] with the *Anns* decision in the United Kingdom and *Feutry* in France representing key turning points in the march of organisational responsibility. Twentieth-century courts viewed the activities of subcontractors in terms of a delegation of public activities and, as such, that public authorities should be held liable either for negligence or on the doctrinal basis of breach of statutory duty. This is the public face, as it were, of organisational liability. Thus, on an organisational model, the real addressee of liability ought to be the state. This mirrors developments on the private side, so to speak, as like the employer in vicarious liability or the firm in the case of product liability, the state was ultimately imputed responsibility when that risk materialised in harm. Organisational liability might be understood as a 'secondary normative remodelling' of tort law that made it more reflexively oriented for a society of (hierarchical) organisations.[9] None of these changes could have been conceived or realised without reference to changing ideas of risk.[10] However, while two distinct models of liability have developed, they tend to inadequately grasp the contemporary 'landscape of fact'.

7 In other words, quite apart from the codifications of product liability law, the development of the tort of negligence in the twentieth century can be understood in these terms. Brüggemeier (n 6). So, incidentally, can developments within contract and corporate law. This is because all areas of private law have reacted in a dynamic and contingent way to their environment.

8 But not exclusively. Important US pivotal judgments will be examined as well, eg *MacPherson v Buick Motor Co*, 217 NY 382, 111 NE 1050 (1916); *Escola v Coca Cola Bottling Co*, 24 Cal2d 453, 150 P2d 436 (1944). The United Kingdom, apart from being the major legal system I am most familiar with, is also a good example of a legal system where the individualistic model has the most lasting impact, especially at a scholarly level; see P Benson, 'Misfeasance as an Organizing Normative Idea in Private Law' (2010) 60 *University of Toronto Law Journal* 731. For this reason, it is a good testing ground for our argument.

9 See Ladeur (n 2). That is, a society of rational organisation. We will develop the concept of secondary normative remodelling later in our theoretical framework section, Section C.

10 F Ewald (S Utz trans), 'The Return of Descartes Malicious Daemon: An Outline of the Philosophy of Precaution' in T Baker & J Simon (eds), *Embracing Risk: The Changing Culture of Insurance and Responsibility* (Chicago, IL: University of Chicago Press, 2002), 273.

As we enter the society of networks, the existing models of tortious responsibility are failing to adequately respond to their environment. Networks, and their governance, do not respect national boundaries and so the focus of our investigations turn to the context of the EU legal order. Understood as an *avant garde* experiment in transnational governance, it is the site for developing a theory of network responsibility.[11] It will be shown how the inchoate beginnings of an idea of network responsibility can, indeed, already be detected. Today, in the context of EU law, while the hard and fast distinction between public and private is blurring, effacing even, the models of both individual and organisational responsibility are strained. They are strained because neither model of liability adequately reflects the societal knowledge base, which has migrated from organisations to networks. These networks, unlike in the society of organisations, cannot neatly divide into public and private spheres. Secondly, the society of networks is also a society of risk in which classical understandings of causation become increasingly difficult to apply to harms occasioned by 'network failures'.[12] Thirdly, networks have broken out of the frame of the territorial state and, it is argued, a form of liability law that takes the concept of network as its 'frame of reference' in a multi-level legal order is required. This line of reasoning will be pursued in Chapters 3 and 4 with specific focus on the New Approach to Technical Standards (NATS) which is a characteristic example of 'network governance'[13] in a risk society.[14] Ultimately, it will be argued that what is now required is a concept of network responsibility for network failures, which is normative in substance, and represents an overall cupola for which individual responsibility and organisational liability form constituent elements. In the final chapter, it will be demonstrated how by recasting and reimagining *Francovich* liability, expanding on how its principles have already been applied to both public and private actors, it can be repurposed as a new form of secondary liability within an overarching concept of network responsibility, which can contribute to rethinking tort liability, more generally, in a transnational society of networks.

[11] See, seminally, KH Ladeur, 'Towards a Legal Theory of Supranationality – the Viability of the Network Concept' (1997) 3(1) *European Law Journal* 33, 44.

[12] See Teubner (n 5).

[13] Indeed, it will be argued that thinking in terms of public and private is not an adequate theoretical frame of reference; see GP Calliess & P Zumbansen, *Rough Consensus and Running Code* (Oxford: Hart Publishing, 2012).

[14] See U Beck (M Ritter trans), *Risk Society: Towards a New Modernity* (London: Sage, 1992), esp part 1.

TABLE 0.1. *The transformation of tort law in the context of the transformation of society*

Modernity	Tort law	Model of liability	Case law examples
Society ofindividuals (nineteenth century)	Individual wrongdoing: moralistic	Individual responsibility	*Winterbottom v Wright; Geddis v Bann Reservoir*
Society of organisations (twentieth century)	Strict(er) liability (risk creation)	Organisational responsibility	*Anns v Merton LBC; Donoghue v Stevenson*
Society of networks (twenty-first century)	Liability for risk enhancement	Network responsibility: network liability, organisational liability and network liability as components	*Francovich liability Schmitt*

These preliminary observations can be presented in the form of a matrix (Table 0.1), which forms the entry-point and foreshadows the argument to come.[15]

The rest of the chapter will be devoted to explaining how I reached this position on contemporary tort law. It will distinguish a systems theory frame of reference from those more commonly associated with tort theory. Then its basic assumptions will be outlined before returning to the main argument about how European law offers the promise of law of torts for a society of networks.

B BREAKING ACADEMIC FRAMES OF REFERENCE

Tort law is in many ways a subject revitalised due to the processes of Europeanisation and globalisation of law. The process of Europeanisation has provoked scholars of private law to once more focus on the question of legal evolution and the social embeddedness of private law.[16] This 'irritates'

15 See Ladeur (n 2).

16 N Jansen & R Michaels, 'Private Law and the State: Comparative Perceptions and Historical Observations' in N Jansen & R Michaels (eds), *Beyond the State: Rethinking Private Law* (Tübingen: Mohr Siebeck, 2008), 15; D Caruso, 'The Missing View of the Cathedral: The Private Law Paradigm of European Integration' (1997) 3(1) *European Law Journal* 3. On embeddedness, classically, see K Polanyi, *The Great Transformation: The Political and Economic Origins of Our Time* (Boston, MA: Beacon Press, 2001, orig 1944).

private law theory that for a long time has been in the grip of what White describes as 'neoconceptualism' – primarily, the seemingly intractable debate between legal economists and moral philosophers of tort law.[17] In the debate, stripped back to its most essential assumptions, moral philosophers build their model of tort law around the individual, and their obligations in accordance with a theory of individual right and reciprocity, while legal economists focus on aggregative individual preferences, largely arguing how tort law does or should correspond to economic efficiency. In this respect, they argue for tort law's function as a proxy for contract when transaction costs prevent *ex ante* voluntary exchange from taking place.[18]

Our starting point, inspired by systems theory, is different. To be sure, individual and aggregative concerns are germane to tort law, hence the impasse in scholarship. Our point can be summarised quickly: there is no law of torts *in abstracto*, which requires explanation. Instead, tort law is a dynamic and contingent system. Earlier common law theorists grasped this insight. As Holmes argued:

> What has been said will explain the failure of all theories which consider the law only from its formal side; whether they attempt to deduce the corpus from *a priori* postulates, or fall into the humbler error of supposing the science of the law to reside in the *elegantia juris*, or logical cohesion of part with part. The truth is, that the law is always approaching, and never reaching, consistency. It is forever adopting new principles from life at one end, and it always retains old ones from history at the other, which have not yet been absorbed or sloughed off. It will become entirely consistent only when it ceases to grow.[19]

It is well-known that while Holmes pointed to the 'bricolage' of the common law, he went on to provide his own formal theory dividing tort law neatly into negligence, strict liability and intentional torts.[20] Nevertheless, he was at least cognisant of the importance of the diachronic dimension to law to

[17] GE White, *Tort Law in America: An Intellectual History* (New York: Oxford University Press, 1980). It is also 'parochial', even if it seems to make 'universalist' claims; see B Bix, 'The Promise and Problems of Universal, General Theories of Contract Law' (2017) 30(4) *Ratio Juris* 391–402.

[18] R Cooter & T Ulen, *Law and Economics* 6th ed (Boston, MA: Pearson, 2012).

[19] OW Holmes, *The Common Law* (1881; reprint New York: Barnes & Noble, 2004), 36. This common law tradition stretches back to Coke's 'artificial reason of the law', noted by Luhmann (n 2), 311–12.

[20] White (n 17) focuses on Holmes' place in American legal scholarship as a bridge, as it were, between Langdellian formalism and legal realism. More recently, Holmes has been claimed by those who advocate naturalism for his supposed classical realism. See B Leiter, 'Holmes, Nietzsche and Classical Realism' (2000) University of Texas School of Law Publications Law

furnish a good explanation of current law and its various apparent inconsistencies in objectives not to mention the 'real' social problems that legal changes were responding to. What the existing approaches in moral theory of tort law lack, it is submitted, is a focus on this practical dimension, suggesting either that these questions are beyond the province of private law or that a pre-political private law has precedence over them.[21] Law and economics (or economic analysis of law – EAL), on the other hand, offers an instrumental theory of private law suggesting it is merely a tool in a regulatory arsenal that might serve in a complementary fashion to public regulation.[22] Whereas public regulation is one way to achieve regulatory objectives, private law is an institutional complement to these ends. In the radical form of this argument, private law, tort law in our case, is public law in disguise.[23] Yet, as the legal pluralists of tort law have shown, neither theory seems to 'fit' tort law on its own terms.[24] Fit is achieved at the expense of some questionable stretching of existing doctrines,[25] reformulations that seem to

Working Paper No 003. For 'bricolage' see N Simmonds, 'Bluntness and Bricolage' in H Gross & R Harrison (eds), *Jurisprudence: Cambridge Essays* (Oxford: Clarendon Press, 1992), 1.

21 H Dagan & A Dorfman, 'The Justice of Private Law' (unpublished manuscript, 24 July 2015), make a valiant effort to incorporate such a perspective into tort law. Their argument is that the justice that tort law embodies is relational. To simplify, while formal equality is often a good proxy for substantive autonomy as self-determination (what they claim to be the normative ends of a liberal, as distinct from libertarian private law), it is not always so. As such, modification is required to ensure 'real' (material), as distinct from 'abstract' justice is done. Heavy reliance is , at least implicitly, placed on Durkheim's theory of social interdependence. While it is cited, the link between organic solidarity and private law is not explored overtly, although it would appear that the notion of relational justice can be read as at least similar to solidarity.

22 S Shavell, 'Strict Liability versus Negligence' (1985) 9(1) *Journal of Legal Studies* 1.

23 L Green, 'Tort Law as Public Law in Disguise' (1959–60) 38 *Texas Law Review* 257. Cafaggi has helpfully distinguished between 'functional equivalence' and 'functional complementarity'; see F Cafaggi, 'A Coordinated Approach to Regulation and Civil Liability in European Law: Rethinking Institutional Complementarities' in F Cafaggi (ed), *The Institutional Framework of European Private Law* (Oxford: Oxford University Press, 2006), 191. The radical version seems to blur into functional equivalence per his terminology. As we see it, Teubner has described the dark side of functional equivalence when noting the problem of the over-socialisation of law. See G Teubner, 'After Legal Instrumentalism? Strategic Models of Post-Regulatory Law' in G Teubner (ed), *Dilemmas of Law in the Welfare State* (Berlin: de Gruyter, 1986), 299.

24 G Schwartz, 'Mixed Theories of Tort Law: Affirming Both Deterrence and Corrective Justice' (1996–97) 75 *Texas Law Review* 1801; G Schwartz, 'Reality in the Economic Analysis of Tort Law: Does Tort Law Really Deter?' (1994) 42 *UCLA Law Review* 377; C Robinette, 'Can There Be a Unified Theory of Torts? A Pluralist Suggestion from History and Doctrine' (2004–5) 43 *Brandeis Law Journal* 369. More recently, see J Goudkamp & J Murphy, 'The Failure of Universal Theories of Tort Law' (2015) 21 *Legal Theory* 47–85, persuasively debunking EAL, and rights theories.

25 E Weinrib, *The Idea of Private Law* (Oxford: Oxford University Press, 1995). His explanation of the doctrine of strict liability, *eg* vicarious liability, seems unconvincing. See Robinette's

ignore the actual history of their development,[26] or through marginalising developments in the law[27] and, in particular, by ignoring the way courts justify their development.[28] Indeed, Lord Hoffmann describes this as a tension in tort law between individual wrongdoing and compensation as social justice that is not fully reconciled. This fits into a pluralist understanding of the tort system. It is worthy of extended quotation:[29]

> the law of negligence attempts simultaneously to pursue two quite different objectives. The first is to attribute responsibility on the basis of moral fault and the second is to award compensation by way of redistribution of loss. Responsibility on the basis of moral fault requires that one should have regard to the actual physical and mental ability of the defendant as far as it is practically possible to do so . . .. But redistribution of loss is a matter of social justice which does not require any moral fault at all. It depends upon the proposition that it would be fairer for the loss to be allocated to the insurers or customers of the enterprise which caused it than to be borne by the victim alone. And since no moral fault is required, it does not matter that the defendant was doing his individual best. The question is simply whether his conduct fell below whatever standard the law prescribes for the protection of the plaintiff.[30]

That a celebrated judge should point to the diverse aims of tort law is largely ignored by neo-conceptualist theories of tort law favouring an approach that, like their scholastic antecedents, largely places a gloss on tort law. But, then, what do we propose in its stead? With a reading of tort law inspired by systems

criticism in CJ Robinette, 'Can There Be a Unified Theory of Torts? A Pluralist Suggestion from History and Doctrine' (2005) 43 *Brandeis Law Journal* 369.

26 Ignoring how, for example, product liability law was theorised first in terms of loss spreading by, *eg*, Fleming James and how the intellectual drive here was legal realists on the progressive left who pointed to the real-world inequalities that tort law reinforced. White (n 17).

27 Coleman's strategy in *Risk and Wrongs* regarding market share liability pushing it to the 'periphery' of tort law. J Coleman, 'Justifiable Departures from Corrective Justice' in *Risks and Wrongs* (New York: Cambridge University Press, 1992), 386–406.

28 W Lucy, 'Method and Fit: Two Problems for Contemporary Philosophies of Tort Law' (2007) 52 *McGill Law Journal* 605. In law and economics, the infamous 'surface froth' accusation, but Lucy is equally scathing of certain moral philosophical accounts of tort law that purport to take an 'internal point of view' but then largely ignore it or take the perspective of certain participants to the exclusion of others without a clear reason for doing so. As an addendum, it might be argued that in a practice such as tort law that has developed over time, the field is inevitably contested, such that it might be implausible to speak of a singular 'internal point of view': tort law is simply not that homogeneous or is no longer so.

29 G Williams, 'The Aims of the Law of Tort' (1951) 4(1) *Current Legal Problems* 137; today, this approach has been rendered more sophisticated by adopting the concept of pluralism.

30 L Hoffmann, 'Anthropomorphic Justice: The Reasonable Man and His Friends' (1995) 29 *Law Teacher* 127, 130.

theory, are we not culpable of exactly what we criticise, namely, placing yet another gloss on tort law – indeed, it might be argued, one that is considerably more obscure and abstract than the valiant attempts of the systematisers? I argue that the 'added value', as it were, of an approach informed by systems theory is to better conceptualise the fact that tort law is a 'historical machine', which has developed layers of complexity remodelling itself to changes in the knowledge base of society.[31] From this perspective, the controversy that Lord Hoffmann touches on in the earlier quote is the evolutionary pressures placed on tort law by the development of the 'practical knowledge base' of society from one of individuals to one of organisations. Before examining this evolution more closely in Chapters 1 and 2, the basic features of our theoretical standpoint will be unpacked. Once unpacked, it should be apparent that this approach locates tort law in the more general evolution of society in modernity.[32] This meta-theory aims to provide an analytical frame of reference through which tort law can be reconstructed and provides, it is submitted, an instructive and original lens through which to view and conceptualise contemporary tort law. These latter theme will be developed in chapters 3 and 4. Thus, by adopting a systems theory approach, which stresses tort law as a system in a dynamic and contingent relation to its environment, an interpretation of tort law not primarily based on the individual is proffered, whether conceived in terms of abstract right or an aggregation of preferences.

C UNDERSTANDING SYSTEMS THEORY AS AN ANALYTICAL 'FRAME OF REFERENCE' RATHER THAN A GRAND THEORY

1 *Tort Law from Individuals to Systems: Ladeur's Debt to Luhmann*

It is now germane to make the theoretical commitments explicit by situating the approach in a systems theory 'frame of reference'. Within systems theory, the argument is 'Ladeurian' because it is concerned with the relationship between the internal differentiation of the legal system and its relationship with changes in the knowledge base of society.[33] To unpack these theoretical commitments, however, some central features of Luhmann's theory require

[31] Ladeur (n 2).

[32] *Ibid*, 12.

[33] Although it departs from Ladeur's perspective discussed in Chapters 3 and 4 insofar as he argues normatively for the 'cognitivisation' of law, *ie* that it is desirable to treat law as a 'learning system', as both an explanation of postmodern law because of radical knowledge heterarchy and a plea for the law of the twenty-first century. Perhaps I am still too much a lawyer to give up on the function of law as a normative system.

explanation. Once explained, the theoretical commitments of this book will be clearer. At the outset, it should be noted that the systems theory approach does not offer a grand theory of society; although it is clearly a meta-theory, as it is a sociological theory about sociological theories. It is viewed as an *analytical frame of reference* rather than positing an explanation in the sense of the philosophy of tort law or EAL. We do not attempt to find 'fit' between our theory and the actual practices of a legal system as understood by participants, whether by explaining particular doctrines as instantiations of deeper philosophical commitments (deontological or utilitarian) or by drawing out the implicit philosophical foundations of the tort system.[34]

Systems theory is meant to be 'an observation of observations', second-order observations of legal 'communications' rather than reconstructions of the internal point of view.[35] It is not an external point of view, properly speaking, but rather relies on existing legal theory but reclassifies these theories according to its second-order observation methodology. Legal theories become, in this light, self-descriptions and are relegated to the level of law's observations. A crucial methodological step in this approach resituates the individual no longer as a sovereign will shaping laws to their ends, or a group of 'participants' within a practice; rather, the law's individual forms part of law's self-description. To put this in other terms, Luhmann is not concerned with the individual or groups of individuals (including their purported 'internal point of view'); instead, his analysis occurs at the level of communicative systems. As King and Thornhill state: 'Luhmann's primary unit of analysis is not the individual or groups of people but systems. And these systems consist not of people, but of communications.'[36] It should be stressed that Luhmann constructs a communicative theory that departs from methodological individualism. Instead of searching for the internal point of view of participants, systems theory examines societal communication.

It is radically different to EAL or philosophy of private law in this respect. 'The individual' is not the centre of society and nor should they be the basic unit of social analysis. The individual, according to this approach, is a constructed category, a fiction that can be subdivided into three distinct elements: the living, the psychic and the social system:

[34] Some of the difficulties in terms of the way these theories explain the tort system are analysed by Lucy (n 28).

[35] Whose internal point of view is the obvious question: judges, legal scholars? Additionally, there are problems when distinguishing core from periphery, orthodox from heterodox accounts, *etc*.

[36] M King & C Thornhill, *Nicklas Luhmann's Theory of Politics and Law* (Basingstoke: Macmillan & Palgrave, 2003), 2.

> In this schema people, as we have seen, become living systems, which exist as bodies and bodily parts, and 'psychic systems', which produce meaning through consciousness. Society, on the other hand, consists of interdependent social systems which make sense of their environments through their communications. The two remain always quite separate, although dependent on and 'structurally coupled' to one another.[37]

The focus in Luhmann's theory is on how communicative systems interact with one another, which follows from his strict separation of psychic systems ('consciousness') from social communication.[38] This assumes, of course, that there are distinct systems of communication independent of 'psychic' systems. The presence of multiple communicative systems is explained in terms of modernity. The move from a stratificatory to a functionally differentiated society leads to the emergence of several communicative systems to solve coordination problems[39] leading to multiple interpretations of the same 'event'.[40] The emergence of societal sub-systems is explained on the basis of the double contingency problem transposed from bilateral exchange to the level of societal communication. These communicative systems constitute society, as such, because society is defined in terms of communications. The communicative system defines its environment. I will return to this issue when we discuss the place of the legal system in this scheme. Suffice it to say, in this context 'functional' does not refer to purposive or goal-directed rationality, as it more commonly denotes, but in Luhmann's terminology it refers to the role of each differentiated communicative system, which produces meaning although different communicative systems produce different sub-systems of meaning (*Sinnwelten*). Function obtaining to law, in this sense, denotes law's role in providing counterfactual normative expectations over time, upholding these normative expectations in the face of experiential disappointment.[41] This is important for social 'learning' because normative

37 *Ibid*, 7.

38 *Ibid*. They stress that this does not downplay 'humanity', but describes how consciousness and communication are autonomous worlds of meaning (citation omitted).

39 The so-called double contingency problem.

40 At this point, there is a certain echo of Weber. The various communicative systems can be thought of as structures that subsume events according to their distinct codes. These events are new information that is subsumed into their structures, rendered 'redundant' or excluded. See King & Thornhill (n 36), 49–50.

41 King & Thornhill (n 36), 56, on learning within the legal system in particular, but with a broader import. See also, M Renner, 'Death by Complexity: The Financial Crisis and the Crisis of Law in World Society' in P Kjaer, G Teubner & A Febbrajo (eds), *The Financial Crisis in Constitutional Perspective: The Dark Side of Functional Differentiation* (Oxford: Oxford University Press, 2011), 93. How the cognitivisation of law threatens law's normative role

counter-expectations help other systems 'anticipate', 'adjust' and 'plan'.[42] Radical separation of communication discourses assumes, paradoxically, interdependence. His examples of these various systems include law, politics, economy, art and so on. In terms of meaning, law produces normative expectations 'in the face of actions that contradict such expectations'.[43] Differentiation is explained by King and Thornhill thus:

> Systems are functional, therefore, in so far as they are able to organize communications and disseminate them in ways that they and other communicative systems may make use of them. In very general terms, function systems create order out of chaos: they give meaning to events which otherwise would be meaningless for society. Their functionality relates exclusively to communications and is in no way affected by the quality of their performance assessed on any other basis.[44]

From this account, it is clear that for systems theory the function of the legal system is to provide society with normative expectations that help stabilise or 'de-complexify' society. While in common with classical legal positivists, Luhmann regards law as 'operationally closed' communication, his overall theoretical approach is different. He does not attempt to furnish an internally coherent system of rules, referable to the will of a legislator or participants' point of view, but rather sees law as 'a contingent and infinitely alterable system of communication'.[45] Law does not exist in isolation from 'society' according to this view; rather it reconstructs its environment by internal legal means while maintaining its 'identity' *qua* system:

> Closure is not to be confounded with impermeability to influence from outside: the system is permanently 'irritated' from outside, i.e. by its natural unstructured environment or by other systems. But systems do not share a common reality – they have to and are only able to observe and operate on

such that trust and reliance on law is no longer possible. This normative counter-expectation function for law is important for learning (coordinating systems) otherwise a crisis of normativity occurs.

42 N Luhmann, 'Operative Closure and Structural Coupling: The Differentiation of the Legal System' (1992) 13 *Cardozo Law Review* 1419. Note how he reconstructs the 'institution' of property in this way, and how it has different meanings for legal, economic and political systems. King & Thornhill (n 36), 11.

43 King & Thornhill (n 36), 11.

44 Although on the question of 'performance' see GP Calliess & M Renner, 'From Soft Law to Hard Code: The Juridification of Global Governance' (ssrn, 20 July 2016).

45 King & Thornhill (n 36), 38. Incidentally, this marks his approach out from philosophical treatises on tort law, which argue a distinct 'justice' for private law embodied by tort law, and distinct from the concerns of public law or morality more generally.

> certain elements of reality – because their own 'identity' does not have a stable objective character, they are a product of their own operations using certain distinctions and neglecting others.[46]

It is at this point that a distinction between code and programme is introduced. The code denotes the differentiation of a system from other systems into a functional system. It is akin to its 'DNA' and gives a system its identity. Programmes are more variable depending on 'contingent choices' and represent the cognitive openness of the law: 'One needs to appreciate the role of programmes for system operations and the possibility of programmes becoming highly complex in response to the growing complexity of the system's environment.'[47] Programming allows for the environment to re-enter the system but in a way that does not undermine its code.[48] The code law/non-law still determines how the environment, as constructed by the system itself, will be meaningfully understood.[49] However, programmes reformulate information from law's environment and reframe them to be consistent with law's binary code.[50] As King and Thornhill explain: 'Programmes exist as organizers of information which allow the application by the system of its binary code.'[51] Hence, if in law the binary code depends on the distinction between law/non-law, then what counts as law is organised by the law's programmes which provide criteria of selectivity for law's code. Although there is no direct

46 KH Ladeur, 'The Theory of Autopoiesis as an Approach to a Better Understanding of Postmodern Law', EUI Working Paper LAW No. 99/3, 11. G Teubner, 'Alienating Justice: On the Surplus Value of the Twelfth Camel' in D Nelken & J Pribán (eds), *Consequences of Legal Autopoiesis* (Aldershot: Ashgate, 2001), 21–44, has framed this self-reference in terms of the paradox of self-foundation of communicative systems: law, politics, economy, *etc*.

47 Ladeur (n 46), 25.

48 *Ibid*, 12. In his terms: 'The extreme and unstructured complexity is only accessible to the system if it develops a "translation"-system of its own which does not correspond to its external reality.' 'Re-entry' is a systems theory term which implies that which has been excluded can be reconstructed internally within the systems programmes. One might think of 'policy arguments' in tort law in these terms, *ie* the re-entry of politics and economy into a tort law where its normative programmes are oriented to developing rules of interpersonal justice.

49 A good example here might be the way law/non-law is applied to mental illness. The programme for dealing with mental illness is normally the insanity defence, which asks a fundamentally different question to that of health professionals focusing on legal capacity (programme) rather than on the question of efficient treatment. Another perhaps more directly relevant distinction is the famous law versus morality distinction in *Donoghue v Stevenson*, but these examples can be multiplied.

50 Paraphrasing King & Thornhill (n 36), 59. Ladeur (n 46), 15, gives specificity: 'The system needs programmes, e.g. a legal act for its functioning which specifies its distinctions between law and non-law and allows for the generation of patterns, such as legal dogmatics' (citation omitted) .

51 King & Thornhill (n 36), 23.

relationship between the legal system, in terms of input–output, and other systems, such as law and the economy, the legal system 'experiences' irritation in its environment and this provokes internal reactions at the level of its programmes. Programmes relate to law's function by making the law a 'historical machine', allowing for law's binary code to be applied.[52] These programmes create 'redundancy', meaning the law can incorporate 'events' (information) into its 'structures', which allow for normative stabilisation over time.[53] Luhmann locates the centre of these legal communications in courts; it is here that the programmes of legal communications are primarily unfolded.[54]

2 *Ladeur's Models of Modernity: Programmes and Paradigms*

(i) The Individual and Organisational Paradigms

Thus, the law as a distinct communicative system with its own 'internal complexity' (internal differentiation) emerges with modernity. This is the level at which Ladeur's analysis becomes germane. The fundamental break here in modernity is the introduction of the *liberal law*, which is the law of a 'society of individuals'.[55] Liberal law, with its separation of the right and the good, is an internal legal programme that reflects the functional differentiation of society.[56] This is the case, first, because what is legally valid (law/non-law) is determined entirely by the legal system itself, rather than by appeal to an extra-legal source, meaning the law itself is functionally differentiated from other communicative systems.[57] In other words, no *finis ultimus* outside legal communication is a source of law, rather the law simply links operation to

[52] Ladeur (n 46), 12. As Ladeur stresses, the law links to its own operations. It has no 'holistic view of reality'.

[53] King & Thornhill (n 36), 49. Another way to put this is that law's programmes enable the law to incorporate information but are also sufficiently open to allow for variation on the basis of new information. Standards such as reasonableness or good faith allow for this balance. However, this is not a precise or clear process.

[54] This would seem commonplace to common lawyers. However, given the tradition of codification in civil law countries, this is a novel approach.

[55] Ladeur (n 2), 12, citing J Appleby, *The Relentless Revolution: A History of Capitalism* (New York: WW Norton, 2010).

[56] Ladeur (n 2), 11: 'These rules are decoupled from substantive values, and allow for the co-ordination among agents who pursue their self-chosen goals.'

[57] What Kaarlo Tuori refers to as 'the essential positivity of modern law'. K Tuori, 'Fundamental Rights Principles: Disciplining the Instrumentalism of Policies' in AJ Menéndez & EO Eriksen (eds), *Constitutional Rights through Discourse: On Robert Alexy's Legal Theory – European and Theoretical Perspectives*, Arena Report No 9/2004, 55.

operation.[58] Second, the liberal law's programmes (subjective right; private will) supports 'space' for heterarchical communicative systems and, in addition, relies on these systems to enrich its programmes (internal differentiation). Thus, with Luhmann the basic insight follows the claim that while modern law is operationally closed, it is cognitively open. Ladeur's paradigms of modernity attempt to explain the law's internal differentiation going beyond Luhmann's rather more limited examination of the internal dimension to law, and its relationship to its epistemic knowledge base.[59] The relationship between cognitive assumptions of normality and legal norms is close and complicated. To understand Ladeur's approach, this is a key (epistemological) methodological assumption. I will expand on this distinction presently.

Within the legal system, programmes develop patterns as a result of 'events' and these programmes include what Ladeur refers to as 'legal dogmatics'. The liberal law is the law for a heterarchical society, without a stable concept of collective order imposed from above or by tradition.[60] Instead, central 'institutions' such as the subjective right support what Ladeur refers to the relational rationality of the society of individuals in which the 'play of ideas' lead to the emergence of innovation.[61] In other words, the non-instrumental form of the subjective right which refers to 'relationships in terms of rules' buttresses decentralised cooperation by allowing for future-oriented planning of relations.[62] The subjective right provides a normative structure for decentralised cooperation because its *formal* equality allows for the forming of 'stable

58 Of course, *pace* Tuori (n 57), this does not mean that the legal system does not develop, internally, dogmatic concepts of fundamental rights. Tuori locates these at the level of deep legal culture to be contrasted with surface-level law.

59 Whereas Luhmann was apt to show how law is a distinct system, he was less detailed regarding his examination of the content of law's programmes.

60 This insight appears to be the main point of departure for his criticism of discourse ethics because the latter, Ladeur argues, attempts to construct a notion of the collective good on the basis of stable rules that can be universalised. Because liberal law assumes an 'acentric' social order, linking operations to operations rather than a concept of the good, this precludes access to objective values. As Ladeur (n 2) notes at page 14, 'Such a system cannot work on unstructured values or moral discriminations.'

61 Ladeur (n 2) cites Appleby (n 55), 240, for this phrase.

62 Ladeur (n 2), 11. He borrows this terminology from M Oakeshott, *On Human Conduct* (Oxford: Clarendon Press, 2003), 140 (Ladeur cites the 1975 edition, but the pagination is identical). There is an analogy here in terms of planning with, Macneil's notion of discreteness and presentiation providing for binding the future in his theory of classical contract law; see I Macneil (D Campbell ed), *The Relational Theory of Contract: Selected Works of Ian Macneil* (London: Sweet & Maxwell, 2001). With Macneil, Ladeur shares the idea that the egoistic man of the classical legal order is not an accurate representation of contracting. However, Ladeur seems to argue it is an important institution that helps solve coordination problems.

patterns of relationships between legal actors'.[63] It is a background 'architecture' that facilitates cooperation outside the legal system understood as state law.[64] Another important but subsidiary 'institution' in this respect is 'classical' tort law, that is, tort law limited in scope by a strict distinction between misfeasance and nonfeasance.[65] There is a strong focus in classical tort law on individual active conduct; causation of harm alone will not ground legal responsibility. Tortious responsibility requires fault, most clearly in the civil law where it is conceptualised as an excess of the will.[66] The legal 'institution' of the subjective right and the misfeasance/nonfeasance concepts in tort law do not impose thick moralistic duties on parties to care for one another.[67] Rather, they facilitate horizontal cooperation without impediments based on feudal institutions or on the basis of state-reinforced customs.[68]

Ladeur, in addition, views decentralised cooperation as giving rise to 'conventions' (or cognitive assumptions of normality, interpersonal standards) that can then be incorporated into the law and normatively coded. Hence, while liberal law provides 'space' for decentralised cooperation, the latter produces social conventions that can then be incorporated into law in a 'feedback loop'.[69] In tort law, for example, the standard of care fulfils this function.

63 Ladeur (n 2), 21.

64 The term legal system is employed here to mean state law. In some systems theory scholarship, legal system is meant to denote what is ordinarily called the legal system and law-like patterns outside the legal system. Instead, when I use legal system it refers to state law (courts and legislature made law). For the totality of legal communications, I use 'legal communications'.

65 The term that Ladeur (n 2), 23, actually uses is responsibility based on the harm 'in the stricter sense as opposed to negative externalities which cannot be regarded as restricting the subjective rights of third persons'. What I think he means here is the distinction between negligence for direct injury versus indirect injury, as discussed by Brüggemeier (n 6). This will be treated in Chapters 1 and 2. I will defer comment until then.

66 F Ewald, *L'Etat Providence* (Paris: Grasset, 1986).

67 The focus on subjective right is a very 'continental' approach to common lawyers: G Samuel, 'Le Droit Subjectif and English Law' (1987) 46(2) *Cambridge Law Journal* 264. However, notwithstanding the absence of a subjective right in English law, *stricto sensu*, there is overlapping protection and philosophical orientation. In other words, it is plausible to refer to classical contract and tort law in liberal terminology. For contract PS Atiyah, *The Rise and Fall of Freedom of Contract* (Oxford: Clarendon Press, 1979); for tort law, White (n 17).

68 P Kjaer, 'Post-Hegelian Networks: Comments on the Chapter by Simon Deakin' in M Amstutz & G Teubner (eds), *Networks: Legal Issues of Multi-Lateral Co-operation* (Oxford: Hart Publishing, 2009), explains well the transition from feudalism to modernity within a framework of functional differentiation.

69 Ladeur (n 2), 13, alternatively uses the phrase 'factual normality' to denote the dependence of the legal norm on social conventions about what is good, reasonable, *etc* as a basis for constructing collective order. He is, though, quick to caution that the relationship is one of 'oscillation' or of feedback between norms and 'fact'. For example: 'This does not mean that normal knowledge is just blindly introduced into the legal system. On the contrary, the legal

What is normal and what is reasonable behaviour are closely linked.[70] In this light, the collective order is constructed 'bottom-up' out of 'cognitive assumptions of normality.'[71] This architecture, Ladeur argues, limits 'the centralisation of legal material', by which he means: allows for the development of legal transactions outside the legal system; for example, private contracting that creates complex structures of cooperation.[72] This inverts the classical account of law, whereby legal norms are deductively applied to facts.[73] In Ladeur's account, by contrast, practical knowledge informs the development of legal rules, not the other way around.[74] The deductive modelling of the law, classical legal formalism, conceals the legal system's dependence on its practical, social knowledge base. In this regard, Ladeur refers to a 'reverse process of norm generation', with the construction of norms dependent on practices beyond the law rather than by means of the more classical understanding of norms applied to facts that the deductive model supplies.[75] It should be clear that this is not a simple 'input' model, however, because the law reconstructs these 'events' or data internally through its programmes consistent with law's autonomy or operative closure.[76] 'Open norms'[77] ('bridging concepts') such as reasonableness or good faith[78] assist in linking law's

system can, and has to, observe whether these practical rules are sufficient, reliable, have to be modified upon the basis of new experience, etc. Normality and normativity are closely linked, and this link is continuously observed, revised and re-modelled' (18).

70 B McMahon & W Binchy, *The Law of Torts* 4th ed (Dublin: Bloomsbury, 2013).

71 Ladeur (n 2), 6.

72 Indeed, it was such complex contracting out from which the modern firm developed before it gained legal personality, eg *Salomon v Salomon & Co Ltd* [1896] UKHL 1.

73 And this is probably more radical than Oakeshott's subtler account of *lex*, in which he dismisses deductivism in favour of analogical reasoning as a process of amplifying the *meaning* of *lex*. Oakeshott (n 62), 130–41.

74 To be precise, there is an interaction, a 'feedback loop' between norms and normality. KH Ladeur, 'From Universalistic Law to the Law of Uncertainty: On the Decay of the Legal Order's "Totalizing Teleology" as Treated in the Methodological Discussion and Its Critique from the Left' (2011) 12(1) *German Law Journal* 525, 539: Legal norms and their 'application' in decisions is viewed somewhat like a feedback loop, whereby state law norms and the non-state practical knowledge base are 'reciprocally penetrable'. He speaks of 'order from fluctuations'.

75 Ladeur (n 2), 5, referring to administrative law, but this is a general point.

76 Ladeur (n 74), on the notion of a feedback loop.

77 See, for an instructive analysis, S Taekema, 'Private Law as an Open Legal Order: Understanding Contract and Tort as Interactional Law' (2014) 43(3) *Netherlands Journal of Legal Philosophy* 140. Taekema argues (or at least seems to argue) here against legal positivism building on Fuller's ideas about human interaction. This is not our task.

78 Although there is no general doctrine of good faith in the English common law, many scholars maintain that casuistic reworking of classical law approaches this concept, eg the concept of reasonableness, especially 'the reasonable expectations of honest men'; see R Brownsword, *Contract Law: Themes for the Twenty-First Century* 2nd ed (Oxford: Oxford University Press, 2006), and H Collins, 'Implied Terms: The Foundation in Good Faith and Fair Dealing' (2014) 67 *Current Legal Practice* 297; for the phrase 'reasonable expectations of honest men' see

programmes to shared 'cognitive assumptions of normality'; in other words, the law is linked to the decentralised 'collective order of modernity'.[79] The task of Chapter 1 is to give shape to the programmes of the liberal law, which is situated in a society of individuals. The liberal law gives rise to a particular type of individualistic attribution/imputation in tort law. This is explored in Chapter 1, drawing on examples from the United Kingdom, France and the United States in product liability and state liability law.

For as long as this practical knowledge can be derived from distributed 'experience', the liberal law's subjective right – the society of 'individuals' – is an adequate[80] normative modelling of society.[81] This practical knowledge base is 'dynamic', meaning that the law, a normative stabilisation of this knowledge base, will be impacted by changes in this knowledge base. However, as soon as the knowledge base fragments with the rise of the 'society of organisations', this stable framework of *rules of just* (individual) *conduct* is undermined.[82] The society of organisations is a development in the knowledge base of society, breaking the symmetry between the liberal legal system's individualism and factual normality. In Ladeur's words, a 'rupture' occurs, which he defines in these terms:

> A distinction has to be made between the continuous flow of information which emerges from the permanent variation within societal knowledge basis, and the momentary suspension of normality by the rise of new factual paradigms which induce a kind of 'break of symmetry' in the interrelationship between technical normal knowledge and the feedback loops which have to be designed within the legal network of networks.[83]

J Steyn, 'Contract Law: Fulfilling the Reasonable Expectations of Honest Men' (1997) 113 *Law Quarterly Review* 433.

79 Ladeur (n 2), 6.

80 Both in terms of its function of providing stable normative rules to facilitate and regulate society (function) as well as in terms of its performance *qua* system. On performance, see Calliess & Renner (n 44).

81 Although one cannot speak of a subjective right, strictly speaking, in the common law the systematic and deductive model came to prominence in the mid-to-late nineteenth century, on both sides of the Atlantic. The functional equivalent for the subjective right in Anglo-American law is an objective law organised around the misfeasance/nonfeasance distinction in tort law and the 'will theory' in contract. On the relationship between subjective right and English law see Samuel (n 67); for prominent systematic approaches to law in the United States and United Kingdom respectively see discussion of Langdell, and Pollock in Roseberg, in White (n 17).

82 FA Hayek, *Law, Legislation and Liberty: A New Statement of the Liberal Principles of Justice and Political Economy* (London: Routledge, 1982; 1998 reprint), esp chs 8 & 10. His normative theory for what a legal order should comprise provides a good analogy with the liberal law of the society of individuals. Oakeshott (n 62), 230–41, his account of *lex* is more precise.

83 Ladeur (n 2), 21.

The legal system, then, receiving feedback from society, experiences a 'rupture' caused by a change of paradigm in the practical knowledge base of society, develops its internal programmes. This constitutes a second normative remodelling in order to adjust to the new knowledge paradigm such that the legal system can continue to fulfil its function. The basic shift from the society of individuals to the society of organisations is the change in how social 'reality' or 'normality' is perceived. In the common law, at least, Holmes is an important thinker in this regard. However, as Kennedy has noted, the main intellectual impetus comes from France and, as such, we will examine Duguit, Saleilles and Josserand in Chapter 2 as illustrative. There is a move from a view of reality that is premised on the idea of chance,[84] in which case the loss lies where it falls, absent positive (human) conduct, to one based on accidents as statistical regularities, probabilities to be calculated and losses to be socialised, most clearly represented in the rise of insurance.[85] The injuries that occur to individuals remain a question of misfortune but are rendered statistically predictable and therefore the subject of prevention *ex ante* or deterrence and loss spreading *ex post*.[86]

'Society' comes to be viewed, in other words, as an aggregate and the question becomes one of risks and their fair distribution. Especially with the rise of insurance, the emphasis shifts from fault to risks, their distribution and the justification for such a distribution. This is what Ewald means when he refers to risks as a '*mal à répartir*'.[87] This impacts profoundly on tort law, because it provides a basis from which to argue beyond individuals about who the best risk avoider *is* and *why*. Different factual worlds make for different normative conclusions regarding *is* and *why*. The emergence of risk calculation, of course, led to what Weber calls rationalisation in both private firms and public bureaucracy. These emerging structures became subjects of law, although not legal subjects in the earlier, liberal sense. Artificial or legal personality concealed, somewhat, the way in which risk calculations succeeded rules of just conduct with regard to organisations. Thus, it is the

84 This will be elaborated on in Chapter 2. Suffice it to say, it bears a residuum of the Christian world view.

85 This might, as an aside, cast doubt on Honoré's outcome responsibility relation to tort law as an adequate approach to twentieth-century tort law, never mind contemporary tort law. His basic argument is that we should bear the risk of our bad luck, as well as benefit from the gains that accrue to us should our risk taking not result in harm to another. This approach seems at odds with the welfare state and an approach to tort law that aims at compensation/risk spreading. See T Honoré, *Responsibility and Fault* (Oxford: Hart Publishing, 2002).

86 F Ewald, 'Philosophie Politique du Principe de Précaution' in F Ewald, C Gollier & N de Sadeleer (eds), *Le Principe de Précaution* 2nd ed (Paris: PUF, 2008).

87 Ewald (n 66), 24.

hierarchical organisation to which decision-making is attributed in the secondary normative remodelling. But we must remember that it is not the organisation X or Y *per se* that is the target but the group to which the organisation belongs. In legal doctrine, this is both explicitly the case (product liability) and implicitly achieved (the doctrine of vicarious liability). Both examples will be explored in Chapter 2. Suffice it to say, the aim was internalisation of costs in industries. However, the model of organisational liability that developed was also applied, with modifications, to the state.[88] This *normative* model of liability will be denoted by the term organisational responsibility, where the legal model looks beyond immediate actors to the groups and their activities, in which acts are ensconced. To put this otherwise, the emergence of collective or corporative structures irritates the law and how normality is understood. As Ladeur states:

> The knowledge base is increasingly processed and channelled by representative groups, organisations and a homogeneous technical infrastructure beyond the open processes of self-coordination among individuals and small organisations as used to be the case in the case of the liberal order.[89]

Linking normativity and facts is more 'proceduralised', with the legal system coordinating groups rather than individuals. There is, thus, an emphasis on 'the harmonisation of competing interests' in an interdependent society.[90] If the society of individuals developed rules of just conduct, the society of organisations developed rules of just conflict. Thus, Ladeur argues that in the society of organisations, the legal system developed 'a set of "rules of conflict" for the management and co-ordination of different types of rules (individualistic v collective)'.[91] In his words, '[n]ew types of rules and judgments evolve which try to balance the liberal individualistic rationality against the new collective logic'.[92] The society of organisations, and the notion of organisational responsibility, coincide with the apogee of the welfare state as the primary societal institution of 'positive integration'.[93]

88 Drawing on Gert Brüggemeier's analysis, see Brüggemeier (n 6), 150–56. He makes a strong and persuasive argument to this end.

89 Ladeur (n 2), 57–58.

90 *Ibid.*

91 KH Ladeur, 'The Social Epistemology of Risk Observation and Management – Modern Law and the Transformation of Its Cognitive Infrastructure' in HW Micklitz & T Tridimas (eds), *Risk and EU Law* (Cheltenham: Elgar, 2015), 49, 57.

92 *Ibid.*

93 Kjaer (n 68), tying 'positive integration' to the 'Hegelian State'.

In tort law terms, at the level of the law's programmes, this meant that individual litigants are understood as representatives of conflicting groups within society. This moulded the law of negligence and strict liability, building on earlier models of corrective justice towards a model of what has been described as weak commutative justice.[94] Thus, stricter forms of liability emerge that decouple legal responsibility from fault in the classical sense. The language of the law may remain rooted in concepts such as fault, but fault is redefined as running an unreasonable risk as distinct from directly and unreasonably acting in the world.[95] And faulty conduct or acts are replaced by 'fault' in activities, whether production processes or in the imprudent hiring of subordinates who are not sufficiently controlled. In both cases, the internalisation of costs within an organisation is what matters and the task of the courts is to determine which risks are unreasonable and which are reasonable and must fall on the 'victim'.[96] This involves courts in the complex task of determining reasonable risk taking relying on an economic and sociological (aggregative) perspective but ultimately with a view to making a normative judgment.[97] This presupposes an epistemology in which risks are calculable and collective, and injuries can be converted into a monetary value.[98] The nub is that accidents are considered as ordinary instances of social

94 C Schmid, 'The Thesis of the Instrumentalisation of Private Law by the EU in a Nutshell' in C Joerges & T Ralli (eds), 'European Constitutionalism without Private Law, Private Law without Democracy', ARENA Report No 3/11 RECON Report No 14, 17.

95 Although disputed, it is sufficiently established that the transition from the nineteenth to the twentieth century involved a transition from the pre-eminence of direct to indirect injuries. The latter led to the need for the development of the 'control mechanisms' of foreseeability and proximity in tandem, as Fleming calls them. See J Fleming, *The Law of Torts* 6th ed (Sydney: Law Book Co, 1983); Brüggemeier (n 6), 93–115. For the idea that the move from nineteenth-century to twentieth-century law involved a shift from subjective to objective fault see D Ibbetson, *A Historical Introduction to the Law of Obligations* (Oxford: Oxford University Press, 2001). It might be a question of emphasis or degree, rather than a transformation of kind.

96 As Ewald remarks in *L'Etat Providence*, the victim as a general term for those who suffer accidents only makes sense when the world is viewed as interdependent. He is the victim of the inevitable accidents of industrial society rather than an unfortunate victim of *fortuna* or the excess of individual will. Indeed, accidents has a similar situativity, *ie* before they were 'wrongs', now 'accidents', which implies the secularisation of tort law.

97 Renner (n 41); on the interaction between custom and legal norm see, inter alia, Brüggemeier (n 6), 65–70.

98 F Ewald, 'Insurance and Risk' in G Burchill, C Gordon & P Miller (eds), *Studies in Governmentality* (Chicago, IL: University of Chicago Press, 1991), 197. Ewald refers to injuries as 'a capital' (204) Unlike civil liability, full reparation is not required by the paradigm of insurance, which is a pricing mechanism and not a moral principle, although it may in fact be achieved. Interesting here, for a philosophic and economic analysis, is G Calabresi, 'Torts – the Law of the Mixed Society' (1977–78) 56 *Texas Law Review* 519.

interdependence, not acts of nature or the individual will.[99] Ewald traces this changed view back, at least in France, to the rise of factory accidents in mid-nineteenth-century France, culminating in the law of 9 April 1898, which led to the internalisation of ordinary costs of activities within firms.[100] As we will see, the theorists of this approach were Saleilles and Josserand, who attempted to refashion French law in light of the 'machine age'. This move to stricter forms of liability, meaning liability on the basis of risk creation which locates responsibility in hierarchies, such as firms, has parallels in other leading jurisdictions.[101] It is not only by means of legislation, but by means of reinterpreting judge-made law that transformations occurred to reflect this changing understanding of accidents, their causes and the best way to deal with their consequences. Most importantly, it represents a transformation through which the law harnessed the collective and special knowledge of organisations to achieve public ends. This transformation from the first modern tort law to the second is treated in Chapters 1 and 2 respectively.

Kennedy's concept of globalisation of the law finds neat expression in this transformation. The change from legal formalism to the social, reflecting a different understanding of the causes of accidents in the context of tort law, might be considered to reflect the way these changes were intellectualised by their leading proponents.[102] However, it should be noted *pace* Ladeur that the aim is not to supplant the liberal order with a different model but to construct a functional equivalent model to that of the nineteenth century.[103] The aim

99 The concept of 'interdependence' is noted by D Kennedy, 'Three Globalizations of Law and Legal Thought: 1850–2000' in D Trubek & A Santos (eds), *The New Law and Economic Development: A Critical Appraisal* (Cambridge: Cambridge University Press, 2006), 63, as animating the language of the social, which we argue corresponds to Ladeur's 'society of organizations'. Philosophically speaking, Durkheim's definition of his science of morals, following Comte, is a strong exposition of this tendency whereby morals are defined as observable social facts, rather than by means of an *a priori* theory. Revisited recently in G Comparato & R Condon, 'The General Transformations of Private Law since Léon Duguit: Autonomy, Responsibility and Sovereignty in European Private Law' in L De Almeida et al (eds), *The Transformation of Economic Law: Essays in Honour of Hans-W. Micklitz* (Oxford: Hart Publishing, 2019), 115–36.

100 F Ewald discusses the importance of this law in Ewald (n 10), 277: 'Thus, the result of the new law was to make the firm legally "responsible" not only for accidents arising from personal imprudence or negligence, but also for those arising even when the firm has taken all precautions to avoid them, and those for which the worker is the cause (absent tortious intent on the worker's part).'

101 G Brüggemeier, 'Risk and Strict Liability: The Distinct Examples of Germany, the US and Russia', EUI Working Paper Law 2012/29. He draws parallels between Germany, the United States and Russia in this respect. Similar social legislation is found in the United Kingdom.

102 In Kennedy's terms, at the level of 'legal consciousness', see Kennedy (n 99).

103 *Ibid*. For example, it is often noted that legal realists in the USA, who can be fitted well into the social, were 'fixers', progressives, who wanted to revise the law in the light of social science responding to the 'felt necessities of the time', rather than 'breakers', who want to expose the

remains that of facilitating decentralised coordination. To this end, the remodelling of normative rules to the 'patterns' of the practical knowledge base is required. This pattern is now pre-eminently organisational and, as such, legal programmes evolve to facilitate coordination between organisations, and between organisations and 'individuals'.

That is not to say that such secondary normative remodelling was not achieved without difficulty.

One might consider Luhmann's central preoccupation concerning the distinction between contingent programming and purposive programming in this light. The former refers to the 'if/then' structuring of legal reasoning, whereas the latter replace 'if/then' with open-ended objectives – ends to be achieved. The contingent programming of the law is historicised by Ladeur, who considers it to correspond, more or less, to liberal law. In this book, we follow that approach. Luhmann contends that the latter, purposive programming, can potentially undermine law's operative closure, leading to 'de-differentiation' or 'cognitivisation'. With the emergence of 'world society', these tendencies are magnified.[104] While it is surely correct that once one replaces rules of conduct with end-dependent rules there is a blurring between law and non-law, it is also the case that the organisational paradigm of the twentieth century remained strongly normative. We will examine the way in which factual normality was integrated into legal reasoning in Chapter 2.

(ii) Beyond Individuals and Organisations: The Society of Networks and Its Tort Law

In Chapters 3 and 4, the salience of 'the society of networks' for tort law is examined. The society of networks is understood as a third rupture in the knowledge base of society in modernity. The society of networks as the knowledge base for twenty-first-century society is one in which our understanding of risk has become reflexive, heterarchy has replaced hierarchy as the main ordering structure in both public and private governance and, whether public or private governance is at issue, networks have surpassed the confines

internal contradictions in the law, something that incidentally distinguishes them from later trends in American scholarship such as critical legal studies. A possible harbinger for the later approach is René Demogue's theory of the legal subject. See HW Micklitz, 'The Legal Subject, Social Class and Identity-Based Rights' in L Azoulai, S Barbou des Places & E Pataut (eds), *Constructing the Person in EU Law: Rights, Roles, Identities* (Portland, OR: Hart, 2016), 285.

104 N Luhmann, 'The World Society as a Social System' (1982) 8(3) *International Journal of General Systems* 131.

of the territorial state and its centrality for the regulation of society.[105] The loss of regulatory centrality of the state requires a *methodological* shift from the national and comparative to a transnational orientation. Legal communication occurs not only within territorial states but, as Ladeur and Teubner argue, within and between functional systems in global society.[106] The EU legal space, and EU law in particular, will be used as the testing ground for a theory of network responsibility because, *theoretically*, it is considered an example of a post-Hegelian 'state' in which 'positive integration' is no longer feasible.[107] Ladeur conceptualises the European Union's multi-level structure as a 'network of networks' that attempts to coordinate a heterarchical 'society'. This understanding is, then, applied *mutatis mutandis* to its legal order.[108]

The role of court-based law *viz* other sources of law is radicalised in the network society, with court made law conceived of as peripheral to legal communication outside the state.[109] However, while courts are a 'last stop' peripheral to networks, it is argued that they *should* retain an important role as a site for strategic public intervention in disrupting 'network pathologies'. These 'pathologies' arise where networks are captured by particular discourses crowding out others. In our context of public and 'private' product regulation the danger is that in the definition of acceptable levels of risk in certain discourses, notably the economic discourse, comes to dominate to the detriment of other discourses within networks, ultimately leading to 'network failures'.[110] The role of courts, then, *should* be to disrupt these pathologies by creating normative counter-expectations.

105 G Teubner, 'Breaking Frames: Economic Globalisation and the Emergence of Lex Mercatoria' (2002) 5 *European Journal of Social Theory* 199.

106 KH Ladeur, 'The State in International Law' in C Joerges & J Falke (eds), *Karl Polanyi, Globalisation and the Potential of Law in Transnational Markets* (Oxford: Hart, 2010), 397; A Fischer-Lescano & G Teubner, 'Regime-Collisions: The Vain Search for Legal Unity in the Fragmentation of Global Law' (2004) 25 *Michigan Journal of International Law* 999; G Teubner, *Constitutional Fragments* (Oxford: Oxford University Press, 2012).

107 KH Ladeur 'The State in International Law' in Joerges & Falke (n 106), 397. See Chapter 3 for the substantive argument.

108 *Ibid*. Also, in this direction, see M Amstutz, 'In-Between Worlds: Marleasing and the Emergence of Interlegality in Legal Reasoning' (2005) 11(6) *European Law Journal* 766.

109 See also Calliess & Zumbansen (n 13). However, like Ladeur and Kjaer, I view the EU as an emergent 'order' in the society of networks.

110 P Kjaer, 'The Multiplicity of Normative Orders in World Society' in *Constitutionalism in the Global Realm: A Sociological Approach* (London: Routledge, 2014), 41–62. He argues that Luhmann's world society thesis is under-determined. What is required is an examination of governance structures 'defined as frameworks of transfer located in between normative orders which are characterised by legal and organisational heterarchies' (41). It is in these interfaces between normative orders (*Sinnwelten*, we think discourses in Teubnerian terms) that analysis

Failing to do so, it will be argued, contributes to the 'cognitivisation of law'; that is, the law's programme becomes dependent on knowledge from other social systems, most notably the economic system, as the market-leading discourse in world society,[111] rather than fulfilling its traditional stabilising function of providing normative counter-expectations. Thus, courts in this perspective are viewed as having a role in interrupting 'negative' patterns in networks, unblocking their dependence on particular discourses that have 'external effects' for society. This will be explored in Chapters 3 and 4 in the context of the New Approach to Technical Standards by focusing on Court of Justice of the European Union (CJEU) case law. The regulatory regime of the New Approach to Technical Standards combines private self-regulation by firms and certification bodies, and transnational public supervision and is considered an example of network governance beyond the state.[112] The fundamental argument advanced in this book is that the CJEU case law *conceptualised* in its best light furnishes a nascent concept of network liability. How is this the case? Taken together, a number of trends in the way the CJEU constitutionalises private law, treats the public/private divide and understands risks can be recast into a new normative model of responsibility.

It will be argued, first, that emerging and promising trends in the constitutionalisation of private law can offer a potential path to 're-normativise' 'private' law, tort law in our case, beyond the frame of reference of the nation-state.[113] *Boston Scientific* is an important case study in this respect because of how the CJEU approaches the issues of scientific uncertainty and market access through a rights-based discourse that, in essence, imposes liability based on the enhancement of a risk.[114] It is argued that it provides a

should be directed. The governance structures are referred to as 'autonomous *Eigenstructures*' or, alternatively, in terms of their 'nomos', at p 46.

[111] P Kjaer, *Between Governing and Governance* (Oxford: Hart, 2010), 67. But not only the economic system – what is an acceptable level of risk and its corollary, namely what attracts legal censure, is ultimately *for law* a legal question.

[112] Characteristic of these regimes additionally is private standards. See H Schepel, *The Constitution of Private Governance: Product Standards in the Regulation of Integrating Markets* (London: Hart, 2005).

[113] However, constitutionalisation of private law understood in terms other than 'total constitutionalisation. The argument from total constitutionalisation underestimates the way in which, in the EU for example, the legal order does not correspond to a federal state, and the role of the CJEU within the legal order. For the 'total constitutionalisation' argument, see M Kumm, 'Who Is Afraid of the Total Constitution? Constitutional Rights as Principles and the Constitutionalization of Private Law' (2006) 7 *German Law Journal* 341.

[114] See Joined Cases C-503/13 and C-504/13, *Boston Scientific Medizintechnik v AOK Sachsen-Anhalt* (2015) ECLI:EU:C:2015:148. More recently, and perhaps more radically, on the issue of risk, see *NW and Others v Sanofi Pasteur MSD SNC and Others* (2017) ECLI:EU:C:2017:484

path for the for 're-entry' of other functional discourses into EU law.[115] This provides a route to 're-norm' EU law's 'programmes' – fundamental rights that apply to public bodies, but also indirectly to private parties through legal interpretation. It is argued that constitutionalised rights-based reasoning provides placeholder rights for mediating colliding discourses of economics, politics, safety and law. In a sense, it expands the 'protected interests' of tort law, but in the context of different systems discourses instead of a discourse of individual right. By reframing consumer expectations in terms of rights, EU law turns policy arguments into principled collisions of norms. This allows for 'strategic public interventions' to disrupt pathologies in other functional systems based on an open, and case-by-case experimentalism.[116]

Notwithstanding the potential that constitutionalisation holds,[117] by providing strong normative backstops against cognitivisation, it alone furnishes no model of liability. An important second feature of CJEU case law in recent years[118] has been, in the tort law context, the increasing willingness of courts to translate principles of state liability to 'private' parties in governance networks. The *Schmitt* judgment is illustrative and important because it 'applies' *Francovich* liability to 'private' actors.[119] The CJEU indicates that whether the regulator (secondary actor) is a private certifier or public body, a liability regime should be developed by member states for omissions' liability for failure to exercise discretion.[120] This ties the private liability of certification bodies to the public (administrative) liability of states in EU law. This is distinct from organisational liability because it takes account of the secondary role of the certifier and the state by calibrating the standard of care – sufficiently serious breach – to a *'faute lourde'* level in recognition of its secondary or network role.

[115] For example, how recitals are read in the light of the Charter as a means to enhance consumer protection.

[116] See O Gerstenberg, 'Justification (and Justifiability) of Private Law in a Polycontextural World' (2000) 9(3) *Social & Legal Studies* 419.

[117] In our context, we will develop these arguments in Chapter 3 by reference to *Boston Scientific* (n 114).

[118] Although it has long been a feature of EU law, retraced in L Azoulai, 'The Court of Justice and the Social Market Economy: The Emergence of an Ideal and the Conditions for Its Realization' (2008) 45 *Common Market Law Review* 133.

[119] C-219/15, *Schmitt v TÜV Rheinland LGA Products GmbH* (2017) ECLI:EU:C:2017:128.

[120] The fact that the court did not set a European-level 'rule' has been criticised as a missed opportunity. See M Rizzi, 'The Court as Pontius Pilate: Reflecting on Missed Opportunities in the PIP Decision' (2017) 1(1) *European Pharmaceutical Law Review* 42–48. I disagree; it reflects the multi-level network architecture of EU law. The CJEU sets the frame of reference, and member states calibrate their national laws per effective judicial protection.

Therefore, the CJEU is developing principles of network *liability* for circumstances in which secondary actors enhance, as distinct from create, a risk that eventuates in harms. The main dogmatic trigger for an enhanced liability for secondary actors stems from the constitutionalisation of tort law, but the application of these principles to secondary actors is based on applying principles developed in the context of state liability to both 'public' and 'private' actors.[121] 'Sufficiently serious' failure to exercise 'discretion' – in other words, failure to regulate at all or adequately – in normative terms can be conceptualised as liability for enhancing a risk. In this way, secondary actors in networks – whether 'public' or 'private' – are subject to a regime of network liability. However, while network liability creates legal responsibility for the specific role played by secondary actors, it is not yet a regime of network responsibility. It needs to be reconciled with individual liability and organisational liability within an overall framework of network responsibility.

When one combines network liability with principles of individual liability (*AGM.Cosmet*)[122] and organisational liability (producer's liability) in the context of network governance, the overall cupola of network responsibility emerges, which combining elements of individual, organisational and 'network' liability. The CJEU takes account of the collective dimension of risk in networks, but *normatively* distinguishes primary and secondary actors within this overall cupola. Because network responsibility is *normative* – in other words, it draws on the law's internal programmes of responsibility – it is consistent with the law's requirement of coherence.[123]

This is the positive argument. By developing a regime of secondary, normative liability the CJEU is providing a template for liability in networks. The attitude towards risk evident in judgments such as *PIP*, *Boston Scientific* and, more recently, *Sanofi* shows a shift from risk creation (organisational liability) to risk contribution or enhancement (society of networks). By broadening the addressees of liability through rights (constitutionalisation), by shifting emphasis to the justification for the exercise of discretion (*Francovich*, *Schmitt*) and by relaxing causal rules (*Boston Scientific*, *Sanofi*), the CJEU is creating a tort law for a network society. Importantly, liability of secondary actors formerly invisible and based on risk enhancement, as distinct from risk

121 They are normative secondary actors. The problem is understood, sociologically, as a collective failure of regulation, and regulation is understood in encompassing terms as a combined task spanning public and private actors in an overall governance regime.

122 Although it is not currently theorised in this way *de lege lata*. However, the point of a tripartite division between individual, organisational and network is what counts.

123 Additionally, it does not subvert a social practice because it does not question the underlying design, nor should it have minimal impact because the threat of liability provides incentives to act. Teubner (n 23).

creation, completes a new responsibility regime into which personalised and organisational liability may be subsumed. The sociological literature which reconceptualises governance structures as networks, when translated into EU law, results in a new, emerging normative model of tort for the twenty-first century.[124]

Table 0.1 should now be clearer. The model developed will, of course, require a deeper engagement with both the evolution of knowledge base of society and a positive and persuasive argument as to why systems theory offers a new, distinctive and illuminating way to view tort law in its societal context. Each chapter will contribute to reconstructing tort law and pointing the way towards a new concept of tort liability both beyond the individual and beyond the frame of reference of the state.

Let's take stock. It has been argued so far that once one moves from the internal point of view to a systems theory approach to tort law, one is confronted with the social embeddedness of tort law and its models of liability. A focus on these models of liability demonstrates a clear evolution from an individualistic model to an organisational model of liability within the frame of the nation-state. In both respects, tort law and the legal system help to coordinate society by providing a normative framework for society. When one moves from the society of organisations to the society of networks the position of the legal system in performing this task is challenged. In the society of networks, regulation cannot be confined within the boundaries of the nation-state, and instead governance networks have emerged that are, strictly speaking, neither public nor private in the traditional sense. The networks are sites of discourse collisions; unregulated, they impose 'externalities' upon society. The existing models of legal responsibility are ill-equipped for the task of providing liability rules for structures that go beyond market and hierarchy. A tort law for the twenty-first century requires a distinctive form of secondary liability for network actors that fulfil normatively 'secondary' roles in networks as well as, conceptually, an overall regime of network responsibility. This book argues that a regime of network liability is emerging in CJEU case law; however, an overall concept of network responsibility – Teubner's invisible cupola – is missing. This book, for the first time, shows how the bits and pieces, the fragmentary elements of network responsibility, can be congealed into a third normative model of responsibility fit for the problems of tort law today.

[124] I share with Micklitz, and others, the idea that EU law is 'experimentalist', or a laboratory, which breaks with traditional legal concepts. See HW Micklitz, *The Politics of Justice in European Private Law: Social Justice, Access Justice, Societal Justice* (Cambridge: Cambridge University Press, 2019).

1

Tort Law and the Society of Individuals

A INTRODUCTION

The French Revolution marks an important break-even point in the emergence of functional differentiation as the 'the primary scheme of differentiation'.[1] Although the roots of modern law and society can plausibly be traced back to the high middle ages,[2] the structural transformation of society from 'stratificatory' to 'functional' differentiation occurred gradually from the sixteenth century onwards.[3] Two fundamental differences between societal differentiation by strata and by function are relevant.[4] The first is that in the former, knowledge rests on tradition and authority, while in the latter, knowledge is distributed, and emerges from bottom-up experimentation. The second is that in a stratified society, societal communication is holistic,[5] while in a functionally differentiated society, communication is fragmented and

[1] N Luhmann, 'Differentiation of Society' (1977) 2(1) *Canadian Journal of Sociology* 29–53, at 40. But see P Kjaer, 'From the Private to the Public to the Private? Historicizing the Evolution of Public and Private Authority' (2018) 25(1) *Indiana Journal of Global Legal Studies* 13–36, noting, like De Tocqueville, the continuity of essentially feudal institutions into the late nineteenth century in the West, and noting that the West is the exception rather than the rule. These are important qualifications to nineteenth-century stadial thinking, but nothing turns on these qualifications for my argument.

[2] H Berman, *Law and Revolution: The Formation of the Western Legal Tradition* (Cambridge, MA: Harvard University Press, 1983), noting how the law 'must be seen also as an important part of the basic structure of Western Society' (43), and gains autonomy in the twelfth century as well as the Church–State dialectic; see Kjaer (n 1), who also argues persuasively that the *fons et origo* of differentiation of law is the investiture crisis.

[3] Kjaer (n 1).

[4] Luhmann (n 1).

[5] *Ie*, there is no clear demarcation between law, economy and morality, and institutions such as guilds tend to fulfil religio-social, legal, political and economic functions. Teubner's evocation of *il buon governo* is apt, see G Teubner, 'Contracting Worlds: The Many Autonomies of Private Law' (2000) 9(3) *Social & Legal Studies* 399–417.

partitioned into the different, autonomous sub-systems of society.[6] By the early nineteenth century, these profound structural changes were programmed into the law. The modern law, in other words, presupposes 'an acentric society the collective order of which resides in the permanent emergence of innovations that establish a "play of ideas", a pool of variety that contains an excess of possibilities over reality generated from the practices of cooperation, competition, imitation, and experimentation in society'.[7]

The *Code Civil* is exemplary insofar as it institutionalised the subjective right: 'les conventions légalement formées tiennent lieu de loi à ceux qui les ont faites'.[8] This re-programming of law, as it were, represents a reflexive form of second-order observations of the societal self-organisation inherent in modernity whereby the social system 'patterns its own infrastructure with meta-rules and stabilising institutions'.[9] In other words, while the law's function remained that of providing normative expectations for society,[10] its programmes now modelled the acentric 'society of individuals' in which no one was in charge or steering the collective order.[11] However, while functional differentiation emerged as the 'primary scheme of differentiation' after the French Revolution[12] and is reflected in, and *protected* by, its legal system, it was 'counterbalanced' by the Westphalian territorial differentiation of states, and it was in emerging Western states[13] 'that functionally-differentiated society

6 For a comprehensive explanation of these sub-systems, see N Åkerstrøm Andersen, 'Contract as a Form of Intersystemic Communication' in A Febbrajo & G Harste (eds), *Law and Intersystemic Communication* (London: Routledge, 2013), 144.

7 KH Ladeur, 'The Evolution of General Administrative Law and the Emergence of Postmodern Administrative Law', Osgoode CLPE Research Paper 16/2011, at 11, citing J Appleby, *The Relentless Revolution: A History of Capitalism* (New York: WW Norton, 2010), 156. The quote continues: 'Clearly, this process generates not only spontaneously, but also in a reflexive form of second order observations of the very rules and patterns its own infrastructure, meta-rules and stabilising institutions.'

8 *Code Civil*, art 1134 ['Agreements legally entered into serve as law for those who have made them'. RC trans].

9 Ladeur (n 7), 20.

10 Kjaer (n 1), very plausibly, retraces the emergence of law as a functional system to the investiture crisis.

11 Ladeur (n 7) 'The legal norms basically do not "steer" society in modernity, but protect the self-organisational potential inherent in the unrest which it introduces in the "society of the individuals"' (12). The same impulses are clearly illustrated in political economy ('invisible hand') and philosophy (Hegel and differentiation).

12 N Luhmann, 'Differentation of Society' (1977) 2(1) *Canadian Journal of Sociology* 29–53, at 40.

13 Kjaer (n 1). Very few nation-states existed prior to the twentieth century. In most cases, the private law society pre-dates the *de facto* emergence and consolidation of the nation-state, *eg* in France, the revolution and *Code Civil* 'made' modern France.

unfolded'.[14] But it should be remembered that, even so, the 'structural coupling' of law, politics and economy occurs in all leading Western states, and it is plausible to refer to the constitutional structure as reflecting a 'society of individuals'.[15]

The subjective right is the legal programme *par excellence* of the society of individuals. It is, in a fundamental sense, based on the premise of societal self-organisation.[16] The basic idea of self-constitution of future relationships, inherent in the executory contract and serving as the general law for all social intercourse, is the central pillar of 'classical contract law'.[17] This programming of law reflects a society that 'no longer accepts a privileged point of observation, which is either "given" by tradition or claimed to be possessed by the political sovereign power in the European absolutist states'.[18] Instead, personal or self-constitution through private autonomy is constitutionalised as the fundamental norm of freedom of contract,[19] *autonomie de la volonté* or *privatautonomie*.[20] While the valences are, of course, different in common law, and in France and Germany, the emergence of a 'classical contract law' ultimately concerned with private autonomy follows a similar pattern.[21] In legal 'self-observation', private autonomy frees individuals to pursue their

[14] P Kjaer, 'Post-Hegelian Networks: Comments on the Chapter by Simon Deakin' in G Teubner & M Amstutz (eds), *Networks Legal Issues of Multilateral Co-operation* (London: Hart, 2009), 75–85, at page 81, Kjaer uses territorial differentiation, but segmentary differentiation is used in International Relations (IR) systems theory literature.

[15] Ladeur (n 7). One might also say, a 'private law society' in which private law is constitutionalised, but it has particular German connotations.

[16] G Samuel, '"Le Droit Subjectif" and English Law' (1987) 46(2) *Cambridge Law Journal* 264–86. Of course, the common law fits inelegantly into this scheme due to the lack of an institutional system comparable to civil law countries. Nonetheless, freedom of contract, which is discussed at some length in this chapter, fulfils a functionally equivalent role.

[17] PS Atiyah, *The Rise and Fall of Freedom of Contract* (Oxford: Clarendon, 1979), ch 14, esp 405ff.

[18] Ladeur (n 7), 12.

[19] The first norm, namely freedom of contract, is axiomatic. See, for a recent and informed discussion, S Swaminathan, '*Mos Geometricus* and the Common Law Mind: Interrogating Contract Theory' (2019) 82(1) *Modern Law Review* 46–70. For a discussion of the private autonomy substrate to freedom of contract at a point at which it was on the wane, see L Fuller, 'Consideration and Form' (1941) 41(5) *Columbia Law Review* 799–824.

[20] HW Micklitz. 'On the Intellectual History of Freedom of Contract and Regulation' (2015) 4(1) *Penn State Journal of Law & International Affairs* 1–32.

[21] Although see PS Atiyah, noting in particular the distinct emergence of the executory contract, and the civilian influence. See Atiyah (n 17), 399–400, 405–6. Also JM Perillo, 'Robert J Pothier's Influence on the Common Law of Contract' (2005) 11 *Texas Wesleyan Law Review* 267–90 on this point. *Compare* W Swain, 'The Classical Model of Contract: The Product of a Revolution in Legal Thought?' (2010) 30(4) *Legal Studies* 513–32.

diverse projects *inter se*.[22] Legal programmes are, then, denuded of substantive moral commitments, which frees the individual from the bonds of status-based relationships. The subjective right is also unfolded in a discourse of legal formalism – conceiving of legal relationships in terms of uniform rules.[23] This combination of subjective right and legal formalism means that in the society of individuals, 'experience' is no longer a given, but is generated bottom-up through processes of cooperation and competition.[24]

Thus, from the early nineteenth century, a distinctive normative model of individualistic attribution is programmed into legal discourse, which becomes in the nineteenth century the *dominant* legal model of normative ascription in private law.[25] Legal relationships come to be defined as a question of demarcating individual, abstract and formal rights and duties, 'territories of the self',[26] which apply without distinction of rank (stratificatory differentiation) and without reference to social context (segmented differentiation).[27] In this

[22] *Ie*, legal self-observation denotes legal communication about legal communication. More plainly, in legal theory as distinct from doctrine.

[23] Adams & Brownsword write in terms of the 'rule book' of classical contract law. See J Adams & R Brownsword, *Understanding Contract Law* 5th ed (London: Sweet & Maxwell, 2004), 3–4.

[24] HS Maine, *Ancient Law* (New York: Henry Holt, 1906), 163–65. However, as S Deakin & F Wilkinson, 'The Origins of the Contract of Employment' in *The Law of the Labour Market: Industrialization, Employment, and Legal Evolution* (Oxford: Oxford University Press, 2005), point out, this is not the whole picture. Employment relationships maintained their vestiges of hierarchy well into the twentieth century: '[T]he predominant legal form of work relations in the nineteenth century was not the employment contract, but, instead, the disciplinary and hierarchical model of the master–servant relationship' (42). This shows the hazard of over-generalisation of the move from status to contract; nevertheless, it is submitted that it remains largely correct *qua* paradigmatic transformation. Deakin & Wilkinson at page 43 acknowledge that their account is nuanced and the general trend was towards 'will theory' and private autonomy, citing D Ibbetson, *A Historical Introduction to the Law of Obligations* (Cambridge: Cambridge University Press, 2001). In addition, it dovetails with Marshall's account of the emergence of civil rights. See TH Marshall, *Citizenship and Social Class and Other Essays* (Cambridge: Cambridge University Press, 1950).

[25] Dominant, not exclusive. See Deakin & Wilkinson (n 24). See also Ibbetson (n 24, ch 12), noting how the will theory never fully fit the legal realities, and resulted in distortions and fragmentation in both contract and tort law, but *semble* distortions and fragmentations *in its light*. See also Ladeur (n 7) on the way in which nineteenth-century public law, *ie* administrative law, borrows from this structuration of relations.

[26] E Goffmann, 'The Territories of the Self' in *Relations in Public* (New York: Basic Books, 1971), 28–61, esp 60–61. Although Goffman's theory is complex, I take demarcating territories of the self to mean boundary setting as a means of exercising psychic self-determination and personhood. This might be referred to as the internal dimension of rights for present purposes.

[27] Relationships are defined in terms of formal qualities – formal justice – the opposite pole of which is defining legal relationships in terms of 'multiplex relationships' of belonging to particular social groups, families or tribes; see M Gluckman, *The Judicial Process among the Barotse of Northern Rhodesia (Zambia)* (Manchester: Manchester University Press, 1955), 81.

edification of contract law and theory, tort law is positioned in a subsidiary role, particularly in the common law.[28] While contract is pre-eminent in providing a constitutional basis for the acentric, modern society, tort law polices its outer limits.[29] It provides 'just rules of *interpersonal* conduct' in the absence of agreement justified in terms of excesses of the will. The increasingly systematised tort law is a mirror to the increasingly systematised contract law; both follow a logic ascribing legal rights and duties to 'individuals'.

However, this 'internal' face of the subjective right should not obscure its equally important 'external' face. The 'architecture' of modern law,[30] which conceptualises relationships in terms of rules, also reinforces other societal sub-systems. It is notably facilitative of the economic system. As Simmonds has argued, formal contractual equality rested on a conception of justice that leaves questions of the distribution of wealth to the market; whether a particular distribution is fair or unfair depends on 'the way in which it has come about'.[31] But, perhaps less obviously, a constitutionalised subjective right also facilitates other sub-systems such as art, health and so on, because *as a constitutional supposition* of self-organisation it is inherently self-limiting.[32] This is achieved by delimiting the thicker social dimensions of bilateral disputes,[33] effectively instituting a thin procedural form of (corrective) justice

[28] In France, although 'subjection' of tort to contract is less evident, the unitary fault standard placed an emphasis on affirmative action, limiting the scope of tort law; see F Ewald, *L'Etat Providence* (Paris: Grasset, 1986) for a reconstruction, especially focusing on the philosophical background or embeddedness to nineteenth-century tort law in France. In common law, this represents a historical turnabout from the erstwhile relationship between contract and tort. See Ibbetson (n 24).

[29] It might be said that it regulates, without being regulatory. See R Brownsword, 'Regulatory Fitness: Fintech, Funny Money, and Smart Contracts' (2019) 20 *European Business Organization Law Review* 5–27, at 11–14, distinguishing coherentism and 'regulatory instrumentalism'. In my sense, it provides basic, negative *ordre public* rules but is secondary to contract law in the overall coherentist design or 'law's programmes'.

[30] One might say, alternatively, its methodology. See MH Hoeflich, 'Law & Geometry: Legal Science from Leibniz to Langdell' (1986) 30(2) *American Journal of Legal History* 95–121, esp at 107.

[31] N Simmonds, *The Decline of Juridical Reason: Doctrine and Theory in the Legal Order* (Manchester: Manchester University Press, 1984), 27.

[32] This is not to say that prior to the French Revolution there was no sub-system of art, science, *etc*. That would be absurd and ahistorical. The point is, rather, that the modern legal system constitutionalises autonomies, see Teubner (n 5). In the nineteenth and, indeed, for much of the twentieth century, this was held together within the 'social unity' of territorial differentiation.

[33] *In extremis*, Gluckman (n 27) gives an example of segmented differentiation: 'Men live in villages with their kinsmen or quasi-kinsmen, and *by virtue of kinship ties* they acquire their rights and obligations' (18; emphasis added). But, in a European context, the regulatory role of

inter partes in both contract and tort.[34] Critiques that emphasise the 'negative externalities' generated by this model of responsibility[35] dismiss too readily the 'positive externalities' of experimentalism and innovation that modern law facilitates.[36]

However, it is important not to overlook that, notwithstanding the formalism of individual rights and duties, which might be criticised as an 'operational closure' of the legal system *in extremis*, the modern law itself is 'cognitively open'. Apart from being a 'second-order observation' of modernity, and thus *statically* modelled on its knowledge base, it is also *dynamically* linked to this 'cognitive infrastructure'[37] through its concepts.[38] This conceptual openness links norms to normality through dynamic and iterative feedback. The most obvious[39] examples are the so-called open norms of the legal system – reasonableness, good faith, fault – which act as cognitive bridging concepts through which distributed knowledge is translated into the law and normatively modelled into individual rights and duties.[40] Fault, in particular, encodes into tort law knowledge emerging from 'society' as to appropriate and safe standards of care which were generalised by the law through its 'rules of just conduct'.[41] In this sense, normality and normativity are

guilds, religion and the aristocracy, formed an overall feudal 'mindset' (stratificatory differentiation). See Kjaer (n 14).

34 *Compare* H Dagan & A Dorfman's version of relational justice in 'The Justice of Private Law' (unpublished manuscript, 24 July 2015), which is contextual. For an elaboration of procedural, as distinct to substantive justice, see R Brownsword, 'The Theoretical Foundations of European Private Law: A Time to Stand and Stare' in R Brownsword et al (eds), *The Foundations of European Private Law* (Oxford: Hart, 2011), 159, 161–64.

35 The controversial 'Horwitz thesis': see M Horwitz, *The Transformation of American Law 1870–1960: The Crisis of Legal Orthodoxy* (New York: Oxford University Press, 1992). Much ink has been spilt in an attempt to discredit this thesis, *eg* G Schwartz, 'Tort Law and the Economy in Nineteenth Century America: A Reinterpretation' (1980) 90 *Yale Law Journal* 1717.

36 Ladeur (n 7), 11–12. His discussion of intellectual property law is illustrative.

37 *Ibid*, 20.

38 What the Critical Legal Studies movement would later criticise as the indeterminacy of law. See, *eg*, D Kennedy, 'The Political Stakes in "Merely Technical" Issues of Contract Law' (2001) 1 *European Review of Private Law* 7–28.

39 All legal concepts are operationalised, so to speak, by 'the reasonable man', which is a constant of legal discourse from 'primitive' to modern society, see Gluckman (n 27).

40 G Brüggemeier, *Common Principles of Tort Law: A Prestatement of Law* (London: BIICL, 2004), at 66, regarding how the standard of care, while drawing on custom, is ultimately a normative standard.

41 What should not be underestimated is the role of law as a means to generalise local knowledge. In this respect, the building of the nation-state, its legal system and the diffusion of knowledge are intertwined. Kjaer (n 14) places particular stress on this dimension to the law, namely, the role of law as a means to 'distribute' technical knowledge. KH Ladeur, 'The Postmodern Condition of Law and Societal "Management of Rules": Facts and Norms Revisited' (2006) 27

intertwined.[42] These 'fact-ridden'[43] concepts help to bridge the gap between normality and legal norm and, in time, lead to ever greater sophistication in legal reasoning. Private law's cognitive infrastructure is,[44] in other words, comprised of 'complex layers of social knowledge, conventions and professional practices all of which were enshrined in public order at large or in social and technical experience'.[45] This entanglement of normality and norm[46] also helps the law to reduce uncertainty by creating 'order from noise' through signalling to other societal sub-systems the outer normative limits of their communication.[47] The law's function in providing counterfactual normative rules is, in other words, sustained by the dynamic and iterative interaction with normality through its *legal* concepts.

However, because the law in modernity is 'positive'[48] – it is a second-order, institutionalised 'observation' of the acentric or heterarchical knowledge base of society – when its knowledge base changes it places pressure on law's programmes to evolve or internally differentiate. The emergence of a 'society of organizations', and its epistemology of risk, results in a change in the function of negligence from a backward-looking analysis of *individual* conduct to a policy-led and forward-looking question of *socially* acceptable risk.[49] For now, it suffices to say that the will and fault structuring of the law rested on a vision of society permeated by the ascription of action or, more precisely,

Zeitschrift für Rechtssoziologie Heft 1 87, 90, notes in the German context the role of technical bodies which fulfilled an analogous, or even more important, function.

42 Ladeur (n 7), 17. Ladeur is strongly opposed to the concept of rational subsumption, citing A Lefebvre, *The Image of Law: Deleuze, Bergson, Spinoza* (Stanford, CA: Stanford University Press, 2008), 138.

43 See Ladeur (n 7), 34.

44 See *ibid*. This is true also in the public law of the society of individuals, noting how in administrative law, 'the "acte administrative" corresponds to the distributed logic of the "private law society"' (13).

45 *Ibid*, 20.

46 *Ibid*.

47 As Collins explains, this information is reconstructed internally by the various sub-systems. See H Collins, *Regulating Contracts* (Oxford: Oxford University Press, 1999), esp ch 2. It is not a simple input/output model. Often overlooked or perhaps under-stressed is how law's normative models also structure reality, see G Hodgson, 'The Legal Nature of the Firm and the Myth of the Firm–Market Hybrid' (2002) 9(1) *International Journal of the Economics of Business* 37–60.

48 Ladeur (n 7). Positive law should not be confused with legal positivism. Ladeur elaborates his concept of positive law at page 11: 'In a deeper sense, a law that . . . rests on the assumption that "nobody is in charge of the collective order" is "positive". As a consequence, it is "non-instrumental", in the sense that it refers to a "relationship in terms of rules". These rules are decoupled from substantive values, and allow for the co-ordination among agents who pursue their self-chosen goals' (citations omitted).

49 Ewald (n 28), who chronicles the transition from fault to (social) risk.

'acts' to individuals. A view that presupposes *(une) vie collective* had not yet emerged when the drafters of the *Code Civil* or the systematisers of the common law commenced their reorganisation of the classical law.[50] Rather, accidents were either ascribed to nature as 'natural' misfortune or to man as positive intervention in the world.[51] This chapter will proceed by sketching the emergence of a distinct law of torts within the tradition of 'legal science', and examine the main bridge between law and normality before, finally, examining areas in law in which the individualistic model most clearly impacted the nature of the legal relation, which today would be considered in a collective dimension. This construct will be referred to as the individual model of responsibility. It has left a lasting imprint on the law, and continues to frame legal thinking even if, today, it no longer exclusively dominates contract or tort thinking.

B RE-PROGRAMMING THE LAW: THE CONTRIBUTION OF LEGAL SCIENCE TO AN ACENTRIC LEGAL ARCHITECTURE

These introductory remarks can be rephrased: in the modern era, the legal system distinguishes clearly between the right and the good through its programmes.[52] While seventeenth- and eighteenth-century natural lawyers did not for the most part adhere to Aristotelian–Thomist metaphysics, they retained the doctrines developed by the late scholastics. By contrast, in the nineteenth century doctrines that appeared to be justified by reference to a final end were reinterpreted as based on the will of the parties.[53] Demarcating

50 *Ibid*, 22.

51 Ewald (n 28) notes the various misfortunes that befell the eponymous hero in Voltaire's *Candide*, which aptly capture this mix of natural and man-made perils. Fault was attributed to moral, individual shortcomings at the opening of the nineteenth century, while misfortune was considered 'natural' whether based on popular and antique notions of *fortuna* or providence or more modern or scientific notions of natural, social laws. Eg T Malthus, *An Essay on the Principle of Population* (London: Johnson, 1798).

52 This is paralleled in classical liberal political philosophy. As Larmore states, drawing on deeper philosophical congruencies between Locke, Kant and JS Mill. See C Larmore, 'The Moral Basis of Political Liberalism' (1999) 96(12) *Journal of Political Philosophy* 599–625, at 603: 'Our status as political subjects or citizens should be independent of whatever view of the human good we affirm, because in that way political principles respect as Locke, Kant, and Mill would have said the fallibilist, autonomous, or *experimental attitude* which we as persons should maintain at the deepest level of our self-understanding' (emphasis added).

53 J Gordley, *The Philosophical Origins of Modern Contract Doctrine* (Oxford: Oxford University Press, 1991), ch 7, distinguishing between the continued reliance by natural lawyers on the concept of virtue inherited from the late scholastics and, ultimately, Aristotle, in contradistinction to the rise of the will in nineteenth-century doctrinal scholarship. Gordley

clearly between contract and tort is of central importance for this normative, anthropocentric model: Will is the basic institution that supported an acentric society,[54] while fault is its outer limit, defined in its light as an 'excess of the will' as exemplified in the French tradition[55] or obligation absent agreement in the common law.[56] These basic concepts were unfolded through 'legal science', which reordered legal programmes around these axiomata.[57]

Legal science, as Bell and Ibbetson remark, 'did not look directly at social values and consequences, but sought coherence in doctrinal legal principles'.[58] In this vein, Kennedy refers to the period stretching roughly from 1850 to 1914 as the era of legal formalism.[59] German 'legal science', with its

shows, convincingly, how the recasting of the law as resting on the will of the parties led to confusion and distortion.

54 Atiyah (n 8) captures this idea by his connection of the will theory of contract to the economic organisation of society for the first limb of this formula. He comments that in the early nineteenth century, owing to the specialisation, not to mention urbanisation and the attendant breakdown of feudalistic bonds, industrial society unleashed: 'Relationships that were formerly taking place within some kind of institutional framework were now taking place on an individualized basis through the medium of contract' (259). This was the impetus, he argues, to 'individualism as a social mechanism'.

55 Ewald (n 28).

56 Ibbetson (n 24), 172–73 (or by operation of law as distinct from agreement).

57 This presentation of the development of the law is not free from controversy. On the will and fault side of the debate among modern authors are, notably, D Kennedy, 'Three Globalizations of Law and Legal Thought: 1850–2000' in D Trubek & A Santos (eds), *The New Law and Economic Development: A Critical Appraisal* (Cambridge: Cambridge University Press, 2006); GE White, *Tort Law in America: An Intellectual History* (New York: Oxford University Press, 1980); and Ibbetson (n 24). Where these authors see discontinuity, OW Holmes in *The Common Law* famously saw a long-standing emphasis on fault. R Kaczorowski, 'The Common Law Background of Nineteenth Century Tort Law' (1990) 51 *Ohio State Law Journal* 1127, interjects on the side of Holmes in the debate, tracing fault-based reasoning in the common law which was established at least by the eighteenth century. I do not pretend to resolve this dispute; however, it suffices to say that by the nineteenth century the accent placed on fault, whether by exegesis (Kaczorowski, especially his discussion of contributory negligence) or by invention, had increased to the extent that it was the central organising principle in the law of torts. By the latter half of the nineteenth century the consolidation of the law of torts into a systematic and independent field of law centred on fault had been achieved, replacing disparate torts with a law of tort in scholarship, and to a certain degree in practice. This progress was accentuated during the twentieth century.

58 J Bell & D Ibbetson, *European Legal Development: The Case of Tort* (Cambridge: Cambridge University Press, 2012), 43.

59 Kennedy (n 57). It should be noted that Kennedy's divisions of what he refers to as the 'legal consciousness', or what I would call the modelling by law of its cognitive environment, are overlapping and inexact. They do not have sharp ends, with one period ending and another beginning, but rather approximate the dates that Kennedy ascribes to them. White (n 57) would place the starting point for modern tort law around 1870.

emphasis on legal principles and deductive reasoning,[60] is considered its most developed and influential instantiation.[61] It is especially prominent in the continental law,[62] with an emphasis on the 'subjective right' and reparation for fault.[63] But the will theory of contract and the gradual emergence of negligence premised on fault is paralleled in the common law too.[64]

60 *Ibid*, per Kennedy, 'Between 1850 and 1914 what globalized was Classical Legal Thought (CLT). It had no essence. But among its important traits were that it was a way of thinking about law as a system of spheres of autonomy for private and public actors, with the boundaries of spheres defined by legal reasoning understood as a scientific practice' (21–22).

61 In this regard, 'German legal formalism' of the nineteenth century was defined as much by its catholicity as by its coherence with several divergent schools of thought. In addition, its 'reception' into Anglo-American legal thought was not straightforward. See M Reimann, 'Nineteenth Century German Legal Science' (1990) 31 *Boston College Law Review* 837 on this point. For an elaboration on the link between the methodology of German legal science and common law reform, see White (n 57). See D Ibbetson, 'The Law of Business Rome: Foundations of the Anglo-American Tort of Negligence' (1999) 52(1) *Current Legal Practice* 74, esp 108 on the influence of continental sources on the common law and how these sources were used selectively rather than systematically in reshaping tort law.

62 In its many instantiations, the point here is not that 'continental law' is all the same, but rather that it follows a similar institutional pattern; see G Samuel, '"Le Droit Subjectif" and English Law' (1987) 46(2) *Cambridge Law Journal* 264–86.

63 Fault was the main organising concept, especially in France. This is not to say that there were no tensions between Arts 1382/3 and the antecedent, customary law. Many of the types of vicarious liability, *ie* liabilities for the acts of others, were based originally on an objective view of liability, but fault encroached on this territory, *eg* liability for the acts of children in one's care, or liability of employers. See Bell & Ibbetson (n 58), esp 59–62. See also L Josserand, *De La Responsabilité du Fait des Choses Inanimées* (Paris: Rousseau, 1897), for a discussion of how isolated areas of non-fault liability, *ie* Article 1386, were later generalised and expanded. In Germany, although fault was the main organising concept in the *BGB*, because of the relatively late unification of the country, codification arrived at the end of the 'society of individuals' and already the *Bürgerliches Gesetzbuch* (*BGB*) appeared outdated by the time of its enactment. See HW Micklitz, 'Do Consumers and Businesses Need a New Architecture of Consumer Law? A Thought-Provoking Impulse', EUI Working Papers LAW 2012/23, especially the discussion of the defects of the *BGB viz* social law.

64 Hoeflich (n 30). On the will theory of contract in the common law, see Ibbetson (n 24), ch 12, and Atiyah (n 17). To be precise, in the common law the main organizing device was the emerging duty of care, but note ch 12 of Ibbetson's book: 'The equation that negligence with the actor's failure to live up to the standards reasonably to be expected of individuals in society meant that legal liability was significantly identified with personal moral shortcoming' (181), focused on fault, as negligence moved to the centre of tort law in the nineteenth century. For further elaboration on the duty-based formulation of the law and its origins see N Jansen, 'Duties and Rights in Negligence: A Comparative and Historical Perspective on the European Law of Extracontractual Liability' (2004) 24(3) *Oxford Journal of Legal Studies* 443–69. Jansen traces the duty concept of tort law back to ambiguities in the thought of Grotius, but the main precursor to the nineteenth-century view is declared to be Pufendorf. 'Civil liability, he [Pufendorf] argued, was a private sanction necessary in order to ensure compliance with duties of care that were not penalized criminally. Deterrence had become the aim of claims for damages; the old Thomistic ideas of restoring equality and ensuring fair compensation were, at

Nineteenth-century legal science borrowed significantly from the natural lawyers when formulating the law as a 'rational science'.[65] Simmonds concisely summarises these borrowings in a common law context:

1. Law is, or may be, capable of justification in terms of principles. These principles are extracted from cases and the cases may be justified in relation to these principles.
2. Rules of law are justifiable in terms of their content, and not simply by reference to principles requiring, for example, respect for the decisions of a court of law, or a democratically elected legislature.
3. Law embodies moral values in a non-instrumental way. In other words, the positive rules must be related to the values that they serve deductively not instrumentally. That is to say, the rules must be specific applications of wider moral principles, not simply means to a desirable goal.[66]

In France, of course, the code, rather than case law, is the primary source of law.[67] In Germany, Von Savigny, father of the German school, intended to create a science of positive law deriving inspiration from historical sources to explain the existing law, not chronologically but conceptually and systematically.[68] The historical development of the law, therefore, was instrumentalised in a manner, in order to serve the search for the underlying principles which explained the law in a coherent manner.[69] Nevertheless, the overriding similarity with the natural lawyers is the emphasis on a self-sufficient private law, sustained by the conceptual coherence of individual rights and duties. However, it was pure will that held this post-Aristotelian, positivistic schema together.[70]

best, secondary' (458). Therefore, delictual duties were reduced to those based on individual behaviour: '[H]e was the first to formulate the fault principle: if liability is regarded as a private law sanction, this does indeed follow' (458) .

65 Hoeflich (n 30).

66 These three points are a partial quotation/partial summary of Simmonds' description. For his argument see Simmonds (n 31), ch 2, esp 19–22. This description comes close to Oakeshott's description of *lex* in M Oakeshott, *On Human Conduct* (Oxford: Clarendon Press, 2003), ch 2.

67 In France, and related codifications. In Germany, of course, the story is somewhat different. See Reimann (n 61).

68 *Ibid*, 'The empirical method required attention to actual data, the systematic goal the demonstration of an order in them' (847–48).

69 Reimann (n 61) puts it that history was used not to venerate the past but to detect the law's 'innermost principles' (854).

70 It is going far beyond this book to analyse German legal thought in the nineteenth century *in toto*, and we hope the reader might excuse this passing reference. A comprehensive treatment of the birth and development of German legal thought from the historical school to the

Thus, the will theory of contract, and fault in tort, instantiated in different but comparable ways in common law and civil law, unfolded within an understanding of relationships 'in terms of (interpersonal) rules', without recourse to the substantive good, contribute to an 'individualised' private law.[71] This re-programming of law, as Kennedy argues, rests on 'an attempt to identify the rules that should follow from consensus in favour of individual self-realization'.[72] The common law example, on which this chapter is mainly focused, is illustrative because the transformation of the law was so pronounced.[73] From the perspective of legal science, an anarchy of different forms of action was refined, and rationalised according to doctrines and, at base, general principles that eventually concretised a sharp contract–tort divide. While the common law never achieved the systematisation through codification of French or German law,[74] a distinctively individualistic and formalist law of contract and tort emerged.[75] Table 1.1 explains the main juridical basis of classical tort law.

Both French and German law constructed tort law around a generalised concept of fault, whereas in English law the notion of a duty of care leavened

Pandectists is found in Reimann (n 61). There, Reimann points to the Kantian critique of natural law as based on experiential reason confusing 'is' and 'ought'. For a more recent analysis, see G de Almeida Ribeiro, *The Decline of Private Law: A Philosophical History of Legal Liberalism* (Oxford: Hart, 2019), ch 2.

[71] D Kennedy, 'Legal Formalism' in N Smelser & P Baltes (eds), *International Encyclopedia of the Social and Behavioral Sciences*, vol 13 (New York: Elsevier, 2001), 8634, 8635: 'According to the critics, the mainstream saw law as having a strong internal structural coherence based on the two traits of "individualism" and commitment to legal interpretive formalism. These traits combined in "the will theory". In the sociological jurists' version, the will theory was that the private law rules of the "advanced" Western nation states were well understood as a set of rational derivations from the notion that government should help individuals realize their wills, restrained only as necessary to permit others to do the same.'

[72] Kennedy (n 57), 26. This movement was part of a greater effort to turn the whole mechanism of the state, but particularly its laws, towards this goal, *ie* AV Dicey, *Introduction to the Study of the Law of the Constitution* (Indianapolis, IN: Liberty Classics, 1982, orig. 1885).

[73] While lines of continuity could be drawn in both France and Germany due to their institutional traditions, the common law transformation was relatively sudden; see Gordley (n 53); Atiyah (n 17).

[74] Nor does Kantian thinking play an important role in common law legal science. In contract and in tort law, the more obvious inspiration comes from Pothier and Pufendorf in terms of both content and formalistic style. See Ibbetson (n 24). *Compare* Ribeiro (n 70), ch 2.

[75] The precise relationship between the formalism of nineteenth-century common law and economic doctrines is contested; compare Gordley (n 53), Atiyah (n 17) and Collins (n 47). Gordley doubts the direct impact of economic liberalism on the law, Collins refers to classical contract in economic terms but qualifies this as perhaps an ideal type, whereas Atiyah is more direct in connecting legal formalism and economic liberalism.

TABLE 1.1. *Classical tort law in comparative perspective*

Fault/duty of care[a]	Germany	France	United Kingdom
Source	BGB	*Code Civil*	Case law
Example	Article 831	Article 1382/3	Emergence of negligence

[a] Duty of care, because of the more rigorous distinction between these two concepts, namely fault and duty, in Anglo-American law. However, as Ibbetson (n 24) persuasively shows, the distinction was more fluid than is generally assumed, with ideas of wrongful conduct infecting the duty of care question especially after the judges sought to take questions of legal responsibility away from juries.

fault.[76] Nevertheless, in all major jurisdictions, while contract provided support for experimentation, offering a facility for individuals to assume duties, a 'libertarian' ('negative freedom') tort law drew its minimal outer limits. In the common law, this is manifested in the strong emphasis on duty and, at base, misfeasance in classical tort law.[77] Duty was an important limiting device on the boundaries of an otherwise 'dangerously open-ended' fault.[78]

1 *The Emergence of a Distinct and Subsidiary Tort Law: The Radiating Effect of the Will of the Parties and* Winterbottom v Wright

The emergence of the duty of care in negligence closely mirrors the emergence of duty in contract law premised on the will of the parties. *Winterbottom v Wright* is a break-even point because although it is a case decided on a contractual basis,[79] it came to stand for a wider proposition that no duty of care

[76] Ibbetson (n 24), 170–74, on duty. Albeit German law included a notion of unlawfulness, and protected interests, which meant that notwithstanding its continental starting point in fault, it actually came closer to the common law approach in reality.

[77] See White (n 57), who explains this in terms of discerning the rules for accidents between strangers. The pre-modern affirmative tortious duties rested on assumed obligations through status and therefore nonfeasance for breach of a status-duty. The modern, open-ended duty of care towards strangers required some limitation, and misfeasance is the relevant delimiting factor since it ties wrongfulness to positive acting in the world. How convincing this essentially liberal limit is may be debated, see KS Abraham & L Kendrick, 'There Is No Such Thing as an Affirmative Duty', University of Virginia School of Law Public Law and Legal Theory Paper Series 2018-59.

[78] D Ibbetson, 'How the Romans Did for Us: Ancient Roots of the Tort of Negligence' [2003] 26 (2) *University of New South Wales Law Journal* 475–514, referring to Pufendorf's notion of fault, which he attributes as influential on the development of modern tort law. Pufendorf framed fault in terms of social duty towards others, and as such fault, even if open-ended in his theory, must be interference-based.

[79] *Winterbottom v Wright* (1842) 10 M&W 109.

in *negligence* should be imposed where the tort arises in a contractual matrix.[80] This impeded both the development of 'product liability' law and the emergence of a general duty of care in negligence. However, it sharpened the idea that the central organising division in private law is what Winfield calls the 'contract-tort catena' in which *individualistic* duties are voluntarily undertaken by contract or imposed absent agreement via tort for *individual*, wrongful misconduct.[81]

The defendants in *Winterbottom* were suppliers of mail coaches, subcontractors who provided the Postmaster-General (Royal Mail) with mail coaches and contracted to ensure that the mail coaches were to be 'kept in a fit, proper, safe, and secure condition for the said purpose' and, in addition, the defendant undertook to repair the coaches where necessary. By a separate contract, the Postmaster-General hired Atkinson and others to convey the coaches from Hartford to Holyhead. The plaintiff, an employee of Atkinson and others, brought his action *on the contract* against the defendant for negligent failure to maintain the mail coach, resulting in personal injury to the plaintiff. The essential question was: Given the negligent failure of the defendant to maintain the mail coach, contrary to his contract with the Postmaster-General, could this presumptive fault give rise to a tortious duty of care *on the contract* allowing the plaintiff to recover?

The rather circuitous framing of the dispute as a tort arising from a contract resulted from the fact that in the mid-nineteenth century a general duty of care in negligence was not yet recognised, and indeed a hard-and-fast distinction between contract and tort was only just emerging. Existing law tended to base recovery on incidents flowing from status relationships, rather than on the notion of a general duty.[82] The only *available* route to recovery was to argue that *Levy v Langridge*[83] stood for the proposition that where an article supplied is negligently ('imperfectly') constructed and in this way dangerous, recovery should follow for third parties to the contract of supply.

The claim was firmly rejected. Notably, Lord Albinger stressed, first, that the *Levy v Langridge* analogy for a concurrent duty of care in *negligence* was

80 P Winfield, 'Duty in Tortious Negligence' (Jan 1934) 34(1) *Columbia Law Review* 41–66. This section largely relies on Winfield's analysis. But see V Palmer, 'Why Privity Entered Tort – An Historical Reexamination of Winterbottom v. Wright' (Jan 1983) 27(1) *American Journal of Legal History* 85–98.

81 A similar story could be told in relation to employers' liability and the holy trinity of defences.

82 As Winfield (n 80), states, at pages 45–46, these were based on 'the custom of the realm' or common law, not on general principles of liability, and the custom of the realm and the common law was concretised in the forms of action.

83 (1837) 2 Meeson & Welsby 519.

not good because of the absence of fraud and direct injury.[84] Secondly, and more broadly, he rejected the analogy with *Levy* by rehearsing a 'floodgates argument'.[85] Thirdly, he added for good measure, logically, that in the absence of privity of contract, concurrent duties in tort are excluded. Again, more broadly, he emphasised the unsettling effect that the claim would have on what is nowadays referred to as 'the contractual matrix':[86]

> By permitting this action, we should be working this injustice, that after the defendant has done every thing to the satisfaction of his employer, and after all matters between them had been adjusted, and all accounts settled on the footing of their contract, we should subject them to being ripped open by this action being brought against them.[87]

In language no less clear, Alderson B. stated that although the absence of recovery constituted 'hardship' for the plaintiff, 'that might have been obviated, if the plaintiff had made himself a party to the contract'.[88] The robustness of the dismissal of a *concurrent* duty of care in tort, whether it was intended or otherwise, later served as ballast to deny an *independent* duty of care in negligence.[89] Recognising such a general duty of care would circumvent the contractual allocation of risks, lead to indeterminate liability and blur the line with the province of the emerging contract law.[90]

The significance of the case, then, is twofold. First, it was deployed later to harden the notion of a clear 'contract–tort' divide as the central structuring device of private obligation. Either a case was based on will-as-agreement and privity, or it is a tort absent agreement. By extension, this 'catena', secondly, requires a clear basis of tort, which can be distinguished from will-as-agreement. Much of the later nineteenth century, in fits and bursts, aimed at developing this parallel structure of recovery in tort through the duty of care in negligence.[91] But, importantly, developing the notion of a general duty of

84 In fact, Lord Albinger used contractual reasoning to state that, in *Levy*, the plaintiff was 'really and substantially the party contracting' (114) because the contract was made between the defendant and his father presumably for his benefit, the plaintiff lacking the capacity to contract, and the defendant was aware of his identity; consequently, *semble* that judgment was not truly an exception to the privity of contract rule.

85 See *Winterbottom* (n 79), 113, 'an infinity of actions'.

86 J Fleming, 'Tort in a Contractual Matrix' (1995) 33(4) *Osgoode Hall Law Journal* 661.

87 *Winterbottom* (n 79), 115.

88 *Ibid*.

89 *Eg Longmeid v Holliday* (1851) 6 Exch 761.

90 That is to say, the notion of a *general* contract law in a Langdellian or Willistonian framework.

91 Important, *George v Skivington* (1869–70) LR 5 Ex 1 (1869) (analogy from *Levy* from fraud to negligence, but representation and known plaintiff); *Heaven v Pender* (1883) 11 QBD 503 (Brett MR) (from known plaintiff to 'remoteness'), who uses classical legal science methodology to

care in tort was stymied by the view that tort should not trespass into the province of contract law. This had two dimensions. First, it limited third-party claims in a contractual context. This effectively blocked the emergence of product liability law,[92] and, of course, of a general duty of care at all.[93] The second, and perhaps more important, dimension is that if contract is premised on recovery for nonfeasance – a failure to perform an undertaking given – then tort *should* be premised on misfeasance. This is unproblematic when fraud as deliberate, wicked conduct is proven, and might plausibly be extended to inherently dangerous things because it is a fraud of a sort, that is, recklessness, to introduce something known to be dangerous without adequate warning.[94] These can, to use continental terminology, be characterised as excesses of the will, which *directly* harm others outside contract. However, where the thing that causes harm is not *per se* dangerous, and especially where the defect is latent, then it may be characterised as an omission as distinct from an affirmative act and, by extension, there is no recovery for malfeasance outside contract or the narrow set of pre-existing assumed obligations absent contract.[95] Relatedly, courts struggled to conceive of the possibility of recovery for *indirect* harms not a result of a voluntary undertaking of some sort whether in contract or by assumed obligation in tort.[96] Indirect injury is too far removed from the acts of an individual to fit into a scheme of just rules of interpersonal conduct absent a positive

state a general duty of care in negligence, *ie* inductive generalisation. But see the slew of authorities against the general duty of care in negligence, *eg Le Lievre v Gould* [1893] 1 QB 491; *Longmeid*; *Earl v Lubbock* (1905) 1 KB 253; *Blacker v Lake & Elliot* 106 LT 533.

92 *Donoghue v Stevenson* [1932] AC 5, Lord MacMillan esp. (608–9).

93 See Rolff B's short judgment in *Winterbottom*, 116. *LeLievre v Gould* is instructive in this respect. In that case, it was held that either the plaintiff had to show that the fault was parasitic on contract, or that it fell within one of the recognised and narrowly defined categories of pre-existing duties.

94 There is a long and instructive discussion in *LeLievre v Gould* about how recklessness is not fraud, but evidences fraud, citing *Derry v Peek* (1889) LR 14 App Cas 337.

95 The classic example of this type of reasoning is *Longmeid*; but this omissions' thinking, so to speak, had a wider application than simply failure to inspect for latent defects. It also worked injustice in cases of botched repairs. See the plaintiff's struggle to circumvent this limitation in *Earl v Lubbock* in his attempt to characterise the relevant negligence as the defendant's act. The court rejected the argument on omissions' grounds, *ie* the good was not visibly out of repair on delivery.

96 The established categories of recovery such as bailment, common calling or occupiers' liability involved some assumption of responsibility even if no contract existed. Similarly, public duty could be viewed as falling into that category too. Libel and slander, like fraud, are a *direct* injury to another's reputation. Even *Heaven v Pender*, on its facts, involved quite a close relationship.

undertaking.[97] Thus, the 'contractualist' mind-set of the society of individuals greatly impeded the development of a fully fledged tort law based on negligence as *indirect* or foreseeable harm to another, even if there some promising signs it was in the offing.[98] This was only resolved by re-characterising putative omissions in terms of a breach of a pre-existing and general duty of care in the twentieth century, with the boundaries of indirect injury set by proximity, which is a mixed factual and normative standard. However, the legacy of individualistic omissions-thinking has never been fully expunged from the law, even if the notion of negligence as fault by commission or omission gained centrality in twentieth-century law.[99]

2 *Secondary Remodelling of Distributed 'Experience' through the Tort Standard of Care*

While the protective scope of tort law was determined by, and dependent on, the primacy of contract law as a reflexive and *static* modelling of society in the nineteenth century, the standard of care in tort was 'opened' to the *dynamic* and distributed knowledge base of society.[100] This was achieved by formulating a single, community standard of care,[101] which created a bridge between normality and legal norm.[102] At the start of the nineteenth century, negligence could be divided into gross negligence, ordinary negligence and slight negligence.[103] This blurred the lines between negligence and fraud, and also between tort law and criminal wrongdoing.[104] By the century's end, if not

97 G Keating, 'Products Liability as Enterprise Liability' (2016) USC Gould School of Law Legal Studies Research Papers Series No 16-38, 1–44, at 6, has described it in terms of tort law based on 'individuals undertaking isolated risky acts' rather than business activities.

98 *Heaven v Pender*; the inherently dangerous case law is a tenuous type of fraud.

99 In some respects, there are parallels to the contract law tension between classical law and modern contract law. See H Collins, *The Law of Contract* (Cambridge: Cambridge University Press, 2003), 3–10.

100 While the duty of care was subsequently enlarged, a crucial step in modernising tort law via an objective standard of care is the purpose of this section. A limited duty of care also came under strain from changes in the knowledge base, particularly when new ideas about responsibility were confronted with a 'rigid' contract law formalism. See B Markesinis, 'An Expanding Tort Law – the Price of a Rigid Contract Law' (1987) 103 *Law Quarterly Review* 354.

101 R Brownsword, *Contract Law: Themes for the Twenty-First Century* 2nd ed (Oxford: Oxford University Press, 2006), 135, distinguishing community and critical morality redolent of Hart's distinction in HLA Hart, *Law, Liberty and Morality* (Stanford, CA: Stanford University Press, 1963).

102 Ladeur (n 7), 34.

103 Ibbetson (n 24), 169.

104 Or at least one could say that because it hints at a state of mind, it is apt to lead to confusion between criminal and civil standards.

earlier, it was clear that the standard of care in negligence was unitary, and it was stripped of its connections to *subjective* moral culpability even if it remained wedded to a strong notion of *individual* misconduct.[105] The combination of a community standard of care and a notion of individual and general duty formed the first modern model of liability in tort.

In legal doctrine, the decisive shift to a community standard of care can be retraced through two leading judgments. The first mover, *Vaughan v Menlove*,[106] was reaffirmed decisively in a second important judgment *Blyth v Birmingham Waterworks*.[107] In *Vaughan*, the plaintiff and defendant were adjoining landowners. Owing to the defendant's want of care, which included ignoring several warnings as to the fire hazard inherent in the placement of his haystack, a haystack ignited, destroying plaintiff's property. The legal issue on appeal was whether the plaintiff should be held to the standard of reasonable prudence or whether his subjective, *bona fide* judgment as to the risks involved should determine the standard of care.[108] Tindall CJ overruled the trial judge, stating that the appropriate standard of care was 'in all cases a regard to caution such as a man of ordinary prudence would observe'.[109] This approach was later confirmed in *Blyth* as the appropriate standard of care in all negligence cases, where the court held that '[n]egligence is the omission to do something which a reasonable man, guided upon those considerations which ordinarily regulate the conduct of human affairs, would do, or doing something which a prudent and reasonable man would not do'.[110] One should not be misled, however, by the rejection of subjective standards of care and presuppose that the reasonableness standard was, in the nineteenth century, decoupled from knowledge accessible to ordinary members of a jury. The reasonableness standard was not yet a handmaiden of 'policy'.[111] Rather, it is clear from the facts of *Menlove* that the reasonableness standard was premised on individual conduct, and was a judgement pre-eminently based on individual moral shortcoming, albeit judged in the light of community standards of

[105] For a discussion as to Holmes' role in dismissing the Austinian personal fault/responsibility standard in favour of a community standard of interpersonal wrongdoing, as well as the relationship between contract and tort, see G Gilmore, *The Death of Contract* (Columbus: Ohio State University Press, 1974, 1995 ed), 15–19.

[106] (1837) 132 ER 490 (CP).

[107] (1856) Ex Ch 781.

[108] The trial judge had held that since the case was not one that fell under contractual principles, if it were held that gross negligence was the appropriate standard of care, this involved proof of a subjective recklessness.

[109] *Vaughan* (n 106), 475.

[110] *Blyth* (n 107), 784.

[111] Seminal, OW Holmes, 'The Path of the Law' (1897) 10 *Harvard Law Review* 457, 469.

reasonable conduct, knowledge of which was accessible to any ordinary member of the community. This, of course, meant that fault in negligence was embedded in a wider social understanding of what constitutes good, interpersonal moral conduct for individuals. Individuals should be responsible for their culpable *acts or omissions*, judged against what the reasonable man would *do*, but not yet for the putative regular risks associated with their *activities*.[112]

The notion that individuals should be held legally liable for their culpable acts or omissions which foreseeably harm others appeared to crystallise in the sixteenth century,[113] and displaced a pre-modern *encompassing* concept of *fortuna*.[114] It had certainly gained a foothold by the time *Blyth* was decided insofar as it represents a judgment that those culpable acts which are reasonably foreseeable should be imputed to individuals. However, while personal responsibility as reasonable foreseeability was embedded in the nineteenth-century law, the legacy of *fortuna* had not been fully expunged for the common stock of knowledge.[115] Either accidents should be attributed to individuals or they were attributed to *fortuna*. While one could be rightly admonished where one's acts foreseeably harmed another, one could not reasonably be expected to account for happenstance. The corollary is that those who were injured where their injury could not reasonably be attributed to another individual were themselves culpable of a lack of foresight and

[112] See Keating (n 97), and G Keating, 'The Idea of Fairness in the Law of Enterprise Liability' (1997) 90 *Michigan Law Review* 1266.

[113] See Ibbetson (n 24), retracing this to late Spanish scholastics. Although, obviously, it had antecedents in canon law notions of sinfulness and providence. See Berman (n 2). There was, it seems, a struggle between providence and *fortuna* in the Western imagination that lasted until the modern period. See A Brenndecke & P Vogt, 'The Late Fortuna and the Rise of Modernity' in A Brenndecke & P Vogt (eds), *The End of Fortuna and the Rise of Modernity* (Berlin: De Gruyter, 2017), 1–14, referring to Machiavelli's ambivalence.

[114] For a fascinating reconstruction of the history of *fortuna* and its decline, see Brenndecke & Vogt (n 113). Even in antiquity, the relationship between the God *fortuna* and individual, prudent behaviour was ambivalent.

[115] Ewald (n 28) has explored this in relation to the fault standard in France, but I think this analysis applies *mutatis mutandis* to the emerging classical tort law in the common law. Both regimes reflect what Ewald calls a 'liberal legal order'. Ewald, like Giddens, uses *fortuna* and fate *qua* providence interchangeably to stand for a certain pre-modern cosmology. See A Giddens, *The Consequences of Modernity* (Cambridge: Polity Press, 1990), 130 ('providential *fortuna*'). In more recent scholarship, these are seen as rival concepts with providence superseding *fortuna* before risk and chance took hold. See Brenndecke & Vogt (n 113), 1–14. In any case, the idea that nature was an impersonal force, and that man's virtue was determined by his ability to exercise prudence or foresight of potential calamitous perils was not fully expelled in nineteenth-century thinking, *eg* Malthus (n 51). In his case, natural laws superseded natural agency. But the externalisation of impersonal forces remains a constant.

should have taken their own precautions against happenstance.[116] The contemporary idea that accidents are inevitable regularities arising in the course of everyday activities, and may be attributed to business and governmental activities, only became current in the last decades of the nineteenth century.[117] This mode of thinking was the consequence of the rise of social statistics and, relatedly, insurance as a generalised regulatory mechanism.[118] Rather, when tort of negligence was forming, the image of the world that prevailed on tort law was one of acts and not activities, which corresponded to a 'society of individuals' in which the individual, not business or governmental activities, was the main locus of attribution.[119] Indeed, the focus on the paradigm of the individual obscured the emerging firm and mass accidents, at least within the

[116] Eg by insuring themselves, or in the case of workplace accidents a related argument was that they had actually assumed the risks that came with their employment. Man's relationship with *fortuna*, and the degree to which he can exercise control over it, has been a constant theme from antiquity. See Brenndecke & Vogt (n 113).

[117] For a reconstruction, in an American context, see JF Witt, *The Accident Republic: Crippled Workingmen, Destitute Widows, and the Remaking of American Law* (Cambridge, MA: Harvard University Press, 2004), ch 2.

[118] Ewald (n 28); F Ewald (S Utz trans), 'The Return of Descartes Malicious Daemon: An Outline of the Philosophy of Precaution' in T Baker & J Simon (eds), *Embracing Risk: The Changing Culture of Insurance and Responsibility* (Chicago, IL: University of Chicago Press, 2002), 273. While the origins of proto-maritime insurance can be retraced to the fourteenth century, which came into its own in the sixteenth century, the idea of insurance as a generalised mechanism did not fully develop until the nineteenth century. Its relevance for fault as culpability were not clearly unpacked until the early twentieth century. These were presaged by legislative development, see ch 2. But they also impacted directly on tort law and not simply as a patina of legislation surrounding tort law; see J Smith, 'Sequel to Workmen's Compensation Acts' (Jan 1914) 27(3) *Harvard Law Review* 235–59. On the history of insurance, see WS Holdsworth, 'The Early History of the Contract of Insurance' (1917) 17(2) *Columbia Law Review* 85–113.

[119] Josserand (n 63) also stressed the vestiges of *fortuna* in classical tort law in France. This supported the attribution of responsibility only in cases of fault, *ie* human action. For a legal philosophical analysis of this distinction see Keating (n 112): The author emphasises the distinction between acts and activities with the latter 'modern' conception of tort law particularly evident in product liability and vicarious liability per Keating. Ewald (n 118) picks up on this theme, which linked responsibility to providence in the nineteenth century, referring to it as a paradigm: 'Providence is the great virtue of the nineteenth century. It is the foundation of responsibility in the conventional sense of the term (except in the case that it is due to the fault of another). Indeed, when the term was coined in the nineteenth century, "responsibility" did not designate, as it does today, a general principle of blaming others for mishaps, but precisely the opposite' (276). The argument goes: If nature is governed by immutable laws beyond the knowledge of the fallible human mind, one's only recourse is to take precautions against the potential unwieldly power of happenstance, and consequently one is personally responsible for failing to take prudent precautions against such vicissitudes of life; this view of responsibility therefore encouraged self-reliance and could not lead to moral or legal obligations in the absence of fault, the loss therefore was meant to lie where it fell.

province of tort law.[120] All this implies that losses *naturally* lie where they fall in the absence of fault,[121] with the latter implying 'affirmative negligent conduct'.[122] This was common-sense knowledge in the nineteenth century and, as such, coloured the standard of care in negligence. The prevailing view of 'normality', so to speak, had yet to place injuries as normal and natural consequences of (industrial) activities[123] as distinct from depending on unavoidable providence or *fortuna*, and attributable only where external force is brought to bear on another through faulty conduct.[124]

In the society of individuals no one else is responsible for one's misfortunes in the absence of fault. That negligence was premised on fault underscores the fact that 'the primary function of tort liability had been seen as one of punishing or deterring blameworthy civil conduct'[125] as distinct from compensating injured 'victims', but blameworthiness was interpreted according to a 'community standard'.[126] In an important sense one can argue that tort law of the nineteenth century was backward-looking, focusing on the conduct of the parties to a dispute. Once their conduct breached a certain threshold, tortious liability would be inferred.[127] It was only later in the century that it was

[120] Legislative interventions can be traced back to Germany, which began experimenting with strict liability as early as the 1830s with respect to the railway. See, G Brüggemeier, 'Risk and Strict Liability: The Distinct Examples of Germany, the US and Russia', EUI Working Paper Law 2012/29. But, even so, the core German codification, the *BGB*, was largely premised on individual responsibility.

[121] Keating (n 112), on the modern conception: 'That conception holds that the characteristic risks of the modern world are the inevitable by-products of planned activities – not the random consequences of discrete acts – and seeks to make activities – not actors – bear the costs of the accidental injuries that they occasion' (1267). Of course, Holmes saw clearly the policy choice involved, but preferred the allocation of risks that this implied. From my perspective, I view Holmes as an important harbinger for the social insofar as he viewed the world through a scientific lens. See OW Holmes, *The Common Law* (1881; reprint New York: Barnes & Noble, 2004), 36.

[122] A phrase taken from J Stapleton, *Product Liability* (London: Butterworths, 1994), 19.

[123] It also tracked the structure of business activity in which the same firm dominated as distinct from the vertically integrated firm, which had sophisticated risk management capabilities. See G Viney, *Introduction a la Responsabilité* 3rd ed (Paris: LGDJ, 2008): 'En effet dans un monde ou l'activité économique demeurait principalement artisanale, les relations de droit privé mettaient généralement en présence des individus et, en cas de dommage, c'était donc un litige entre individus qu'il fallait, le plus souvent, trancher' (22).

[124] Ewald (n 118). In the twentieth century, by contrast, 'Injuries are "normal" – which does not mean inevitable' (279). In a conflictual and prejudicial social life where business activity results in injury to another, the costs occasioned by such activities need to be distributed.

[125] White (n 57), 62.

[126] Brownsword (n 101), 135.

[127] Simmonds (n 30), 27: 'The doctrinal writer expounds a body of principles that assess the justice of a situation by reference to the way in which it came about. The law is regarded as containing a complex moral theory that defines and delimits the legitimate spheres of conflicting interests,

TABLE 1.2. *The emergence of classical tort law'*

Tension: pre-modern legacy v nineteenth-century law: common law illustration	Pre-modern	First modern model of individual responsibility
Contract and tort	Forms of action (remedies not wrongs)	Nonfeasance/misfeasance (strangers)
Duty in tort	Duties (status)	Emerging, general duty of care in negligence
Injury/harm	Direct (duty or deliberate acts)	Largely direct, rationalising existing forms of action, but emerging concept of indirect harms
Knowledge base: *fortuna/* providential	Encompassing (in medieval period, changes gradually post-Renaissance)	Foresight for oneself; otherwise happenstance

redefined in terms of statistical probabilities.[128] That the concept of reasonableness was tied to an objective standard of care, however, smoothed the path to the imposition of a 'critical' standard of care.[129]

The argument to this point is summarised in Table 1.2.

The legacy of legal science is that of a model of normative ascription which is premised on affirmative wrongful conduct, involving an intense focus on individual acts, and a reluctance to extend recovery much beyond direct injuries. When the duty of care finally gained an autonomy of sorts from contract law, proximity acted as a spatio-temporal and normative limit on recovery for foreseeable harms. The individual-centred focus of classical tort law also contributed to a rather sharp distinction between acts and omissions, which continues to impact on the boundaries of negligence.[130] However, the

fair and unfair forms of competition and cooperation.' Simmonds refers to this as resting on a '*particular type* of conception of justice' which he calls historical justice. It might also, it is argued, be referred to as corrective justice.

128 Holmes (n 121).

129 Community versus critical, relying on Brownsword (n 101), 135. The community standard reflects ordinary pre-critical community standards of ascription of responsibility to individuals, whereas the critical standard reflects a proceduralised form of ascription, meaning a standard not readily accessible to ordinary judgment such as an economic or 'social justice' standard.

130 It is patent today in relation to supply chain liability cases such as *Vedanta* in which the courts struggle to reconcile distant torts with the notion of assumed responsibility, or in the cases post-

emergence of negligence as a personalised or individualistic tort in a legal science or universalistic form – as 'a comprehensive theory of (tort) liability'[131] – should not only be considered from an internal perspective; it also radiated through tort law resulting in, in many cases, theoretical muddle.

C HOW INDIVIDUALISED ASCRIPTION BECAME A NORMATIVE MODEL FOR A GENERAL LAW OF TORT

The momentous changes to nineteenth-century tort law not only formed the first modern model of normative ascription in tort – negligence in the common law, *faute* in French law and fault as unlawfulness in German law – but also radiated through tort law as a whole. Pre-modern forms of liability were recast in terms of fault-based, individualised responsibility or were marginalised.[132] The liability of public authorities, and the state, was also formulated in individualistic terms. In the classical model of legal responsibility, in other words, there was no room for a concept of liability which emphasised individual acts and the regular accidents flowing from public or private bureaucratic activities.[133]

1 *Private Bureaucracy: The Doctrine of Vicarious Liability*

The doctrine of vicarious liability makes a master liable for the torts of his servant and in the common law is a form of secondary liability which exists in the absence of fault on the part of the master.[134] Ibbetson argues that prior to the nineteenth century, while not logical, the existence of the doctrine of vicarious liability in the common law was unproblematic.[135] It was a legal means to make a master pay for the torts of his servants, and sounded in case.

Michael on the liability of public authorities. See *Michael v CC of South Wales Police* [2015] UKSC 2; *Lungowe v Vedanta Resources plc* [2019] UKSC 20.

131 White (n 57), 15.

132 In France, the Romanist doctrines of *faute d'autrui*, and fault for things, became marginal exceptions to Arts 1382 & 1383. They were only revived, and became centrally important, in the late nineteenth/early twentieth century. The *BGB* discussed also followed an individualised model of vicarious liability, see Brüggemeier (n 40), 119–21.

133 This Diceyan equality principle has been recently reaffirmed in English tort law, see *Michael* (n 130).

134 Although this remains in dispute, the master's tort version of the doctrine of vicarious liability is a minority view.

135 Ibbetson (n 24): 'The earlier common law had dealt with these [cases] without any apparent difficulty: so long as the common law could reflect popular ascriptions of responsibility, legal liability could straightforwardly be imposed in those cases where it was considered appropriate, and there was no need for any soul-searching analysis to justify this' (181), citing *Hern v Nichols* (1708) 1 Salk 289; *Jones v Hart* (1698) 2 Salk 441; *Kingston v Booth* (1685) Skinner 228.

With the rise of large-scale enterprises and the attendant accidents they caused in the nineteenth century, notably in the railways industry, the doctrine of vicarious liability drew renewed attention as a means by which to empty the deep pockets of railway companies and induce them to better monitor their employees.[136]

Ibbetson demonstrates that as individualised fault spread to dominate tort law, it gradually invaded areas of the law which had previously rested on different foundations.[137] Vicarious liability was traditionally justified either on an identification theory or based on agency thinking, both of which were viewed as inconsistent with a law based on individual responsibility. Both justifications, of course, were status-based, namely focusing on the implications of the master–servant relation and more broadly the duties of the *bonus paterfamilias*. For the doctrine to be accommodated in the era of individual responsibility, it was, first, restricted to the employment context, and secondly the scope of recovery was limited to a narrowly construed 'course of employment' test. Thus, the doctrine of vicarious liability became an ill-defined and ill-justified exception to the broader regime of individual responsibility for fault. Because of the dominance of individualised responsibility in tort, by the twentieth century it could not be justified except as a concession to 'rough justice', policy and convenience, which lay outside the fault-based core of the law of torts.[138]

The rise of the classical model of responsibility, in other words, led the justification of the doctrine of vicarious liability into a theoretical muddle that lasted the course of the twentieth century, as those who viewed its foundation as pragmatic and based on policy vied with those who viewed (inter-)personal fault as indispensable as a limiting factor on the expansion of the tort. This main debate focuses on whether in fact vicarious liability should be conceptualised as the masters' tort (primary liability) or servants' tort (secondary liability).[139] Even on a servants' tort concept, if the moral underpinning of the law is based on individual fault then the doctrine should be construed narrowly.[140] It seems that as a consequence of its narrowness, other doctrines

[136] Brüggemeier (n 120), 15.

[137] Ibbetson (n 24); PS Atiyah, *Vicarious Liability in the Law of Torts* (London: Butterworths, 1967).

[138] Atiyah (n 137), 221.

[139] Although most favour a servant's tort conception of the doctrine of vicarious liability, the most recent contribution in favour of a 'master's tort' conception shows how this debate is far from over. R Stevens, 'Vicarious Liability or Vicarious Action?' (2007) 130 *Law Quarterly Review* 30–34.

[140] This is not only a common law dispute. See Viney (n 123): 'Dans l'optique d'un système fondé sur la faute, il est en effet naturel d'exiger que, pour engager la responsabilité du commentant, l'acte du préposé ait été autorisé ou au moins toléré par l'employeur . . .. En revanche, dans la

that rest on fault were developed, such as employers' non-delegable duties. But a fully fledged enterprise liability could not be allowed to develop, or perhaps even be conceived, in the classical law.[141]

Whereas the influence of 'fault' contributed to the otherwise pragmatic common law, judges limiting the reach of both vicarious liability and the 'scope of employment', German jurists went one step further in Art. 831 *BGB* by requiring an employer to be personally at fault, in addition to the fault of his employee. This led to 'the specific structure of [Article] 831(1) *BGB* as a compound cause of action consisting of an employee's wrongful behaviour, regardless of fault, plus the principal's own fault'.[142] Brüggemeier states that the effect of this prescription was to 'localise' liability with the employee. From the beginning, this individualisation of fault led to problems of attributing fault to corporations, and it took many years of inventive judgments by the German judges to remedy what were even in 1900 outdated notions of individualised fault.[143]

But even in this era, too close a focus on the law in the books distorted the rise of special legislation to deal with specific industrial accidents. Brüggemeier states that even in the nineteenth century, the application of strict liability had emerged through legislation in respect of railroads in Germany.[144] This pointillist manner of conceptualising strict(er) liability, as an exception to the rule, was extended to, *inter alia*, automobiles, aircraft and energy installations in the twentieth century.[145] The rule/exception approach to strict liability, although particular to German ways of conceptualising tort liability, is not exclusive to Germany. These peripheral irritants which sought to internalise the costs of activities of large-scale industries placed pressure on the individualised conception of tort law. They came into conflict with the fault paradigm and began to reverse the consequences of private law reasoning

perspective d'un système fondé sur la corrélation entre le profit de l'activité d'autrui et le risque engendré par celui-ci, ce qui importe c'est de déterminer quels sont des risques qui doivent normalement peser sur l'entreprise' (996, 997).

141 J Morgan, 'Liability for Independent Contractors in Contract and Tort: Duties to Ensure That Care Is Taken' (2015) 74 *Cambridge Law Journal* 109. See D Ibbetson, 'The Law of Tort in the Nineteenth Century: The Rise of the Tort of Negligence' in Ibbetson (n 24), 170–87, esp 181–84, arguing that *Rylands v Fletcher* can be viewed as a circumnavigation of the limits of vicarious liability. At least, in the United Kingdom, its march was stalled, if not ended, in *Read v Lyons* [1947] AC 156.

142 Brüggemeier (n 40), 119.

143 See *ibid*, 118–32, for Brüggemeier's extensive treatment of the jurisprudence.

144 Brüggemeier (n 120): 'The German answer to the "age of railways" was a sort of strict civil liability (1838/1871), out of which the modern *Gefahrdungshaftung* developed' (3).

145 *Ibid*.

alone. An equivalent English *harbinger* of things to come is the Workmen's Compensation Acts, which viewed the firm as an organisation with responsibilities towards workers.[146] As Collins argues, this peripheral legislation came to the centre in the twentieth century and began to influence how arguments were made and how judgments were given in the courts.[147] From isolated regulations that dealt with the consequences of industry on the railroads and socially ameliorative measures for workers, the regulatory technique became dominant in the twentieth century, and was coupled with a new conceptualisation of the role of law as a corrective to social and economic problems. In the background is an organisational concept of liability which interacts with questions of insurance to shape the scope of tort liability. This muddle could have been avoided but for the nineteenth-century systematisers who equated the law of torts with individual fault.

2 *Public Bureaucracy: A Public Law of Tort*

In the nineteenth century a distinctive public law of tort emerged in France. In England, by contrast, judges grappled with existing grounds for recovery. Again, the issue of fault has cast a long shadow over the liability of public authorities and the state. It is instructive to compare both approaches as the same underlying classical concept of individual responsibility impacted on the articulation of recovery. If one assumes that the state should be liable, how can the state be accommodated within this individualised model of liability?

(i) France

In nineteenth-century France, *le roi ne peut mal faire* was replaced by a general principle of state liability in tort. This was achieved in 'small steps'.[148] The reasons for the reluctance of the administrative courts to allow for tortious recovery against the administration relate mainly to the slow emergence of

[146] See D Brodie, *Enterprise Liability and the Common Law* (Cambridge: Cambridge University Press, 2010). Brodie details the historical influences on the emergence of enterprise liability in the common law in his introduction. On the Workmen's Compensation Act, 1897: 'The Act was a remarkable piece of social legislation and imposed a form of strict liability on employers. Compensation for industrial injuries was now seen as the responsibility of enterprise' (3) .

[147] H Collins, 'Utility and Rights in Common Law Reasoning: Rebalancing Private Law through Constitutionalizaton', LSE Law, Society and Economy Working Paper 6/2007. Collins was not the first to notice the profound implications of special legislation for the law, see Smith's (n 118) prescient paper in 1914.

[148] D Fairgrieve, *State Liability in Tort: A Comparative Law Study* (Oxford: Oxford University Press, 2003), 9.

independent administrative courts, the particular French conception of the separation of powers, and the traditional concept of sovereignty.[149] Harlow emphasises the latter as particularly important: 'At the political level, the idea of the Nation-State, whose fundamental attribute is Sovereignty, formed a serious obstacle to imposition of legal liability on the State.'[150] However, as Harlow equally notes, this principle of unfettered sovereignty exists in tension with the notion that the state is a legal entity subject to the rule of law.[151]

The state immunity from tort was first chipped away and gradually replaced. In *Blanco*, the case was framed as one of individual liability of an employee and the vicarious liability of the state. The claimant argued the *Code Civil*'s principle of *respondeat superior* should be extended from a private law context to the state. The court rejected the principles applicable to civil liability in the *Code Civil* and '[t]he rules of administrative liability were held to be of a distinct and special character'.[152] That they were distinct and special, of course, justified the Conseil *d'État*'s jurisdiction. The relevant test was whether the tort was committed in the *service public*. This was intended, initially, to *restrict* liability by taking account of the 'need to balance the exercise of private rights with the general public interest'.[153]

Hence, civil liability of the administration could be neither 'general nor absolute'. What the court in *Blanco* did, in effect, was to allow for a special regime of administrative liability to be carved out 'for damages caused by the actions of persons which [the state] employed in the public service'.[154] Its justification was based on the separation of powers. Hence, the decision was both expansionary, developing a general principle of state liability, and restrictive, suggesting that liability would be more limited than that of private parties.[155] *Pelletier* added to this the distinction between personal acts and *fautes de service*, with the latter attracting the liability of the state. Finally, in

149 *Ibid.* Harlow notes that this traditional concept of sovereignty was challenged by L Duguit, who reconceptualised the role of the state as a provider of services. see C Harlow, 'Administrative Liability: A Comparative Study of French and English Law' (PhD thesis, 1979), 12.

150 Harlow (n 149) cites for the origins of the rule of law argument: N Johnson, 'Law as the Articulation of the State: A German Tradition Seen through British Eyes' (unpublished paper); HC Dowdall, 'The Word "State"' (1923) 39 *Law Quarterly Review* 98; E Borchard, 'Governmental Liability in Tort' (1924–25) 34(1) *Yale Law Journal* 129; GDH Cole, *The Social Contract; and Discourses* (London: Dent, 1973), 236; Fairgrieve (n 148), 11.

151 Harlow (n 149), 12, citing Bodin.

152 Fairgrieve (n 148), 11.

153 *Ibid.*

154 Harlow (n 149), 13.

155 Harlow relates this restrictiveness to the sanction, as distinct from compensatory, rationale for state liability. It was also restrictive in this period due to the *acte d'autorité* doctrine which persisted until the *Tomaso Grecco* case.

the *Feutry* decision, the *Tribunal des Conflits* 'extended the jurisdiction of the administrative courts to local authorities based on a unitary conception of the State'.[156] This provided the basis of a corporate view of the state which distinguished state liability from ordinary civil liability viewed on individual conduct with a doctrine of vicarious liability to attribute liability to the 'master'. In other words, these decisions differentiated administrative liability from delictual responsibility. However, the *faute de service* was to be judged according to the standard of fault or gross fault and therefore the distinction was more apparent than real. In this sense, by tying the liability of the state to the fault of an individual servant, this was a principle of vicarious liability not dissimilar to the type of liability in Article 1384. The difference lay, apparently, in the special nature of the employment contract between a state employee and the state. This was a limiting principle. Second, the state retained the right to sue the individual tortfeasor. Third, not all tortious acts of employees were sufficient to fall under the heading '*faute de service*'. The court took it upon itself to reconcile 'public needs with private interests'.[157]

Despite the court's remonstrations that state liability did not depend on the rules of the *Code Civil*, in the early days at least, it was dependent on its conceptual framework. Harlow refers to this as the 'gravitational pull' of the *Code Civil*.[158] Hence, an action could be brought against the state understood as a corporate entity only if fault of an employee could be demonstrated. This is similar to the notion of *faute d'autrui* whereby the latter must trigger the civil responsibility of the principal. The difference in *Blanco*, at least, is that there were further reasons to limit this type of recovery. This was, as stated, based on balancing the public interest with the private rights of the citizen.[159] If it is correct to argue that at this stage of legal development (late nineteenth century) fault remained an individualised concept, then the state's liability depended on an *individualised and moral* view of the tort law.[160] In the early days, it was not yet appropriate to speak of recovery for systemic failure – this would come later. Second, the rationale for recovery according to Harlow was to sanction the state, as distinct from compensate or repair the injured party. Harlow argues that because it was developed in tandem with an abuse of

[156] Here, I closely follow Harlow's (n 149) characterisation of developments at pages 27–28.

[157] Harlow (n 149), 26.

[158] *Ibid*, 30.

[159] Per *Blanco* (www.legifrance.gouv.fr; 5 March 2014): 'Que cette responsabilité n'est ni générale, ni absolue ; qu'elle a ses règles spéciales qui varient suivant les besoins du service et la nécessité de concilier les droits de l'Etat avec les droits privés.'

[160] It is probably accurate to say that in 1873 it did, but it is evident that *Blanco* was decided on the eve of great change.

powers doctrine, it came to be seen as a sanction for maladministration rather than a compensatory remedy. While state liability later developed towards compensation, there remains a tension between a sanction-based view of liability and a compensatory one.

However, this initial emergence of an individualised fault-based state liability was not to last. In fact, the fault-based liability of the *Conseil d'État* coexisted alongside other forms of strict recovery against the state. Because they were based on statute, these 'exceptions' to the general rule of no recovery in the nineteenth century were developed piecemeal and covered areas such as war damage compensation and compensation for losses caused by public works such as road, canal and railway construction.[161] Harlow argues that they could have been the basis for a general principle of risk or strict governmental liability but the prevailing emphasis on fault in the late nineteenth century prevented its emergence. However, by the early twentieth century Duguit had proffered just such a theory. Harlow demonstrates how Duguit in the early years of the turn of the twentieth century reconceptualised the law of state liability, giving it a fresh and stricter basis centred on the concept of public service. No longer was public service a limit to recovery, but justified wider recovery than that which arose in a purely private context. Duguit argued that liability of the state cannot be premised on fault because the state, as a corporate body, cannot commit a fault. In other words, it would be to submit the state to a version of the pathetic fallacy.[162] This led to the reformulation of state liability on the basis of equality before public charges deriving ultimately from the protection of private property mandated in the post-Revolutionary period. Ironically, the emphasis on the 'special' nature of state liability once the basis for restricting recovery became a motor of liability. The shift was indeed swift because *Blanco* was decided on the precipice of the transformation from the society of individuals to the society of organizations which impacted on the discussion as to the functions of tort law by stressing the limitations of the classical model of private law.

(ii) England

In England by the nineteenth century it was firmly established that the Crown enjoyed immunity in tort law: 'The King can do no wrong'. This is the

[161] Harlow (n 149) outlines the various provisions.

[162] This undercurrent in scholarly debate is noted also by G Williams, 'Vicarious Liability and the Master's Indemnity' (1957) 20(3) *Modern Law Review* 220 when he discusses the tendency to view the firm in a similar anthropomorphic light. This, it is argued, is symptomatic of what Ladeur refers to as the society of organisations.

common historical basis from which the two jurisdictions depart. For Harlow, the subsequent differences that emerged are overstated. What Fairgrieve refers to as the 'injustice of Crown immunity' was meliorated by special legislation to deal with specific incidents of liability. 'A practice evolved whereby the Crown would stand behind the individual Crown servant and pay the damages and costs if a private employer would have been vicariously liable in similar circumstances.'[163] Therefore, if there is a difference between the two jurisdictions it is in consequence of the fact that in English private law a distinction between the personal liability of individual public servants and immunity of the state was copper-fastened, in contrast to France where a model of liability developed which came to stress the corporate liability of the state.[164] The latter, as noted, comprehends the notion of *faute de service* (fault in the administrative system) and, as such, has an expansionary dynamic.[165] Second, although the Crown could do no wrong, a distinction was made between the Crown as sovereign and the acts of public authorities. As Harlow points out, it was curtailed in *Mersey Docks and Harbour Board v Gibbs*.[166] The judgment concerned damage caused by negligence of a harbour authority. The House of Lords deprived the shield of Crown immunity to a large number of public corporations which offered ordinary commercial services to the public.[167] Another notable judgment from this period is *Geddis v Proprietors of Bann Reservoir* which muddied the waters somewhat by indicating that public authorities may be liable for their acts or omissions where they are based on statutory duties, but this was again premised on an individualised view of tort law.[168]

[163] Fairgrieve (n 148), 10.

[164] Harlow (n 149). On the deeper significance, see JWF Allison, *A Continental Distinction in the Common Law: A Historical and Comparative Perspective on English Public Law* (Oxford: Oxford University Press, 2000). Harlow shows that the difference is overstated because the *Conseil d'État* deploys a number of control mechanisms, which produce similar outcomes.

[165] My point here is that by diverting from the interpersonal conception of tort law, it allows questions of distributive justice more scope.

[166] (1866) LR 1 HL 93.

[167] As cited and explained in Harlow (n 149), 43.

[168] *Geddis v Proprietors of Bann Reservoir* (1878) 3 App Cas 430 This is at least how the judgment came to be seen retrospectively. In *Home Office v Dorset Yacht Co Ltd* [1970] AC 1004, Lord Reid accepted that statutory duties were duties owed to the Crown and not to private individuals: 'I would agree [that statutory duties are owed to the Crown], but there is very good authority for the proposition that if a person performs a statutory duty carelessly so that he causes damage to a member of the public which would not have happened if he had performed his duty properly he may be liable' (1031).

Therefore, '[f]rom the middle of the nineteenth century, it became clear that public bodies could be liable for the torts of their servants'.[169] However, whether for expediency or principle, the *Public Authorities Protection Act 1893* placed limitations on this form of recovery including rules regarding costs to discourage claims.[170] It was not until the *Crown Proceedings Act 1947* that liability of the Crown returned to the fold.[171] In that Act, the Crown was equated with a private person of full age and capacity in respect of tortious liability. However, this equality principle meant that the Crown was read into a private law based on individuals and their transactions rather than stressing the unique role of the Crown (or state) in the provision of public services. This included the use of the doctrine of vicarious liability against the Crown.

However, no 'special' concept of Crown liability was established. By the mid-twentieth century, though, the state as service provider was an increasingly plausible account in light of the previous half-century of social legislation, and the new impetus for corrective legislation given by the Beveridge report.

In sum, the courts were less willing than their French counterparts to abandon an individualised view of tort law to meet the needs of claimants in actions against the state. However, the law of torts was transforming in any event such that the question of state liability, in the absence of a concept of the state, would re-emerge. Dicey's conceptualisation, based as it was on the parity or equality principle, was unsuited to the activities of the state because the legislative, democratic state's main torts can be described as omissions. These omissions in activities of the state were accommodated in the framework of individualised torts or acts by a great deal of casuistry.[172]

D CONCLUSION

No sooner had the individualised model emerged than it was breaking down. However, an individualised view of legal responsibility remained an important, distinctive means to view ascription. It provides a powerful normative model of liability, which continues to influence the law, existing in tension with what will be referred to in the next chapter as an organisational model of

[169] Fairgrieve (n 148), 11.
[170] *Ibid*.
[171] *Ibid*, 12.
[172] Although, more recently, see *Michael* (n 130).

liability.[173] In the nineteenth century, the legal systems of all main Western jurisdictions refocused their private laws on individual self-realisation, through the will theory and its limit, in fault. This both provides a static or constitutional structural support for an experimental, acentric society and prescribes its normative limits. Fault, in this schema, is subsidiary, such that it would not undermine the basic acentric programming of modern law. However, fault *qua* norm is a bridging device through which normality enters and re-enters the law when demarcating the scope of interpersonal justice.[174]

This model, of course, ignored the rise of the vertically integrated enterprise, and indeed the 'regulatory' and welfare state, the activities of which lay behind the acts of tortfeasors. This is unsurprising because at the start of this period neither the vertically integrated firm nor the regulatory state had emerged as an institutional form, and knowledge had hardly differentiated into specialisms.[175] Enterprise was conducted by merchants in partnerships,[176] not yet by corporations, and the state had not yet assumed wide and intrusive 'social functions'.[177] In consequence, the need for a corporate form of liability did not yet exist. Without large bureaucracy – public or private – specialist, aggregative knowledge had not yet emerged. When the changes in the knowledge base at the end of the nineteenth century were perceived, and found troubling, this model of individualised fault came under pressure. This was because knowledge was increasingly technical in nature, and could not be scrutinised by simply reconstructing behaviour as what a *bonus paterfamilias*, or reasonable man, would have done in the circumstances. This was the case in terms of liability as it applied to both public and private actors. The moral, individualised view of tort law was about to be changed utterly.

173 Its legacy is clearly visible in the career of *Rylands v Fletcher* [1868] UKHL 1 in the United Kingdom, which has wavered from quasi-strict liability, and back towards fault-based recovery over the past 150 years.

174 Both in a dynamic sense, namely by changing concepts of what constitutes reasonable interpersonal conduct, and in the more technical, systems theory sense of re-entry, *ie* the system's internal modelling of its environment.

175 See White (n 57) on this point.

176 For a fascinating retelling of the private company, see P Ireland, 'Limited liability, Shareholder Rights and the Problem of Corporate Irresponsibility' (2010) 34 *Cambridge Journal of Economics* 837–56.

177 A Chandler, *The Visible Hand: The Managerial Revolution in American Business* (Cambridge, MA: Harvard Belknap, 1977), 28: 'Specialization in Finance and transportation, unlike that in distribution, led to an important institutional development: the growth of the incorporated stock company.' This corporate form was required in areas where large amounts of capital were needed such as banking, turnpikes and canals.

2

Tort Law and the Society of Organisations

A INTRODUCTION

No sooner had the classical model of tort liability emerged than it began to strain and bend.[1] While classical legal positivism assumes a strict separation of fact and norm, which is a necessary consequence of the operative closure of the legal system, this 'self-observation of the legal system', so to speak, drastically underestimates the embeddedness of the normative legal system in its cognitive knowledge base.[2] There is a strong connection between 'normal' expectations and legal norms whether, to use the categories of the common law, one refers to the duty of care or the standard of care in negligence. In other words, what Ladeur refers to as 'bridging' or 'hybrid' concepts such as negligence are sufficiently cognitively open to adapt to newer understandings of normality or 'fact', which is then normatively coded in the legal system as duties of reasonable care.[3] In the late nineteenth century the emerging generalised duty of care and the standard of care were products of a liberal legal order that, on the one hand, provided the basic modern architecture of experimentation, particularly through elevating contract-as-will, and, on the

1 This tension is already present in Holmes' account of tort. Although Holmes, in his early writings, developed a fully fledged doctrine of negligence premised on fault, later he introduced a particular statistical understanding of tort law in the common law. For a good analysis of early and late Holmes, see J Witt, *The Accident Republic* (Cambridge, MA: Harvard University Press, 2004), ch 2.

2 See KH Ladeur, 'The Postmodern Condition of Law and Societal "Management of Rules": Facts and Norms Revisited' (2006) 27 *Zeitschrift für Rechtssoziologie Heft* 1 87.

3 See KH Ladeur, 'The Social Epistemology of Risk Observation and Management – Modern Law and the Transformation of Its Cognitive Infrastructure' in HW Micklitz & T Tridimas (eds), *Risk and EU Law* (Cheltenham: Elgar, 2015), 49, at 53. Although Ladeur refers to 'danger' as a bridging concept, he also remarks: '*Erfahrung*' is, by itself, a typical hybrid concept which integrates informational, practical and normative elements. Its role in public law can be compared to the rules defining 'negligence' in private law' (citation omitted).

other hand, set its outer limits in excess of the will in tort. However, tort law had not been fully extricated from more atavistic notions of naturally occurring harm and the implication that losses should lie where they fall absent affirmative, individual negligent conduct. The emergence of a community-based (objective) standard of care, however, set the scene for the excision of pre-modern notions of subjective and individualised wrongdoing.[4] But, the general model of classical tort liability was rule-oriented and individualistic (just rules of interpersonal conduct), drawing on distributed experience to ascribe legal responsibility to individuals; it was, as such, blind to the possibility that certain individual 'acts' are better captured in terms of a social concept of 'activities'.[5]

This changed fundamentally at the turn of the twentieth century when 'a new type of group-based knowledge ... which relies upon rules of probability which imposed order on and allowed for recognition of patterns in phenomena which hitherto had been regarded as subject to blind chance'.[6] This group-based knowledge assisted forward-looking planning and facilitated the rise of governance structures,[7] chiefly public bureaucracy and its counterpart,

4 To be clear, regarding the common law, a general concept of negligence emerged only towards the end of the legal formalist period. Its rise corresponds to the rise of mass accidents. Its conceptual tools, fault and the concept of a *general* duty, are creatures of the nineteenth-century rationalisation of the law. It came to prominence as a rationalisation of due care, because trespass concerned with property damage was inadequate to a rising industrialising society. This is true at the level of the scholarship, *eg* Pollock and Holmes – and in certain judicial pronouncements such as that of Brett MR in *Heaven v Pender* (general duty), *LeLievre v Gould* ('proximity'). It was not until the twentieth century that they were generalised in legal doctrine in *Donoghue v Stevenson*. Although this was certainly a gradual process, as B Hepple, 'Negligence: The Search for Coherence' (1997) 50(1) *Current Legal Practice* 69, avers, citing J Salmond, *Salmond on Torts* 6th ed (London: Sweet & Maxwell, 1924), who was still referring to subjective states of mind as required for negligence. To be clear, *pace* G Brüggemeier, *Common Principles of Tort Law: A Prestatement of Law* (London: BIICL, 2004), 66, reasonable care is a normative concept, albeit one highly dependent on cognitive definitions of normality.

5 F Ewald, *L'Etat Providence* (Paris: Grasset, 1986). Although when one notes that the legal system was 'blind', one is speaking anachronistically, because the collective attribution of responsibility required the emergence of a concept of risk, the subject of this chapter. Ewald makes this point clearly.

6 Ladeur (n 2), 87. See J Gordley, *The Jurists: A Critical History* (Oxford: Oxford University Press, 2013), 92–93, for how among the late scholastics strict liability was denied as a matter of commutative justice because it was said to rest on 'chance' as distinct from will. This framework was taken over into early modern law.

7 See P Kjaer, 'The Multiplicity of Normative Orders in World Society' in *Constitutionalism in the Global Realm: A Sociological Approach* (London: Routledge, 2014), 41–62, uses the German term *eigenstructures*. This indicates that they have emerged from within existing structures, *eg* the firm from the joint stock company unlimited by guarantee, and the state from the feudal order. Nothing turns on this historiography.

the private, vertically integrated firm in which hierarchical decision-making occurred.[8] Society itself became conceptualised as an 'organisation of organisations' in which different organisations fulfilled distinctive and interdependent social functions.[9] Territorial differentiation remained the main 'frame of reference' within which functional differentiation unfolded; however, the state took on a progressively more interventionist role in the economy and society, and its regulatory role increasingly 'irritated' the classical liberal law.

However, the most fundamental pressure on liberal law was not state *dirigisme*, but rather the more profound 'rupture' between liberal legal normative programmes and the law's observation of cognitive 'reality'. The advent of group-based knowledge may be described as an epistemological 'break of symmetry' or 'rupture' between the 'feedback loops' of the legal system and the knowledge base of society. In the 'society of organisations', a dichotomy emerged between distributed 'experience' and 'expert knowledge'. What is normal and, closely related, normatively acceptable, could no longer be based on everyday experience, but became a question of risk calculation not accessible to ordinary people. The upshot, as I will argue, is ultimately a secondary normative remodelling of the legal system through the establishment of a new organisational model of liability as a *rival and supplement* to individualised responsibility.[10] In tort law terms, the blind chance of *injury* is replaced by a notion of statistically regular *accidents*, which do not fit the anterior dichotomy between fault as affirmative action and *fortuna*.[11] The law, in addition, began to 'look' beyond individuals, and their fault, to the place of the individual within representative groups, and gradually diminished the notion that injuries can be attributed to 'act of god' or *vis major* in the absence of individual fault. Accidents are the consequence of human (collective)

[8] *Ibid*. A Chandler, *The Visible Hand: The Managerial Revolution in American Business* (Cambridge, MA: Harvard Belknap, 1977), for the 'firm', and his path-breaking conceptualisation of the firm as 'private bureaucracy'.

[9] The sociology of E Durkheim is exemplary of holism, interdependence and the distinctive role of intermediate organisations. E Durkheim, *De la Division du Travail Social* 2nd ed (Paris: PUF, 1930). On the connection between Durkheim and Léon Duguit see G Comparato & R Condon, 'The General Transformations of Private Law Since Léon Duguit: Autonomy, Responsibility and Sovereignty in European Private Law' in L De Almeida et al (eds), *The Transformation of Economic Law Essays in Honour of Hans-W. Micklitz* (Oxford: Hart, 2019), 115–36.

[10] This also involved the internal differentiation of the legal system. See H Collins, *The Law of Contract* 4th ed (Cambridge: Cambridge University Press, 2003), 37–39. The universalism of contract and tort was replaced by the emergence of, *eg*, distinct labour, employment and tenancy law. For Germany see F Wieacker (T Weir trans), *A History of Private Law in Europe* (Oxford: Clarendon Press, 1995).

[11] Ewald (n 5).

activities rather than individual acts or the 'natural' order. Accidents, in short, are *social* phenomena.[12]

B COGNITIVE RUPTURE AND ORGANISATIONAL RESPONSIBILITY

Rules derived by a process of logical deduction from pre-established conceptions of contract and obligation have broken down before the slow and steady action of utility and justice.[13]

The liberal legal order's knowledge base was individualised, distributed experience. In the society of organisations, by contrast, knowledge became disembedded from quotidian 'experience'. The implications of this 'rupture' impacted on both contract and tort law's observations of 'reality'. Instead of viewing relationships in terms of rules of just interpersonal conduct, a collective perspective of social interdependence became currency in the early decades of the twentieth century.[14] From the cognitive observation of 'reality', a *normative* organisational model of liability developed, increasingly looking beyond the individual and towards the position of individuals within overarching groups.[15] This change in law's normative programmes in tort was enabled by the new 'reality' that firms, and indeed the state, were well placed to make rational, risk management decisions and their expertise could be channelled to reduce the likelihood of accidents, and also because it was *just* to place the typical costs of their activities upon them. These organisations could, *additionally*, better shoulder the costs of accidents through third-party insurance and self-insurance.[16] The emerging product liability law is a paradigmatic example.[17] Beyond product liability, the doctrine of vicarious liability, whether

[12] *Ibid.*

[13] B Cardozo, *The Nature of the Judicial Process* (New Haven, CT: Yale University Press, 1921), 99–100.

[14] The concept of 'interdependence' as a *leitmotif* is noted by D Kennedy, 'Three Globalizations of Law and Legal Thought: 1850–2000' in D Trubek & A Santos (eds), *The New Law and Economic Development: A Critical Appraisal* (Cambridge: Cambridge University Press, 2006), 25–71, at 63.

[15] See G Keating, 'Products Liability As Enterprise Liability', USC Gould Legal Studies Research Papers Series No 16-38, 1–44. In Keating's colourful terminology, enterprise (normative) liability is not 'a bizarre regulatory or insurance scheme' (6). I prefer organisation responsibility to capture its place within wider social epistemology, and because it applied not only to enterprises, but across the public/private divide.

[16] Although how states shoulder the costs is more complicated as they cannot use insolvency as a last resort. There is therefore an overt solidaristic element to state liability.

[17] Ladeur (n 2), 96, notes that 'within individualistic rules of liability, problems of the collective attribution of responsibility re-appear; this applies to product liability'.

applied overtly to employers or deployed *mutatis mutandis* against the state is also salutary. It was, of course, these areas of law – namely product liability (mass accidents, the counterpart of mass production), the doctrine of vicarious liability and state liability – in which organisational liability was apt to emerge, because they can easily be seen to touch directly upon the firm and the state as centres of (expert) decision-making, as distinct from individual agents, in the industrialised welfare state. The emergence of the organisational form occurred in both public bureaucracy and 'private bureaucracy', and the model of organisational liability was applied regardless of the liberal public–private divide.[18]

The background to the emergence of 'expert knowledge' can be retraced to the rise of 'social statistics' and, relatedly, the use of insurance as a *generalised* social mechanism.[19] The providential tone of self-reliant *prūdentia* in classical tort law was gradually superseded by a view of accidents as *inevitable* consequences of activities that can and should be insured against. All social problems, it seems, could be explained in terms of iron-clad social laws: probabilities (risks) of accidents, crime, health and so on that remained reasonably constant year on year, which enabled preventive forward-planning and, indeed, insurance.[20] As Ewald states, in consequence, prevention replaced providence as the turn-of-century *leitmotif*:

> Prevention (the vocabulary of which henceforth replaced that of providence) presupposes science, technical control, the idea of possible understanding, and objective measurement of risks. Thus, the problem is no longer that of compensating for practically inescapable losses but of reducing the probability of their occurrence.[21]

[18] Of course, in the United Kingdom, given the equality principle, there was an inevitable spillover effect, albeit not without significant controversy. Elsewhere, in France, in particular, a special organisational regime of liability was developed for the state. The point is not that the details of the regimes of state liability and vicarious liability were identical, but rather the basic organisational model of liability underpinned the expansion of tort liability to the state.

[19] Ewald (n 5) notes at length the seminal important role of Queletet in France in forming the new social sciences, in direct tension with earlier metaphysical views of causation. More recently, Ken Oliphant has conducted an insightful survey of late nineteenth- and early-to-mid twentieth-century common law developments emphasising the somewhat implicit role of liability insurance, see K Oliphant, 'Tort Law, Risk, and Technological Innovation in England' (2014) 59(4) *McGill Law Journal* 819–45, esp 839–40.

[20] Ewald (n 5).

[21] F Ewald (S Utz trans), 'The Return of Descartes Malicious Daemon: An Outline of the Philosophy of Precaution' in T Baker & J Simon (eds), *Embracing Risk: The Changing Culture of Insurance and Responsibility* (Chicago, IL: University of Chicago Press, 2002), 273, at 282.

This expert knowledge of risk, of course, could not be ascertained by reference to distributed experience, but lay in a domain accessible to firms and governments.[22] Brüggemeier states the rupture from providence to prevention in the distinction between danger and risk. For Brüggemeier, '*[d]angers* are the natural events, which have always imperilled mankind: tempests, wild animals on land and sea, epidemics, earthquakes and tsunamis. By contrast, *risks* are man-made contingent perils, in particular in relation to industrial or technical development'.[23] Thus, the concept of prevention is tied to that of risk, and risks are considered subject to rational planning aiming to achieve optimum levels of safety and spread the inevitable costs when risks materialise as accidents.[24] Ultimately, prevention aimed to reinforce individual security.[25] This cognitive rupture – the rise of the social concept of risk – contributed to the new horizon of twentieth-century tort law, and a new concept of organisational liability. However, the shift in emphasis from individualised fault to fair, social risk management did not occur first in juridical tort law and theory;[26] rather, the setting was, across all relevant jurisdictions, the large swathe of social legislation adopted at the end of the nineteenth century, which was aimed at increasing the security of workers, minimising accidents and spreading the costs of industrial accidents through private and social insurance.[27] This new strict liability legislation aimed explicitly to

[22] As Witt points out wryly, statistics is etymologically grounded in the state. See Witt (n 1), 139–40.

[23] See G Brüggemeier, 'Risk and Strict Liability: The Distinct Examples of Germany, the US and Russia', EUI Working Paper Law 2012/29, p 1.

[24] G Calabresi, 'Torts – the Law of the Mixed Society' 56 (1977–78) *Texas Law Review* 519.

[25] Ewald (n 21): 'The nineteenth century's dream of security is tied to a scientific utopia ever more capable of controlling risks. While one cannot eliminate risks altogether (there is never zero risk), they will have been reduced sufficiently to be able to be dealt with collectively: accidents are the by-product, necessary although always more marginalized, of scientific and technical progress. These are special or abnormal risks, the responsibility for which should be spread over the community. Our concept of assured public health and safety involves prevention, the dream of an ever more complete reduction of risk. It is not, at least not on purpose, a measure designed to take on all human misfortunes' (282).

[26] Although Holmes heavily hinted in the direction in *The Common Law*. German scholarship appeared more advanced.

[27] As well as pacifying an increasingly enfranchised working class. In this respect, German law was at the forefront. See *RHPflG*, 1871 on enterprise liability and the introduction of compulsory state insurance for accidents in the workplace in 1884, which as Brüggemeier informs us was the basic model for French legislation, 1898, and the Workmen's Compensation Acts in the United Kingdom and United States. Brüggemeier (n 23) states that technical innovation which led to a proliferation of accidents was the engine of change: 'This new technical-industrial world with its industry – and transport – related accidents forced legal practitioners and legislatures to seek new regulatory strategies for dealing with these risks outside of well-trodden paths of roman-pandectist legal doctrine' (3). The emphasis in

provide security from the risks of the industrial society was,[28] subsequently, enlarged within the post-war welfare state to provide a minimum level of security to citizens from 'cradle to grave'.[29] These legislative efforts introduced a new risk- and group-based logic into statutory law, which then found its way into juridical law in the course of the twentieth century.[30] In Germany, this took the form of special legislation outside the core of civil liability because the civil code (the *BGB*) rested on a liberal constitution which favoured freedom of contract and fault.[31] Elsewhere, parallel steps were taken to reassign the outcomes of contract and tort rules redistributing the benefits and burdens of industrial activity; for example, both France's *loi* 1898[32] and the United Kingdom's Workmen's Compensation Act 1897[33] were a direct riposte

Germany was on social insurance and no-fault statutes, whereas in the common law jurisdictions a greater role was given to compulsory enterprise private insurance as a means to transfer risk, and spread it among the relevant class, and ultimately to pass on the cost to consumers. Brüggemeier also notes pre-1870s harbingers, such as the Prussian Railway Act, 1838, but these should not be overstated, *ie* they rested not on risk, but on '*receptum*' liability, which allowed for contractual waiver.

28 Brüggemeier (n 23), 11, argues that in respect of the German model it had two tracks 'state social insurance and stricter forms of civil liability (enterprise liability and *Gefahrdungshaftung*) beyond the fault principle. The first was in the Bismarck era not to be separated from the political context of the attempted state domestication of the new class of industrial workers and their organisations (socialist parties; trade unions) and their integration into the society of imperial Germany. The special legislation on no-fault liability came from politics, too'.

29 Influential, see TH Marshall, *Citizenship and Social Class and Other Essays* (Cambridge: Cambridge University Press, 1950).

30 See D Priel, 'British Politics, The Welfare State, and Tort Liability of Public Authorities', Warwick School of Law Research Paper No 2010/14. Priel notes on mid-twentieth-century legal scholarship: 'Academic lawyers writing at the time started talking about the area of law in terms of what it "does" (instead of what it "is"), and increasingly this question has come to be examined within the context of its role within the welfare state' (10). And 'The consensus years and the expansion of the welfare state were reflected not only in the creation of new public institutions such as the National Health Service and the Industrial Injuries Scheme, but also in a slow but steady expansion of tort liability against the state and employers, an expansion that effectively reoriented tort law towards becoming a mechanism of insurance concerned with the optimal allocation of risks among different groups in society' (10).

31 Brüggemeier (n 23): 'The different heads of liability for technical risks developed before and after 1900 in the shadow of the great systematic codification of the *BGB*. This lay in the hands of pandectist academics and practitioners . . . Political attempts to incorporate strict liability into the *BGB* failed' (11).

32 Ewald (n 5) notes, in particular, its influence on Saleilles and Josserand.

33 One should not overlook the Employers' Liability Act 1880, which made inroads into the common law defences to a tort action.

to classical contract and tort law and, one might add, its cognitive model of reality.[34] As Cafaggi explains:

> In the last part of the nineteenth century and the first part of the twentieth, the emergence of regulation, and in particular that of welfare regulation, was primarily due to significant limits of compensation. These shortcomings were associated with the *internal structure of civil liability* and the weaknesses of other branches of private law, especially contract and labour law. Worker compensation regimes for industrial accidents are only one example of an emerging body of legislation stimulated by the combined weaknesses of civil liability and labour law.[35]

The 'shortcomings' of the internal structure of civil liability, in our terms the individualistic model of liability premised on fault, 'irritated' tort law.[36] In other words, pointillist social legislative interventions into the internal governance of the firm – how risks were distributed between 'employer' and 'employee' (internal) – had a wider impact on tort law's programming towards 'manufacturers' and 'consumers' (external).[37] Not only did they obliterate the spell of contractual allocation of risks[38] but, more importantly, they challenged the individualised, act-based view of contract and tort introducing risk-based, stricter liability into tort law's former domain. This radiated into juridical tort law's observation of third-party harms.[39] Increasingly, tort liability was viewed as fulfilling a regulatory function, which saw tort liability as a mechanism to indemnify or *compensate* 'victims' for inevitable accidents.[40]

34 See D Brodie, *Enterprise Liability and the Common Law* (Cambridge: Cambridge University Press, 2010). Brodie makes the point that the concept of enterprise liability – what we call organisational liability – owes its origins to the Workmen's Compensation Act.

35 F Cafaggi, 'A Coordinated Approach to Regulation and Civil Liability in European Law: Rethinking Institutional Complementarities' in F Cafaggi (ed), *The Institutional Framework of European Private Law* (Oxford: Oxford University Press, 2006), 191, 192–93 (emphasis added). For similar movements in German, American and Russian law see Brüggemeier (n 23).

36 For detail see GE White, *Tort Law in America: An Intellectual History* (New York: Oxford University Press, 1980); Hepple (n 4).

37 And, indeed, *accident* 'victims' of torts. Note the de-personalisation/de-individualisation.

38 The anterior regime was premised on, *inter alia*, the contractualist doctrine of *volunti non fit inuria*.

39 Jeremiah Smith was an early, and prescient, observer of the reverberations for general tort law of making workers 'a specially protected class'; see J Smith, 'Sequel to Workmen's Compensation Acts' (1914) 27(2) *Harvard Law Review* 235–59, at 237, and see also 253–54 for the rationale of extending recovery to third parties based on the 'theory' of the Workers' Compensation Acts.

40 There is certainly a clear link in Saleilles' treatment of tort law, see R Saleilles, *Les Accidents du Travail et la Responsabilité Civile (essai d'une théorie objective de la responsabilité délictuelle)* (Paris: Rousseau, 1897).

This inexorably requires taking a *normative* view on typical *and* acceptable business risk-taking, as opposed to right, individual conduct. Such a view displaces the individual from the centre of tort law, and instead requires taking an organisational view of activities. The normative role of law becomes that of designating and intermediating between 'active' (risk takers) and 'passive' (risk bearers) groups within society.[41] The standard of care becomes stricter, and where fault is retained, it is casuistically redefined from a question of individual conduct to the running of an unreasonable risk, which is informed by a critical standard of care that draws on expert knowledge – that is, ordinary intuitions about right conduct gleaned 'bottom-up' from social practice (community, distributed knowledge) versus expert or top-down knowledge gleaned from statistics, and a theory of societal interdependence – and which is accessible to the firm and the state. Both the firm and the state become organisational, normative addressees of liability.[42]

The first, sustained scholarly attempts to realign tort law in the light of this emerging risk paradigm occurred in French scholarship, which developed a concept of enterprise liability.[43] Vanguard scholars included Josserand and Saleilles, and, in particular, Duguit, clarified the link between the law and its

41 There are strong parallels in contract law, and Saleilles' theory of the 'contrat d'adhésion', later popularised by Kessler in the common law world. F Kessler, 'Contracts of Adhesion – Some Thoughts about Freedom of Contract' (1943) 43 *Columbia Law Review* 629.

42 See, on the deeper consilience between the new role for public law and private law, L Duguit (F & H Laski trans), *Law in the Modern State* (New York: Huebsch, 1919), 49: 'Public law has become objective just as private law is no longer based on individual right or the autonomy of a private will, but upon the idea of a social function imposed on every person. So government has in turn a social function to fulfil' (49). See also L Greene, 'Tort law Public Law in Disguise' (1959–60) 38 *Texas Law Review* 259; for contract, F Kessler, 'Contracts of Adhesion – Some Thoughts about Freedom of Contract' (1943) 43 *Columbia Law Review* 629.

43 Kennedy (n 14) allots German, French and US scholarship pre-eminent influence at various historical junctures in the shaping of Western 'legal consciousness'. This is somewhat of a simplification. Indeed, to be fair, Kennedynotes the influence of Jhering on French scholarship (37). Nevertheless, it is certainly true that a rich and influential wellspring of French scholarship emerged in the first decades of the twentieth century, and was broadly read outside France. Wieacker offers an explanation as to why the scholarship was most developed in France: F Wieacker, 'The Degeneration of Positivism, and Legal Naturalism' in F Wieacker (T Weir trans), *A History of Private Law in Europe* (Oxford: Clarendon Press, 1995), 442, 456: 'In France, Duguit, Saleilles, and Gény put forward a new theory of interpretation based on law's *fonction sociale*, the need for a new theory being felt earlier in France than in Germany or Switzerland, since the Code there was a hundred years older.' Jhering, in addition, influenced common law scholars. In particular, Cardozo (n 13) noted Jhering's 'great contribution', namely 'a conception of the end of the law as determining the direction of the growth … finds its organon, its instrument, in the method of sociology. Not only origin but goal is the main thing' (102).

social function in order to fashion a principle of strict liability.[44] This paved the way for a law viewed in a regulatory dimension beyond the provision of universalised 'rules of just conduct'.[45] Saleilles and Josserand's development of *La théorie du risque profit* or *théorie du risque d'activité* is of particular importance.[46] This theory of risk–profit rested on a social conception of responsibility infused with a view of the allocation of benefits and burdens of industrial society between active and passive parties.[47] Josserand's justification for the expansion of *la responsabilité* gives an insight into such thinking:

[44] These scholars were not, of course, all in agreement, with some favouring an entirely new socialist and realist law while others concerned themselves with intermural development of the existing legal categories. L Duguit, *La Transformation Générales du Droit Prive depuis le Code Napoléon* (Paris: Alcan, 1912): 'On essayait de justifier le système en torturant quelques textes du Code Napoléon, notamment les articles 1384 et suivants.' This was Duguit's criticism of L Joserrand's *De la Responsabilité du fait des Choses Animées*, and Saleilles' *Les Accidents du Travail et la Responsabilité Civile*. Duguit notes that his inspiration comes from Auguste Comte's *Système de Politique Positive* (1890). See Hayek on what he perceived to be Comte's 'fatal conceit', which we liken to Duguit's methodology: FA Hayek, 'The Fatal Conceit' in WW Bartley III (ed), *The Fatal Conceit: The Errors of Socialism* (London: Routledge, 1988), 66, 68: 'Confusion about justification also stems, particularly so far as the issues that mainly occupy us are concerned, from Auguste Comte, who supposed that we were capable of remaking our moral system as a whole, and replacing it by a completely constructed and justified (or as Comte himself said, "demonstrated") body of rules.'

[45] Kennedy (n 14), stressing the unifying point of critique: 'Their basic idea was that the conditions of late nineteenth-century life represented a social transformation, consisting of urbanization, industrialization, organizational society, globalization of markets, all summarized in the idea of interdependence. Because the will theory was individualist, it ignored interdependence, and endorsed particular legal rules that permitted antisocial behavior of many kinds. The crises of the modern factory (industrial accidents, pauperization) and the urban slum, and later the crisis of the financial markets and the Great Depression, all derived from the failure of coherently individualist law to respond to the coherently social needs of modern conditions of interdependence' (38). Although note Saleilles's attempt to balance subjective and objective law. R Saleilles, *De la personnalité juridique* 2nd ed (Paris: Rousseau, 1922).

[46] These were the leading French scholars who formulated the risk-compensation theory on two bases. Saleilles by a redefinition of fault on the basis of risk, and Josserand by an expansive reading of the *code civil*, art 1384. There were other attempts however, as B Cirhuza Nyamazi notes very precisely in his 'De la responsabilité sans faute de l'administration en droits compares francais, belge et congolais': 'Ces deux doctrines aboutissaient en définitive, à substituer à la notion de la faute un principe de responsabilité plus large, celui du risque. Mais en réalité, il y eut plusieurs théories du risque dont le seul dénominateur commun était la recherche de solutions favorables aux victimes en dehors de toute idée de faute.' www.memoireonline.com/12/09/2953/De-la-responsabilite-sans-faute-de-ladministration-en-droits-compares-francais-belge-et-congol.html (18 July 2016).

[47] However, it is important to note, as Jutras does, that this activity/passivity criterion was not simply liability for being active, but for setting in motion a thing which subsequently causes damage to another party. Jutras goes on to discuss the ambiguity in Josserand's concept of risk–profit, particularly its weaknesses, but it need not detain us here as we are concerned with the

> il arrive tout naturellement que, dépourvus de la sécurité matérielle, nous aspirons de plus en plus à la sécurité juridique ; puisque nous courons de sérieux risques d'être accidentés, ayons, du moins, la certitude d'obtenir à l'occasion, une réparation, nous-mêmes si nous sortons vivants du fâcheux fait-divers, nos héritiers, si notre destin est scellé.[48]

The kernel is that liability law should be modified in the light of the inevitability of accidents wrought by industrialisation. Josserand added that 'l'accident devint anonyme', i.e. not retraceable to individual conduct, but to industrial processes, and therefore fault of the 'patron' or of the company cannot be established in accordance with the traditional subjective or individual fault principle.[49] This is largely because the type of injury that occurs in industrial society no longer corresponds to a direct act – what earlier was referred to as fault as affirmative action – but is an indirect consequence of lawful industrial activity.[50] Therefore, Josserand proposed that legal responsibility should be based on 'cause' alone, founding this principle on 'équité'.[51] Cause in this theory had a particular meaning. It was not individual causation as such: rather, it stands for the principle that he who creates a risk should indemnify those who suffer injury should that risk materialise: the 'théorie du risque crée'.[52] Its rationalisation rested on the idea that the industrial world is a world of activities and in consequence accidents were inevitable; as such,

transformation itself, and not the strengths or weaknesses of a particular theory. See D Jutras, 'Louis and the Mechanical Beast or Josserand's Contribution to Objective Fault in France' (ssrn, August 2014), 321–22. Originally published in K Cooper-Stephenson & E Gibson, *Tort Theory* (York: Captus Press, 1993), 317–41.

48 L Josserand, *L'Évolution de la responsabilité (conférence donnée aux Facultés de Droit de Lisbonne, de Coimbre, de Belgrade, de Bucarest, d'Orades, de Bruxelles, à l'institut français, aux centres juridiques de L'Institut des Hautes Etudes marocaines à Rabat et à Casablanca), Evolutions et Actualités Conférences de Droit Civil* (Paris: Recueil, 1936), 32. This was not, however, only a French phenomenon. See D Ibbetson, *A Historical Introduction to the Law of Obligations* (Cambridge: Cambridge University Press, 2001), n 87: 'Legal Commentators began to stress that negligence liability depended not on a moral principle but on a social one; it was based not on something internal to the defendant but on failure to live up to an external standard, and that external standard was something that be determined by public policy' (197).

49 Josserand (n 44), after examining several alternative approaches, concluded that the fault principle had to be replaced: 'Il faut faire un pas de plus et s'attaquer ouvertement à l'antique notion de la faute aquilienne; il faut dégager la responsabilité de l'idée de faute qui l'enserre dans un domaine devenu trop étroit, et l'asseoir sur une plus large base' (5, 52).

50 Saleilles (n 40) makes this point clearly by contrasting direct and secondary cause: 'Il s'agit donc d'une cause immédiate et directe qui n'est le fait positif de l'auteur responsable, ni le fait des choses, mais qui se rattache cependant, comme cause seconde, a un fait d'imprudence de la part de l'auteur responsable' (51).

51 Josserand (n 44), 103–4. See also Saleilles (n 40), 54–61, especially for Saleilles's consideration of 'participation indirecte et lointaine' (60).

52 Josserand (n 44), 113. Josserand attributed this theory to Saleilles (n 40), 105.

because certain activities impose inevitable accidents on its passive victims as a cost of social progress, it was only right and fair to impose an indemnity on those actors who generated the risks of harm when they materialised as injury.[53] In other words, law has a role in safeguarding the interests of those upon which non-reciprocal risks have been placed.[54]

Saleilles referred to this concept as 'causalité industrielle',[55] which was premised on the notion of social justice as justice *qua* risk distribution.[56] Translated into French law, it gave rise to a principle of strict liability for business activities through an expansive reinterpretation of articles 1384–86 of *Code Civil*. Yet its influence can be felt beyond strict liability in the way

[53] Notably, this normative 'passive'/'active' distinction was later exploded by Coase, at least on one reading of his thesis see R Coase, 'The Problem of Social Cost' (1960) 3 *Journal of Law & Economics* 1.

[54] There is a certain consistency here with his argument regarding abuse of rights. Jutras (n 47) argues that this protection of the weaker party dimension meant that as a general theory of strict liability it ran into difficulty in those situations in which such differences of power did not exist: 'For Josserand, this objective liability was meant to protect the "weaker party". It did not make sense to invoke it when both parties had been creating identical risks for one another. For that reason, it could only be applied in the context of the imposition of nonreciprocal risks' (323). See G Priest, 'The Invention of Enterprise Liability: A Critical History of the Intellectual Foundations of Modern Tort Law' (1985) 14 *Journal of Legal Studies* 461. In the context of the American twentieth century, expansion of product liability makes the link between the 'myth' of freedom of contract and product liability directly. Discussing Kessler, he states that if one assumes that unequal bargaining power means that contract is not a reliable protection of an individual's interest, then tort law has a regulatory role to correct contracts brought about by asymmetries of power: 'The narrative [Kessler's] persuaded the courts that the nineteenth-century nation of independent and equal merchants had disappeared and had been replaced by a twentieth-century nation of product consumers who, because lacking in bargaining power, are uninformed, unable to influence manufacturer behavior, and thus totally dependent on courts for protection. It follows directly that nineteenth-century contract law must also be replaced with law more responsive to modern problems' (494–95). J Stapleton, 'A New Theory of Strict Moral Enterprise Liability' in *Product Liability* (London: Butterworths, 1994), 185, 196, explicitly draws the parallel with consumer protection, *ie* the parallel between employer liability and the Unfair Contract Terms Act, 1977: 'Although not imposing strict liability, other UK legislation, including the important Unfair Contract Terms Act 1977, has placed those who act in the course of business in a more demanding position in terms of civil liability than those who do not, and EC measures have followed this pattern' (citations omitted).

[55] Saleilles (n 40). If the particulars of his argument differ, Saleilles is consilient with Josserand in terms of its justification. 'La vie moderne, plus que jamais, est une question des risques. . . . Le point de vue pénal est hors de cause, le point de vue social est seul en jeu. . . . forcément, en raison et en justice, il faut que ce soit celui qui en agissant a pris à sa charge les conséquences de son fait et son active' (5).

[56] Fault becomes objective under this conception referred to as an *obligation légale*. It is, per Saleilles (n 40), an 'obligation imposée par la loi pure et simple de l'obligation légale, obligation imposée par la loi sur le fait du rapport de causalité industrielle, en raison seulement de la loi de justice sociale sur la répartition des risques' (12).

negligence came to be interpreted. As Ehrenzweig puts it: 'Exposing the community to risk, rather than causation of the individual harm has become the basis of liability in both fields [negligence and strict liability], even in countries in which fault has been called "'the mother of all enterprise liability".'[57] This meant, in brief, that apart from providing just rules of interpersonal conduct, tort law was now viewed as a form of indemnity justified by the actions of an active party vis-à-vis a passive victim.[58] So long as the active–passive distinction between risk creator and victim remained good, organisations that were in a better position to prevent risks materialising should be legally responsible on a test of 'causation'.[59] It is crucial to note that this is at base a normative model of ascription to groups *qua* their organisational actors: first, it establishes that risks should be attributed to organisations as a normative premise; second, that this assists risk spreading. It is liability based on a materialised or social approach to accidents and might be described as 'moral enterprise liability'.[60] Thus, tort liability is reconceived in social terms as a means to intermediate between different social groups *qua* their organisational form, for example manufacturers/consumers, employer/employee. Although this resulted in a secondary normative remodelling of tort law, often changing outcomes that follow from the liberal law's 'just rules of conduct', the law did not simply negate that which came before and start again from first principles.[61] In all main jurisdictions, the core private law – contract and torts – evolved in a more casuistic manner.[62] Doctrinal tort law remained on its face

57 AA Ehrenzweig, 'Negligence without Fault' (1966) 54(4) *California Law Review* 1422.

58 In this respect the French scholars were solidaristic, most clearly expressed in Duguit's treatment of the concept of duty, whether this concerned the duties private parties owed each other or those which the state owed private parties. In the USA, on the other hand, the approach appeared to be more directly utilitarian. Although Priest avers that the approach that developed before, but more especially after, the Second Restatement aimed at indemnifying the poor and reducing accidents, it had a more important economic basis, namely the Pigovian thesis about the efficiency gains of internalizing externalities. See Priest (n 54).

59 Josserand (n 44), 88: 'De là l'idée de faute objective qui n'est plus qu'un rapport de causalité entre le dommage réalisé et une activité considérée comme constitutive de risques.'

60 Stapleton (n 54), 186.

61 It did not constitute a 'revolution' also within juridical law. *Compare* G Priest, 'The Modern Expansion of Tort Law: Its Sources, Its Effects, and Its Reform' (1991) 5(3) *Journal of Economic Perspectives* 31: 'The legislative intervention in tort law, however, itself constituted a revolution. Tort law scholarship gained a novel dimension: If the worker injury component of tort law could be changed to achieve some social gain, what other part of tort law should also be changed?' (33).

62 The reformulation most explicitly departs from the individualist model in France under the influence on the public side of the theory of service public, and on the private by the concept of risk. See Duguit (n 42). In a fascinating paper, Deakin refers to casuistry as the evolutionary salient term of 'exaption': S Deakin, 'The Evolution of Vicarious Liability', Allen & Overy

interpersonal, but the interpersonal law was embedded in an organisational framework. The concept of *weak commutative justice* – interpersonal justice framed by a social concept of duty and care – aptly captures the transformation. In the common law, the duty of care (protective scope of tort law) was enlarged and extended to indirect or remote accidents, and the standard of care was reframed to capture organisational risk management. This ultimately results, of course, in the decentring of the individual in tort law through the emergence of a second normative model of ascription.[63] This chapter will, again, draw primarily on common law examples, but refer also to continental law examples to underscore the point.

1 *Materialised Social Responsibility:* Donoghue v Stevenson

The old forms remain but they are filled with new content.[64]

The English courts never went as far as to fully embrace strict liability, at least not overtly.[65] However, the courts did embrace a type of hybrid negligence regime in which the social dimension of activities is evident, while the standard of care is increasingly critical, namely, a standard of care that does not rely exclusively on a community standard of care, but rather imposes liability in the absence of fault as classically understood because the enterprise is a better position to reduce costs of accidents, through risk spreading and insurance.[66] The loss shifting and spreading approach as a general policy prefers enterprise liability and places burdens on enterprises not only in terms of the cost of accidents, but as a way to ensure prospective improvements to safety standards such as to avoid further third-party harm. Liability as deterrence strong-arms industry expertise to innovate and is, in systems theory

Lecture, University of Cambridge, 8 November 2017 https://resources.law.cam.ac.uk/privatelaw/the_evolution_of_vicarious_liability_(lecture%20text).pdf (accessed 23 June 2021), 5.

63 KH Ladeur, 'The Financial Crisis – A Case of Network Failure?' in P Kjaer et al (eds), *The Financial Crisis in Constitutional Perspective: The Dark Side of Functional Differentiation* (Oxford: Oxford University Press, 2011), 63, at 72, in which Ladeur refers to the role of law in the society of organisations as that of 'the mediator of Exchange processes among representative "encompassing" groups and organisations with their own internal and external stable cognitive infrastructure'.

64 Cardozo (n 13), 101.

65 *Read v Lyons* [1947] AC 156 is often considered a line in the sand, so to speak. However, the calibration of the standard of care, which Lord MacMillan suggests in *Read*, may very well come close to 'strict liability' in an appropriate case.

66 Ehrenzweig (n 57).

terms, a normative support for cognitive learning.[67] Before focusing on the 'critical' standard of care, however, the expansion of the duty of care from direct to indirect or remote injury will be examined.

(i) The Duty of Care and the Organisation

The post-*Buick*,[68] post-*Donoghue* 'escape out of contract law' allowed for direct actions to be brought against manufacturers, 'leapfrogging' retailers at least with regard to personal injuries.[69] The duty of care was, first, extended to remote accident 'victims'. Secondly, accidents are viewed in a social dimension. *Manufacturers qua* groups that introduce risks (active parties) into society should be responsible when those risks materialise as harm towards *consumers qua* groups (passive parties). While the standard of care is fault, it is a fault in manufacturing processes, and not attributed to individual behaviour. In fact, it is the firm that is being held legally responsible. Therefore, despite appearances, there is a great deal of consistency between the underlying structure of legal reasoning in *Donoghue v Stevenson*, and the French scholarship that emphasises so called *causalité industrielle* and anonymous injury. Industry in the form of firms should pay its way for the typical or business risks it introduces, and this moral- or fairness-based argument is supported by loss spreading through insurance and pricing, and deterrence, that is, internal risk management.[70] While, on its surface, legal reasoning remained wedded to justice *inter partes* – who is law is *my* neighbour – courts began to view individuals in their social roles, thus weakening the concept of individual right and tort law as reparation for its violation inherited from classical law. *Donoghue v Stevenson*, in effect, created a necessary relational link between a manufacturer and end-consumer, moving from a direct-act injury model to

67 M Renner, 'Death by Complexity: The Financial Crisis and the Crisis of Law in World Society' in Kjaer et al (n 63), 93–111.

68 But perhaps more importantly, post-*Palsgraf v Long Island Railroad Co*, 248 NY 339, 162 NE 99 (1928) given its emphasis on 'relational' victims, *ie* remoteness.

69 For 'Escape' see B Markesinis, S Deakin & A Johnston, *Markesinis and Deakin's Tort Law* 7th ed (Oxford: Oxford University Press, 2012). Leapfrogging is Stapleton's terminology. See Stapleton (n 54).

70 The highpoint of this thinking is the 1960s in the USA with the Restatement (Second) of Torts. Within tort law scholarship, this was challenged due to cognitive feedback of an insurance crisis, but more profoundly by a certain interpretation of Coase's (n 53) famous article, which suggested that the notion of causation, and the moral basis of enterprise liability, was unscientific.

one concerned with typical business risks in activities, from externalisation of the costs of accidents to their internalisation.[71]

Lord Atkin's celebrated judgment in *Donoghue* pronounced the neighbour principle, which provided a general test of duty of care premised on reasonable foreseeability and proximity.[72] This refocused the law to questions of *remote* injury to individuals beyond a contractual relationship, expanding the province of tort law considerably to relationships between strangers.[73] The test, in other words, both de-coupled tort from contract, and the model of liability on which the classical contract–tort catena rested,[74] and from direct to indirect injury, setting the agenda for twentieth-century courts as one of charting the outer boundaries of firms' responsibility. This would somewhat inevitably lead to a policy-oriented and social tort law.[75] In this vein, Lord Atkin reveals in the first pages of his judgment the public health and liability-systemic context of

[71] P Cane, 'Distributive Justice and Tort Law' (2001) 4 *New Zealand Law Review* 401. See also G Keating, 'The Idea of Fairness in the Law of Enterprise Liability' (1997) 95(5) *Michigan Law Review* 1266, in which he criticises the corrective justice scholars, especially Fletcher, Fried and Weinrib. In particular, he argues that the distinction between act and activities is the basis for a fairness account of enterprise liability that fixes on the concept of commutative justice. Oddly, given its early French articulation, in a later article, he remarks that this is enterprise liability is a distinctively American contribution to tort law, see Keating (n 15), 10. *Donoghue* was influenced by *McPherson*, and Benjamin Cardozo, it is clear, read, and was influenced by, François Gény, Raymond Salleilles, and Léon Duguit. See Cardozo (n 13), 16, 19, 26, 34, *etc*.

[72] *Donoghue v Stevenson* [1932] AC 562: 'The liability for negligence, whether you style it such or whether you treat it as in other systems as a species of culpa, is no doubt based on the general public sentiment of general moral wrongdoing for which the perpetrator must pay' (580).

[73] See esp Ewald (n 5) and Brüggemeier (n 4) on the difference between the responsibility paradigm of the liberal and welfare states. In tort law terms, Brüggemeier states that the main transformation in the twentieth century was from direct to indirect injuries. 'The actual revolution in liability law in the twentieth century took place, both nationally [Germany] and internationally, in the field of indirect injuries . . .. We need merely mention environmental, manufacturer, dealer and workshop liability, the entire field of "media torts", the situations of nervous shock and interruption of public supplies and the internationally controversial set of cases on noncontractual liability for pure economic loss. The list goes on' (93).

[74] P Winfield, 'Duty in Tortious Negligence' (1934) 34(1) *Columbia Law Review* 41–66, at 56. In classical private law, the scope, justification and purpose of contract and tort were interconnected. See Chapter 1B(1) for an elaboration on this theme.

[75] M Davies, 'The Road from Morocco: Polemis through Donoghue to No-Fault' (1982) 45(5) *Modern Law Review* 534. Davies refers to the change from direct acts towards indirect acts as 'Kuhnian' in proportion. In the USA, Priest (n 54) refers to the influence of Kessler on the transformation of the law of torts by undermining the justification for freedom of contract. See Kessler (n 42). Although this pertains more to the post-Traynor J in *Escola v CocaCola Bottling Co*, (1944) 24 Cal2d 453, 150 P.2d 436 policy turn in the law, as distinct from the exception to the privity rule in *MacPherson v Buick Motor Co*, (1916) 217 NY 382, 111 NE 1050, which is more akin to the *Donoghue* judgment.

the question before the court.[76] In other words, from the manner in which the case was framed it is clear that the judge was looking beyond the immediate case, and examining a world of manufacturers and consumers, and the extent to which the former owed obligations towards the latter as a matter of social policy. That is, in essence, a question of distribution of rights between groups or classes for typical or systemic risks, which encases corrective justice between individuals or persons in a broader social dimension. This is evident when Lord Atkin states:

> The question is whether the *manufacturer* of an article of drink sold by him to a distributor, in circumstances which prevent the distributor or the ultimate purchaser or *consumer* from discovering by inspection any defect, is under any legal duty to the ultimate purchaser or consumer to take reasonable care that the article is free from defect likely to cause injury to health.[77]

The language of manufacturers and consumers reappears many times in Lord Atkin's judgment. The individual litigants are understood in their materialised, social roles as manufacturers and consumers.[78] The group context informs the scope of just rules of conduct, as a primarily inter-individual model is supplemented by a model which looks beyond the individual to their place within a larger, encompassing group. These are relations the law must regulate to achieve justice between the parties.[79]

Thus, *social* policy is at work beneath the neighbour principle.[80] Additionally, Lord Atkin indicates that the needs of society favour a particular

76 Per Lord Atkin in *Donoghue*: 'I do not think a more important problem has occupied your Lordships in your judicial capacity: important both because of its bearing on public health and because of the practical test it applies to the system under which it arises' (579).

77 578.

78 Stapleton (n 54), 202. Her treatment of *Donoghue v Stevenson* makes clear: 'If we choose to focus on the individual's existing cause of action against an individual defendant, we can describe it in terms of securing corrective or commutative justice. If we choose to focus on who (*as individual(s) or as a class*) is enriched by the legal change as *intended* to secure the redistribution of risks, *ie* intended to secure distributional justice, and our reasons for the law must establish why it is fair to make this redistribution.'

79 This has analogies with the differentiated areas of law, labour, tenancy and so on, that replace references to individuals with references to (materialised) group-based categories, *eg* 'tenant', 'employee'.

80 Consider P Cane, 'Corrective Justice and Correlativity in Private Law' (1996) 16(3) *Oxford Journal of Legal Studies* 471–88. On *Donoghue v Stevenson* he argues that it is not corrective justice principles *per se* which is at question but rather a question as to who should bear the risk: 'These are not principles of corrective justice because they are not dependent on the particular interaction between the defendant and this plaintiff – they are general principles which may apply, and which have subsequently been applied to a multitude of interactions between manufacturers and consumers. But they are consistent with the structural principle of

interpretation of the relevant authoritative judgments:[81] 'I do not think so in our jurisprudence to suppose that its principles are so remote from the ordinary needs of civilized society and the ordinary claims it makes upon its members as to deny a legal remedy where there is obviously a social wrong.'[82] This statement is redolent of Cardozo J's judgment in *MacPherson v Buick*, which also draws on social need.[83] In that judgment, Cardozo J held that precedents should be interpreted with a view to contemporary social conditions, not merely as an outworking of juridical reason. Cardozo J stated famously:

> Precedents drawn from the days of travel by stage coach do not fit the conditions of travel today. The principle that the danger must be immanent does not change, but the things subject to the principle do change. They are whatever the needs of life in a developing civilization require them to be.[84]

In sum, even if one supposes that the neighbour principle is a rule of conduct between 'neighbours', which it undoubtedly is, one should remain mindful of several key points. First, the question is posed as one of social welfare with respect to manufactured goods. In other words, Lord Atkin looks beyond the facts of the case, and the particular relationship between the parties, to the social consequences of allowing the manufacturer to escape liability, thus depriving the plaintiff of a remedy. It should be apparent that this breaks new ground by recognising the need to compensate 'victims' and reverses *Winterbottom*'s *damnum abseque iniuria* thinking.[85] The import of the judgment is to rebalance tort and contract, leading to the expansion of the scope of

corrective justice because they concern the relative positions of the two parties. More than that, they are, in an important sense, principles of distributive justice because they are principles about who, as between manufacturers and consumers, should have an entitlement: should the consumer have an entitlement to be free from injury or should the manufacturer have an entitlement to inflict injury?' (481). And: 'Let us assume that before that case the relevant rule of law was that a bystander could not recover against a manufacturer in respect of injuries caused by the negligence of the manufacturer in producing a product. After that case the relevant rule imposed such liability. An effect of the case was, therefore, to redistribute resources (in the form of legal rights) from one group (manufacturers) to another group (bystanders). Therefore, to say that the meaning of private law is corrective justice is to give an incomplete account of the structure of private law' (482, 483).

[81] See Lord Buckmaster's rebuke, at 567.

[82] 583.

[83] Indeed, Lord Atkin seemed to obtain guidance from that judgment, which he refers to as 'the illuminating judgment of Cardozo J. in *MacPherson v Buick Co.* … in which he states the principles of the law as I should desire to state them' (598).

[84] *MacPherson* (n 75), 391.

[85] Indeed, it was part of a general trend to increase the protection of consumers that was transforming contract law. See Stapleton (n 54).

the former into *terra incognita*. This adjustment has the practical effect of creating new legal bonds that previously did not exist. Second, Lord Atkin's new bonds are not between individuals *qua* individuals, but between groups, consumers and manufacturers. Although by no means explicit in the judgment, tort law becomes a means to identify justified balances between the interests of different groups in society.[86]

In *Donoghue*, therefore, the protective scope of tort law is a distributive question in the last analysis. Thus, what was developed was a form of weak commutative justice out of the duty of care. While courts argue analogously from case to case, unfolding justice *inter partes*, the courts additionally embed this argument in concerns of social responsibility, utility and distributive fairness, particularly regarding whether the scope of tort law should be widened. *Donoghue* is not far from the idea of *moral* enterprise liability[87] albeit without embracing stricter enterprise liability.[88]

It should be stressed, for clarity, that this concept of weak commutative justice is different from Gardner's concept of localised distributive justice. Gardner's localised distributive justice stands for the analytical proposition that in the doing of corrective justice between individuals, the chief task of private law, there is an inevitable and *subsidiary* distributive justice dimension.[89] This is because in the outworking of the common law, the drawing of analogies results in the redistribution of rights and duties according to the rule of law. Gardner argues that:

> Under the rule of law judges must decide cases according to law, which means (minimally) that [they] must not separate the rules from the ruling, either by declaring what the rule is or will henceforth be while declining to apply it to the case in hand, or by denying that there is a rule. It follows that no judge may rule in favour of any plaintiff except by locating the plaintiff

86 To be clear, I am not arguing that the neighbour principle is 'surface froth', and my argument is not an 'error theory' in which the court simply gives effect to social policy. Rather, my argument is that the neighbour principle is more complex than simply demarcating just interpersonal conduct between individuals; instead, it is embedded in an organisational and social view of responsibility. It is, in other words, a layered judgment.

87 See J Stapleton, 'A New Theory of Strict Moral Enterprise Liability' in Stapleton (n 54), 185, 191.

88 A major implement in this respect in the United Kingdom is the fact that the courts did not extend the principle of *res ipsa loquitur* to product liability claims in negligence. For discussion, see S Deakin & Z Adams, *Markesinis and Deakin's Tort Law* 8th ed (Oxford: Ooxford University Press, 2019), 580–83, esp 582.

89 One might say, on Gardner's analysis, it is the *effect* of doing corrective justice rather than the *reason* for the legal rule. See J Gardner, 'What Is Tort Law For? Part 2. The Place of Distributive Justice', Oxford Legal Studies Research Paper No 62/2013, 12.

> within a class of imaginable plaintiffs who would, according to the judge, be entitled to the same ruling. … [and to make this judgment they are confronted with the question.] How do we dole out the right to proceed in tort among various candidate classes?[90]

In other words, if class A can recover, why not class B in an analogous situation? If an apt analogy exists and gives reason for an extension of recovery, then a redistribution of rights occurs and, in this sense, a minimum of distributive justice is done. This conception of the connection between the rule of law and justice recalls Lord Diplock's very similar incremental and cloistered account of common law reasoning in *Dorset*, in which if policy is to play a role at all, it is policy inherent to the law.[91] However, this so-called traditional common law approach[92] underestimates the influence of the social concept of responsibility because the very concept of responsibility between A and B, tortfeasor and claimant, is dependent on their social roles *qua* consumer or manufacturer. It is not a question, in short, simply of extending recovery to consumers as a class by analogy: the very idea of the relevant classes is itself informed by views of social responsibility. This idea rests, in turn, on the crucial distinction between active and passive actors, tortfeasors and victims. Enterprise or organisational 'moral' responsibility assumes this distinction and aims at channelling liability to organisational addressees, which breaks with a concept of individual responsibility that unfolds by analogy. Rather, the question is one of the impact of social interdependence (materialisation) on the concept of responsibility.[93] This social concept of responsibility reverses the distribution of rights of A and B, placing the parties within their social roles as consumer and manufacturer. Manufacturers *qua* manufacturers owe duties to consumers: once an accident occurs, the role of the court is to restore this social distribution of rights. Thus, doing corrective justice between the parties becomes entangled in the overall distribution of risks and, in this sense, is weakened. It is interpersonal justice with an eye to a sociological concept of responsibility. This is clearly the case in Cardozo's pioneering work when he argues how the appropriate grounds and bounds of tort law are to be determined.[94] I do not think, respectfully, that this can be

[90] *Ibid.*

[91] *Home Office v Dorset Yacht Co Ltd* [1970] AC 1004. But note, Lord Diplock was a dissenting voice in *Dorset*.

[92] D Nolan, 'The Duty of Care after Robinson v Chief Constable of West Yorkshire Police' (2019) 9 *UK Supreme Court Yearbook* 174–205, which Nolan alternatively refers to as 'standard common law reasoning' (198).

[93] Gardner (n 88), 14. It is closer to Calabresi's position, which Gardner criticises.

[94] Cardozo (n 13).

explained simply as the outworking of the liberal rule of law, but represents a new way to conceptualise responsibility in its own right.

(ii) The Social Standard of Care

Once it is accepted that a legally relevant relation or *vinculum iuris* exists between different groups of individuals understood in terms of their social roles, then the question of standard of care reappears. But it does so primarily in terms of the imposition of a reasonable risk rather than in terms of individual wrongful conduct. Ehrenzweig refers to twentieth-century negligence as bearing 'Siamese-twin functions', and, at least in my view, this can be characterised as the supplementing of an individualised, normative model of liability with an organisational, normative model of liability.[95] This manifests in the tension between fault as wrongful conduct and fault as (unacceptable) risk resulting in a standard of care that balances different interests *and* models of liability; it is negligence all things considered: fairness between the parties (its application to the particular facts), between groups (compensation justification), custom (expertise), cost–benefit analysis, particularly questions as to which is the best cost avoider (economic utility).[96] In the final analysis, a normative standard of reasonable care is supplied, which is additionally a social standard of care because of its emphasis not only on individual right but, additionally, materialised justice and aggregative utility when attempting to hold the enterprise liable for typical business risks.[97] The twentieth-century refinements of the fault standard, which strip it of 'much practical meaning', is, additionally, difficult to understand without the rise of enterprise liability insurance – a device 'devised for the injurer's protection, [which] has widely been adapted to secure recovery of the injured'.[98]

95 Ehrenzweig (n 57), 1422, 1445.

96 H Collins, 'Utility and Rights in Common Law Reasoning: Rebalancing Private Law through Constitutionalizaton', LSE Law, Society and Economy Working Paper 6/2007, criticising the way in which this is in effect economisation. Although the extent to which cost/benefit analysis actually occurs is disputed. It is more often than not an impressionistic justification adduced for restricting or expanding the law: usually the former in recent years.

97 Ehrenzweig (n 57), 1423. Typical business risk is a sociological concept, strongly influenced by the availability of insurance. Also Brüggemeier (n 23), 8: 'The chance to externalise the risks of business activities on insurers made it more sensible for the courts to internalise the losses caused by these activities as costs on the risk creating enterprises.'

98 *Ibid.*

While the language remained the same, namely fault or reasonable care,[99] reasonableness *in the context of group or organisational activity* was an increasingly exacting standard premised on technical knowledge as to what constitutes an unreasonable risk.[100] Nevertheless, the standard of care is ultimately a normative standard such that custom, although highly influential, is not coterminous with due care. In this vein, Ladeur argues that it fell to the judge to determine the appropriate balance between groups: 'The judge, in particular, should act as a mediator between conflicting interests beyond the stable orientation provided by abstract legal norms.'[101] The fact that judges engage in these balancing exercises is rarely acknowledged, but is something of an open secret.[102]

Thus, in order to effect this policy-oriented change, enterprise negligence was finally shorn of its subjective or objective just rules of conduct element, which opened the door to reshaping fault in light of higher standards of care for typical business risks.[103] Twentieth-century courts subtly began to refocus the question to '"Whose risk was it that this damage might occur?" in place of ... "Whose fault was it that this damage did occur?"'[104] The 'ill-defined objective standard of care' divorces reasonable care from ordinary notions of fault, as a species of *culpa* or of some community standard of just conduct.[105]

99 Ehrenzweig (n 57), 1428: 'If this be the trend today [enterprise liability], the courts, at least in their language, have failed to concede the change, since the rules of enterprise liability are still couched in terms which imply reprehensible conduct.' Or, as Markesinis, Deakin & Johnston (n 69) remark, the standard of ordinary care, *ie* reasonable man or person, is 'little more than an anthropomorphic conception of justice as perceived by judges or juries' (198). In other words, the individual is a device through which the courts deliberate over 'justice'. I argue that this is a socialised, or social justice.

100 M Lee, 'Safety, Regulation and Tort Law: Fault in Context' (2011) 74(4) *Modern Law Review* 555: the precise relationship between technical standards, custom and regulatory standards is highly ambiguous. The courts often defer but may revise these standards as well. Medical negligence shows that, while very important, what is customary by reference to medical standards is not decisive.

101 Ladeur (n 2).

102 *Eg Smith v Eric S Bush* [1990] UKHL 1; particularly in shipping, *eg Mark Rich and Co AG v Bishop Rock Marine Co Ltd, The Nicholas H* [1996] AC 211. See, also Oliphant (n 19), 840, points to Denning LJ's explicit recognition of balancing interests as exceptional. Judicial and scholarly debate is more explicit in the USA, *eg Escola*, and the legal realists.

103 Ehrenzweig (n 57), 1457, with regard to railways but making a more general point: 'What the law wants to know is whether liability can be imposed on the railroads in those cases because the harm was typical for its activities and thus calculable and typically insurable.' This influences how concepts of proximity and due care are interpreted (1458).

104 JA Jolowicz, 'Liability for Accidents' (1968) *Cambridge Law Journal* 50–63, at 58. Jolowicz, it is argued, underestimated the extent to which the fault standard was becoming a placeholder for policy-based decision-making.

105 *Ibid*, 58, citing Ehrenzweig (n 57).

It now depends on expert, customary practice, for example, the professions or technical standards in production processes, supplemented by the general justificatory arguments about which is the least cost avoider. It is supposed that the enterprise is in a better position to control risks, as subject and object of law.[106] Subject because particular enterprises are held liable for systemic failures to control risks,[107] object because the question is one of balancing group interests between industry and consumer safety.[108] This role is well captured by Renner when he argues that it involves stricter, if not strict liability, with cognitive expectations placed inside a framework of normative expectations (liability).

> [I]n order to impose strict liability for certain types of activities, the courts necessarily had, more or less scientifically, to evaluate social risks rather than indulge in the normative questions of intent and negligence. In doing so, they specifically had to pay due regard to the technical feasibility and to the costs of preventive measures. Thus, cognitive expectations with regard to the technological–scientific state of the art, industry-specific standards and economic calculus soon found their way into legal reasoning.[109]

While Renner refers to strict liability, it is not only in strict liability that these calculations were made.[110] The Learned Hand test is important here, mainly as a heuristic though. The Hand test compares the (marginal) costs of

[106] It is only later that a tension emerged between a moral enterprise theory and the deterrence theories, including the Posner v Calabresi dispute.

[107] Once again, Brüggemeier (n 4) brings much-needed clarity here, which, incidentally, dovetails with Ladeur's concept of the knowledge base in the organisational society. The choice for internalisation implies: 'He, the business owner, and the judge or state agent, must decide whether, considering the (internalized) risk of damage, he should continue his business unchanged (and pay compensation), take insurance coverage and apply better preventive measures, or convert or cease activities' (159).

[108] I imagine that the greater emphasis on the classical fault in the United Kingdom reflects the idea that this balance should favour the freedom of enterprises more than the rights of consumers in tort. This is a little impressionistic, however. For broad comments in this direction see C Van Dam, *European Tort Law* 2nd ed (Oxford: Oxford University Press, 2013), 106.

[109] Renner (n 67), 103.

[110] Indeed, with respect to strict liability one might argue that there is a distinct blurring. If we focus only on doctrine, one might suspect that strict liability is liability for causation, a much lower threshold than fault. However, if one removes the fault requirement one is left in all likelihood with causation as a more exacting 'control mechanism'. This is the French experience, see C Harlow, 'Administrative Liability: A Comparative Study of French and English Law' (PhD thesis, London School of Economics and Political Science, 1979); D Fairgrieve, *State Liability in Tort: A Comparative Law Study* (Oxford: Oxford University Press, 2003). It might be argued that strict liability, then, is also a question of partitioning risks, but emphasises a choice of emphasis, *ie* solidarity v liberty.

precautions with the probability or risk of harm and its gravity. B v PL in shorthand. As Learned Hand J recognised, his test is not precise and cannot avoid contentious interpersonal utility comparisons:

> All these are practically not susceptible of any quantitative estimate, and the second two (seriousness of the injury, cost of precautions) are generally not so, even theoretically. For this reason a solution always involves some preference, or choice between incommensurables, and it is thought most likely to accord with commonly accepted standards, real or fancied.[111]

While Posner finds an immanent economic logic of the common law in the Learned Hand test, Brüggemeier cautions in this respect that the Learned Hand test was a sophisticated formulation of the standard of care that, in the end, rested on the assumption of measurable typical business risk and was aimed at large organisations capable of making such calculations or, indeed, their insurers.[112] The cost–benefit analysis, then, seemingly is a prospective test aimed at ensuring businesses take optimum levels of precautions. However, Brüggemeier doubts businesses have sufficient information to factor in optimum levels of cost,[113] and following Calabresi states that judges are not in a position to make marginal cost–benefit analyses and, as such, the rule is instead a justification for cost internalisation with the best risk avoider.[114] The aim is to channel liability such typical business risks to the organisation and the test is, as such, 'perfectly suited to "depersonalized" enterprise negligence liability a la *MacPherson*'.[115] In the twentieth-century law of torts, what was 'normal' can no longer be gleaned from distributed knowledge, but refers to expert calculations of probabilities and harm.[116] In the background was, of course, the question of insurance, which was increasing the threshold of 'reasonable' or 'fault'-based liability.[117] However, in the final analysis, '[c]ourts

[111] *Conway v O'Brien* (1940) 111 F2d, 611, 612. Reproduced in Markesinis, Deakin & Johnston (n 69), 199.

[112] Brüggemeier (n 4), 70–73. Indeed, citing Calabresi, Brüggemeier argues that judges are not in a particularly good position to make cost–benefit analyses and, as such, the question should be who is in a better position to make risk-avoiding decisions, which usually is the enterprise.

[113] Citing R Dworkin, *Law's Empire* (Cambridge, MA: Harvard University Press, 1986), 281–82, in this respect.

[114] See, G Schwartz, 'Reality in the Economic Analysis of Tort Law: Does Tort Law Really Deter?' (1994) 42 *UCLA Law Review* 377.

[115] Brüggemeier (n 4), 73.

[116] Eg USA, the transformation of *Rylands v Fletcher* into strict liability recovery for ultra-hazardous risks. Liability for risk creation *qua* strict liability has not been so clear-cut in the United Kingdom. More generally, Ladeur (n 2).

[117] See Oliphant (n 19), 891, 840. Particularly his discussion of Denning LJ's 'candour' regarding how insurability influenced 'victim' compensation in *Nettleship v Weston* [1971] 2 QB 691.

are not regulatory agencies that set general standards. They decide concrete cases. In such situations, they determine *"correct" behaviour, appropriate to the situation and the defendant*'.[118] Therefore, while the test may be formulated in general terms, it is applied to a particular factual nexus that involves contextual adjudication.[119] This means it retains a corrective justice dimension even if a general policy of internalisation is being pursued.[120] That is why the courts do not simply avoid the 'administrative costs', so to speak, of lengthy adjudication over cause and fault: the guiding principles for formulating the particular standard of care *in abstracto* may be social justice as compensation or utility, but the actual application of the test is fact-sensitive. Another way to put this is that the rise of the organisational entity, the enterprise usually, meant that courts increasingly imposed an exacting standard of care cognisant of their social role vis-à-vis consumers, but the dispute remained a question of achieving justice *inter partes*.[121] It is, in short, materialised private law.

Thus, it is sufficiently clear from the foregoing that while the new social concept of responsibility indicated that the duty of care should be enlarged to groups *qua* organisational actors, the standard of care owed is determined according to a critical standard, not accessible to community, distributed knowledge. While this risk-based thinking has obvious implication for industry, the rise of the welfare state as a service provider in parallel led to an enormous expansion of the activities undertaken by the state in the twentieth century. The model of organisational liability was applied to the state by extension, quite clearly in France and in fits and bursts in England.[122] The scholarship in France explicitly emphasised these links between private and

[118] Brüggemeier (n 4), 67 (emphasis original).

[119] See Deakin & Adams (n 88), 184, distinguishing setting the standard of care and applying it.

[120] *Compare* R Demogue, 'La Notion de Sujet de Droit : Caractère et Conséquences' (Extrait de la Revue Trimestrielle de droit civil, no 3, 1909), who views the legal subject, and the structure of private law, as a mere technique through which other aims are achieved. This is a simplification. Aims must not only be framed in terms of legal categories, but must interact with the underlying normative structure of law. Of course, this is more controversial in overtly functionalist legal orders such as the EU, see HW Micklitz, 'The Legal Subject, the Social Class and Identity-Based Rights' in L Azoulai et al (eds), *Constructing the Person in EU Law: Rights, Roles, Identities* (Oxford: Hart, 2016), 285–310, and, for discussion, Chapter 3.

[121] *Compare* two illustrations of how the court used 'inferences of negligence', namely *Grant v Australian Knitting Mills* [1936] AC 85, and *Evans v Triplex Safety Glass Co Ltd* [1938] 1 All ER 282. Inferences of negligence will render the defendant business negligent for faults in production processes relieving the plaintiff of the requirement to show particular, individualised fault, but not if there is doubt on the particular facts as to whether the default arises from the manufacturing process. The facts still matter even when pursuing broader policies.

[122] Most recently, *Armes v Nottinghamshire Co* [2017] UKSC 60.

public tort law.[123] In English law, the link is even clearer due to the equality principle.[124] This parallels the application of an organisational model to private actors and public actors in Section C3. What is reasonably clear is that an individualistic model of liability was overlain with an organisational model aiming at the internalisation of risk for businesses and, indeed, the state. The moral basis of liability was the distinction between active and passive parties, while the scope of negligence and vicarious liability was determined according to a test of typical business risks. Strict liability was concerned with risk creation, and the social responsibilities that followed therefrom. The transformation of tort law into two tracks of individualised responsibility and organisational responsibility is captured in Table 2.1. These tracks are non-linear; they are two models of responsibility that, while they emerged at different historical moments, coexist in modern law: organisational responsibility is a specific regime for firms and the state; individualised responsibility is for natural persons. However, although they may be analytically and conceptually distinguished, in legal practice the lines between these two models of liability are more blurry.[125]

The rest of this chapter will be devoted to expanding on organisational responsibility through case law in private and 'public' law.

[123] G Ripert, *Le Régime Démocratique et le Droit Civil Moderne* 2nd ed (Paris: Pichon, 1948). In particular, his chapter on responsibility and ch 1 and ch 2 explaining the influence of democracy by universal suffrage on law.

[124] This golden thread is present in Josserand's view of how mechanisation changes tort law, and how Duguit discusses the change from a sovereigntist to a public service-based theory of the state and its laws. See Duguit (n 42), esp 44–46, regarding the characterisation of the state as a relationship of interdependence, as distinct from sovereignty as a personalised concept, and the attendant need due to changing circumstances, or 'flux', to move beyond simply national defence, internal security and order, and justice as the functions which the state is required to perform. In particular: 'The profound economic and industrial change that has taken place over the world has created new governmental obligations. The clear interdependence of peoples, the circulation on all hands of intellectual ideas and scientific discoveries, impose on the state the duty of organizing such public services as will permanently assure such international communication' (45, 46). This is but one example of interdependence fostering a need for greater governmental, regulatory involvement. Another is the labour movement. For gaining acceptance of the concept of flux, see Cardozo (n 13), who argued for a pragmatic method in law and social justice as the dominant aim: 'Nothing is stable. Nothing absolute. All is fluid and changeable. This is an endless "becoming". We are back with Heraclitus' (28).

[125] See H Collins, 'Ascription of Legal Responsibility to Groups in Complex Patterns of Economic Integration' (1990) 53(6) *Modern Law Review* 731, 732. Noting the 'confusion and injustice' arising from the fact that the common law has no principle of group responsibility, G Brüggemeier, 'The Civilian Law of Delict: A Comparative and Historical Analysis' (2020) 7(4) *European Journal of Comparative Law* 339–83.

TABLE 2.1. *Two models of normative ascription*

	Nineteenth century: individualised responsibility	Twentieth century: organisational responsibility
Duty in tort	Emerging general duty of care (individualistic)	General duty of care (socialised and group identity)
Injury/harm	Largely direct	Indirect or remote injury
Standard of care	Community morality: the *vir diligens*	Critical morality: technical knowledge and acceptable risk
Wrongful conduct	Wrongful individual conduct	Creation or imposition of a risk
Knowledge base: *fortuna*/providential	Individual prudence, legacy of providence	Inevitable accident and insurance

C THE ECLIPSE OF THE INDIVIDUAL: ILLUSTRATIONS OF THE TURN TO ORGANISATIONAL LIABILITY

The basic structure of tort law in the twentieth century was reconfigured to leapfrog the individual and capture organisational addressees that were placeholders for group-intermediated justice and utility. This had a profound impact not only at the level of the general test for negligence, but across tort law.[126] Writing in the middle of the twentieth century, Glanville Williams bemoaned the de-personalisation of tort law.[127] What he perceived was in our terms the gradual emergence of organisational liability, which he considered a perversion of the interpersonal framework of tort law. As Brüggemeier observes, organisational liability has two tracks: '(i) it is vicarious liability to the extent that it involves liability for direct injury through the wrongful action of concrete employees; (ii) it is, within certain bounds strict liability to the extent anonymous production and service processes are involved'.[128] In other

[126] Stapleton (n 54), 191, where Stapleton discusses 'causation' with regard to vicarious liability, *eg* 'What I am arguing for here is that the special circumstances which may justify the imposition of vicarious liability on the employer even in the absence of uniform agreement that the employer's conduct was a 'cause' of the harm, is the profit motive of the employer in creating the opportunity for the employee to act.' This rationalisation of vicarious liability could easily have been taken from Josserand or Saleilles discussed earlier.

[127] G Williams, 'Vicarious Liability and the Master's Indemnity' (1957) 20(3) *Modern Law Review* 220. 'Man's progress has been associated with increasing emphasis upon the value of the individual, and collective punishment tends to deny this value' (234). Williams thought this an inadequate justification of the doctrine of vicarious liability.

[128] Brüggemeier (n 4), 158.

words, it is vicarious liability for employee 'fault' increasingly broadly construed and, eventually, no-fault liability for production processes.[129] Additionally, the rise of organisational liability cannot be sensibly divorced from the rise of third-party liability insurance.[130] In France, this was informed by solidaristic thinking; in other jurisdictions by a socially tinctured concept of fairness.[131]

The expansion of both vicarious liability and product liability will be examined in a common law context. Both examples, however, largely mirror developments on the Continent (Germany, France) although developments occurred at different speeds and along different paths.[132] In the case of a product's liability, there is a clear systemic approach to the organisation. In the case of vicarious liability, the trend has been to stretch the doctrine to its limits in order to shift losses to the organisation insofar as is possible.

1 *Product Liability* qua *Organisational Liability*

Through the development of separate legal personality for firms at the end of the nineteenth century, the corporation as distinct from the individual entered the law.[133] The firm entered a law that relied on the language of individuals, to be sure, but nevertheless reshaped tort liability towards an internalising model. The particular context is, of course, the development of large, vertically integrated firms.[134] Brüggemeier exemplifies this transformation in a tort context when he contrasts *Thomas v Winchester* and *MacPherson v Buick*.[135]

[129] *Ibid*, 161.

[130] *Ibid*, 8. Additionally, Van Dam (n 108), 265, refers to insurance as 'the fuel of modern tort law'.

[131] Ewald (n 21): 'Social solidarity, more generally, allocates risk by shifting it to the firm, thereby creating a new balance between rich and poor, consumers and producers' (278). In a world of probabilities and statistical measurement, in which scientific knowledge is considered objective, the parameters of such solidarity can be determined.

[132] J Bell & D Ibbetson, *European Legal Development: The Case of Tort* (Cambridge: Cambridge University Press, 2012), referring to product liability and medical negligence: 'Changes have not always taken identical form, since at any moment each legal system has had its own particular rules, principles, values and institutional structure against the background of which changes have occurred. But these differences aside, it is possible to paint a coherent picture of convergent legal development across Europe' (74).

[133] Saleilles (n 45) on the subjective rights of firms.

[134] Bell & Ibbetson (n 132), 175: By the 1930s, at the latest, 'the structure of the manufacturing industry was moving towards larger undertakings which had a greater capacity to absorb losses and pass them on to their customers, and liability insurance was generally available to spread losses (as it had not been in the nineteenth century), though it is impossible to find data demonstrating that this was in fact the cause of the changes in the law'.

[135] (1852) 6 NY 397. Brüggemeier (n 4), 133–34. The analogy with *Donoghue* should, it is submitted, be patent. Here, Brüggemeier argues that it is a move from vicarious liability to

In *Thomas*, the defendant sought to deny liability in negligence on the basis of the privity rule. There, a pharmacist sold the plaintiff a poisonous substance, mistakenly assuming that the substance was benign.[136] The plaintiff suffered personal injury. The mislabelling in actual fact was occasioned by Winchester, a third party to the contract between the pharmacist and the injured party. Thus, under the privity rule in *Winterbottom*, recovery would be denied. Ruggles CJ fashioned an exception to the privity rule for inherently dangerous goods. However, in order to do so he stated that the pharmacist was an 'agent' and Winchester his 'principal'. By the time *MacPherson* was decided, such a principal–agent link had disappeared. The question was simply whether a manufacturer owed a duty of care to an injured party.

MacPherson concerned a situation that traditionally would have failed due to an absence of privity of contract. Instead of coating the judgment in terms of agency, a direct duty of care was imposed on the manufacturer to take reasonable care in manufacture. Cardozo J extended the scope of the concept of 'inherently dangerous' beyond poisons, explosives and deadly weapons, 'things whose normal function it is to injure or destroy',[137] broadening the test: 'If the nature of the thing is such that it is reasonably certain to place life and limb in peril when negligently made, it is a thing of danger.'[138] The enterprise as an organisational unit is, in principle, from this point onwards tortiously liable for the reasonably foreseeable consequences of its failure to comply with an objective standard of care.[139] It is therefore a de-personalised concept of fault, not required to rest parasitically on employee fault or requiring the fiction of an agency-type relationship. It is a nascent organisational liability for production processes. The 'manufacturer' as distinct from a specific individual was held liable in fault. By providing a direct cause of action against the manufacturer, 'legal policy channels liability to the "correct" address, the enterprise owner, and at the same time to reach the "deep pocket"'.[140] The subsequent use of the doctrine of *res ipsa loquitur* in US product liability cases also blurs the line with strict liability.[141] *Res ipsa*, a rule

direct responsibility; although I think he does not mean the 'doctrine of vicarious liability' but uses the term more loosely to include agency.

136 'The plaintiff' for convenience. The action was brought by the husband of the injured party on her behalf.

137 *MacPherson* (n 75), 387.

138 *Ibid*, 389.

139 This de-personalisation can be traced back to *George v Skivington* (1869) LR 5 Exch 1 per Bell and Ibbetson (n 132).

140 Brüggemeier (n 4), 135.

141 In the United Kingdom, 'inferences of negligence' fulfil a similar function, but it is a much narrower doctrinal basis. See *Grant v Australian Knitting Mills Ltd*.

of evidence, became a procedural means to make recovery easier for 'victims' of defective products. This was to place the burden of proof on the manufacturer once a clear inference of negligence could be made from the circumstances.[142] It is, naturally, favourable from a victim's recovery perspective. Second, the standard of care was 'surreptitiously' raised, because of the relative ambiguity of concepts such as reasonableness.[143] As argued already, the focus was increasingly placed on reasonable risk, and thus reasonableness became entangled in questions of policy, that is, deterrence and risk spreading. The subsequent twentieth-century expansion of liability, which Priest, *inter alia*, documents, demonstrates how what became important was not individual fault but determining which risks should be placed on manufacturers and which should lie with consumers. What emerged after the war was a pro-consumer case law.[144]

Escola v Coca Cola Bottling Co was a decisive turning point in US law and scholarship in this regard. In *Escola*, the plaintiff suffered personal injuries when a carbonated bottle exploded. Traynor J argued that strict liability should apply, going beyond the previous negligence and *res ipsa* approach. Traynor J introduced three main arguments in favour of strict liability for defective products. First, he relied on enterprise moral responsibility. Drawing on parallels with administrative provisions regarding safety that impose criminal responsibility for introducing defective products, he argued for an analogous heightened standard of liability. Secondly, the enterprise is in a better position to anticipate and reduce hazards vis-à-vis the public and in a better position to spread the costs of accidents. Thirdly, Traynor J states that while in *McPherson* there was manifest negligence, the principle laid down was more extensive than the facts before Cardozo J such that implied warranty should be extended beyond parties in privity, justifying a stricter standard of care between manufacturer and consumer. Finally, warranty can be classified as a species of tort or contract. It is quasi-tort or quasi-contract and Traynor J seems to locate it properly in tort law. The net result is that manufacturers are strictly liable for defective products in their ordinary use. This judgment was highly influential

[142] See Bell & Ibbetson (n 132), 78, citing *Grant*; and S Whittaker (ed), *The Development of Product Liability* (Cambridge: Cambridge University Press, 2010).

[143] Stapleton (n 54), 22, though, notes that warranty is preferable because it is strict, whereas negligence-in-fact remains difficult to prove. For an early, extended discussion of this trend see Ehrenzweig (n 57).

[144] From the 1960s especially, 'The liability of manufacturers for product-related losses was vastly increased and the obligations of consumers vastly diminished.' Per Priest (n 54), 462.

on the Second Restatement twenty years later, creating stricter liability for products.[145]

While the transformation of UK tort law was less dramatic, remaining wedded to 'negligence' as distinct from strict liability, the threshold of reasonableness gradually increased. In the end, Directive 85/374/EEC drew the US and European approaches closer together.[146] Both focus on the standard of care a person is entitled to expect, the so-called consumer expectation test, taking all circumstances into account.[147] This is a flexible standard meant to mediate traditional negligence and strict liability, balancing consumer and manufacturer interests. And they both waver somewhere between negligence as a 'risk–utility' test and strict liability as enterprise liability *simpliciter*. It is not so distinct in this respect of the general evolution of fault towards a hybrid standard, although the European regime seems more weighed in favour of the consumer *on paper*.[148]

2 *The Slow Emergence of 'Enterprise Risk' Liability in the Common Law: Vicarious Liability*

The doctrine of vicarious liability is a hybrid between individualised responsibility and enterprise liability. The long-term trajectory of vicarious liability has moved subtly from determining the outer boundaries of the agency (interpersonal) relationship towards determining the outer boundaries of firms' (organisational) responsibility for typical business risks.[149] This has meant that in legal practice courts have gradually downplayed a close analysis of employee duties, and focus instead on business activity – the boundaries of the firms' activities – and the connection between those activities and the torts committed. In the process, the courts have all but abandoned the so-called Salmond test, and have replaced it with a test of *enterprise* liability.

145 *Ibid.*

146 M Reimann, 'Liability for Defective Products at the Beginning of the Twenty-First Century: Emergence of a Worldwide Standard?' (2003) 51(4) *American Journal of Comparative Law* 751–838.

147 Product Liability Directive, art 6.

148 The above comments are impressionistic. For more critical remarks, see Stapleton (n 54). See also M Reimann, 'Product Liability in a Global Context: The Hollow Victory of the European Model' (2003) 11 *European Review of Private Law* 128, who regards the EU regime as a paper tiger.

149 There are parallels in recent years in the expansion of non-delegable duties outside employment *stricto sensu*, see *Woodland v Essex County Council* [2013] UKSC 66, which, as Deakin has rightly noted, focuses more squarely on 'organisational fault'. See Deakin (n 62).

The Salmond test is the traditional formulation of vicarious liability for torts within the course of employment where the act is: 'A wrongful act authorised by the master, or (b) a wrongful and unauthorised mode of doing some act authorised by the master.'[150] Salmond elaborates that the duty is greater in the case of a master as opposed to the relationship between a principal and agent because, unlike ordinary agency, a master is responsible 'for acts which he has not authorised, provided they are so connected with the acts which he has authorised, that they may rightly be regarded as modes – although improper modes – of doing them'.[151] This additional responsibility is justified based on the control that a master exercises over his servant. However, it is clear that Salmond treats vicarious liability as a 'particular form of agency'.[152]

While the first limb of the test is uncontentious,[153] the focus of twentieth-century vicarious liability was on the second limb, namely, an 'unauthorised mode' of doing an act that is explicitly authorised. It is instructive to compare two judgments on this point. The first, *Conway v George Wimpey & Co Ltd*,[154] is firmly rooted in 'agency thinking'. In that case, a practice emerged whereby employees of the defendant company would transport workmen of another firm, contrary to the defendant's instructions, to a work site. The plaintiff was badly injured when he was alighting from the defendant's lorry. While the defendant's employee clearly permitted the plaintiff to ride the defendant's lorry, the defendant argued that the injured party was a trespasser and they were not vicariously liable. Much of the legal analysis focused on the fact that there was no liability towards trespassers in tort. More relevantly, however, Asquith LJ treated the potential vicarious liability of the employer entirely in terms of ostensible authority. In other words, notwithstanding the express prohibition, could it be said that that the employer had constructive notice of the practice of using their lorries as an omnibus? This focuses squarely on the scope of authorised acts treating the second limb as concerned with ostensible *authorisation*: either vicarious liability rests on what has been actually authorised or what has been impliedly, or ostensibly authorised. In other words, the focus is on the personal relationship between employer and

[150] JW Salmond, *The Law of Torts* (London: Stevens and Haynes, 1907), 83.

[151] *Ibid*, 84.

[152] *Ibid*, 75. *Compare* T Baty, *Vicarious Liability* (Oxford: Clarendon Press, 1916), who vigorously disputes this claim, and views agency as contractual reasoning that has illegitimately become commonsense in tort.

[153] Most tort scholars agree that it is not properly vicarious liability in *tort*. However, this depends on one's conception of vicarious liability. If one's conception of vicarious liability is agency-centred, then it is properly vicarious liability.

[154] [1951] 2 KB 266.

employee – the course of employment – and its implications for liability towards third parties, rather than on the scope of typical risks incidental to business activity. In *Rose v Plenty*,[155] in contrast, there is a subtle shift of emphasis to the 'business purpose'.[156] In that case, a milkman, again contrary to his employer's instructions, transported a boy on his milk rounds and paid him to deliver milk. Notwithstanding the employer's express prohibition, on this occasion the employer was held vicariously liable on the second limb of the Salmond test when the boy was injured while dismounting from the milk van. Lord Scarman justified his interpretation of the Salmond test decision in the following way: '[T]he matter must be looked at *broadly*, not dissecting the servant's tasks into its component activities – such as driving, loading, sheeting and the like – by asking: what was the job on which he was engaged for his employer.'[157] This retains an agency focus, but interprets it widely.[158] Lord Denning, by contrast, went further, stating explicitly that vicarious liability is engaged if an act is done in furtherance of the business purpose.[159] This was sufficient to distinguish the case from *Conway* as well as the fact that the common law no longer denied recovery against trespassers *tout court*. Lord Denning's stressing of the business purpose breaks with the agency thinking of earlier case law because it focuses not the scope of actual or implied or ostensible authority as such, but rather on the broader notion of a connection between the tort and the business activity. It is not particularly far from the modern approach to vicarious liability, which emphasises the 'close connection' between the employee's tort and the business' 'field of activity'.[160]

The gradual expansion of the doctrine of vicarious liability might, indeed, be viewed as a spill-over from product liability, from Salmond-agency thinking to enterprise liability proper.[161] At first in the Californian Supreme Court, later in the Commonwealth and Ireland, courts began to rationalise vicarious liability in terms of social fairness as between employer and victim – even

155 [1976] 1 WLR 141.

156 Lord Denning MR highlights how the origins of this approach are in the nineteenth century in *Limpus v London General Omnibus Co*, 158 ER 993 (1862).

157 *Ibid*, 147–48. (emphasis added).

158 Compare, Lawton LJ's dissent in which he adopts a narrow approach to agency: 'The driver had been employed to drive the milk float and deliver the milk. He had not been authorised to sub-contract his work' (145).

159 At 145.

160 *Mohamed v Morrisons* [2016] UKSC 11, [para 44]; *WM Morrison Supermarkets plc v Various Claimants* [2020] UKSC 12, [para 31].

161 HJ Steiner, *Moral Argument and Social Vision in the Courts* (Madison: University of Wisconsin Press, 1987), regarding spill-over in terms of justification.

when this included criminal acts by employees![162] The underlying idea that the doctrine of vicarious liability is a question of primary liability is, of course, out of step with how it is formally rationalised.[163] It is secondary liability for the fault of an employee. However, developments in the law from the mid-twentieth century onwards casts doubt on this explicit basis. To explain the shift of *emphasis*, and if we use the terms of the debate for a moment, there has been a move from a 'servant's tort' conception of vicarious liability to a 'master's tort' conception. Giliker distinguishes the two bases:

> The first and most popular explanation is that it is indeed liability imposed on one person for the wrongful act of another. This is sometimes known as the 'servant's tort' theory. The second (the 'master's tort' theory) holds that the master is liable for the torts of the servant by reason of the attribution of the servant's acts to the master.[164]

When the master's tort is translated into modern terminology it places emphasis on the enterprise's 'field of activities' and how closely the servant's tort is connected to that field of activities.[165] If the tort can be properly said to be closely connected to these activities then it is fair and just to impose liability on the firm, and this fairness rationale is supported by policy reasons.[166] In other words, the modern regime is concerned with charting the outer boundaries of the *firm's* responsibility.[167] This is a quite distinct question from closely examining the duties of the employee and asking whether those express duties were advanced through 'improper modes'.[168]

162 Or, one should say, criminal acts seemingly unconnected with the business purpose. There has long been recovery for fraud, and criminal assault if it can be shown to further the business purpose. See *Lloyd v Grace Smith & Co* [1912] AC 716.

163 England: *Staveley v Jones* [1956] AC 627.

164 P Giliker, *Vicarious Liability in Tort: A Comparative Perspective* (Cambridge: Cambridge University Press, 2010), 13. The 'confusion' between primary and secondary liability constantly appears in doctrinal scholarship post-*Lister* as a critique of the court's approach. *Lister v Hesley Hall Ltd* [2001] UKHL 22.

165 *Eg Mohamed v Morrisons* (n 160), para 44; *WM Morrison Supermarkets plc* (n 160), para 31. The latter judgment may, however, be viewed as a retrenchment back to a more 'conservative' approach, see D Nolan, 'Reining in Vicarious Liability' (2020) 49(4) *Industrial Law Journal* 609.

166 See Keating (n 15), esp 15–18. Ultimately, the fairness-based argument is the primary argument for enterprise liability whether in the context of product liability or vicarious liability.

167 This is all the more apparent in the 'akin to employment' case law; see, *eg*, *Barclays Bank v Various Claimants* [2020] UKSC 13; and, outside a commercial context, *Various Claimants v Catholic Child Welfare Society* [2012] UKSC 56, *Armes v Nottinghamshire Co* [2017] UKSC 60; *Cox v Ministry of Justice* [2016] UKSC 10.

168 See R Stevens 'Vicarious Liability or Vicarious Action' (2007) 30 *Law Quarterly Review* 123, *ie* masters' tort. See, in addition, Williams (n 127). Additionally, since exemplary damages can be

The fact that vicarious liability should be viewed as liability for typical business risks has a long history and is firmly anchored in a notion of enterprise moral responsibility. Laski furnishes one of the earliest formulations of the doctrine of vicarious liability in these terms: 'If the employer is compelled to bear the burden of his servant's torts even when he is himself personally without fault, it is because in social distribution of profit and loss, the balance of least disturbance seems thereby best to be obtained.'[169] This approach was influenced, in turn, by French scholars such as Saleilles, who had developed a concept of a moral enterprise liability.[170] Therefore, while formally a servant's tort, it appears incongruous to argue that the doctrine of vicarious liability is not concerned with group justice. As Brodie argues, it rests on an appeal to (social) fairness: 'The appeal to fairness proclaimed by enterprise liability is predicated on the capacity of the courts to render an enterprise responsible for the risks engendered by it.'[171] This 'logic' can be observed for the first time in the jurisprudence of the Californian Supreme Court in *Hirman v Westinghouse Elec Co* in which the court expressed the rationale for a broad doctrine of vicarious liability:

> They are [the losses caused by the torts of an employee] placed upon the employer because, having engaged in an enterprise which will, on the basis of past experience, involve harm to others through the torts of employees, and sought to profit by it, it is just that he, rather than the innocent injured plaintiff, should bear them; and because he is better able to absorb them, and to distribute them, through prices, rates or liability insurance, to the public, and so to shift them to society, to the community at large.[172]

The framing of enterprise liability as a question of where a *loss* should lie between a risk creator and an innocent plaintiff rests on the social concept of fairness between active and passive parties where active parties are held liable for accidents incidental to their activities. The legal test remains situational, however, because policy arguments alone do not result in liability; there must be a sufficiently close connection between the employee's 'job-created authority' and the tort.[173] If the enterprise provided a framework in which power or

awarded against employers based on vicarious liability, this demonstrates that the servant's fault alone is an inadequate conceptualisation, see *Rowlands v Chief Constable of Merseyside Police* [2006] EWCA Civ 1773.

169 H Laski, 'The Basis of Vicarious Liability' (1916–17) 26 *Yale Law Journal* 105, 112.

170 *Ibid*, citing Saleilles and Duguit, in particular.

171 Brodie (n 34), 27.

172 This section owes a large debt to *ibid*, ch 3. He cites this judgment at 28–29. See *Herman v Westinghouse Elec Co* (1970) 2 Cal 3d 956, 959–60.

173 Brodie (n 34), 34.

authority is exercised, this is the justification for the imposition of liability. While in California this broad enterprise liability approach has waned, its influence has spread beyond the USA.

The Canadian Supreme Court in *Bazley v Curry* further refined the test of vicarious liability as a mix of policy and principle. However, it is clear that the main thrust of the judgment is that where a firm not only introduces a risk, but through its delegation of authority to employees 'materially enhances' it, liability should follow. Material enhancement is operationalised based on a 'close connection' test, which essentially inquires as to whether the employer has created or enabled the exercise of authority over vulnerable victims. McLachlin J, in *Bazley*, identified enterprise liability as the key policy reason for vicarious liability. This has two dimensions, namely (social) fairness and deterrence. As well as placing the burden of liability with the risk creator, the greater scope for liability is meant to incentivise the firm to take precautionary measures to ensure an employer will not act negligently, or even criminally.[174] The *Bazley* approach was adopted by the House of Lords in *Lister* but without discussion of its rationale in risk.[175] There is, as was noted earlier, a fundamental tension between vicarious liability understood as personal responsibility of an employee for activities in the scope of his employment which should be borne by his *master*, and the idea that the third-party effects (their costs) of activities undertaken by *enterprises* should be borne by those enterprises. This tension is evident in *Catholic Child Welfare* where Lord Philips states that the policy factors – essentially enterprise liability – and the legal test 'overlap'.[176] This, in essence, dissolves the primary/secondary liability distinction. It is an organisational way of viewing the enterprise's activities. One is concerned with the moral basis of tort law as individual conduct (whether regarding the *master* or the *servant*), the other, the question of how to regulate organisational activity fairly and the issue of who should bear the burden of losses created by lawful but risky activity. In short, it is a move from *master* to *organisation* as the frame of reference. In *Bernard v Attorney General for Jamaica*, for example, this 'move' is pellucid:

[174] There is a strong economic strand running through this incentive argument. MacLachlin J for the majority in *Bazley v Curry* [1999] 2 SCR 534 cites AO Sykes, 'The Boundaries of Vicarious Liability: An Economic Analysis of the Scope of Employment and Related Legal Doctrines' (1988) 101 *Harvard Law Review* 563.

[175] *Lister* per Lord Steyn: 'Wherever such problems are considered in future in the common law world, these judgments [*Bazley* and *Jacobi*] will be the starting point. On the other hand, it is unnecessary to express views on the full range of policy considerations examined in those decisions' (para 27).

[176] *Catholic Child Welfare Society* (n 167), para 34.

> The correct approach is to concentrate on the relative closeness of the connection between the nature of the employment and the particular tort, and to ask whether looking at the matter in the round it is just and reasonable to hold the employers vicariously liable. In deciding this question a relevant factor is the risks to others created by an employer who entrusts duties, tasks and functions to an employee.[177]

The parameters of what is constituted 'material' enhancement of a risk (*Bazley*) or 'close connection' (*Lister*) is ultimately based in equity or fairness – not equity between individuals but equity between firms and victims harmed by their activities. Therefore, an aim of the tort law approach is favoured that abstracts from the individual case and looks to general policy questions, and then returns to the case to make fact-sensitive judgments.[178] This is an admixture of policy and principle typical of our times. Thus, the problem remains how to integrate enterprise liability into interpersonal law. Certainly, the expansion of vicarious liability is to be explained in this manner, as a thinly disguised form of organisational liability (using the language of individuals and their responsibility) with the parameters of the scope of employment largely influenced by policy reasoning. But the tensions remain with the extant interpersonal law, as the doctrine of vicariously liability has not fully migrated to strict liability for simply the creation of a risk. The employee fault requirement continues to be important but is no longer the most important factor, with risk-context reasoning coming to the fore, and the close connection test policing the outer boundaries of the *firm's* responsibility. Recently, a partial retreat has occurred,[179] but it should be understood in the context of the expansion of alternative and analogous avenues of recovery.[180]

In Germany and France, a similar transformation of vicarious liability may be documented. In Germany, as noted in Chapter 1, the personalisation of responsibility in tort law extended to the requirement that in addition to the employee, the employer must be personally at fault (Article 831, *BGB*). These

[177] [2005] IRLR 398, para 18. Cited in Giliker (n 164), 168.

[178] This is the tension between the moral basis of enterprise liability and the policy basis, often today the economic justification (allocative efficiency as distinct from risk distribution *simpliciter*, although the latter can overlap with the former). I would argue that this is a problem that occurs when one grafts economic or policy arguments onto a legal system which operates according to the organizing principle of justice as an interpersonal concept. For a comprehensive moral theory of enterprise liability see Keating (n 71).

[179] Back to *Dubai Aluminium* only.

[180] *Ie* the dramatic expansion of non-delegable duties outside employment post-*Woodland*, and the use of assumption of responsibility, post-*Vedanta v Lungowe* (2019) UKSC 19, both aimed at organisational fault. For a discussion of the latter, see Chapter 4.

rules were contorted in the case law leading to strict liability.[181] Whereas in France, via Article 1384(5), a strict form of enterprise liability based on risk was developed.[182] This elevates risk reasoning to most important justification for vicarious liability. All these developments tended to place greater burdens on enterprises, with a movement from a focus on the functions of employment towards liability where there is some connection with the employment context.[183] That is not to say that the legal test so framed is clear; it is not.[184] It rests on an uneasy accommodation of policy and juridical reasoning, which from a traditional lawyer's perspective is a recipe for uncertainty. The driver appears to be victim compensation and policy arguments, including the availability of firms' liability insurance, which support the enterprise as the relevant risk bearer.[185] The notion of being a relevant risk bearer is both (a) a justification based on (social) 'fairness' and (b) a justification based on good economic sense.

3 *Direct Action against the State via Negligence: The Rise of the State* qua *Organisation*

Brüggemeier states that '[t]he result of enterprise liability is the consequence of the change in values undergone by society with the transition from externalization of damages (nineteenth century) to internalization of damages (twentieth century)'.[186] Accompanying these trends is a certain tendency to view the state as a large organisation like any other that began to prevail even upon common law judges before this tendency was reined in from the 1980s onwards, a striking parallel with the general retrenchment in negligence liability vis-à-vis private parties.[187] In Brüggemeier's terms, governmental or

[181] Brüggemeier (n 4), ch E.

[182] This is especially the case since the 1980s. See Giliker (n 164), 181–88. 'The 1988 decision [of the *Cour de Cassation*] represents not simply a new formula, but an acceptance of the principle of vicarious liability as a means of responding to the risks arising from misconduct of employees' (186).

[183] Or even 'akin to the employment' context, see *Catholic Child Welfare Society* (n 167), and subsequent judgments. Most recently, *Barclays Bank* (n 167).

[184] This has been openly acknowledged by the courts. See, Lord Toulson in *Mohamed v Morrisons* (n 160): 'To try to measure the closeness of connection, as it were, on a scale of 1 to 10, would be a forlorn exercise and, what is more, it would miss the point' [para. 45]. Instead, it is an evaluative question bearing in mind decided cases, and the policies behind vicarious liability.

[185] See Giliker (n 164), ch 6.

[186] Brüggemeier (n 4), 72–73.

[187] *Dorset*; *Dutton v Bognor Regis Urban District Council* [1972] 1 QB 373; *Anns v Merton London Borough Council* [1978] AC 728.

state liability, or what is referred to in the common law as the liability of public authorities (*inter alia*, 'the Crown'), constitutes '[a] special case of organizational liability' comprising 'objective liability for unlawful acts'.[188] It is certainly true that governmental liability, with its focus on unlawfulness/discretionary power additionally moved away from a concept of personal fault towards a concept of breach of public duty.[189] The precise relationship between the state's public functions and tort law has remained ambiguous throughout the twentieth century. Periods of treating the state, or public authorities, as if an ordinary tortfeasor alternates with periods of treating the state, or public authorities, as *sui generis*.[190] However, in those circumstances in which the state has been held liable in negligence, the state is conceptualised as a direct tortfeasor, albeit a 'special' tortfeasor given the statutory context in which the state conducts its activities.[191] Nevertheless, the case law even in England evidences a tendency by judges to hold the government 'vicariously liable' as the sphere of state activities expanded.[192]

Dorset, *Dutton* and *Anns* demonstrate this tendency through the expansion of recovery in negligence against the state in the guise of public authorities. *Dutton*, indeed, is probably the high point in this respect by explicitly relying on the concept of control, which neatly parallels the doctrine of vicarious liability. State liability *qua* organisational liability never, of course, reached the

188 Brüggemeier (n 4), 162. See Deakin (n 62), 8, referring to the *Armes* decision, 'In the light of their managerial capacities and access to insurance, there is no reason in principle to exclude the application of the concept of enterprise liability to public sector bodies, in the context of which it might be helpful to refer to "organisational" rather than "enterprise" liability'.

189 Brüggemeier (n 4), 150–54, even more so at the European level in which the 'state' or the 'EU' is held liable for breaches. However, it should be noted that in common law acting *ultra vires* is not a condition precedent for negligence.

190 The UK case law is well-known. Certain important judgments: *Murphy v Brentwood District Council* [1991] 1 AC 398; *Hill v Chief Constable of West Yorkshire* [1988] 2 WLR 1049; *X v Bedfordshire* [1995] 2 AC 633; *Osman v United Kingdom* [1998] EHRR 101; *Stovin v Wise* [1996] 3 WLR 389.

191 In recent years, the UK courts have viewed the statutory context not as a policy bar to recovery *ex ante*, as in *Hill*, but as a reason to limit the equal application of private law to the state *ex post*. See *Poole v GN* [2019] UKSC 25.

192 This is not vicarious liability but organisational liability via various means, eg breach of statutory duty, negligence. This way of viewing state liability is, incidentally, shared by C Harlow & R Rawlings, *Law and Administration* 3rd ed (Cambridge: Cambridge University Press, 2009), 751, referring to crown immunity as traditionally exceptional. With the erosion of this exception via the Crown Proceedings Act, 1947, the equality principle came under pressure because of the developing organisational dimension to tort liability, particularly in negligence: 'This exception [Crown Immunity] was to assume greater importance as tort law moved from a system of "corrective justice" in which individuals sued individuals to a system where the objective was to fix vicarious liability on corporate entities able either to meet or insure against the substantial awards of damages made in personal injury actions.'

extent it has in France, but it would be remiss to ignore attempts to view the state in this de-personalised manner and straightforwardly ascribe responsibility for its activities even in the common law![193] The basic insight was that insofar as the state was 'a complex public service corporation' the role of the law was to provide an assurance against the consequences of its activity for those individuals who were prejudiced by its operations.[194] This accorded to the theory of enterprise liability expounded by Laski, among others.[195] This implied setting aside concerns about state sovereignty and applying a stricter form of tortious responsibility to the state. In the case of England, a transformation of the role of the state, similar to that which occurred in France, took place from the late nineteenth century but came to fruition after the Beveridge report. In other words, one should not overlook the context for the rise of state liability, namely, the rise of the welfare state during the twentieth century which increasingly regulated many spheres of social and economic activity.

(i) England: From Dorset to Dutton to Anns

The Diceyan equality principle – that the same standards that apply to citizens should apply to the state – has had a profound impact on, and is a recurring theme in, English law.[196] Given that twentieth-century negligence law took on a distinctively organisational hue, the question as to whether this 'Kuhnian transformation' wrought by *Donoghue v Stevenson* should be extended to the liability of public authorities became a pressing one. The question first arose for decision in the seminal *East Suffolk v Kent* judgment.[197] The essential question was whether statutory powers could be converted into common law duties of care, providing the requisite proximity between the tortfeasors and

[193] JWF Allison, *A Continental Distinction in the Common Law: A Historical and Comparative Perspective on English Public Law* (Oxford: Oxford University Press, 2000). One should recall Harlow (n 110), who argues that the state in France has other control mechanisms apart from duty, *ie* causation and degrees of fault, such that differences in the actual application of state liability can be overstated. In the United Kingdom, there remains an idea that governmental liability is somehow distinctive of general tort law, Markesinis, Deakin & Johnston (n 69), 313–18.

[194] Duguit (n 42), 240.

[195] Indeed, Duguit explicitly makes the connection to Laski's work on vicarious liability in this respect.

[196] Allison (n 193). Of course, Harlow & Rawlings (n 192) clarify that Diceyan equality was somewhat a fiction given contemporary crown immunities.

[197] *East Suffolk Catchment Area v Kent* [1941] AC 74, HL (E).

the injured party. The House of Lords majority resisted the analogy.[198] In *East Suffolk* the relevant local authority pursuant to a statutory power assisted in the reconstruction of a dam after the plaintiff's land was flooded. The reconstruction was carelessly undertaken and had it been properly undertaken it would have been completed at a much shorter interval, which resulted in cost and inconvenience to the plaintiff. While the judgment is not particularly clear, it appears that the court refused recovery based on three arguments: causation, that it was a pure omission case, and the related distinction between statutory powers and duties.[199] For the majority, there can be no duty where a local authority acts pursuant to a statutory power where that act merely does not improve the position of the claimant as distinct from actively harming them.

In his dissenting judgment, Lord Atkin criticised the failure to distinguish between breach of statutory duty and the common law duty of care.[200] The former is, traditionally, a narrowly defined tort requiring the plaintiff to demonstrate membership of a particular protected class for whose benefit the statute is enacted. However, Lord Atkin stated an independent and additional common law *Donoghue* duty to care. One must conduct oneself 'with reasonable care so as not to injure someone liable to be affected by your conduct'.[201] This duty applies whether an individual is exercising a public duty or power, or acting 'in pursuance of his ordinary rights as a citizen'.[202] Thus, it would appear to be a duty that applies to *individuals* with respect to their conduct. However, notwithstanding this manner of framing the duty, Lord Atkin goes on to state:

> I treat it therefore as established that a *public authority*, whether doing an act which it is its duty to do, or doing an act which it is merely empowered to do, must in doing the act do it without negligence, or, as it is put in some of the cases, must not do it carelessly or improperly. Now quite apart from a duty owed to a particular individual, which is the question in this case, I suggest that it would be difficult to lay down that *a duty upon a public authority to act without negligence* or not carelessly or improperly does not include a duty to act with reasonable diligence, by which I mean reasonable despatch.[203]

198 *Ibid.*
199 The court is unclear as to whether it was decided on the basis of causation or duty of care.
200 See especially 88: 'I cannot help thinking that the argument did not sufficiently distinguish between two kinds of duties: (1) A statutory duty to do or abstain from doing something (2) A common law duty to conduct yourself with reasonable care so as not to injure persons liable to be affected by your conduct.'
201 *Ibid.*
202 *Ibid*, 89.
203 *Ibid*, 90 (emphasis added).

The significant slippage between the initial framing of the duty of care in individualised terms and the subsequent formulation of the principle in terms of the direct duty of a public authority, then, demonstrates that the duty is an organisational one. The public authority, in other words, is conceptualised as a unit, a subject of law, and its obligations flow from its putative negligent discharge of those functions. In terms of the duty of care, Lord Atkin's approach posited the presence or absence of proximity as the decisive issue in the case,[204] albeit without invoking the concept explicitly:

> But we have to deal here with relations between the plaintiffs and the Board, which I suggest are much closer than the general relations of members of the public to a public authority. The Board were engaging themselves in repairing the plaintiffs' wall with the object of preventing the further flooding of the land of the plaintiffs.[205]

This gives rise to a duty to conduct the work with 'reasonable dispatch'.[206] As Markesinis and Deakin emphasise, in Lord Atkin's dissent, 'the central question was not whether the board was under a pre-existing statutory duty to act, but whether the relationship between the two parties was sufficiently close to give rise to a duty of care at common law'.[207] Lord Atkin's dissent is significant for two reasons. He applied the general principles laid down in *Donoghue* to public authorities. Second, in echoes of *Donoghue* he provided a direct action against the public authority leapfrogging, so to speak, the negligent acts of individual public servants. Of course, Lord Atkin's finding of proximity in *East Suffolk* could not have been made outside the statutory context even if it did not rely on the statutory powers as the basis of the duty of care. This approach was subsequently applied with some qualifications by Lord Reid in *Home Office v Dorset Yacht Co Ltd*.[208]

The *Dorset* judgment was given at the highpoint of the welfare state. The welfare state as a 'direct service provider' undertook social services through its servants, and via third parties, and it was thought that given the fact that these individuals further the aims of the state, the state should therefore be liable for

[204] There is, of course, in this respect a strong emphasis on the concept of assumption of responsibility in the manner the duty is framed. This became an important factor in later jurisprudence, *eg* implicitly *Dorset*, *Anns*, and in certain pro-plaintiff post-1980s judgments, explicitly, *eg Reeve* [1998] 2 WLR 408. Although assumption of responsibility is not decisive, *eg X v Bedfordshire*, *Murphy v Brentwood* and so on.

[205] *East Suffolk* (n 197), 91.

[206] *Ibid.*

[207] Markesinis, Deakin & Johnston (n 69), 320.

[208] [1970] AC 1004 (Lord Reid, Lord Morris & Lord Pearson maj, Lord Diplock and Viscount Dilhorne dissenting).

their torts, either primarily or vicariously.[209] Additionally, this era marked the highpoint of the general approach to the duty of care in negligence.[210] Thus, no longer was general principle a residuum to cover situations outside of the existing category-based duties, but the general duty became the relevant test. As Smith and Burns state, 'the courts . . . gradually shifted their approach from that of ascertaining a specific duty of care for each kind of situation or class of relationship, to that of starting from the position of the general duty of care as enunciated in Donoghue v. Stevenson, and in particular Lord Atkin's formula'.[211] *Dorset* concerned the escape of seven borstal boys from an island under the control and supervision of three officers, who left the island at night and boarded a yacht, casting it adrift. The claim was twofold: as against the borstal officers in negligence, and assuming officer negligence, as against the Home Office in vicarious liability; against the Home Office directly in negligence. But whether based on vicarious liability or negligence, the obvious preceding question was whether a duty of care could exist at all.

The claimants, in brief, argued that where there is a power to control a person there is a corresponding duty to take reasonable care in the exercise of such control.[212] The defendants, on appeal, argued that there was no common law duty independent of statute, and that the only duty recognised whereby third parties may be liable for the actions of others was that of the parent–child relationship. In addition to the fact that there was no duty, policy should, *prima facie*, militate against the imposition of a new duty.[213] In his judgment, Lord Reid dismissed the defendant's category-based, analogical approach.[214] He accepted the 'steady trend towards regarding the law of negligence as depending on principle so that, when a new point emerges, one should ask

[209] Harlow & Rawlings (n 192), 338, where the authors refer to the welfare state in these terms: 'at the time the classic welfarist model of direct service provision by integrated, hierarchical, public bodies'.

[210] Post-*Hedley Byrne & Co Ltd v Heller & Partners Ltd* [1964] AC 465. Ibbetson (n 48), 199 writes of negligence and its 'satellites'.

[211] JC Smith & P Burns, 'Donoghue v. Stevenson: The Not so Golden Anniversary' (1983) 46(2) *Modern Law Review* 147–63, at 150.

[212] *Dorset* (n 91), 1020.

[213] *Ibid*, 1011.

[214] The defendant had argued against the general duty of care: 'It is not sufficient to establish a duty of care, merely to consider whether the damage was foreseeable. If that were a permissible question, the duty of care would be open-ended in a way which the courts never recognised' (1010). And 'The court must, before it applies the test of foreseeability, make a policy judgment as to whether or not it desires to create the duty in question. The proper approach is to consider whether a duty of care situation exists which the law ought to recognise and whether, in the situation, the defendant's conduct was such that he should have foreseen that damage would be inflicted on the plaintiff' (1011).

not whether it is covered by authority but whether recognised principles apply to it'.[215] This was accepted unless there was some valid explanation or justification for its exclusion.[216] Importantly, Lord Reid considered the legal problem as not, first, about the justifiable limits of common law cases on responsibility for the acts of others[217] but, on a *Donoghue* reasonable foreseeability approach, as one of remoteness. Given that the officers had carelessly failed to supervise and control the boys under their charge, was it reasonably foreseeable that harm would occur? In this way, the criminal acts of the borstal trainees could, at most, constitute a *novus actus interveniens*.[218] The question of statutory policy came in at a second stage of analysis in terms of policy reasons to deny recovery, but since the case concerned the officers' (statutory) duty to supervise and control the boys, and not a statutory power, there was no bar to a negligence action.[219] Lord Reid added that in certain circumstances the unreasonable exercise of a statutory power could also give rise to liability.[220] If not quite as bold as Lord Atkin in *East Suffolk* who *entirely* conceptually distinguished breach of statutory duty from common law negligence, its effects in expanding negligence against public authorities was largely the same. Additionally, whether framed as a direct duty or in terms of the vicarious liability of the Home Office, it is difficult to gainsay Harlow, who views the decision as 'the starter motor of state liability' and sees it as the emergence of a view which places the state 'in the position of guarantor'[221] The state, or public authorities, was increasingly treated as 'vicariously' liable whether based on a direct and corporative duty towards third parties or via the doctrine of vicarious liability.

This 'vicarious' liability reasoning was extended dramatically in *Dutton v Bognor Regis*.[222] In that case, a home purchaser sought recovery against a

[215] *Dorset* (n 91), 1026–27: This is the learned judge's explanation of *Donoghue v Stevenson*.

[216] It ought to apply 'unless there is some justification or valid explanation for its exclusion' (1027), eg special treatment of pure economic loss cases.

[217] *Compare*, concurring, Lord Morris, who views the case as an 'illustration' of this special relation case law, *eg Smith v Leurs* (1945) 70 CLR 256; *Carmarthenshire County Council v Lewis* [1955] AC 549, *Holgate v Lancashire Mental Hospitals Board* [1937] 4 All ER 19.

[218] *Dorset* (n 91), 1027.

[219] This duty/power distinction goes back to *Geddis v Proprietors of Bann Reservoir* (1878) 3 AppCas 430, and was endorsed by the majority in *East Suffolk*.

[220] Thereby inaugurating fifty years of increasingly byzantine case law on duties and powers, policy and operational decisions. As Harlow has noted, the addition of unreasonableness into the mix introduces a public/private divide element into tort law, which had not previously existed. See C Harlow, *State Liability: Tort Law and Beyond* Ch 1 (Oxford: Oxford University Press, 2004).

[221] *Ibid.*

[222] [1972] 1 QB 373.

builder, and also against a local authority where its surveyor had negligently certified a house as sound. The house proved structurally defective because it had been built on a rubbish tip. The purchaser was not in privity with the builder or the council because she had bought the property on resale. The council had acted pursuant to by-laws based on the Public Health Act 1936; a statute specified that it was the function of local authorities to enforce building regulations. It was unclear, however, whether this function should be classed as a statutory duty or power.[223] Lord Denning MR, however, rejected that the power/duty distinction was dispositive: 'This argument assumes that the functions of a local authority can be divided into two categories, powers and duties. Every function must be put into one or other category. It is either a power or a duty. This is, however, a mistake. There is a middle term. It is control.'[224] Control, for Lord Denning MR, was a common currency sufficient to give rise to a duty of care in negligence. This is because actual control entrusted to local authorities was so extensive, ranging from by-laws, the approval of planning permission, the employment of a surveyor to ensure that the construction complies with the by-laws, to the eventual demolition of structures which fail to comply. Policy arguments were dismissed, openly based on the availability of insurance and the council's broad shoulders.[225] As Priel argues: 'When the state was put in charge and has extensive control, it matters little whether the risk was *created* by the state, for the state was given (or has taken) control for the sake of *reducing* risks. Having failed to do so, "its shoulders are broad enough to bear the loss".'[226]

Dutton is at odds with the traditional common law distinction between acts and omissions, and the general rule against recovery for pure economic loss. It seems to overtly align the approach towards *corporative* public authorities' liability more with the rationale behind vicarious liability as enterprise liability, by which the enterprise or, more accurately, organisation (in this case the state) is held liable for the risks it has created and/or has failed to manage. Responsibility for risks is laid at the door of the state because of the position of control it assumes. This is, of course, radically inconsistent with the act- and fault-based theory of the liberal state.[227] This was the true highpoint of the

[223] Entitled, 'Power to prohibit erection of buildings on ground filled up with offensive material.' See www.legislation.gov.uk/ukpga/Geo5and1Edw8/26/49/section/54/enacted (accessed 3 April 2021).

[224] *Dutton* (n 187), 391.

[225] *Ibid*, 398: *semble* builders' insurance, and council's broad shoulders.

[226] Priel (n 30), 13 (citation omitted).

[227] Indeed, it is at odds with the manner in which Dicey, with characteristic brio, conceptualised the responsibility of public servants, which was personalised and based on acting *ultra vires*. AV

expansion away from the traditional law, although the House of Lords further developed, albeit cautiously in *Anns*, an expanded recovery against public authorities.

Anns v Merton extended the law of negligence into the problems of the administration of the welfare state and consumer protection. The law of torts is instrumentalised in order to effectively correct bad contracts by implying a warranty of merchantable quality into buildings constructed at the behest of local authorities.[228] This, in effect, expands tort law into the domain of contract law and is a feature of the judgment that drew the ire of the judges in the *Murphy* judgment in which *Anns* was overturned.[229] The facts in *Anns* were slightly different to *Dutton*; in *Anns*, the council had negligently failed to undertake any inspection of the the building work. The claimants argued that this was contrary to their function under the Public Health Act, 1936. A third party had inspected the foundations, but they had done so negligently. The upshot was structural damage including subsidence, cracks and other defects. Again, the duty was framed as if it was a form of primary liability of the local authority which could be described as an omission, although it resembled vicarious liability, broadly understood, as it was, in effect, liability for the negligent acts of third parties, that is, independent contractors by an expanded reading of the statute.[230] The objection to such a use of tort law which grasps at the expanded function of the state is captured by Goodfellow QC, who reminds us of the individualistic act-based origins of tort law:

> It is one thing to hold that there is a duty of care if a person creates a danger or induces a breach of the byelaws, another to hold there is a duty if a person fails to detect someone who has broken the byelaws. If a building inspector

Dicey, 'The Rule of Law' in *Introduction to the Study of the Law of the Constitution* (Indianapolis, IN: Liberty Classics, 1982, orig. 1885): 'With us every official from the Prime Minister down to a constable or a collector of taxes, is under the same responsibility for every act done without legal justification as any other citizen. The Reports abound with cases in which officials have been brought before the courts and made in their personal capacity liable to punishment or the payment of damages for acts done in their official capacity but in excess of their lawful authority' (178). In general, there is a tendency in English law to make the state servant, rather than the state as a corporate body, responsible.

228 This analysis accords with the learned Law Lords interpretation in *Murphy v Brentwood*.

229 As argued in Chapter 1, the traditional emphasis was on personal autonomy with tort less prominent. One can argue that this move from contract to tort evident in *Donoghue v Stevenson*, is now taken to more radical conclusion in *Anns*.

230 Goodfellow QC in *Anns* (n 187) anticipated this distortion of the individualistic basis of tort law if a duty were to be imposed on the inspector of building works: 'The inspector is not the creator of the thing. The prime villain would not be liable and therefore someone whose fault must be less would be under a wider duty than the person primarily at fault' (748).

> simply fails, negligently, to notice that the foundations are only 2 feet 6 inches deep instead of 3 feet there should be no liability.[231]

Nevertheless, the court held the local authority liable based on, in effect if not explicitly, *respondeat superior*. Lord Wilberforce's reasoning was more modest than Lord Denning MR's in *Dutton*. Because of the public law context, duties of care could only arise where the negligent act or omission was pursuant to an operational decision; that is to say, a decision that did not involve policy decisions about the distribution of resources. However, once the case fell on the operational side of the policy/operational divide, the claimant could sue on ordinary *Donoghue* grounds of reasonable foreseeability and proximity. This was the case even for pure economic loss.[232] In consequence, Priel is correct to state: 'The wide reading of *Donoghue* in the context of *Dorset Yacht* and *Anns* established the idea that as far as the citizen is concerned the state is its "neighbour" for much of what it does.'[233] Hence, by the creative development of duties of care out of statutory duties, or more accurately that statutory duties created the necessary degree of proximity to create a duty of care, the law by the early 1980s was developing, aside from personal responsibility or an invocation of the doctrine of vicarious liability, a type of state corporative or primary responsibility. To be sure, this was oblique if compared to the *dans les fonctions auxquelles* test in France, which more directly superimposed primary responsibility on the state, but nevertheless it was a significant adaptation of the existing legal materials to the society of organisations.[234]

The abrupt halt to this progress occurred in *Yuen*, which was one of many judgments in the 1980s that brought this expansive organisational approach to an end.[235] Notwithstanding its specific context, financial services, in which

[231] *Anns* (n 187), 748. It is important to note that *Anns* is also the beginning of an attempt to distinguish torts committed in the context of a legislative framework from those torts committed by private actors. Thus, focus was placed on a distinction between policy/operation of a statute. This meant that special rules were being developed for public authorities. Public–private divisions in tort liability remain very contentious to this day.

[232] Although, like Lord Denning in *Dutton*, Lord Wilberforce considered the case was not a case of pure economic loss. See *Murphy v Brentwood* for criticism.

[233] Priel (n 30), 13. There is a debate as to the manner in which from *Anns* onwards the judges attempted to carve out a public/private divide which is well rehearsed. For our purposes, it will not be examined. Suffice it to say, the judges increasingly made arguments about the intention of the statutory framework to counteract negligence claims. The highpoint of this approach was in *X v Bedfordshire Co Compare, Michael v CC of South Wales Police [2015] UKSC 2*; *Lungowe v Vedanta Resources plc* [2019] UKSC 20.

[234] Fairgrieve (n 110).

[235] *Yuen Kun Yeu v A-G of Hong Kong* [1988] 1 AC 175, others cited in *Yuen* include *Governors of the Peabody Donation Fund v Sir Lindsay Parkinson & Co. Ltd.* [1985] AC 210; *Leigh and Sillavan Ltd v Aliakmon Shipping Co Ltd (The Aliakmon)* [1986] AC 785.

courts are at all times reticent to impose a duty of care, its reasoning subsequently influenced a series of judgments that eventually led to the overturning of *Anns*. The Privy Council's denial of proximity is its most decisive blow to *Anns*. In effect, *Yuen* among other cases reversed the tendency for statutory powers to form, without difficulty, the background to the imposition of a duty of care. Therefore, this case implicitly denies the control or organisational template as a structure for recovery. Secondly, if policy-based reasoning had been behind the expansion of negligence, then policy was now used to retrench the law in the 1980s.[236]

The *Yuen* depositors argued that the regulator, the Commissioner of Deposit-taking Companies, had failed in their duties under the relevant legislation, the Ordinance of 1976, because, in circumstances where they knew or ought to have known about the fraudulent activities of the bank in question, they failed to revoke the authorisation of the bank.[237] This should have been apparent before the plaintiffs made their deposits with the bank and therefore the conduct of the regulator was considered a cause of the plaintiffs losing their deposits.[238]

The claim was based on the statutory powers incumbent on the regulator under the Ordinance, which included the power of control and supervision.[239] In the circumstances, the plaintiffs relied on *Anns* for the proposition that the breach of statutory powers could be the basis of a duty of care, and further argued that it was fair, just and reasonable that 'when legislation is passed with the express object of conferring powers on a public body to protect depositors from loss that if such loss occurs from the negligent exercise of

[236] J Stapleton, 'Tort, Insurance, and Ideology' (1995) 58 *Modern Law Review* 820, makes this point clearly. Lord Keith in *Yuen* is alive to this policy dimension: 'The issues in the appeal raise important issues of principle, having far-reaching implications as regards the potential liability in negligence of a wide variety of regulatory agencies carried on under the aegis of central or local government and also to some extent by non-governmental bodies. Such agencies are in modern times becoming an increasingly familiar feature of the financial, commercial, industrial and social scene' (189).

[237] The preamble of the Ordinance reads: 'To regulate the taking of money on deposit and to make provision for the protection of persons who deposit money and for the regulation of deposit-taking business for monetary policy purposes.'

[238] The essence of the claim related to depositors who made 'substantial deposits' with a deposit-taking company, American and Panama Finance Co Ltd. These deposits were made in 1982 but by 1983 the relevant deposit-taking company was in liquidation. As a result, the depositors lost their deposits in full. The plaintiffs also claimed that the company should not have been registered in the first place.

[239] The court rehearses the plaintiffs' central argument at p 180: 'The commissioner's failure to exercise properly his statutory powers of control and supervision led to the plaintiffs making deposits with a company which should not have received that money, and so the plaintiffs suffered loss.'

those powers a claim should lie'.[240] The defendants sought, *inter alia*, to confine *Anns* to the context of health and safety regulation, argue that a special relationship was required before recovery could be granted in pure economic loss, and that for policy reasons liability should be denied. The defendant had to reconcile the interests of 'multiple' parties and this would be inhibited by a negligence action.

First, Lord Keith cautiously side-stepped the approach in *Anns*, stating that it 'is not to be regarded as in all circumstances a suitable guide to the existence of a duty of care'.[241] Lord Keith then focused on proximity. In this respect, although it was foreseeable that the plaintiffs would be at risk of losing their deposits, this was a necessary but not sufficient condition of a duty of care. Lord Keith took the day-to-day control or narrow interpretation of *Dorset*, which counselled against liability.[242] That approach confined *Dorset* to the proposition that a duty of care would lie in circumstances where a defendant exercised day-to-day control over the activities of a third party, as distinct from general regulatory powers.[243] Therefore, no special relationship (or proximity) was created in the circumstances.[244] Secondly, the plaintiffs' claim on the basis of *Hedley Byrne* was dismissed as there was no voluntary assumption of responsibility towards the plaintiffs. The regulator was not in a quasi-contractual relationship with the plaintiff in which he guaranteed the creditworthiness of the deposit-taking company. The duty on the commissioner was to supervise in the general public interest, and not in the specific interest of individual members of the public.[245] Lord Keith stated further that policy ran against the plaintiffs because of the

[240] The plaintiffs also noted the reliance that they place on the commission (the regulator) owing to the latter's access to information not available to the plaintiffs, at p 181. In addition, it is clear from the submissions of the plaintiffs that they were sensitive to the changing tide towards policy arguments and framed their claim accordingly. They noted at p 179 the various judgments delivered since *Anns* that could be considered a 'retrenchment' from the *Anns* position. Second, while denying that this was a case of pure economic loss, they further argued that 'If the purpose of the legislation is, and can only be, to prevent economic loss, then that is the only type of loss which can be envisaged to result and be the subject of a claim in these circumstances' (181).

[241] *Yuen* (n 235), 194. It was later explicitly distinguished in *Murphy v Brentwood*.

[242] *Yuen* (n 235), 196.

[243] This is to keep negligence and vicarious liability distinct: 'In contradistinction to the position in the *Dorset Yacht* case, the commissioner had no power to control the day-to-day activities of those who caused the loss and damage. As has been mentioned, the commissioner had power only to stop the company carrying on business, and the decision whether or not to do so was clearly well within the discretionary sphere of his functions' (196).

[244] 'To hark back to Lord Atkin's words in *Donoghue v Stevenson* [1932] AC 562, 581, there were not such close and direct relations between the commissioner and the plaintiffs as to give rise to the duty of care desiderated' (196).

[245] See also *Hill* on this point.

'distortion of judgment' that the spectre liability might give rise to, and wider implications of liability for other supervisory bodies.[246]

Lord Keith's judgment, in effect, broke the spell that converted the state into a guarantor, a type of corporate actor which creates or enhances risks and must indemnify individuals for their consequences. Now, it might be argued that the particular facts in *Yuen* make this statement too broad. In other words, the *Yuen* facts disclose a situation in which it cannot be said an organisational context exists, the bank is simply too distant from the state to fit into the organisational model. Perhaps. And yet, when the *Murphy* case was decided a few years later, on facts in line with *Anns*, the *Anns* decision was overruled. Hence, in *Yuen* what one can see is a far more radical *volte face* – a rejection of the organisational or corporate model of responsibility. This was achieved by narrowing the proximity requirement, and the rise of a policy first, duty second type of reasoning which owes considerable debt to the *Yuen* decision.

It might be convenient to argue this use of breach of statutory duty to canalise corporative responsibility broke down with the end of the welfare state but such a causal claim should be treated with caution.[247] Nevertheless, there is a striking parallel between the evolution of the welfare state towards a regulatory state and retrenchment in the law of torts away from an expansive use of breach of statutory duty as a basis for a negligence claim. Once again, the role and function of the state was changing, and with it the corporative model seemed outmoded and inapt. In sum, in the English common law it is clear that the organisational model of state responsibility developed obliquely. No sooner had it developed than it seemed to provoke retrenchment. Applied to the state, the organisational approach in its full expansiveness had a short career. I will examine in the next chapter potential reasons why this may have been the case.

(ii) France: Blanco and the Emergence of State Liability

If the English courts developed a direct action against the state in bits and pieces, as it were, before reconsidering the sweeping approach in the 1980s,

[246] *Yuen* (n 235), 198. Here, very much influenced by the policy arguments in *Hill*. See also p 190, where earlier in the judgment Lord Keith notes this wider context: '[Liability would have] far-reaching implications as regards the potential liability in negligence of a wide variety of regulatory agencies carried on under the aegis of central or local government and also to some extent by non-governmental bodies. Such agencies are in modern times becoming an increasingly familiar feature of the financial, commercial, industrial and social scene.'

[247] Priel (n 30) notes that the new retrenchment can be explained politically, not as influenced by neoliberalism but by the reassertion of traditional conservative values. It is difficult to tell, in truth.

the French expansion of liability was all the more dramatic and patently derived from an organisational model of responsibility. In France, that which never developed in the United Kingdom, a doctrine analogous to the doctrine of vicarious liability, was developed in respect of public authorities. This was a concept of fault for activities related to public-service. As Van Dam explains: 'A *faute* can be linked to public service if the public service has provided the conditions for the fault. An official's personal fault can also be a service-related fault at the same time.'[248] This *faute de service* can be traced to Duguit's treatment of state responsibility. Notably, Duguit's treatment of state responsibility is no more than a subdivision of his treatment of 'responsibility' more generally. This is clear from chapter 7 of *Law in the Modern State*.[249] He dismisses von Gierke's theory of corporate responsibility as resting on an outmoded theory of individual will. Von Gierke's theory was premised on fault and responsibility, with the corporation being the directing mind and agents the body. In a manner similar to the way in which it cannot be said that the actions of the body are not independent of the mind, therefore, the acts of agents are attributable to the will of the directing mind, the corporation. Jellinek applied this analysis to the state, and Hauriou applied to his analysis French public law. Duguit rightly argued that this rested in a contortion of fault to fit the new context of large, vertically integrated firms. Duguit, on the other hand, argued for the abandonment of a model of corporate responsibility that rested on the paradigm of 'the existence of a conscious willing person'.[250] Instead he argued that '[t]he notion of fault is out of place where we deal with the interrelation of groups with groups; or groups with individuals'.[251] He cited Laski's seminal article on the doctrine of vicarious liability to argue that the responsibility as fault and individual will nexus should be broken and replaced by a general principle that, although '[g]roups have no wills and cannot therefore be responsible persons', group activity:

> is none the less an important aspect of social activity. The tasks it performs doubtless benefits the whole of society, but more particularly it is the members of the group who are benefited. If they so benefit, it is only fair

[248] Van Dam (n 108), 535–36.

[249] And, indeed, his *Les transformations générales du droit privé depuis le Code Napoléon* (Paris: Alcan, 1912), ch 5, 145–47.

[250] Duguit (n 42): 'The idea of responsibility and of fault demand, as is clear, the existence of a conscious willing person. Conscious violation of a rule of law by a free will involves the responsibility of the person endowed with that will. Such is the metaphysics of the ordinary concept of responsibility. Clearly it makes the problem one of ascription' (203).

[251] *Ibid*, 205.

> that they should bear the risk which attaches to the contact of their acts with other individuals or groups.[252]

It is therefore clear that with sovereignty set to one side, Duguit addressed the responsibility of the state as merely a variant of 'private' law corporate responsibility.[253] In the case of the state, responsibility is linked to the service that the state performs and should be premised on causation and not fault.[254] All individuals and groups have duties towards society, as distinct from rights, and the duty varies with one's social role. The social role of the state is to provide public services, and to the extent that it fails to fulfil this duty it may be held responsible in tort. The important question was not the identity of the tortfeasor, but its form: in other words, whether the relationship involved was one between individuals and individuals, or individuals and groups. With the growing state involvement in the economy as service provider, the state as a corporate body should be held accountable. One can therefore speak of a congruence between the private and public law around a notion of organisational responsibility.[255] Those adversely affected by *corporative* activity should be compensated when they find themselves 'prejudiced' by group activity. In

[252] *Ibid*, 206. Interestingly, Duguit avoided a type of anthropomorphic thinking later criticised by Williams (n 127) in relation to attempts to found corporate responsibility on a concept of a collective will. An intermediary step in the argument above, *ie* between critiquing von Gierke and developing a benefit principle, was to devalue responsibility as fault by arguing that neither the individual nor the group can be said to be independently responsible and therefore a new basis for liability is required. Especially: 'The act is doubtlessly [*sic*] put in motion by individual wills, but the end is collective. If a fault is committed by an agent of this collectivity, it is not imputable to that agent since it is for a collective end that it has been committed. Nor is it imputable to the collectivity since the latter outside the imagination of lawyers has no personal existence. The idea of fault and imputability are thus eliminated' (205, 206).

[253] Duguit's argument can be properly said to have two movements. The first is to state that insofar as social fact indicates that sovereignty has limits, sovereignty does not exist. In other words, if it is possible to hold the state responsible, as legal practice indicates it is, then the coexistence of responsibility and sovereignty is a contradiction in terms. Second, Duguit argues that the type of responsibility that is developing cannot be captured by the individualistic concept of responsibility inherited from the 'Imperial' state, which tied responsibility to authorial will. Contemporary social facts indicate organised action towards defined ends, whether in the private corporation or the nascent welfare state and therefore require a new form of responsibility which meets the needs of individuals who suffer damage as a consequence of collective action. Duguit thereby intertwines private and public responsibility under the umbrella of group or organisational liability.

[254] *Ibid*. 'It follows that if the organisation or management of such a service should particularly prejudice a group or an individual, the funds of that service should repair the damage so long as the relation of cause and effect between the act and damage is traceable' (207).

[255] See E Picard, 'The Public–Private Divide in French Law: Through the History and Destiny of French Administrative Law' in M Rüffert (ed), *The Public–Private Divide: Potential for Transformation* (London: BIICL, 2009), 17, 54. Picard clarifies that while Hauriou's theory was

other words, since decision-making regarding activities occurs in groups, it is these groups which should be held accountable in tort for the negative consequences of their activity. The sentence that most places in relief this intertwinement between the rationale for private responsibility and state responsibility is found in Duguit's discussion of the emergence of the *faute de service* doctrine before the *Conseil d'État*. It seems, for Duguit, to rest on a risk–profit basis: 'It meant that the possibility of such faults involve [*sic*] a risk but that if the risk is realised the state must pay.'[256] This is no less than Josserand and Saleilles' theory applied to the state – form not identity is paramount. The form was corporate and the state was 'a complex public service corporation'.[257] Indeed, in the distinction between personal fault and *faute de service* one find an analogue to the control test in vicarious liability with a focus on the connection between the functions performed and the act in question.

The *Conseil d'État* borrowed from the civil jurisprudence on tortious liability but modified these rules where the judges thought necessary. Thus, fault can vary between *faute légère* and *faute lourde* which allows the *Conseil d'État* to take into consideration the particular policy factors which exercise the English courts without providing *a priori* strict policy immunities. *Faute lourde* is, in practice, a high threshold and may make recovery very difficult. For example, *faute lourde* applies in respect of the liability of financial regulators.[258] There has been a trend to relax the *faute lourde* requirement, although the French courts have not taken a consistent position in this respect.[259] In addition to fault-based liability, the *Conseil d'État* has also developed a doctrine of *égalité devant les charges publiques* which results in strict liability in circumstances where citizens can demonstrate that they have

more accurate in terms of the existing law, Duguit's was highly influential on how the law developed. In this sense, I examine Duguit here to explain the underlying assumptions.

256 Duguit (n 42), 240.

257 *Ibid*. Similarly, there was a strong instrumental bent to this reasoning premised on the idea that the burden should fall in fairness on the state which can be considered to insure the citizen against these injuries: '[The] private citizen is so to speak insured against the risks arising from each public department by claims in its special budget' (239, 240).

258 Van Dam (n 108): 'Generally, gross negligence is required for damage caused by a particularly difficult or sensitive task, such as those performed by the police, the tax bodies, and supervisory or regulatory authorities' (536).

259 D Nolan, 'The Liability of Financial Supervisory Authorities' (2013) 4(2) *Journal of European Tort Law* 190. The author notes that whereas initially the French courts were willing to relax the *faute lourde* requirement in respect of financial regulatory authorities, the courts have reversed this initial position.

suffered disproportionate damage by state action. This is based on solidaristic and distributive thinking, and holds the state liable for the unfavourable consequences of its actions in a manner very similar to enterprise liability.[260] Both developments, that is, fault liability and strict liability against the state, represent an organisational view of the state and a principle of responsibility for its actions. The *faute lourde* requirement is a way to address the reservations that English judges express at the duty of care stage towards the burden that tort liability imposes on public finances.

D CONCLUSION

In sum, the ultimate consequence of the rise of organisational liability is that the interpersonal or individualistic tort law was supplemented by an organisational model of ascription. Tort law became, in addition to providing rules of just interpersonal conduct, concerned with managing the negative externalities of large-scale industry by making industry internalise its costs for reasons of fairness and expediency. There are clear analogies to be drawn with the liability of public authorities and the state. This organisational model also can impact on the standard of care in tort: individual moral conduct is replaced by liability for consequences of systems failure which relies, but is not entirely determined by, expert calculations of what constitutes reasonable risk imposition. The problem with this approach is that it is not well adapted to a form of public or private organisation in which a vertically integrated public or private bureaucracy is no longer paradigmatic. There are hints in this direction in *Yuen*, which was decided against the background of an emerging regulatory state. When the organisation is replaced by, or encased within, a governance network, whether public, private or hybrid, the organisational model of liability becomes difficult to normatively justify as a comprehensive model of liability because in the absence of singular, hierarchical 'control', it is not clear why it is fair or expedient to impose liability on 'secondary' network actors. But individual responsibility also appears inapt given the fact that 'network failures' are systemic. Perhaps Duguit anticipated these

[260] G Viney and P Jourdain, *Les Conditions de la responsabilité* 3rd ed (Paris: LGDJ, 2006), aver to the similarity between the two regimes of liability: 'On peut la rapprocher également de la responsabilité de la puissance publique pour le fait des fonctionnaires et agents publics qui relève du droit administratif mais répond à des préoccupations comparables et se trouve soumise à un régime très proche' (976).

incongruences between our models of liability and our contemporary need in his penultimate sentence in *Law in Modern State*, where he speculates on the future of liability: 'Our own system, realist, socialist, and objective represents but a moment in history; and before it is finally builded [*sic*] the keen observer will note its transmutation into a newer code.'[261]

[261] Duguit (n 42), 245.

3

Currents and Counter-Currents in Contemporary Law

A INTRODUCTION

Chapters 1 and 2 showed how modern, positive law is a second-order observation of its acentric knowledge base and co-evolves with it. Because law is, in systems theory terms, a functional system that provides normative expectations, its (normative) programmes model its dynamic knowledge base.[1] This modelling implies the legal mapping of cognitive expectations into stable, counterfactual liability rules of conduct.[2] These rules also have an institutional dimension because they not only reflect their knowledge base, but their crystallisation[3] into stable models of liability provides a framework of (normative) expectations, which different societal sub-systems can rely on. This allows other sub-systems – economic, political, and so on – to gain further cognitive complexity 'delegating' the task of defining normative expectations to the legal system.[4] The constant (cognitive) feedback between systems means that the

[1] Luhmann's idea of 'order from noise', or more accurately Heinz Von Forrester's idea adopted by systems theory, and its impact on the inter-systemic division of labour, discussed at length in N Luhmann, 'Closure and Openness: On Reality in the World of Law' in G Teubner (ed), *Autopoietic Law: A New Approach to Law and Society* (Berlin: De Gruyter, 1988), 335–48, esp 340–41. This 'intervention' from the perspective of other functional systems forms the normative environment of these systems. This allows these systems to develop their complexity while leaving the task of providing the normative expectations to the legal system. The dense 'structural coupling' of law and the economic system through property and contract is a good example. The political system and the legal system are linked via constitutionalism, *etc*.

[2] In systems theory terms, these are legal 'second-order observations' of its knowledge base. Cognitive expectations are legal expectations, but ones that are 'responsive' to the law's knowledge base.

[3] One might say certain expectations densify in law, and the law then develops a self-description of these expectations at the level of its programmes.

[4] This is very well understood in the contract law scholarship, *ie* the idea that (classical) contract law provides default rules (a set of expectations) facilitating transactions. Brownsword refers to it as 'static market individualism'. See, R Brownsword, 'Static and Dynamic Market

basic legal (stabilising) concepts receive ongoing irritation from their environment.[5] The basic categories of private law – property, contract and tort – then are locked into a co-evolutionary dynamic.[6] However, where there is a 'rupture' in the knowledge base of society – a break in symmetry between cognitive expectations and legal systems' normative models – this places a corresponding pressure on the legal system to differentiate its programmes. If the legal system does not develop mechanisms to co-evolve with its knowledge base, the law's *performance* of its function may be undermined.[7] Gains in complexity of other sub-systems of society are the cognitive 'perturbation' for greater complexity in normative expectations in law.[8]

The transition from the 'society of individuals' to 'the society of organisations' follows precisely this dynamic. As a counterpart to the rise of the society of organisations, the legal system underwent a 'secondary normative remodelling' from rules of just interpersonal conduct to rules that aimed to designate and intermediate between groups in order to resolve *systemic* conflicts over the allocation of risks. This differentiation of law's normative programmes resulted in two concurrent normative models of responsibility: individual responsibility and organisational responsibility in tort.[9] In other words, when faced with a

Individualism' in R Halson (ed), *Exploring the Boundaries of Contract* (Aldershot: Dartmouth, 1996), 48.

5 It is a two-way street, of course. The other sub-systems of society receive cognitive irritations from the legal system. Juridification is the pejorative term for these irritations, but in a less loaded sense, the normative expectations are processed cognitively by other systems, *eg* legal liability in contract is treated strategically by the economic system, *ie* efficient breach, see M Renner, 'Death by Complexity: The Financial Crisis and the Crisis of Law in World Society' in P Kjaer et al (eds), *The Financial Crisis in Constitutional Perspective: The Dark Side of Functional Differentiation* (Oxford: Oxford University Press, 2011), 93–111, at 104.

6 Through various 'feedback loops', *eg* through the 'open norms' of the legal system. See *eg* S Taekema, 'Private Law as an Open Legal Order: Understanding Contract and Tort as Interactional Law' (2014) 43(3) *Netherlands Journal of Legal Philosophy* 140.

7 GF Calliess & M Renner, 'Between Law and Social Norms: The Evolution of Global Governance' (2009) 22(2) *Ratio Juris* 260–80. Crisply defined as '[t]he function of law is given by reference to society as a whole, whereas performance denotes the services that the legal system provides to other functional subsystems of society like the economy, politics, and so on' (266). For Calliess and Renner, the great threat to the legal system's performance role is excessive formalism.

8 Because, like all sub-systems, the legal system is an 'observing system'. How it observes in an autopoetic understanding of law is well captured by KH Ladeur, 'The Theory of Autopoiesis as an Approach to a Better Understanding of Postmodern Law: From the Hierarchy of Norms to the Heterarchy of Changing Patterns of Legal Inter-relationships', EUI Working Paper LAW No. 99/3, 6–44, esp 13–14.

9 Not only in tort, consumer protection law in contract follows a similar pattern. Like tort liability law, which develops organisational liability based on risk creators and passive victims, it assumes a normatively significant analogous inequality between businesses and consumers.

rupture in the societal knowledge base, the law internally differentiated, normatively adjusting its programmes to group-based and expert knowledge.[10] This was achieved at a doctrinal level through both processes of 'exaption', pouring new wine into old bottles, through 'bridging concepts' such as reasonableness,[11] and by differentiating legal fields into sub-fields.[12] Organisational responsibility in tort, which essentially observes legal problems as a question of defining the circumstances in which 'vertical vicarious liability'[13] is normatively justified should be considered as a self-standing normative concept of liability that cuts across the public–private divide and sits alongside individual responsibility as a resource that assists the law in performing its function. The contours of organisational responsibility varied by national context, but from a broader perspective are equivalent because they are addressing the same fundamental changes in the 'social epistemology' of the legal system.[14] Additionally, it should be underlined that individual responsibility and organisational responsibility not only 'observe' their knowledge base,[15] but also 'irritate' it by normatively designating problems as individualistic or organisational.[16]

[10] KH Ladeur, 'The Evolution of General Administrative Law and the Emergence of Postmodern Administrative Law', Osgoode CLPE Research Paper 16/2011, 104: 'the pre-structuring of society by the corporatist co-operation of the pluralistic social groups and the big firms and the "representative organisations" of both. This complex group-based infrastructure of the late modern nation state has left its traces in the legal system, which was composed of both an increasing number of laws and the regulation of more and more spheres of societal domains in the welfare state' (33–34) (citations omitted).

[11] KH Ladeur, 'The Role of Contracts and Networks in Public Governance: The Importance of the "Social Epistemology" of Decision Making' (2007) 14(2) *Indiana Journal of Global Legal Studies* 339–51. The concepts of danger in public law and negligence in private law are paradigmatic examples of bridging concepts between 'proto-normative rules of practice, knowledge rules, and societal expectations on the one hand, and normative stabilization of order on the other' (338).

[12] Eg consumer law, in which product liability is being recategorised as forming a part of the overall concept of consumer law from its roots in negligence.

[13] G Teubner, 'The Invisible Cupola: From Causal to Collective Attribution in Ecological Liability' in G Teubner, L Farmer & Declan Murphy (eds), *Environmental Law and Ecological Responsibility: The Concept and Practice of Ecological Self-Organization* (Chichester: Wiley, 1994), 429–64.

[14] One might refer to varieties of individual responsibility or organisational responsibility by analogy to how the literature refers to varieties of capitalism, *ie* PA Hall & D Soskice, *Varieties of Capitalism: The Institutional Foundations of Comparative Advantage* (Oxford: Oxford University Press, 2001).

[15] They are a systems-internal reconstruction of the systems environment. Therefore, they must be modelled according to the internal structure of the legal system's programmes.

[16] See G Hodgson, 'The Legal Nature of the Firm and the Myth of the Firm-Market Hybrid' (2002) 9(1) *International Journal of the Economics of Business* 37–60, which makes a similar argument in relation to the importance of legal form when discussing the (normative)

The stabilisation of the relationship between (tort) law and its knowledge base, however, is a contingent phenomenon. Today, the emergent society of networks challenges (tort) law and represents a second rupture in its knowledge base, and is 'a further rise in the complexity of the knowledge base of society'.[17] The emerging society of networks is one in which *ex ante* rules can no longer easily be formulated under conditions of increased uncertainty, and instead, 'order' emerges *ex post* from 'joint ventures' and processes of ongoing experimentation in cooperation between public and private organisations in open-ended search processes.[18] This leads to '[m]ore and more hybrid modes of organisation which blend forms of the market and organisational closure ("network contracts") spread in society, and have a repercussion on the procedures of administrative decision-making which transcend traditional borders and stable separations'.[19] This network logic also impacts on the definition of risks, which cannot be known precisely before their materialisation into harms, which tends to be catastrophic.[20] This provokes a crisis of normativity in tort law because in the society of individuals, and even in the society of organisations, tort law's programmes were modelled according to experiential rules of conduct or (*ex ante*) and expert calculable risks which could be attributed to individuals or organisations.[21] In the society of networks, in contrast, risks cannot be fully known *ex ante* (and therefore cannot be patterned as conduct rules), and attributing acts or activities to 'actors' – whether individual or group – does not capture the systemic nature of how harms occur in networks.[22] What Beck calls 'the assignment of accountability'[23] becomes strained because it is increasingly difficult, particularly in high technology, to identify causal relationships, and to distinguish between

boundaries of the firm. The law not only responds to the firm, but constitutes its boundaries. More broadly, S Deakin et al, 'Legal Institutionalism: Capitalism and the Constitutive Role of Law' (2017) 45(1) *Journal of Comparative Economics* 188–200. Similarly, see Collins' portrayal of law's autonomy vis-à-vis different discourses in H Collins, *Regulating Contracts* (Oxford: Oxford University Press, 1999), ch 2, capturing the dynamics of closure as well as the dynamic qualities of the legal system.

17 Ladeur (n 10), 24.

18 *Ibid.*

19 *Ibid*, 29.

20 The network society is also a risk society: U Beck (M Ritter trans), *Risk Society: Towards a New Modernity* (London: Sage Publications, 1992), esp ch 1.

21 Calculable risks can be insured against, and this furthers risk spreading.

22 F Ewald (S Utz trans), 'The Return of Descartes Malicious Daemon: An Outline of the Philosophy of Precaution' in T Baker & J Simon (eds), *Embracing Risk: The Changing Culture of Insurance and Responsibility* (Chicago, IL: University of Chicago Press, 2002), 273.

23 U Beck, *World at Risk* (Cambridge: Polity Press, 2009), 26.

perceived harms and actual materialised harms.[24] These changes in the social epistemology of the society of networks, then, put tort law and its conceptual apparatus in the dock.[25]

This task of developing a liability law is rendered even more complicated because functional differentiation has broken out of the frame of the territorial state while liability law has lagged behind. In the twentieth century, the bureaucratic state as the 'organisation of organisations'[26] fulfilled a coordinative role between different functional systems and their discourses[27] through law.[28] This 'political–legal complex' could achieve a high degree of positive integration between different societal sub-systems, which 'unfolded … within the framework of the nation state'.[29] The legal system could rely on corporative structures to which liability could be channelled and through which different sub-systems' logics were made compatible. Organisational responsibility structurally coupled political, legal and economic systems. The organisation was, as has been argued, subject and object of law. This logic was, then, applied to the state itself in the form of organisational state liability as the corollary of organisational enterprise liability. In this way, regulating risks in tort positively integrated the sub-systems of society by establishing *modus vivendi* between the *sinnwelten* of economic, political and legal communication.[30] The state, through law, played a coordinating role in an acentric,

24 *Ibid*; see Beck's discussion of 'organized irresponsibility' on 'invisible side effects' (30) of decisions about acceptable risk in the 'second modernity'. Beck states, in a general sense following Weber, that 'relations of definition' (30) become highly political, *ie* the tension between discourses of risk in law, science and politics, and perceptions of risk, and their impact on citizens.

25 *Ibid*, provocatively, Beck by reference to the concept of 'organized irresponsibility', whereby, *inter alia*, the law's conceptual apparatus contributes to making risks invisible through a process of 'symbolic normalization' (95).

26 This, of course, refers to the nation-state 'moment' in Western, 'developed' states, and may suffer from Eurocentrism. See P Kjaer, 'Law and Order within and beyond National Configurations', Normative Orders Working Paper 02/2010 Goethe University Frankfurt am Main, 1–48, esp 25–31. See also, and more broadly, T Duvé, 'Global Legal History: A Methodological Approach', Max Planck Institute for European Legal History Research Paper Series No. 2016-04, 1–22. https://papers.ssrn.com/sol3/papers.cfm?abstract_id=2781104 (accessed 28 June 2021).

27 In systems theory, their self-descriptions.

28 Expressed paradigmatically in the Durkheimian tradition's understanding of the integrative role of law in the achievement of 'organic solidarity'.

29 P Kjaer, 'Post-Hegelian Networks: Comments on the Chapter by Simon Deakin' in M Amstutz & G Teubner (eds), *Networks: Legal Issues of Multi-lateral Co-operation* (Oxford: Hart, 2009), 81.

30 P Kjaer, 'Law of the Worlds: Towards and Inter-Systemic Theory' in S Keller & S Wiprächtiger (eds), *Recht Zwischen Dogmatik und Theorie: Marc Amstutz zum 50 Geburtstag* (Zürich: Dike Verlag, 2012), 159–75, at 173.

polycontextural society.[31] But because, today, this frame has been broken, and functional differentiation has outpaced the state, the couplings between different sub-systems of society has been weakened. For Luhmann, in the fragmented, 'post-Hegelian' 'world society', in the absence of a 'legal–political complex' to rival the coordinative role fulfilled by the nation-state, the law and its function of providing normative expectation for society is, and will increasingly be, substituted by systems that are more overtly cognitive in orientation. In his view, economy, technology and science gain ground over legal, moral and political communication. In a highly cognitivised 'world society', then, the legal system should become more 'cognitivised' or it will become irrelevant.[32]

Teubner has documented the inter-systemic danger of this diagnosis.[33] Because systems have 'delegated' the production of normative expectations to the legal system, they do not have inherent, normative limits on their communications. Without legal integration of systems through norms, there is a danger that systems' *eigenlogics* will inflate and expand, resulting in a post-modern form of de-differentiation.[34] He strikes a hopeful note that systems are self-constitutionalising, and that the counterpart to the positive integration of the nation-state era is negative integration or conflict law within systems in the post-state era. This develops in court-like institutions, which are proliferating at a transnational level within functional areas. This means that systems, internally, should develop a law of 'regime collisions' rather than following the 'old-European thinking' of external irritation through a conception of a

[31] KH Ladeur, 'Globalisation and the Conversion of Democracy to Polycentric Networks: Can Democracy Survive the End of the Nation State?', EUI Working Paper LAW No. 2003/4, 13. The steering of society by the state was overestimated even in the heyday of the welfare state because the welfare state relied on the management capabilities of corporative structures and 'private' organisations to achieve societal integration.

[32] Ladeur has developed these ideas further in a number of publications. See, most recently, KH Ladeur, 'The Future of Law: "Serial Law"?', Working Paper, EUI LAW, 2016/19. See also GP Calliess & P Zumbansen, *Rough Consensus and Running Code: A Theory of Transnational Private Law* (London: Hart, 2010): the pluralisation of sites of norm generation might be viewed as signs of the loss of significance of legal norms, and law more generally, in the society of networks. In more down-to-earth language, J Steele, 'Risk Revolutions in Private Law' in S Worthington et al (eds), *Revolution and Evolution in Private Law* (London: Hart, 2017), 75–97, detects the adjustment of liability law towards greater 'restraint' in the provision of security in recent years in the light of its position within a wider regulatory/governance framework. I would class this as 'cognitivisation'.

[33] Eg A Fischer-Lescano & G Teubner, 'Regime Collisions: The Vain Search for Legal Unity in the Fragmentation of Global Law' (2004) 25 *Michigan Journal of International Law* 999.

[34] As distinct from reverting to simpler forms of societal structuration, *ie* stratificatory or segementary differentiation. Eigenlogic, or 'eigenlogik' here, denotes the unfolding of the basic code of a given system.

unitary state-based legal system.[35] In other words, the different systems should themselves develop their own differentiated legal, normative orders, which attempt to reconstruct, internally, super-adjacent systems and attempt to maintain 'fragile symmetries of chances of translation' between different 'discourses' in world society.[36] However, perhaps more promising than placing 'the fox (exclusively) in charge of the henhouse'[37] is Kjaer's observation that the dichotomy between the old European nation-state and the world society overlooks the role of governance structures that act, in a functionally equivalent way to the nation-state, as sites for meaning transfer, and contestation, between systems.[38] These governance structures (*eigenstructures*) largely take the form of networks such that one might speak in terms of governance networks.[39] They also govern functional areas: products, finance, telecommunications, sports, the internet, social corporate responsibility, and so on, and are epistemic communities, which define socially acceptable risk. They are interfaces between communicative sub-systems, and attempt to obtain compatibility between the sub-systems of society by charting the boundaries between systems communications.[40] Kjaer views these governance networks as fulfilling a functionally equivalent role to nation-state democratic orders at the transnational level. Just as in the society of organisations, public bureaucracy was the counterpart of private bureaucracy, in the society of networks 'public' governance networks are, it seems, the counterpart of 'private'

[35] Should, and are developing these internal constitutions, which are proliferating in 'Global Bukovina'. See G Teubner, 'Global Bukowina: Legal Pluralism in the World-Society' in G Teubner (ed), *Global Law without a State* (Aldershot: Dartmouth, 1996), 3–28.

[36] G Teubner, 'In the Blindspot: The Hybridization of Contracting' (2006) 7 *Theoretical Inquiries in Law* 1–18, at 14.

[37] G Teubner, 'A Constitutional Moment? The Logics of "Hitting the Bottom" in Kjaer et al (n 5), 3–42, 13. I added 'exclusively' here, although it is not clear whether Teubner thinks that internal self-constitutionalisation is the only solution given the 'Bukovina' of world society, or the primary solution. More recently, he seems to advocate for both internal and external mechanisms, see G Teubner & A Beckers, 'Expanding Constitutionalism' (2013) 20(2) *Indiana Journal of Global Legal Studies* 523–50, at 527: 'Conversely, predicting that these rules on self-limitation are developed voluntarily would imply a false idealism and would overestimate the potential of self-regulation to solve such constitutional conflicts.'

[38] See PF Kjaer, 'The Metamorphosis of the Functional Synthesis: A Continental European Perspective on Governance, Law, and the Political in the Transnational Space' (2010) 2 *Wisconsin Law Journal* 489.

[39] That is to say, as distinct from the 'network firm', which is a different concept and dealt with in detail in G Teubner (M Everson trans), *Networks as Connected Contracts* (Oxford: Hart, 2011).

[40] In other words, negative integration of different sub-systems rather than the positive integration of the state.

governance networks.[41] However, as in the society of organisations, the public/private divide is overstated.[42] In fact, it has become even more marginalised in the society of networks since the state has lost its role as 'organisation of organisations', and instead is one actor among several within more encompassing governance networks.[43]

It is, as Kjaer has pointed out, unsurprising that most governance networks attempt to regulate the relationship between the economic system and other systems since, in the transnational era, the economic system has emerged as 'market leader' among systems, as networks seek to make it compatible with its environment.[44] Corporate Social Responsibility (CSR) is a good illustration of both the marginalisation of the public/private divide and also the design of regimes of network governance, which attempt to embed the economic system into the political and legal environment. A network of firms, states, international and supranational organisations as well as non-governmental organisations (NGOs) and auditors all create (iterative) rules, monitor and enforce them. Similarly, the New Approach to Technical Standards involves the opening of transnational markets by mutual recognition in EU law while at the same time developing new governance structures implicating both private and public actors from rule-making to monitoring and enforcement. In both illustrations, risk regulation is shared between public and private actors in overall governance architectures.[45] These network governance 'intermediary structures' may however suffer from pathologies when they become dominated by particularistic communications, and instead of transferring meaning

[41] Again, not the 'network firm' as such, but rather the larger governance networks of which network firms often form important component parts as gatekeepers. See Chapter 4 for elaboration.

[42] See P Selznick, *Law, Society and Industrial Justice* (New York: Russell Sage Foundation, 1969), on private administrative law. In tort law terms, organisational responsibility delegates risk management to private firms.

[43] The state has, additionally, according to this process, disaggregated along functional lines. See AM Slaughter, 'Global Government Networks, Global Information Agencies, and Disaggregated Democracy' (2003) 24 *Michigan Journal of International Law* 1041–75.

[44] In a sense, like a Polanyian double-movement of disembedding and re-embedding. However, the analogy with Polanyi should not be overstated because, first, Polanyi seems to assume a 'lifeworld', which functional differentiation belies. The state is, as Kjaer has pointed out, a disembedded structure. Secondly, the economic system's breaking free of the nation-state occurs at the same time as the rise of networks. They are not in sequential order as in Polanyi's model. See P Kjaer, 'The Structural Transformation of Embeddedness' in J Falke & C Joerges (eds), *Karl Polanyi, Globalisation and the Potential of Law in Transnational Markets* (Oxford: Hart, 2011), 85–104.

[45] D Chalmers, 'The Government and Citizenship of Self-Regulation' in F Cafaggi (ed), *Reframing Self-Regulation in European Private Law* (Alphen aan den Rijn: Wolter Kluwer, 2006), 161.

between systems, they contribute to asymmetries, 'crowding out' effects, network 'negative externalities', and may even become 'captured'.[46] In other words, there is a danger that the *eigenlogics* of certain sub-systems, most notably the economic system, capture the *eigenstructures* of network governance. In my view, if one conceives of a role for law in regulating governance networks, then one perforce regulates collisions between functional sub-systems. This is the case whether those networks consist of private or public actors, or are, as is almost invariably the case, hybrid networks. The fact that governance networks are actor-centred although they follow a network logic also means that liability law can have a role to play – albeit one that has different objectives than in the society of individuals or the society of organisations.

How, then, might law achieve inter-systemic compatibility? Self-constitutionalisation through 'proceduralisation' is the dominant theoretical strand. Global administrative law fits this pattern by proposing[47] *ex ante* inclusion mechanisms such as stakeholder, participatory approaches in terms of iterative standard-setting and implementation, and designing frameworks for ongoing and iterative observations between network actors through norms of transparency, stakeholder input, notice and comment, which are buttressed by benchmarking, auditing, and so on.[48] This is meant to constitutionalise networks following a logic of systems' *audi alteram partem* within networks.[49] But it is a much looser and more processual and cognitivised form of coordination than that which was achieved within the territorial state. Because this type of self-constitutionalisation is process-driven, rather than outcome-driven,

46 Arguably, the Basel process pre-2008, which transferred the definition of risk to banks. See Renner (n 5). *Compare* A Mascareño, 'The Ethics of the Financial Crisis' in Kjaer (n 5), 333–53, who states that the problem is the politicisation of finance.

47 Although Global Administrative Law is a distinct theoretical standpoint, it shares with some of the systems theory literature the idea of self-constitutionalisation of governance networks as a functional equivalent to democracy. However, G Teubner, *Constitutional Fragments: Societal Constitutionalism and Globalization* (Oxford: Oxford University Press, 2012), 51, 143, sees it as external to the 'regulated sphere', and providing 'impulses' only. But *compare* Ladeur (n 10), who proposes a closer and 'bottom-up' relationship between administrative law and regulated spheres.

48 The most advanced theorisation is found in the GAL scholarship, which theorises multi-level network standard-setting practices in terms of functional equivalents to executive law-making in the nation-state; a seminal study is B Kingsbury et al, 'The Emergence of Global Administrative Law' (2005) 68(3–4) *Law and Contemporary Problems* 15–61.

49 In regime collision terms, this means developing greater reflexivity within networks towards their environments by challenging dominant discourses. See G Teubner, 'The Anonymous Matrix: Human Rights Violations by "Private" Transnational Actors' (2006) 69(3) *Modern Law Review* 327–46.

while important, it can only achieve a weak form of inter-systemic compatibility.[50] It seems, therefore, that there is, a gap between *ex ante* (internal) inclusion mechanisms and *ex post* (external) liability mechanisms in the law of the society of networks. Tort liability's existing normative models of liability, however, fall short or are too encompassing. Individual responsibility completely misses the role given actors hold within encompassing risk communities; while organisational responsibility similarly searches in vain in an attempt to find a risk creator. For when risk management cuts across a network of actors, then this network logic makes it conceptually difficult and normatively unattractive to attribute responsibility to a single actor quasi-*respondeat superior*. The materialisation of systemic risks – the network externalities of network activity – cannot be tied to a single organisational actor or be classified as stemming from individual conduct. This misalignment between our existing models of liability and network failures means that inherited models of liability alone when treated as comprehensive schemes are a blunt and unsuitable instrument for getting networks to internalise their externalities. Liability law, then, largely retreats from the scene, or, perhaps worse, becomes a normatively unconvincing bludgeon.[51] What's missing is a concept of network liability in *tort* as a self-standing third model of normative ascription which, in contrast to the society of organisation's 'vertical vicarious liability', might be conceptualised as a form of 'horizontal vicarious liability'.[52]

The rest of this book will be devoted to imagining a regime of tort responsibility for network governance. The testing ground for this theory will be

[50] What Ladeur might term unblocking partial logics. Teubner might refer to this as self-constitutionalisation as the system internally and reflexively reorientates towards its boundaries. Kjaer thinks these notions – stakeholders, transparency, *etc*, are functional equivalents to democracy on the transnational level. However, E Christodoulidis, 'On the Politics of Societal Constitutionalism' (2013) 20(2) *Indiana Journal of Global Legal Studies* 629–63, makes, in my view, the valid point that in the end, given their functional orientation, *eg* World Trade Organization (WTO), their reconstructions will always be biased. Although Christodoulidis' language is moderate, his criticism appears to be that the self-constitutionalisation idea amounts to a form of apologetics.

[51] The former has been described catchily as 'reticular irresponsibility' by G Teubner, '"And if I by Beelzebub cast out Devils, . . .": An Essay on the Diabolics of Network Failure' (2009) 10(4) *German Law Journal* 395–416, 397. The unattractive bludgeon would consist of, *eg*, market share liability, *ie* adopting an organisational responsibility approach to an entire market, which is inconsistent with the interpersonal dimension to tort liability. This is not the only dimension to tort law, see Section 3.C. I agree with Smits that doctrine, or law's programmes, have a 'disciplining power', *ie* they are constraints on adaption, and simply filling them with any content whatsoever leads to a lack of normative coherence in law. See J Smits, 'Enforcing Corporate Social Responsibility Codes under Private Law, or: On the Disciplining Power of Legal Doctrine', Maastricht European Private Law Institute Working Paper No. 2015/09, 1–13.

[52] See Teubner (n 13).

situated in 'public' network governance. Once developed, it will be argued that in a reverse narrative to the society of organisations, it can be applied to 'private' network governance.[53] Liability law should not be abandoned in the face of complexity, but should, instead, be reimagined in terms of 'irritating' networks by confronting them with alternative systems communications through a regime of legal liability. This follows the logic of 'mutual increase' in complexity.[54] Increased cognitivisation calls for increased normativity in law; however, the form and focus of normative intervention should be reconceptualised in collision terms rather than in terms of individual or group-based justice. This creates new network-wide 'duties of care' provoking networks to better represent non-dominant communicative sub-systems and, by extension, normatively signalling systems' boundaries. *In concreto*, developing principles of network gatekeepers' liability is crucially important because it is normatively justifiable and it sends network-wide signals. While one might, conceptually, *attribute* network failures to networks, one should *impute* liability to specific actors which occupy nodal points within networks. Unlike in the society of organisations, gatekeepers are not understood as fulfilling a hierarchical role, but rather as occupying strategically important positions within more encompassing horizontal networks without a controlling mind. They are conceptualised, in other words, as (normatively) secondary actors within more encompassing horizontal governance networks.[55] Network (gatekeeper) liability represents a tertiary remodelling of legal liability, and just as organisational responsibility did not displace individual responsibility but supplemented it, so

[53] Scare quotes because the public/private distinction hardly makes sense where so-called public governance networks are hybrid, relying on enforced self-regulation, and 'private' governance networks have a strong public dimension. See LC Backer, 'Economic Globalization and the Rise of Efficient Systems of Global Private Lawmaking: Wal-Mart as Global Legislator' (2007) 39(4) *Connecticut Law Review* 1–46.

[54] P Kjaer, Transnational Normative Orders: The Constitutionalism of Intra- and Trans-Normative Law (2013) 20(2) *Indiana Journal of Global Legal Studies* 777–803: 'Existing perspectives tend to understand the relationship between the cognitive and normative dimensions of law on the basis of a zero-sum perspective … [t]he distinction between the cognitive and normative dimensions of law is, however, logically conditioned by the continued relevance of both dimensions' (778); Renner (n 5).

[55] That is to say, the claim is not that they are analytically secondary actors. Indeed, the sociological concept of network does not easily translate to law. Instead, law must internally reconstruct the network as a legal concept. Criticism of the porosity of networks, as an empirically grounded criticism of network thinking in law, miss the mark by assuming an input model of the relationship between law and its environment. The law constructs its environment. For an extensive treatment, see G Teubner, *Law as an Autopoietic System* (Oxford: Blackwell, 1993), esp chs 2 & 4.

should network liability exist alongside existing models of normative ascription in an overall concept of network responsibility.

Making this argument requires a shift of perspective from the national to the European Union level. The EU is considered an avant-garde institutional structure because it represents a highly developed network of networks – an intermediate structure between nation-state and world society – that acts as a public interface of public–private networks.[56] It has, therefore, both state-like or vertical and horizontal dimensions.[57] It has also established a (reflexive) transnational legal order, which integrates national and transnational spaces through a discourse of rights.[58] Its 'private law' (including torts) does not rest on interpersonal foundation whether in the strong or weak sense.[59] This is important because instead of viewing it as a technocratic weakness,[60] it facilitates new ways of thinking about legal problems uninhibited by classical legal foundationalism.[61] It can therefore act as a catalyst and accelerant of legal (internal) differentiation, and feed back into national law different

56 P Kjaer, 'The Societal Function of European Integration in the Context of World Society' (2007) 13(1–2) *Soziale Systeme* 369–80. A 'state', in the systems theory definition, which is located 'in-between' member states 'and an increasingly globalised world society' (370). But which also increasingly undermines segmentary (territorial) differentiation of all functional systems, and seeks to advance the 'convergence' of sub-systems beyond the state (375).

57 P Kjaer, 'Constitutionalizing Governing and Governance in Europe' (2010) 9 *Comparative Sociology* 86–119, distinguishing from the 'radical heterarchy' of other 'global legal structures', which Fisher-Lescano and Teubner detail. Kjaer denotes it in terms of governing (vertical) and governance (horizontal), and that this hybridity should not be discounted: it is part state and part regime of transnational governance. He also adds the inter-state dimension, but it is not relevant to my argument.

58 C Thornhill, 'The Formation of a European Constitution: an Approach from Historical-Political Sociology (2013) 8(3) *International Journal of Law in Context*, 354–93, explaining the constitutive role of rights in EU law.

59 See Chapter 1 (strong), and Chapter 2 (weak).

60 A so-called technolaw, H Collins, 'The Revolutionary Trajectory of EU Contract Law towards Post-National Law' in S Worthington et al (eds), *Revolution and Evolution in Private Law* (Oxford: Hart, 2017), 315–36, esp 317–23.

61 Micklitz has used the term 'experimentalism' and 'laboratory' in HW Micklitz, *The Politics of Justice in European Private Law: Social Justice, Access Justice, Societal Justice* (Cambridge: Cambridge University Press, 2018), esp 246–53. It is post-classical in the sense that it represents, in my view, in important ways, a radical break from Wieacker's (hallowed, if not holy) trinitarian characteristics of Western legal culture, *ie* legalism, personalism and intellectualism. see F Wieacker, 'Foundations of European Legal Culture' (1990) 38(1) *American Journal of Comparative Law* 1–29. Intellectualism denotes coherence and consistency in Wieacker's argument. On the latter point, see HW Micklitz, 'The (Un)-Systematics of (Private) Law as an Element of European Culture' in G Helleringer & K Purnhagen (eds), *Towards a European Legal Culture* (Baden-Baden: Nomos, 2014), 81–114.

concepts of liability.[62] As Micklitz argues, the legal person of EU law should be viewed as *mandataire*:[63] from his perspective this denotes the identity-based construction of rights;[64] from my perspective, the legal person in EU law is a multi-layered construct whose 'subjective rights'[65] can act as a channel through which systems collision within networks can be managed.[66] The dogmatic route to the re-normativisation of law in the transnational space is the constitutionalisation of private law. This constitutionalising process allows for a re-coupling of political and legal systems to, *inter alia*, the economic system, which leads to the opening of the black boxes of network governance by conferring rights on 'individuals'.[67] Advancing this argument is the task of this chapter. In this conception, tort rights-remedies are understood in terms of the law of a 'mixed society'.[68] In other words, their function is to intervene *ex post* to disrupt *ex ante* pathologies acting as normative (environmental or external) signals to networks provoking the reconsideration of the internal balances struck between different communicative discourses.[69] In the next chapter, a close reading of its case law in products safety law under the New Approach to Technical Standards – a paradigmatic illustration of network governance – demonstrates that this opening of black boxes has resulted in the CJEU developing an incipient concept of network *liability* by adapting its state liability law to the problem of private gatekeepers.[70] Developing the law

[62] But cautionary, see G Teubner, 'Legal Irritants: Good Faith in British Law or How Unifying Law Ends Up in New Divergences' (1998) 61(1) *Modern Law Review* 11–32.

[63] HW Micklitz, 'The Legal Subject, Social Class and Identity-Based Rights' in L Azoulai et al (eds), *Constructing the Person in EU Law: Rights, Roles, Identities* (Oxford: Hart, 2016), 285–310. Of course, foreshadowed by R Demogue, 'La Notion de Sujet De Droit: Caractère et Conséquences' (1909) 3 *Revue Trimestrielle de Droit Civil* 1–45.

[64] Micklitz (n 63), building on 'the social' to a form of radical individualism in which persons construct their identity through rights seemingly *ex nihilo*, and the formally equal individual vanishes. From my point of view, the individual in EU law remains, but the individual rights rhetoric takes place within polycontextural (boundary) disputes.

[65] But subjective rights, in this view, have a societal function. This is not new. See Chapter 1. But it gains a difference resonance in the society of networks.

[66] Fischer-Lescano & Teubner (n 33).

[67] See, Section B, in which I discuss the concept of 'individual' rights from a systemic point of view. Teubner's (n 49) multi-layered view of rights matches beautifully with EU law's legal person as *mandataire*.

[68] G Calabresi, 'Torts – The Law of the Mixed Society' (1977–78), 56 *Texas Law Review* 519.

[69] In this sense, one might consider tort standards as the opposite of a sort of 'business judgement rule' for networks.

[70] The New Approach to Technical Harmonisation is viewed as a classical illustration of network governance in which governance through networks aims to re-embed the economic semantics of market access into society. However, without a coherent liability regime, it is a partial success in this respect only.

on state liability can act as a template for solving the problems of network failure from a tort law perspective. Taken together – individual liability, organisational liability and network liability – one may speak intrepidly of an incipient concept of network *responsibility* in tort for a society of networks, which harnesses old and new models of liability to regulate networks. Network liability as a regime of gatekeepers' liability can be constructed out of state liability if state liability is understood as a regime of normative secondary liability or network liability, and it can be applied *mutatis mutandis* to 'private' gatekeepers, which, as will be shown, the CJEU is already doing. However, the main obstacle to revealing this immanent conception of network liability in EU law out of the refracted existing law is the over-cognitivisation of liability law at an EU level.[71] Therefore, to make this argument, it is necessary to first reorient our understanding of the role of individual rights in the network society. Remedies follow from rights, but if rights cannot be formulated in the first place, then no regime of remedies can be conceived: *ubi ius, ibi remedium.*

B COGNITIVISATION IN EU LAW: DE-DIFFERENTIATION IN LEGAL DISCOURSE

A central Luhmannian insight is that in world society normative expectations are being displaced by cognitive expectations.[72] This is both a general shift in terms of the centre of societal communications from politics, morality and law towards economy, technology and science, but also as the 'cognitivisation' of normative systems, which become more adaptive and geared towards 'learning'.[73] The latter denotes *in extremis* that in the context of the legal system, in place of producing normative expectations, the legal system 'operations come to be guided by heteronomous references'.[74] A central critique of EU 'private'

[71] Law is, in systems theory jargon, 'cognitively open'. However, it is normatively closed. If it loses its normative dimension, becoming 'structurally corrupt', then it becomes de-differentiated from society. See Renner (n 5), 109.

[72] See N Luhmann, 'Society and Its Law' in *Law as a Social System* (Oxford: Oxford University Press, 2006), 464–90, esp 468ff. He goes further to speculate as to whether the pre-eminence of the legal system is a 'European anomaly'.

[73] Some of course welcome the transformation of law towards a 'learning law'. See KH Ladeur, 'The Financial Market Crisis – A Case of Network Failure?' in Kjaer (n 5), 63–92, who favours a 'renvoi' of a cognitivised legal system to societal actors.

[74] M Amstutz, 'Eroding Boundaries: On Financial Crisis and an Evolutionary Concept of Regulatory Reform' in Kjaer (n 5), 223–68, at 228. There, referring to the financial system. See later at page 246, where Amstutz distinguishes structural coupling from operative coupling: 'a structural coupling – through which information or mutual "perturbations" are exchanged –

law is that it suffers from this tendency through which legal concepts lose their normative content.[75] Rights, duties and so on, become the servant of their environment and mutual irritation between the legal systems and other societal sub-systems is replaced by risk definitions from outside the legal system contorting 'legal' programmes. The legal manifestation of this over-cognitivisation,[76] or 'structural ... corrupt[ion]',[77] is that the legal system ceases to produce counterfactual normative expectations and, instead, becomes beholden to *external* policy reasoning.[78] Unlike in the society of organisations, these policies are not integrated into legal reasoning, but displace legal reasoning.[79] This, also, involves de-centring the individual from legal communication and replacing the individual as a structuring device for the allocation of rights and duties with economic or political objectives.[80] This is paradigmatically seen in EU 'private law' where the regime of rights and remedies is submitted to the 'meta-goal' of the completion of the internal market.[81] The critique from the left is that EU private law in the pursuit of this

has developed into an operative coupling – in which the operations of one system become dependent upon those of another'.

75 Collins (n 60). Writing on contract law, but of more general resonance: 'traditional systems of contract law combine a broad range of instrumental goals with a concern to ensure justice between the parties to a dispute ... [whereas] technolaw focuses on a relatively narrow set of policy objectives, and those objectives are emphasised almost to the exclusion of the traditional private law's concerns regarding corrective justice and doctrinal coherence' (318–19). See, also, G Davies, 'Democracy and Governance in the Shadow of Purposive Competence' (2015) 21(1) *European Law Journal* 2.

76 This is closely related to Teubner's concept of 'over-socialisation' in his classic rendition of the 'regulatory trilemma'. See G Teubner, 'After Legal Instrumentalism? Strategic Models of Post-Regulatory Law' in G Teubner (ed), *Dilemmas of Law in the Welfare State* (Berlin: De Gruyter, 1986), 299–325, at 311–13.

77 Renner (n 5), 109.

78 I'm not endorsing Beever's or Weinrib's claim that policy reasoning has *no* place in 'private' law, and that the only policies relevant to law are policies inherent to the law. See A Beever, *Rediscovering the Law of Negligence* (Oxford: Hart, 2007); EJ Weinrib, *The Idea of Private Law* (Oxford: Oxford University Press, 1995). Rather, I agree with *inter alia* Collins in his 'Utility and Rights in Common Law Reasoning: Rebalancing Private Law through Constitutionalization', LSE Law, Society and Economy Working Paper 6/2007, 1–21, and more generally Collins (n 16), ch 2.

79 *Compare* Collins (n 16), 47–55, in which Collins reconstructs the 'productive disintegration' of, in my terms, the society of organisations well. The law's environment is reconstructed internally in legal doctrine, its normative programmes, and the legal system 'retains sufficient normative complexity' (55). *Cf* also Chapter 2 for a detailed reconstruction.

80 The individual is not, of course, a pre-political 'thing', but a part of legal communication.

81 O Cherednychenko, 'Two Sides of the Same Coin: EU Financial Regulation and Private Law' (2021) 22 *European Business Organization Law Review* 147–72, at 154.

goal is not political enough, and is dominated by economic functionalism.[82] That critique, however, risks overwhelming legal communication by politicalising it, and is another form of cognitivisation.[83] They are, in truth, two sides of a coin. The deeper critique is that the law is not *legal* enough because its normative programmes become simulacra. The hollowing out of genuine legal normativity in the face of cognitivised economic communication is really what is at issue.[84] In legal dogmatics, this is reflected in policies (policy arguments) of self-restraint whereby the law excludes itself from legal disputes. But there is a wider point beyond simply the disintegration of the legal system's closure. Without mediating through stabilising legal normative expectations, learning law ironically reduces the learning capacity of other societal sub-systems because they lack internal normative constraints that enable them to observe their boundaries.[85]

[82] Illustrative is M Bartl, 'Internal Market Rationality: Private Law and the Direction of the Union: Resuscitating the Market as the Object of the Political' (2015) 21(5) *European Law Journal* 572–98. See also G Brüggemeier, 'Social Justice in European Contract Law: A Manifesto' (2004) 10(6) *European Law Journal* 653–74, where there is more than an undercurrent of the CLS manifesto that 'law *is* politics by other means', *eg* criticism of view that private law consists of merely technical rules.

[83] I Kampourakis, 'Bound by the Economic Constitution: Notes for "Law and Political Economy" in Europe' (2021) 1(2) *Journal of Law and Political Economy* 301–32, writing in reference to different approaches to law and political economy, but consistent with my point: 'Overall, an instrumentalist perspective implies an understanding of the law as non-autonomous, an empty vessel to be filled with substantive content that can either advance or hinder different normative agendas. To give shape and content to the law, which eventually shapes the economy and drives our normative universe, instrumentalism relies on democracy as a core principle' (313). See page 313ff for criticism. The seminal text on the dangers of democratic instrumentalism is the masterful G Ripert, *Le Régime Démocratique et le Droit Civil Moderne* 2nd ed (Paris: Pichon, 1948), esp ch 2, for the impact on legal coherence.

[84] Not only at an EU level, but particularly pronounced there because it is a functionalist legal order, See, for a broader perspective, R Michaels & N Jansen, 'Private Law beyond the State? Europeanization, Globalization, Privatization' (2006) 54 *American Journal of Comparative Law* 843; with particular regard to European law, see S Frerichs & T Juutilainen, 'Rome under Seven Hills? An Archaeology of European Private Law' 32 Legal Studies Research Paper Series (2014 ssrn) (accessed 10 June 2015). In a UK context, TT Arvind, 'Obligations, Governance and Society: Bringing the State Back In' in A Robertson and M Tilbury (eds), *Convergence and Divergence in Private Law* (Oxford: Hart, 2016), 9: 'the law of obligations is withdrawing from having any role in defining the bounds of acceptable conduct in an ever-growing set of areas'. In effect, this is correct. But at a deeper level, it is not withdrawing, but its programmes are being transformed in the light of public interest arguments. *Caparo v Dickman*, one of Arvind's illustrations, is a good example of economisation. See also DT Mitchell, 'From Tort to Finance: Delaware's Sedative Duty to Monitor' in M Hollow et al (eds), *Complexity and Crisis in the Financial System* (Cheltenham: Elgar, 2016), 121–48, for a fascinating account of the financialisation of corporate law and how it expelled substantive tort duties of care from company law.

[85] Renner (n 5). Which is also a reason to be doubtful regarding self-constitutionalisation.

State liability in the area of financial services is exemplary. The question in EU law as to whether an individual right is conferred by a directive is collapsed into economic semantics of financial risk management.[86] Legal rights, and remedies, then lose their anchorage in legal discourse over the appropriate regime of individual or organisational responsibility, or indeed any third conception, and becomes an instrument of *ex ante* policy restraints based on concerns of over-deterrence and precaution.[87] This is the basic point in the seminal *Paul* and *Three Rivers* judgments.[88] In *Three Rivers*, the plaintiffs argued that the Bank of England ('the bank') had failed to adequately supervise *Bank de Credit Commerciale International* (*BCCI*) resulting in losses to the plaintiff. In particular, it was alleged that the Bank ignored a number of warning signs meaning that it negligently failed to respond to clear indications that *BCCI* was in a precarious financial situation. It subsequently emerged that *BCCI* was involved in fraud and money laundering. The basis of the claim was, first, the tort of misfeasance in public office which requires bad faith; second, negligence; and thirdly a claim that the relevant directive, Directive 1977 (the First Banking Directive), implied a right to adequate supervision. In the end, the court held that no right had been conferred and that no remedy was available under national law outside misfeasance in public office.[89]

The *Paul* case was a claim brought by Paul and others against the *Bundesaufsichtsamt* because of the latter's failure to withdraw authorisation from *BVH* Bank. Paul and others held deposit accounts at the bank amounting to sums in excess of the amount covered by the deposit guarantee scheme in Directive 94/17/EC. These sums were deposited in the bank

86 Renner (n 5) goes further, specifying how Basel I with its rules on debt–equity ratios is a process of cognitivisation because 'the concept of liability is largely replaced with the concept of risk. The scope of normative expectations, in contrast, is confined to stabilising the debt/equity ratio itself' (102). The approach whereby banks were left to determine capital requirements on the basis of their own risk models whereby 'even the last residue of normative expectations structures on the financial markets was "cognitivised", and liability, for the most part, left to economic calculus in the end'. Of course, legal (normative) models of risk, exist. Renner's point is that they are being superseded by economic models.

87 This is not unique to EU law. See previous discussion of *Yuen Kun Yeu v Attorney General of Hong Kong* [1987] 2 All ER 705 in Chapter 2 on policy bars to negligence.

88 C-222/02, *Peter Paul and Others v Bundesrepublik Deutschland* [2004] ECR I-09425; *Three Rivers DC v Governor of the Bank of England* [2000] UKHL 16.

89 M Andenas and D Fairgrieve, 'Misfeasance in Public Office, Governmental Liability, and European Influences' in D Fairgrieve, M Andenas & J Bell (eds), *Tort Liability of Public Authorities in Comparative Perspective* (London: BIICL, 2002), 183–206.

between 1993 and 1995.[90] The *Bundesaufsichtsamt* failed to de-list the bank in time, resulting in losses to the claimants. The claimants in *Paul* attempted to rely directly on Directive 94/17/EC, and on a composite of directives enacted between the late 1970s and 1990s, to demonstrate that a right was conferred on them.

It seems that the basic claim underlying both cases was that the regulator was in the position of guarantor, having certain functions deriving from European law, and in this role failed to discharge its duties appropriately. In other words, the claims were an invitation to treat the financial supervisor quasi-*respondeat superior* in EU law. Both the House of Lords and the ECJ dismissed the respective claims, largely for the same reason, apparently bringing an end to the possibility of using a tort action against financial regulatory authorities based on European law.[91] From a narrow doctrinal perspective, both the House of Lords' and the ECJ's judgments have been criticised for restrictive interpretation of conferral of a right, which seems to depart from previous state liability jurisprudence.[92] From a broader perspective, the attempt to fit the state into the normative position of guarantor quasi-*respondeat* superior was rightly dismissed. Organisational responsibility is responsibility for risk creation, and the state supervisory does not occupy a position of hierarchical control and does not 'delegate' responsibility to banks in financial services regulation. Instead, it forms part of a decentralised network of risk regulation. However, rightly dismissing the analogy with organisational responsibility wrongly foreclosed the possibility of developing a new regime

90 See para 13 of the *Paul* judgment for the relevant sums and the dates on which they were deposited.

91 Although in truth, this is probably an overstatement given the contingent nature of the court's reasoning, which emphasised the current level of harmonisation, thereby leaving the possibility of liability in the future if further integration occurs, as indeed it has. However, on this points, see T Tridimas, 'Financial Regulation and Civil Liability in European Law' in O Cherednychenko & M Andenas (eds), *Financial Regulation and Civil Liability in European Law* (Cheltenham: Elgar, 2020), 47–72, 70–71.

92 As Tison states the *Paul* judgment: '[It] seems to depart from previous case law of the ECJ, which suggested that the first condition for *Francovich* liability should be read more flexibly: until now, the Court seemed to be satisfied with the demonstration that the EU rules are intended to protect the interests of private individuals, without it being required that the said rules confer by themselves enforceable rights.' M Tison, 'Do Not Attack the Watchdog! Banking Supervisor's Liability after Peter Paul', Financial Law Institute Working Paper Series 200502.26; N Reich, 'Rights without Duties? Reflections of the State Liability Law in the Multilevel Governance System of the Community: Is There a Need for a More Coherent Approach in European Private Law', EUI Working Paper Law 2009/10, 1, 13 refers to the test as an objective *schutznorm* theory.

of secondary liability.[93] In other words, by failing to deem a 'subjective right' as conferred, the court precluded itself from developing principles of normative imputation appropriate to state supervisors within the context of network governance.[94] *De facto*, in the absence of any regime of legal responsibility at an EU level, the courts left it to member states to develop principles of individual responsibility which, in this context, give rise to a rather chimeric possibility of legal liability.[95]

If one turns to the reason for precluding the conferral of a subjective right, the real obstacle is what Andenas and Fairgrieve refer to as the logic of prudential supervision.[96] Between the 1980s and 1990s, the philosophy of financial regulation changed from the aim of protecting depositors to the prevention of contagion and systemic risk: 'In this new perspective, individual bank insolvency could be acceptable.'[97] Therefore, legislation that was primarily designed to protect depositors was outpaced by changes in the function of banking supervision, which is described as a move towards 'modern methods of banking supervision',[98] effectively precluding recovery in *Three Rivers* outside bad faith. This argument applies, *a fortiori*, with respect to *Paul*, in which the court rejected the argument that the *effet utile* of the directives required the conferral of a right to the claimants.[99] In consequence, forbearance which may be viewed as negligent from the perspective of depositor protection could be viewed as prudent from the perspective of systemic contagion. This risk management logic persuaded the courts against using prudential rules to construct a pro-depositor *prima facie* duty of care based on the requirements of EU law. In both cases, in other words, the Basel network

93 In the United Kingdom, this line of thinking goes back farther in negligence to *Yuen Kun*, where the court found a lack of 'proximity' between supervisor and victim.

94 Like the United Kingdom, the policy question is front-loaded in the test of duty, and the standard of care inquiry is avoided. In *Francovich*, state liability, the equivalent of the standard of care inquiry, is the notion of 'sufficiently serious breach'. See Chapter 4.

95 For an overview of the different member state liability regimes, see D Nolan, 'The Liability of Financial Supervisory Authorities' (2013) 4(2) *Journal of European Tort Law* 190–222.

96 Andenas & Fairgrieve (n 89), 193.

97 *Ibid*, 186.

98 *Ibid*. Heavily influenced by the Basil Committee, creating an 'internally defined normative vision' of how priorities in banking should be ranked. See P Kjaer, 'Between Integration and Compatibility: The Reconfiguration of Cognitive and Normative Structures in Transnational Hybrid Law' in P Kjaer et al (eds), *Regulatory Hybridization in the Transnational Sphere* (Leiden: Martinus Nijhoff, 2013), 283, for this phrase.

99 These changes in the role of the supervision were not exclusive to the approach of the UK regulator, and as Andenas & Fairgrieve (n 89) elaborate: 'The Bank of England developed this [approach] over the years, partly in response to criticism over its handling of the different banking crises, and partly in interaction with international standard setting' (186).

governance orthodoxy as assiduously implemented by national regulatory agencies prevailed.[100] This policy bar to recovery effectively short-circuited the development of state liability law as a regime of secondary liability, and instead of a gain of mutual complexity between cognitive and normative expectations, the law's internal mechanisms broke down.

That this approach is not isolated to financial regulation is evident if one considers *AGMCOS.MET* (*Cosmet*). In *Cosmet*, the claimant, an Italian vehicle lift manufacturer, sued the Finnish state quasi-*respondeat superior* based on the public statements of an errant official. The judgment went deep into the New Approach to Technical Standards and its relevance for state liability law. While the case turned on Directive 98/37/EC, which sets out health and safety requirements regarding, *inter alia*, machinery and safety components within the European Union,[101] the broader regulatory framework in which the directive is situated is the New Approach to Harmonisation. In essence, the European Committee for Standardisation (CEN), a 'private' body, defines minimum standards of product safety that apply across the European Union.[102] Standardisation is supported by a strong market access case law.[103] CEN is entrusted these tasks under the New Approach to Technical Standards which can be described as a delegation of authority in rule-making from member states to the European level.[104] These standards enjoy a presumption of conformity with national health and safety requirements. Once a producer certifies that they have complied with the relevant standard, according to national procedures, this is sufficient to satisfy the presumption of conformity. Presumptions of conformity, of course, do not

[100] In this vein, AG Stix-Hackl's implication in *Paul* that a deposit guarantee scheme is an alternative to liability tends to emphasise how rights are sacrificed to expediency without proceeding to a balancing of interests as a traditional legal test requires. That the claimants have means of recovering some of their losses up to a certain threshold traditionally goes to the quantification of the loss rather than the question of whether a duty of care exists. See AG Stix-Hackl in *Paul* (2003) ECLI:EU:C:2003:637.

[101] C-470/03, *AGM-COS.MET Srl v Finland* [2007] ECR I-2749.

[102] These are voluntary standards, and viewed as minimum specifications with which products must comply. C Joerges, H Schepel and E Vos, 'The Law's Problems with the Involvement of Non-Governmental Actors in Europe's Legislative Processes: The Case of Standardisation under the "New Approach"', EUI Working Paper LAW No 99/9, defines the 'New Approach' as covering 'entire sectors rather than single products, and limits themselves to laying down rather general "essential requirements" of health and safety. The task of harmonising technical specifications is now left to private European standards associations. Products manufactured according to these harmonised standards enjoy a 'presumption of conformity' with the essential requirements' (8).

[103] *Procureur du Roi v Dassonville* Case 8/74 [1974] ECR 837.

[104] Joerges, Schepel & Vos (n 102). Although the author takes issue with the 'delegation' categorisation as potentially misleading.

discharge the state's post-market regulatory function, but they heavily circumscribe it.[105]

Directives such as Directive 98/37/EC establish the relevant standards as minima, and *Francovich* state liability to the extent that it is applicable is the private enforcement side of ensuring member states adhere to these standards. Member state authorities may withdraw machinery from the market pursuant to Article 7(1) of the directive in limited circumstances where the relevant authority determines that the machinery when used 'in accordance with their intended purpose are liable to endanger the safety of persons, and, where appropriate, domestic animals or property'.[106] In the instant case, the Finnish Ministry of Social Affairs did not invoke the market surveillance provision. Instead, a state official, a Mr Lehtinen, went on a 'frolic of his own', making several public statements that a vehicle lift was dangerous, first, when he was acting as in an official capacity, albeit without authorisation, and later after being removed from the case and suspended pending investigation. In any event, the consequence of his statements was that AGM-COS.MET suffered financial losses within Finland and throughout Europe. The company sued the Finnish state, arguing that Mr Lehtinen's statements could be attributed to the state.

Sieburgh argues that the framing of the question as one of attribution and not imputation led the court to ignore the necessity of constructing a normative justification for making the state pay given that it had not, officially, acted outside the Article 7 procedure.[107] Additionally, the framing of liability as primary state liability meant that the question of freedom of expression, a defence made by the state, was not relevant for the court's analysis.[108] The court developed, at paragraph 56, a test of objective attribution, which depends 'on how those statements may have been perceived by the persons to whom they were addressed'.[109] The question then becomes one of whether 'the persons to whom the statements are addressed can reasonably suppose, in

[105] Taken quite far in *Fra.bo*. Case C-171/11 *Fra.bo Spa v Deutsche Vereinigung des Gas- und Wasserfaches*, judgment of 31 December 2012.

[106] Directive 38/97/EC. Cited at para. 8 *COS.MET* (n 101).

[107] This is, of course, explainable by the no horizontal direct effect principle. See C Sieburgh, 'The Attribution of Acts: Towards a Principled Assessment under EU and National Private Law' (2016) 3 *European Review of Private Law* 645.

[108] See N Reich, 'AGM-COSMET or: Who Is Protected by Safety Regulation?' (2008) 33(1) *European Law Review* 85. As Reich remarks, '[t]his is a somewhat reduced approach to fundamental rights in a conflict between free movement on the one hand and safety requirements on the other which should be decided on the merits, and not on matters of formal competence' (94).

[109] *COS.MET* (n 101), para 56.

the given context, that they are positions taken by the official with the authority of his office'.[110] At paragraph 58, the court listed a number of factors that the national court should take into account when making this assessment. If they hold, then there is an infringement of the directive amounting to restriction on trade. Hence, the case is really one of liability for omissions. The state failed in its duty to ensure that there was no obstacle to trade. It is organisational liability coming close to a non-delegable duty.

The imperative behind the judgment was ensuring market access and, to wit, embraced a form of organisational responsibility. But it is an unprincipled and instrumental deployment of organisational responsibility not woven into the fabric of legal discourse. As distinct from the doctrinal niceties of the judgment, its narrow interpretation of Article 7(1) as the only path of review, an important policy preference was articulated. Reich argues that at its core, the judgment concerned the collision of market access and consumer protection.[111] The unrelenting preference for the former, which relies largely on self-regulation, indicates that market functioning takes precedence, and arguments based on consumer protection and freedom of expression are dismissed somewhat summarily. Thus, *Cosmet*, like *Paul* and *Three Rivers*, avoids balancing interests.[112] The acts of the errant employee are attributed as distinct from being imputed[113] to the state in the pursuit of a single policy objective. Legal rights and duties are defined according to the economic semantics of reducing transaction costs.[114]

Contrasting *Three Rivers*, *Paul* and *Cosmet*, it appears that principled legal reasoning is eschewed in favour of a policy of market integration, which sit atop deeper structures of transnational economic network governance. Whether models of quasi-individual responsibility or quasi-organisational responsibility are preferred depends, in the final analysis, on determinations

[110] *Ibid*, para 57.

[111] Reich (n 108). Note Reich's criticism of the decision, and how it perpetuates the weak consumer protection available under the New Approach.

[112] AG Kokott, in COS.*MET* (n 101), is less radical than the court acknowledging a balance is to be struck. The court, on the other hand, does not touch on the question of balancing interests, preferring instead the formulation of a rigid test. See, AG Kokott in COS.*MET* (2007) ECLI: EU:C:2005:693.

[113] The point here is that the test avoids the question of justifying a normative link between employee and employer. This requirement of 'control' (Salmond test) or scope of authority (company law) or 'close connection' (newer test of vicarious liability, is, as Sieburgh (n 107) rightly notes, one of balancing rights.) Whereas, the court in COS.*MET* (n 101) ignored this normative step favouring instead a wide objective test of 'perception', even going beyond a concept of ostensible authority which can be avoided by public notice.

[114] C Hodges, *European Regulation of Consumer Product Safety* (Oxford: Oxford University Press, 2005), has pointed this out at length the pro-market access bias of the new approach.

from outside legal discourse. This is important because it stifles courts from developing more sophisticated principles of secondary liability that take account of the state's role in a more encompassing network governance regime. It defers the authority as to the content of legal rules to the economic system as distinct from incorporating and reconstructing economic semantics in law on an equal footing to other discourses such as consumer citizens' rights. In other words, by bending legal rights and remedies to the singular nomos of the economic system, deeper conflicts at issue in network governance between different normative orders are overlooked. From this analysis of state liability law in network governance, two conclusions are apparent. The first is that a more sophisticated form of legal reasoning is required, which can act as 'shock-absorbers', and re-establish a 'complexity gap' between the legal system and its environment.[115] Secondly, a new normative concept of 'secondary' liability is required within the context of network governance, which takes account of the (normatively) secondary role of gakekeepers that rests on a model of neither individualised responsibility nor organisational responsibility.[116] In both cases, the basic building blocks of each is already present in EU law, but requires amplification. Before turning to the second question in Chapter 4, however, it is worth stressing how the former question might be addressed.

C CONSTITUTIONS AND COLLISIONS: AGAINST 'HEGEMONIC PROGRAMMES' OR A COMMON LAW FOR EUROPE

> [D]ifferent social systems represent the world in different and to some extent conflictual and irreconcilable ways', the question becomes . . . how to deal with the different and colliding representations of reality within the framework of law.[117]

Rights-based reasoning in tort holds the promise for the 're-entry' of different normative orders into legal reasoning by a reflexive re-normativisation of legal discourse. In this way, the complex trade-off between different policy

[115] See M Amstutz, 'Eroding Boundaries: On Financial Crisis and an Evolutionary Concept of Regulatory Reform' in Kjaer (n 5), 223–68, at 228, who compares this to the crises that arise from the alternative, namely 'boundary dissolution'. On the 'complexity gap', see Renner (n 5), 109.

[116] Normatively secondary, it puts the cart before the horse. The assumption here is that to be consistent with law's programmes of imputation, the position of the state or other gatekeepers must be normatively distinguished from so-called primary tortfeasors, see Chapter 4.

[117] Kjaer (n 98): compatibility is required. IJ Sand, 'Changing Forms of Governance and the Role of Law – Society and Its Laws', Arena Working Paper 00/14: www.sv.uio.no/arena/english/research/publications/arena-working-papers/1994-2000/2000/wp00_14.htm (accessed 4 July 2021) (unpaginated).

objectives which has unfolded until now in terms of a zero-sum game is reconstructed in a non-scalar collision of norms. There is no *ex ante* priority of 'policies' in this view, but, instead, situative, case-by-case development of legal norms. The aim is to normatively model a functionally differentiated society *within* legal programmes, which is a gain in normative complexity of the legal system, and also re-establishes the 'complexity gap' between the legal system and the various sub-systems of society.[118] The argument until now has been that there is a real risk that the *eigenlogics* of differentiated systems, most notably the economic system, may 'capture' the *eigenstructures* of the post-nation-state era, namely governance networks. When this is uncritically translated into legal norms, the partial risk definitions of societal sub-systems are, effectively, endorsed by the legal system, which represents a post-modern version of accepting custom as law.[119] This undermines the complex relationship between cognitive and normative expectations in legal programmes on which the legal system relies to perform its function. The productive relationship between normality and norm, which was documented in the context of the society of individuals and the society of organisations, collapses, and the legal system loses its autonomy and relevance in the society of networks. In contrast to Teubner's proposal of internal constitutionalisation within other sub-systems, the idea here is one of 'trans-constitutionalisation' through the legal system of a transnational legal order,[120] namely the EU as a 'network of networks'. That is to say, the EU is conceptualised as an advanced political and heterarchical network that integrates both territorial states and horizontal, functional networks, and links and stabilises (that is, re-embeds)[121] the

[118] Renner (n 5), 109: 'Within legal discourse, cognitive responsiveness must be complemented by a higher-level structure of normative expectations, which fulfils a stabilising role in upholding an adequate complexity of the legal system towards its environment.'

[119] Thornhill notes perceptively how 'external' irritation of the healthcare system through civil and criminal law led the medical profession to develop its own culture of informed consent, which is now an internal rights-based constitution of healthcare. See C Thornhill, 'A Sociology of Constituent Power: The Political Code of A *Sociology of Constituent Power: The Political Code of Transnational Societal Constitutions*' (2013) 20(2) *Indiana Journal of Global Legal Studies* 551–603, at 583, fn 104, citing A Krajewska, 'Global Health on Its Way to Self-Constitutionalisation: Towards a Comprehensive Theory of Global Health Law' (unpublished MS, on file with author), preliminary version presented at University of Cardiff (December 2012).

[120] Recently problematised by L Viellechner, 'The Transnational Dimension of Constitutional Rights: Framing and Taming "Private" Governance beyond the State' (2019) 8(3) *Global Constitutionalism* 1–23. In his article, he refers to internet governance, and the need for 'external constitutionalization' at the level of national courts. In my view, the CJEU bridges the chasm between national law and the transnational regulatory space, and its concepts can reduce the need for a 'transnational legal education' (22) for national judges.

[121] Kjaer (n 57), 111.

interrelation between them through law.[122] In this image, the CJEU has a particularly important role because its judgments straddle these different contexts, and ultimately must decide on the interpretation of EU law. Conceived in these terms, the court has a unique context-spanning position in unfolding the hybrid law of networks. Through a sufficiently developed rights-based approach to legal conflicts it may simultaneously develop normative counter-expectations to perturb and irritate public–private transnational networks such as the New Approach to Technical Standards or the Basel network governance, which 'render[s] transnational governance arrangements "responsive" towards their societal environment',[123] and also irritate member states' legal systems by redefining the boundaries of legal protection in terms of both rights and remedies.[124]

The relationship between 'private' law and constitution is not new. It has been argued in Chapters 1 and 2 that modern society is fundamentally an acentric society in which private law has always been understood as Janus-faced. From a certain perspective, private law *is* constitutional law defining 'territories of the self' by demarcating spheres of freedom between individuals as well as between the individual and the state.[125] While this role is understood in a grammar of individual right or utility, often overlooked is its 'architectural' or 'institutional' role whereby the 'relational rationality' of classical private law models the experimental 'order' of modernity. In the society of organisations, while the basic model remained intact, it was adjusted mainly through legal casuistry to take account of the corporative structuring of society.[126] The normative model of individual responsibility was thereby overlain with a model of organisational responsibility in tort. But as the twentieth century progressed, private law was more overtly 'constitutionalised' by reference to basic, public constitutional values which intervened indirectly or directly in

[122] KH Ladeur, '"We, the European People . . ." – Relâche?' (2008) 14(2) *European Law Journal* 147–67.

[123] Viellechner (n 120), 13.

[124] But, this does not necessarily mean harmonisation at a national level. See Teubner (n 62).

[125] Whether according to a Diceyan equality principle, or with qualifications. On territories of the self, see E Goffmann, 'The Territories of the Self', in *Relations in Public* (New York: Basic Books, 1971), 28–61.

[126] See Chapter 1. Apart from Ladeur, this view is most clearly articulated in the ordoliberal tradition. See F Böhm, 'Rule of Law in a Market Economy' in A Peacock & H Willgerodt (eds), *Germany's Social Market Economy: Origin and Evolution* (London: Palgrave McMillan, 1989), 46; FA Hayek, *Law, Legislation and Liberty: A New Statement of the Liberal Principles of Justice and Political Economy* (London: Routledge, 1982; 1998 reprint), esp chs 8 & 10.

the scheme of tort rights and remedies.[127] This process of re-constitutionalisation,[128] so to speak, aimed to enhance the autonomy of individuals within private law discourse, but did not significantly alter the basic framework or function of tort law.[129] Whether indirectly through developing 'private' legal doctrine or overtly through 'constitutionalisation' of tort law, the two dimensions of tort law – autonomy-enhancing[130] and as part of an institutional modelling of an acentric society – remained. These dimensions cannot be sensibly analytically divorced. Tort law by its normative rules of conduct, whether individualistic or organisational, is both a law of persons, defining the boundaries of subjective rights, and an architecture for societal communications by policing the boundaries of different sub-systems. Brüggemeier elegantly underscores this constitutional dimension, and the fact that it unfolded via the judicial branch:

> Tort Law judges adjudicate the scope of the individual and business freedoms within society. They determine the private consequences of conflicting constitutional positions, such as the priority of freedom of expression and of the media over the freedom of economic activity. They also include the protection of privacy against certain forms of public presentation and journalistic investigation, as well as protection against various types of discrimination. These judicial policies imply a reassessment of the scope of protection of traditional legal rights.[131]

[127] The obvious example is Germany. But this constitutionalisation occurred in most European jurisdictions whether overtly, as in Ireland, or more subtly elsewhere. For Ireland see, recently, G Hogan, 'The Farthest – December 1972' (2019) 62(2) *The Irish Jurist* 1–20.

[128] Or perhaps better put in systems theory terms as reflection on the basic scheme of rights in torts. Nowhere did constitutionalisation result, however, in the rewriting of the basic rules of tort law. Therefore, Kumm's 'total constitutionalization' thesis, where all private law becomes 'applied constitutional law', is misleading. The process of interaction is more subtle and variegated. See M Kumm, 'Who Is Afraid of the Total Constitution? Constitutional Rights as Principles and the Constitutionalization of Private Law' (2006) 7 *German Law Journal* 341, who refers to private law in terms of 'applied constitutional law'.

[129] Although some have misgivings about the process of constitutionalisation from a social justice perspective, because it can cut both ways, and does not inexorably lead to greater protection for the 'weaker' party. While some view constitutionalisation as enhancing the democratic legitimacy of private law, *eg* F Rodl, 'Fundamental Rights, Private Law, and Societal Constitution: On the Logic of the So-Called Horizontal Effect' (2013) 20(2) *Indiana Journal of Global Legal Studies* 1015–34, it must be remembered that in private law, constitutionalisation does not always advance democracy, *eg Lochner*. In the EU law context, D Caruso, 'Lochner in Europe: A Comment on Keith Whittington's "Congress before the Lochner Court"' (2005) 85 *Boston University Law Review* 867.

[130] Or autonomy mediating or coordinating, perhaps.

[131] G Brüggemeier, *Common Principles of Tort Law: A Prestatement of Law* (London: BIICL, 2004), 11, points to the post-war German experience regarding the indirect horizontal effect of private law, the ECHR and the CJEU.

Subjective rights and remedies, and the normative models of ascription in which they are unfolded, then, have both a 'personalist' and societal dimension in modernity.[132] In other words, the fact that tort law adjudicates multidimensional problems is not new. However, as has been argued, in the transition from the stable political–legal complex of the territorial state to the context of transnational network governance, tort law has undergone a cognitivising process which has largely undercut both its personalist and societal role in providing normative counter-expectations that police the boundaries of functional sub-systems. Instead, the complex balancing of policies and rights has receded as the functional logic of the economic system, in particular, and has tended to redefine tort law in its light. This was exemplified in Section B, whereby the models of liability – individualistic or organisational – lost normative coherence and consistency, and were applied arbitrarily in the light of policy reasoning.[133] From a societal perspective, these policies, in turn, largely followed one-sided economic semantics and its framing of acceptable risk.[134] Re-norming tort law through a rights-based reflection mechanism, then, gives tort a renewed role and impetus beyond the state and restarts the dialectical relationship between cognitive and normative expectations. This re-programming of tort law through constitutionalisation confers rights on individuals; these should not be understood primarily or exclusively in terms of *le droit subjective*, however, but rather in terms of tort law's long-standing societal dimension. Against this constitutional and institutional background, Teubner's apparent equation of tort law's subjective right with the grammar of Kantian right seems inapt.[135] It overlooks the broader constitutional and institutional dimension to tort law, and seems to equate tort law with a narrow, and non-institutional, understanding of its

[132] And, as Teubner (n 55), has underlined the legal person is in any event a 'semantic artefact' of the law. There can be no direct communication between the legal system, as a communicative system, and psychic systems.

[133] As Teubner (n 55), 105, puts it: 'Legal conflicts are decided in a fashion arbitrary from the law's viewpoint, according to criteria drawn from outside the legal system.'

[134] In Teubner's (n 55) terms, this leads to a kind of 'Khadi justice', see 105. Economic semantics then enter the 'self-description' of the law in terms of policy programmes, and determine the application of the law's code.

[135] Teubner (n 55), 340: 'Legally, this idea has been most clearly developed in classical law of tort, in which not merely indemnifications, but violations of subjective rights are central. Now, "fundamental rights" in their institutional, personal and human dimensions, as here proposed, differ from "subjective rights" in private law. They are not about mutual endangerment of private individuals, *ie* intersubjective relations, but rather about the dangers to the integrity of institutions, persons and individuals that are created by anonymous communicative matrices (institutions, discourses, systems).'

nineteenth-century programming.[136] Tort law has long ago internally differentiated – it has to a large extent de-individuated,[137] and is no longer simply a body of law of persons, but a law of organisations, and in both cases, in any event, cannot simply be understood in terms of 'intersubjective relations', but needs to be seen in its broader societal role of demarcating and mediating conflicting rationalities.[138] Rather, the main problem in the transnational era of network governance for tort law is not one of 'justiciability',[139] but of fragmentation of meaning outside the positive integration of the state. Managing difference in the absence of a 'supreme court for meaning',[140] as Teubner correctly identifies, and in the absence of an imagined lifeworld of the nation-state,[141] is very difficult.[142] However, turning to the partial rationalities of society – its sub-systems – and expecting them to self-constitutionalise and, in a manner, internalise their externalities, represents wishful thinking. This is not to deny the 'inner normativity of the given sub-system itself'[143] or the capacity of sub-systems to develop collision rules, but in the absence of external 'irritation' that cuts transverse sub-systems, it is an unlikely route to regime compatibility alone.[144] Legal regulation, then, must proceed at the

136 Which, in any event, should be understood 'institutionally' as part of a 'second-order observation' of the acentric, functionally differentiated society.

137 Beck (n 23), 29–30, also seems to view tort law in individualistic terms referring to an uncited German case from the Upper Palatinate region in which claimants were defeated based on classical 'but-for' causal principles in circumstances in which there were multiple tortfeasors. But see *Fairchild v Glenhaven* [2003] 1 AC 32, *etc*. His criticism of the iron cage of law, then, in the light of legal adaptation to 'multicausality', falls somewhat flat.

138 G Teubner, 'Transnational Fundamental Rights: Horizontal Effects' in Teubner (n 47), 124, 143.

139 *Ibid*, 146. On pages 146–49, Teubner lists the difficulty with turning human rights into a law of collisions. However, I would argue, this is not primarily a problem of 'justiciability' – fundamental rights *through* tort law subjective rights have mediated societal sub-systems throughout modernity – but of meaning outside the political–legal complex of the nation-state. Therefore, I distinguish the problem of 'supreme court of meaning' from 'justiciability' *contra* Teubner.

140 *Ibid*, 146.

141 As Kjaer has pointed out perceptively on several occasions, the state itself is a disembedded institution. See Kjaer (n 44).

142 T Vesting, 'Modern Law and the Crisis of Common Knowledge' (2017) 54(217) *Revista de Informação Legislativa* 11–29, makes this point clearly and well when discussing the radical fragmentation of meaning into epistemic communities 'after the nation state'.

143 A Golia & G Teubner, 'Societal Constitutionalism (Theory of)' (14 March 2021), Max Planck Institute for Comparative Public Law & International Law (MPIL) Research Paper No. 2021-08, 1–42, at 12.

144 In the society of organisations, formal organisations did not quasi-spontaneously self-constitutionalise. It required legal-political intervention through rights, whether in terms of judicial review or through liability rules. On the public side, see Selznick (n 42), 243ff. On the

level of governance frameworks, which 'rely on networks as their central organizational form',[145] and which are sites of meaning transfer between the different sub-systems of society.[146] The EU as a network of networks is then in a pole position to achieve this task by developing its own law of collisions. It must do so via the grammar of legal rights that compensate for communicative domination without a 'blueprint'[147] for maintaining 'fragile symmetry' of 'chances of translation' between the sub-systems of society.[148] This is not only concerned with the economic system – although, as the case law illustrated, it is the dominant discourse in EU law – but about rendering EU law sensible to other sub-system communication beyond economic or political communication. Legal disputes, and legal rights, should be considered in a polycontextural way, with rights viewed as points of 're-entry' for excluded discourses.

The role and function of constitutional rights and remedies in European regulatory private law should not, in other words, be considered in hierarchical terms.[149] Kumm's image of the total constitution is misplaced in an EU context.[150] Total constitutionalisation is problematic because its emphasis on unity through the medium of constitutional rights is not apt in a legal order such as the EU in which there is no single state where positive integration can unfold. The EU legal order should, instead, be conceptualised in

liability side, see Chapter 2. Why would one expect, then, anything different in the society of networks? The contemporary problem is rather, as Kjaer has pointed out: '[At] times of structural transition, due to changes in the level of social complexity, the speed of social development and the spatial reach of social processes, tends to lead either to an outright suspension of, or at least to increased pressure on, the legal frameworks which are aimed at stabilising societal exchanges … substantial divergence between societal structures and the internally developed legal stabilisation mechanisms, which is aimed at stabilising these structures, can also create preconditions for unsustainable development, and they highlight the need for a move towards a re-stabilisation of society within a new legal and organisational framework which corresponds to the contemporary structural setting.' See P Kjaer, 'Towards a Sociology of Intermediate Institutions: The Role of Law in Corporatism, Neo-Corporatism and Governance' in MR Madsen & C Thornhill (eds), *Law and the Formation of Modern Europe: Perspectives from the Historical Sociology of Law* (Cambridge: Cambridge University Press, 2014), 117–41, at 136–37.

145 *Ibid*, 132.

146 *Ibid*.

147 O Gerstenberg, 'Justification (and Justifiability) of Private Law in a Polycontextural World' (2000) 9(3) *Social & Legal Studies* 419, 424.

148 Teubner (n 36), 14.

149 Or, in Gerstenberg's rendition, as normativistic reconstructions of practice. This excludes the collisions dimension, as I understand it.

150 See Kumm (n 128). And not just for institutional reasons, *ie* the CJEU is not a supreme court either of meaning or in the orthodox sense.

heterarchical terms.[151] The aim should be discourse compatibility not unity.[152] Second, such a unity–hierarchy approach tends to narrow the function of private law and depreciate its role in forming the architecture for other discourses beyond linking the political and economic systems.[153] It is reductive to convert all disputes into a contest between political and economic systems and, at worst, obfuscates the other discourses at issue in legal disputes.[154] While it is true that 'the political' and 'the economic' are important discourses that require reconciliation, it is equally pertinent to note that they are non-exhaustive of the conflicts that underlie legal disputes. As a theoretical conceptualisation, it is reductive in focus, absorbing private law into constitutional law, leaving little room for its promotion of systemic 'private autonomies'.[155]

Gerstenberg favours a *via media* approach between what he perceives to be the *ad hoc* 'trade-offs' involved in maintaining heterarchical symmetries, and Kumm's hierarchical conception. Accepting the lack of a supreme court of meaning, he views the role and function of constitutionalisation of private law in terms of 'deontological side-constraint' plotting the boundaries of instrumental argumentation against 'individual' rights. He advocates reintroducing the 'public point of view' by iteratively constructing a concept of justice out of diverse private law regimes. In his view, this requires 'developing constitutional norms within private law … the role of courts can be seen as one of providing … "deontological side-constraints" for the autonomous self-regulation of comprehensive social spheres that carry their own internal logic and integrity'.[156] This involves recourse to the open norms of private law, such

[151] The segmentary, territorial state is not an appropriate frame of reference, see KH Ladeur, 'The State in International Law' in Falke & Joerges (n 44), 397.

[152] Kjaer (n 98).

[153] That which developed in the classical period, perhaps idealized in FA Hayek, *The Confusion of Language in Political Thought* (London: Institute of Economic Affairs, 1968), especially contrasting *nomos* and *thesis*.

[154] The 'top-down' focus also tends to underestimate private law's role in creating the *iuris vinculum* of civil society, see G Teubner, 'After Privatization? The Many Autonomies of Private Law' (1998) 51(1) *Current Legal Practice* 393, who argues that this is a mistaken approach for this very reason. Per Teubner: 'Private law's respect of the autonomy of the market sector needs to be expanded to other autonomous spaces' (401). On other discourses, see *eg* G Teubner, 'Art and Money: Constitutional Rights in the Private Sphere? (1998) 18 *Oxford Journal of Legal Studies* 61.

[155] Complete or total constitutionalisation tends to politicise and crowd out different discourses. It also inverts the relationship between the constitution of private law and the public constitution. See Rodl (n 129), although I do not follow his view of legitimating private law through constitutional law. This vision remains anchored in the nation-state, and does not contemplate legal orders such as the EU.

[156] O Gerstenberg, 'Private Law and the New European Constitutional Settlement' (2004) 10(6) *European Law Journal* 766–86, at 767.

as good faith and reasonableness, but ultimately 'a justificatory ascent' is 'always on the cards'.[157] It is difficult to see how this approach, in this way, does not in the end descend, or ascend, into a super-discourse of constitutional rights that prioritises the political, and substantive societal unity, beyond the state.[158] This seems to avoid the dangers of economic domination by counterpoising an image of *buon gouverno* despite Gerstenberg's insistence that his approach constructs justice 'bottom-up' out of practice.[159] However, in contrast to Gerstenberg's Dworkinian turning, I suggest that a closer look at the role of fundamental rights as they impinge on 'private' law in EU law might in fact be more promising. In this view, there is no justificatory ascent, but rights can act as a 'common currency' for mediating and coordinating different partial rationalities. To be sure, they intersect the political and economic,[160] but they are also interfaces for other sub-systems of society.[161]

By contrast, Ladeur's conception of constitutionalisation is a means to allow 're-entry' into a heterarchical law of collisions.[162] Applying Ladeur, the law would build on conceptions of 'public interest' or 'risk' developed in networks beyond the state (*eigenstructures*) in a process-oriented case law, which incrementally builds legal standards that are then reflected in 'a second order reflexive concept based upon the observation and justification of a pattern'.[163] The key distinction from Gerstenberg's perspective, as I see it, is that this process is open-ended, iterative and never at rest. In this way, there can be no justificatory ascent towards a right ordering of spheres, but instead, an open-ended search process, which should confront different rationalities with their antinomies – the excluded other discourses – through a highly situative case

[157] Gerstenberg (n 147), 427.

[158] For Gerstenberg, the political and democracy are very closely tied, and must be articulated beyond the Westphalian state. His approach comes close to Thornhill's (n 119) conception of the EU in this respect, which views rights as constitutive in the European context. *Compare* Teubner (n 138), for whom the political is a much more diffuse concept that runs through different sub-systems of society in his vision of societal constitutionalism.

[159] Resembling a sort of Deweyian experimentalism, but then given a Dworkinian twist! See C Sabel's Dewey, Democracy, and Democratic Experimentalism (2012) 9(2) *Contemporary Pragmatism* 35–55; M Dorf & C Sabel, 'A Constitution of Democratic Experimentalism' (1998) 98(2) *Columbia Law Review* 267, who view rights as experimentalist as 'presumptive rules to be applied until experience provides a better alternative' (457).

[160] On this point, more generally, Thornhill (n 119). However, he focuses too narrowly on the issue of constituent power.

[161] *Eg* constitutionalising health communication, bridging science and politics, *ie* rights and risks, *etc*.

[162] Ladeur (n 10), 38. In his terms, closing 'structural holes' through the use of constitutional principles to reopen patterns of rule and exception.

[163] *Ibid*, 37.

law. In Ladeurian terms, this case law, which is inspired by fundamental rights, does not aim at societal unity, but rather aims to bridge the 'structural holes' between sub-systems and their discourses.[164] In other words, the law's role is one of brokerage through which it extracts a normative surplus value. Re-norming through fundamental rights also provides for coherence and consistency in the formation of institutional memory which enables the law to build up 'redundancy', but keep open 'variety' through a norms-led but heterarchical collision discourse.[165] It is a thoroughly 'common law constitutionalism' aiming not only at collisions of sub-systems through norms, but also at incrementally building a public (second) order in the absence of a blueprint: new rights and, as I will argue, models of liability. In this sense, Micklitz uses the concept of the 'laboratory' for this type of 'institutional (constitutional) experimentation'.[166] In more practical terms, partial policies must not be allowed to exclude individual rights, but rather individual rights understanding the individual as *mandataire* should be easily conferred, and thereby provide fuel to the ongoing and unfolding development of legal normative programmes. These programmes should, in effect, balance different normative discourses or orders via legal rights converting different ways of modes of perception into a legal rule of liability. Through processes of trial and error this should harden into new models of liability.[167]

EU law has certain unique resources to this end. The legal person in EU law does not fit the classical understanding of the legal subject, which is embedded in national law, as concerned with autonomy and its 'latent' societal function. In EU law, this national law image is up-ended, and the legal subject is primarily co-opted or instrumentalised to complete the market from the very start such that one might speak of a post-classical legal order.[168] His autonomy is 'regulated' all the way through and, as such, his legal rights

164 *Ibid.*

165 *Ibid*, 38, insofar as Ladeur refers to internal autopoiesis.

166 In *The Politics of Justice*, Micklitz (n 61), 251, associates the EU, more broadly, with a concept of experimentalism in post-classical law, and refers to this as 'the European advantage' in law.

167 In other words, I disagree with Gerstenberg's Dworkinian-inspired dismissal of Sunstein's notion of 'incompletely theorised agreements'. Contingency, and the iterative development of the law, is necessary where meaning is radically fragmented, not only between persons, but between social sub-systems. The case here has the role of irritation and alarm function.

168 This is in opposition to the moral and universal understanding of rights in classical legal thinking. Captured well by I Kampourakis, 'CSR and Social Rights: Juxtaposing Societal Constitutionalism and Rights-Based Approaches Imposing Human Rights Obligations on Corporations' (2019) 9 *Göttingen Journal of International Law* 537–69, at 544–45. 'It is from this cognitive claim to universal morality, associated with dignity, freedom, and autonomy, that rights-based approaches commence to construct their normative edifice regarding the need to interpret current positive law.' This is, of course, a one-sided presentation of the function of

are more manifestly instrumentalised than in national law. In other words, the multidimensional aspects of legal rights are at the forefront of legal analysis. It is clear from this analysis that until now these legal rights have been primarily considered in the economic semantics of the completion of the internal market. But *tertium datur*? A rights-based reflection on this role of completing the market – and the semantics of the economy system – is what is required. This de-individuation of the legal subject should not be feared, nor is it unprecedented, but it is accelerated in the EU law context where rights more explicitly span what Teubner refers to as harms to personal rights, human rights and institutional rights.[169] This inherent tension in EU law rights should be seized on and used productively to reshape the boundaries of colliding discourses dynamically and iteratively through tort. How might this be operationalised? What does it mean for tort law in the EU? In the next section, the incipient form of constitutionalisation of private law within EU law is examined.

D RIGHTS BALANCING BEFORE THE COURT: THINKING THROUGH NON-COMMENSURABLE DISCOURSES

The *Boston Scientific* judgment can assist us in our reconceptualisation.[170] From a systems theory perspective, the judgment underlines a multidimensional or polycontextural conflict that mediates institutional rights, human rights and personal rights through the deployment of fundamental rights in a 'private law' dispute. First, at the level of institutional rights, what is colliding is political ('legitimate expectation of consumers'), health (the distinction between informed consent and legal causation),[171] scientific (precaution[172]

rights from a systems theory perspective even in classical legal orders. No such claim is made in EU law.

[169] In Teubner's terms, personal rights protect rights of communication of 'the social artefacts called "persons"', human rights protect 'persons' and the environment against harms from societal sub-system communications, and institutional rights protect the autonomy of different sub-systems. See Teubner (n 49), 342.

[170] C-503/13 & C-504/13, *Boston Scientific Medizintechnik GmbH v AOK Sachsen-Anhalt* (2015) ECLI:EU:C:2015:148.

[171] A vexing question in national law, see *eg Chester v Ashfar* [2005] 1 AC 134; *Montgomery v Lanarkshire Health Board* [2015] UKSC 11.

[172] Precaution understood as a second-order reflection of science whereby it observes on its own foundations. It was developed through legal irritation of scientific discourse, and has a different meaning within and outside the scientific discourse. This parallels the concept of informed consent in medicine. Ultimately, though the roots of the precautionary principle are in environmental politics, see F Ewald et al, *Le Principe de Précaution* (Paris: PUF, 2008), 6–26.

and legal causation) and economic discourses (market access).[173] Secondly, these collisions, and their resolution, impinge on human rights – in Teubnerian terms, the relationship between discourses and 'vulnerable' 'persons' – as well as, thirdly, on personal rights because of the difficulty on the facts, which is ultimately transcended by the court, of the claimants to articulate their claim in legal doctrine. The court ultimately gives a complex and nuanced judgment co-opting a fundamental rights analysis to up-end received legal wisdom by deploying the concept of legitimate consumer protection as a composite concept.

In *Boston Scientific*, the relevant legal question was the scope of the duties imposed on producers by the Product Liability Directive.[174] The first respondent imported and sold pacemakers and defibrillators. It transpired that these products were defective. In the case of the pacemakers, a sealant leak meant that over time the battery might be depleted, rendering the device inoperative. The relevant manufacturer, Boston Scientific, following the relevant procedures under the Safety Directive, recalled the product and reimbursed the claimant the cost of a new pacemaker.[175] The claimant, then, sued for the cost of the medical procedure to fit a new pacemaker under the Product Liability Directive.[176] The defibrillators were similarly defective, and the claim was largely consistent with the pacemaker claim, namely, the claimants sought relief for the costs of the replacement medical procedure. The reference was pursuant to three questions of the German federal court, the most pertinent of which involved the interpretation of Articles 6(1) and 9(1) of the Product Liability Directive, 85/374. According to the directive, a producer is liable for a defective product if the claimant can prove damage, defect, and a causal link between damage and the defect. In the circumstances, all that the claimants could demonstrate was a general increased risk of harm as distinct from the specific causation of harm. Indeed, on orthodox principles it is unclear whether harm was occasioned at all! Additionally, assuming that there

[173] Concepts such as informed consent, precaution, *etc*, are what Luhmann refers to as 'generalize media', but of course have different meanings within different sub-systems and their codes. However, they are structurally coupled to law. For an informative reconstruction of informed consent and its different significance in medical science and law, as well as their dynamic co-evolution, see JA Burr & B Gibson, 'Informed Consent in Research Ethics: An Analysis from the Perspective of Luhmann's Social Systems Theory' (2017) *Social Theory and Health*. ISSN 1477-8211. https://eprints.whiterose.ac.uk/122180/3/STH%20Manuscript%20201559 6%20%281%29.pdf (accessed 10 July 2021).

[174] Directive 374/85/EC.

[175] Directive 94/42/EC.

[176] To be more accurate, the insurance company sued by subrogation.

was no provable damage, the claimants were seeking recovery for pure economic loss.[177]

What is interesting is how AG Bot and the court divided the aims of the directive by giving these aims a normative *and* constitutional significance. The court separated the completion of the internal market from consumer protection. Both aims were placed within a constitutional framework. This is particularly patent in the opinion of AG Bot, but also appears in the reasoning of the court. For example, at paragraph 35, AG Bot states that although an objective of the directive is undistorted competition, another main objective of the directive is consumer protection. Although this paragraph might be considered merely a supporting argument, it reveals the deeper balancing at issue.[178] It is not simply a question of balancing costs and benefits (harmonised standards justified in relation to transaction costs), rather the deeper commitment is to balance the values or principles that undergird the EU legal order.[179] These, in turn, reflect 'legitimate consumer expectations' colliding with market access, which in our language is the collision of the discourses of politics (*qua* citizenship), health, science and the economy. The task of the court, then, is one of developing a discourse of rights that goes beyond the internal market *qua* economic constitutional only.

This is, then, a justification for placing the burden of the costs of replacement on the producers. At paragraph 38, AG Bot states that to make safety subject to the occurrence of specific damage undermines the consumer protection regime because it saps the preventative function of the directive and its risk-creation injury and cost-spreading rationales.[180] Furthermore, in a constitutionalising move, AG Bot links his reasoning to Article 35 of the charter and Article 168(1) Treaty on the Functioning of the European Union (TFEU), which aims to guarantee a high level of human health

[177] The CJEU dissolved boundaries between contract and tort, and, in this respect, the judgment shares some affinities with Joined Cases C-65/09 & C-78/09, *Gebr Weber GmbH v Jürgen Wittmer and Ingrid Putz v Medianess Electronics GmbH* (2011) ECLI:EU:C:2011:396. This is not unprecedented as product liability has always straddled contract and tort. The evolution of American product liability law is particularly prescient.

[178] This might be an attempt at providing a 'corrective' to the perceived pro-market bias in previous product liability judgments see Reich (n 108), Hodges (n 114) on the imbalance in the New Approach. In Reich's analysis, however, one should be careful to note that *AGM-COS.MET* was a case of state liability.

[179] See D Kennedy, 'A Transnational Proportionality in Private Law' in R Brownsword, H Micklitz, L Niglia & Steve Weatherill (eds), *The Foundations of European Private Law* (Oxford: Hart, 2011), 185, in particular his analysis of 'neoformalism' and EU law.

[180] At this point, AG Bot rehearses the social's reason for enterprise liability, namely, where X creates a risk she is in a better position to minimise the risk and prevent damage at the lowest cost. See Opinion of AG Bot in *Boston Scientific* (2014) ECLI:EU:C:2014:2306.

protection in the definition and implementation of all EU activities and policies, and states that this should be a guide to interpretation regarding the directive, especially with regard to the concept of defect. This argument was not repeated in court; although it was not repeated, however, the judgment tracks his argument at paragraph 35.

The CJEU's judgment was not as emphatic or explicit in constitutionalizing the dispute. Nevertheless, a number of common strands exist between the AG's opinion and the court. The method of interpretation is largely purposive, examining the articles of the directive and considering its recitals.[181] Unlike the AG's opinion, the vulnerability of the parties is stressed more overtly. Given their vulnerability, 'the safety requirements for those devices which such patients are entitled to expect are particularly high'.[182] At paragraph 40, the court more clearly follows AG Bot by stressing the abnormal nature of the risk as pertinacious to the definition of what safety requires on the facts before the court. In other words, the greater the vulnerability of the claimants, the higher and more abnormal (serious) the risk, the more exacting the standard of care, or, to put it differently, the more broadly the provisions of the directive will be interpreted. This abnormal potential for damage justified the relaxation of the causal requirement. In circumstances where products of the same group/series are defective 'it is possible to classify as defective all the products in that group or series, without there being any need to show that the product in question is defective'.[183] The court, then, at paragraph 42, invoked squarely the balancing this required. Thus, by examining the second and seventh recitals of the directive, the court stated that the objective pursued was 'a fair apportionment of the risks inherent in modern technological production between the injured person and the producer'. Given this objective, there is no requirement to show that a particular pacemaker was defective for the purposes of Article 6(1) of the directive. On the second question, the court followed AG Bot's reasoning such that this broad interpretation of the directive required the cost of surgical operation to be compensated, certainly in the case of pacemakers, and perhaps in the case of defibrillators, the latter being left open to the German federal court.

In *Boston Scientific*, it was not simply that a teleological reading of the directive provided for recovery but that the particularly vulnerable claimants, given their constitutional rights to safety, required this prima facie *contra*

181 The first, second, sixth and ninth recitals to the preamble were considered relevant.
182 para 39.
183 para 41.

legem interpretation. Constitutional arguments were used, in addition to textual ones, to buttress the claimants' right to recovery for additional expenses beyond the cost of removal of pacemakers. This is important because it suggests that passing on costs to the producer is not a global aim but required by the particular facts of the case given the balance of rights at question. The precedential value of this judgment is circumscribed by such a methodology. Such an approach draws outer boundaries on purely instrumental arguments, embedding them in a constitutional discourse, and simultaneously renders a fact-sensitive judgment. This does not mean that the balance achieved can be extrapolated to all claims, but the court decided that the circumstances at issue required this result. It can be interpreted as a form of situational or contextual reasoning aiming to delimit spheres of freedom, but also of discourses (balancing economic argument, political and health, science) in the concrete case.

In Teubnerian terms, this judgment spans institutional rights, human rights and personal rights dimensions to fundamental rights protection. The court is, first, drawing 'negative bounds on societal communication where the integrity of individuals' body and mind' by economic and even legal communication 'that crosses boundaries'.[184] While the limiting role on economic semantics in determining acceptable risk is quite obvious,[185] it should be noted that the court relaxed causation rules so that the individuals' claims could be articulated. It is essentially a claim for the recovery where no causal relationship can be made out, in the orthodox sense, between the putative 'defect' and 'damage', but rather the defendant has exposed the individuals to an increased risk of harm with uncertain consequences for their health and well-being. The route to this end is to constitutionalise the dispute whereby fundamental rights impact on the definition of legitimate consumer expectation and, additionally, the court in this way reconstructs, through legal doctrine, the (institutional) collision of competing environmental discourses on health and science, which have developed sophisticated discourses on precaution and consent as exposure to a risk. Thus, the court not only internally reconstructs its environment, but also 'irritates' the *eigensturcture* of the New Approach by placing greater *ex post* regulatory limits on the predominantly *ex ante* approach. As a matter of legal reasoning, the court used rights to buttress certain policy goals vis-à-vis others in the instant case. Legitimate consumer expectation, in short, is interpreted in terms of balancing norms. In the end, the individual is

[184] Teubner (n 138), 124, 145.

[185] See Reich (n 108) on the structural weakness of the New Approach in which in the overall regulatory architecture market access is preferred to consumer safety.

provided with a legal pathway to articulate their claim (personal rights).[186] In broader terms, the defendant is liable for providing a defective pacemaker, which *enhanced* the risk of harm to the claimants, without actually causing harm. This notion is taken a controversial step further in *Sanofi*, where it was extended to evidential proof of causation *simpliciter* because the court stated that for the purpose of the directive the use of 'circumstantial evidence' of a 'serious, specific and consistent' nature[187] to infer causation did not conflict with the directive and, indeed, the placing of a requirement of scientific proof in circumstances of scientific uncertainty would violate the directive.[188] Additionally, such circumstantial inferences could also go to the defectiveness of the product. In other words, in *Sanofi*, the court's interpretation lowers the threshold requirement for proving causation where on orthodox principles the most that can be said is that a product *may* have enhanced a risk of injury, if at all.

This complex form of legal reasoning assumes no clear priority between competing norms and *sinnwelten* and, as such, might be accurately described as 'post-classical'.[189] Norms are balanced through a discourse of rights in a non-scalar or hierarchical approach.[190] Rights-balancing, in effect, balances the underlying values or norms of the legal system in a highly contextualised manner rather than subsuming the law into an overall (totalising) perspective. This type of reasoning is an important part of the picture because it suggests divergent discourses can be channelled into the medium of rights, with the latter producing a backstop against the domination of one over the other. In *Boston Scientific* and *Sanofi*, this favours precautionary reasoning concerning

[186] I agree with Teubner (n 49) that the individual is a 'semantic artefact' and there is no direct contact between human beings and communicative systems. However, the point of rights-based reasoning in law is to reconstruct the person internally, *among other purposes*.

[187] C-621/15, *NW v Sanofi Pasteur MSD SNC* (2017) ECLI:EU:C:2017:484, para. 38.

[188] *Sanofi Pasteur*, paras 29–30 (in the context of the burden of proof). Perhaps, even more radically, in circumstances of a total lack of scientific certainty, see Rizzi's excoriation of the decision. M Rizzi, 'A Dangerous Method: Correlations and Proof of Causation in Vaccine Related Injuries' (2018) 9(3) *Journal of European Tort Law* 289–307. Rizzi makes a strong case that the decision amounts to an endorsement of quackery. However, that is a view from orthodox tort principles of causation, and from a certain positivistic view of science.

[189] Kennedy (n 179) would refer to this form of legal reasoning as neo-formalist, which he distinguishes from 'the social'. In the 'social', while the law might be conceived as having several ends, 'it is clear that they may conflict. But the conflict is resolved not by compromise but by the choice of a dominant end', whereas in neo-formalist legal thought, norms are balanced without a dominant, or predetermined end. The criticism of the latter is that it descends into proportionality analysis, and ad hockery. See Ladeur (n 10), 25. However, I think that this underestimates the extent to which the legal system can develop principled and coherent norm balancing.

[190] *Ibid*.

risk, that is, liability for defective pacemakers that enhancing a risk of harm under conditions of uncertainty, liability without clear causal evidence, channelled through the medium of rights.[191] In other words, the court closed the 'structural hole' between economic semantics and other discourses on risk, and furnished a new legal approach to acceptable risk. However, *Boston Scientific* and *Sanofi* remain within the field of primary liability where the standard of care is stricter liability. A suite of other problems is thrown up when one considers problems of secondary liability. While rights reasoning may help in this regard, for example by developing positive obligations of state or quasi-state actors, it does not give a clear-eyed view of the network dimension to the problem, especially how this throws up problems of imputation.

E CONCLUSION

In the post-state-centred constellation, the law of tort has receded under the influence of economisation understood as a cognitivisation of the law. However, *Boston Scientific* demonstrates that the law can be re-normativised via rights. Rights are understood, however, not merely in inter-subjective terms or as vertical entitlements vis-à-vis the state. Instead, they are understood as mediating discourse collisions. This does no more than make explicit what is implicit in a private law or 'bottom-up' understanding of rights. They are architectural or institutional in addition to defining 'territories of the self'. This architectural role for rights protection regains vigour after the state loses its central role in coordination society. Transposed into an EU context, the CJEU attempts through rights to reach compatibility between different social sub-systems, fashioning a concept of acceptable risk in law not once and for all, but case by case. However, if *Boston Scientific* stands for enhanced liability vis-à-vis private parties, *ubi ius, ibi remedium*, this does not provide remedies against other regulatory actors in a heterarchical society. I now turn to examine how the new *eigenstructures* are causing problems for tort law in terms of its rules of causation and attribution and how a rights-based approach might assist in the resolution of these problems.

[191] This is not dissimilar to the UK asbestos case law where the defendants are held liable for their material contribution to harm, *eg Fairchild v Glenhaven* [2003] 1 AC 32. The difference here is that the harm itself is uncertain. This is also some parallel with the controversial loss of chance case law in which the defendant is held liable because a risk is unilaterally imposed on a claimant over which the claimant could make no informed decision.

4

Re-norming Tort Law

From Network Rights to Network Remedies

A INTRODUCTION

In Chapter 3, it was argued that recent CJEU judgments such as *Boston Scientific* have converted policy balancing into principled collisions of norms by 'constitutionalising' private law disputes. This resulted in the CJEU imposing liability for enhancing a risk, as distinct from causing a risk to materialise in harm. Constitutionalisation in the light of functional differentiation was explained as a means to counteract 'cognitivisation', namely the domination of law's programmes by the rationalities of other social sub-systems. *Boston Scientific*, more precisely, by drawing an explicit connection between legitimate expectation and fundamental rights protection, shows the way by adding a third layer to tort reasoning alongside juridical and policy-based reasoning.[1] This normative remodelling occurs by reorienting legal categories to the problem of discourse collisions, interposing market integration with discourses of consumer protection and safety. By placing legal argumentation in a constitutional framework, collisions of non-scalar norms can be reconciled in a principled way.[2] More precisely, by understanding competing 'objectives' in

[1] Exclusive reference to policies against recovery may be understood in Teubner's terms as oversocialisation of the law, or in our terms as cognitivisation. See G Teubner, 'After Legal Instrumentalism? Strategic Models of Post-Regulatory Law' in G Teubner (ed), *Dilemmas of Law in the Welfare State* (Berlin: de Gruyter, 1986), 299.

[2] D Kennedy, 'A Transnational Proportionality in Private Law' in R Brownsword, H Micklitz, L Niglia & S Weatherill (eds), *The Foundations of European Private Law* (Oxford: Hart, 2011), s. Reconciliation should not be understood as a 'for all time' answer to these problems. *Pace* N Luhmann, 'Legal Argumentation' in *Law as a Social System* (KA Ziegert trans) (Oxford: Oxford University Press, 2004), 305, law is understood as a historical machine designed to ensure stable normative expectations as well as flexibility. Oversocialisation can be understood as favouring the latter at the expense of the former, constitutionalisation can be understood as disruptive of this problem. See also KH Ladeur, 'The Evolution of General Administrative Law and the Emergence of Postmodern Administrative Law', Osgoode CLPE Research Paper

terms of balancing of norms, rather than policies, the court has significant scope to intervene to counteract the problem of policy arguments as an *ex ante* bar to recovery as well as reviewing settled understandings of legal doctrines such as causation in the light of pervasive uncertainty.[3] This shift in legal reasoning addresses the 'de-differentiation' or 'cognitivisation' of law, with greater internal differentiation of complexity in legal reasoning.[4]

Buttressing the autonomy of legal argument vis-à-vis other social sub-systems is, of course, only one dimension to the problem. Establishing a framework of 'collision' rights does not outline who should be the addressees of liability and on what basis within a framework of network liability. The task of this chapter is to draw on incipient and innovative tendencies in CJEU case law to develop this concept. In the chapter, the argument as to how an incipient regime of network liability is taking shape will be located within the New Approach to Technical Standards considered a site of network governance. When these incipient and implicit dimension to CJEU jurisprudence are drawn together, the outline of a network liability regime emerges.

The NATS illustrates a move from government to governance.[5] This governance regime mixes 'private' and 'public' regulation within an overall network governance architecture.[6] What is missing from this positive account is an overall *normative* framework of network liability that adequately demarcates the distinctively collective role of regulatory actors, but which avoids imposing a model of individual or organisational liability on *normatively*

16/2011, 36–38, who views constitutionalisation as a tool to revise the network of rule/exception in the law.

3 This uncertainty is pervasive, because risks have become reflexive, *ie* because it is increasingly evident that scientific discourse cannot answer normative questions in circumstances in which meaning is fragmented.

4 Luhmann (n 2).

5 It is representative of a broader move to governance in 'world society'. On 'world society', see N Luhmann, 'The World Society as a Social System' (1982) 8(3) *International Journal of General Systems* 131. For examples, see W Mattli, 'Private Transnational Governance' in J Katz Cogan et al (eds), *The Oxford Handbook of International Organizations* (Oxford: Oxford University Press, 2016), 173: 'What is emerging in some areas is a novel type of transnational governance, one that is neither purely private nor public but may best be captured by the term of "joint or hybrid governance".'

6 D Chalmers, 'The Government and Citizenship of Self-Regulation' in F Cafaggi (ed), *Reframing Self-Regulation in European Private Law* (Alphen aan den Rijn: Wolter Kluwer, 2006), 161. This is Chalmers' terminology when referring to self-regulatory regimes, noting the manner in which they should not be described in terms of private ordering given their public salience and enablement. He notes the main danger in SSRs 'is not so much that industry will seek to lower standards, but, more invidiously, that a particular, relatively non-pluralistic worldview dominates ideas of consumer and environmental safety'.

secondary actors. The hesitancy of developing network as a legal category[7] stems, in large part, from the tendency to equate the liability for advancing networks purposes with organisational liability. The sociological network requires,[8] instead, a *normative* model capable of making 'strategic public interventions', not a regime of 'total responsibility'.[9] Networks are not organisations but, it is argued, nor is individual liability an appropriate framework for considering problems of 'network failure'.[10] Drawing on the as yet unrealised potential of CJEU case law, which can be viewed as applying the *Francovich* state liability regime to secondary non-state actors, one can postulate a distinctive secondary regime based on neither individual liability nor organisational liability. This distinctive approach comes into full relief in the *Schmitt* judgment when one compares the CJEU's approach with that of the member states' courts in France and Germany. The CJEU, in short, views private intermediaries in regulation as forming part of an 'overall governance architecture' without subsuming them into a regime of individual or organisational liability.[11] This *supplements* EU law on organisational liability by drawing on analogies from *Francovich* state liability and goes beyond the public/private divide. However, the CJEU held back from following these shifts to their logical conclusion. Therefore, in this chapter we will draw out what is implicit in the court's reasoning and show how it contributes to a concept of network liability. Having done so by reference to the *Schmitt* judgment, it will be argued the '*Francovich* analogy' should then be used to recapitulate the role and function of state liability in EU law, which would create a parallel track of network liability for the state in its co-equal role as a normatively

7 G Teubner, '*Coincidentia Oppositorum*: Hybrid Networks beyond Contract and Organisation' in M Amstutz & G Teubner (eds), *Networks: Legal Issues of Multi-Lateral Co-operation* (Oxford: Hart, 2009), 3.

8 As perceived by the legal system. It is not a question of equating sociological networks with legal remedies. Legal models of liability model their environment, but they must first construct that environment through legal dogmatics. 'Bridging concepts' assist the legal system's cognitive openness, its responsiveness, but do not result in an input/output relationship with reality 'out there'. In other words, although network is not a legal concept, it does not follow that there can be no legal concept or problematisation of networks. *Compare* R Buxbaum, 'Is "Network" a Legal Concept?' (1993) 149(4) *Zeitschrift für die gesamte Staatswissenschaft* 698–705.

9 For these reasons, we oppose what we regard as *ad hoc* solutions such as *Sindell v Abbott Laboratories* Docket No 31063 (LA) (163 Cal Rptr 132 (1980)), especially with regard to network governance.

10 G Teubner, '"And if I by Beelzebub Cast Out Devils, . . .": An Essay on the Diabolics of Network Failure' (2009) 10(4) *German Law Journal* 397. As was argued in Chapter 1, individual liability does not allow for positive duties to be *imposed* on individuals.

11 Chalmers (n 6).

secondary actor within network governance. This will provide a template for liability of peripheral actors in network governance. The final task will be to 'test' its wider application as a template for network liability beyond the New Approach to Technical Standards. This argument requires contextualising the dispute in *Schmitt* and, therefore, before alighting on the concept of network liability the *Schmitt* judgment will be contextualised in the context of the NATS.

B THE NEW APPROACH: THE EMERGENCE OF NETWORK GOVERNANCE

The basic design of the NATS radically alters the anterior division of labour between public and private parties. In the NATS, the state's regulatory role is consigned to one of post-market surveillance under strict conditions, whereas, *ex ante* manufacturers are required to ensure that their products reach appropriate product standards, meeting at the very least the essential requirements specified by directives which refer to CEN requirements. Manufacturers are obliged to enter contracts with notification bodies, intermediaries which are charged with the inspection of products to ensure compliance with those requirements. A certification of compliance, in effect, gives manufacturers a 'European passport' that enables them to export their products within the EU but is not equivalent to a guarantee of safety. Thus, greater responsibility is given to manufacturers, and certification bodies, and a more restricted role is afforded to national supervisors in the overall architecture of the NATS, which aims at product safety and undistorted competition. A brief history of the NATS before turning to relevant case law in the field of product liability.

1 *A History of the New Approach: Building Network Governance*

The NATS developed first in the 1980s aiming to open markets by harmonising standards.[12] Before the NATS was adopted, the European Community made several attempts in vain at specifying product requirements in secondary legislation. According to Schepel, the problem with this approach is twofold: first, the practical difficulty in obtaining agreement at a European level over technical specifications ('Decisional supranationalism') and, second, by the

[12] M Egan, *Constructing the Market: Standards, Regulation and Governance* (Oxford: Oxford University Press, 2001), esp ch 6.

time consensus is reached the standards are often outdated.[13] The latter occurs because of rapid developments regarding the state of the art. Before the NATS was introduced in 1985, 'the creation of a harmonized system of legislation had slowed to a halt, as Directives had needed to be encumbered with detailed technical specifications'.[14] The NATS followed the *Cassis de Dijon* approach, combining market access ('mutual recognition') with proportionate measures in the name of health and safety.[15]

This led the commission to propose a radical new departure, whereby only 'essential requirements' were to be established at a European level.[16] Once these were complied with, they constituted a passport for manufacturers within the EU. A new regulatory framework was established, which Hodges describes succinctly:

> The New Approach system does not involve pre-marketing assessment of a product by a competent authority or the grant of a marketing authorization. Instead, the onus of ensuring and declaring that a product conforms to the legal essential requirements is placed on the manufacturer himself, although in many instances this is subject to approval by an independent technical organization (known as a notified body).[17]

The regulatory system that was established to facilitate the New Approach had an impact on the traditional public–private divide, and the division of responsibility this implies. The determination of product standards was assigned to private standardisation bodies and,[18] especially after the introduction of the Global Approach in the early 1990s, *ex ante* compliance and monitoring was assigned to mostly private notification bodies in accordance with a notification procedure.[19] The notification procedure meant that member states were obliged to list certain competent bodies, and notify the commission which incorporated these bodies into the relevant directive.

[13] H Schepel, *The Constitution of Private Governance: Product Standards in the Regulation of Integrating Markets* (Oxford: Hart, 2005), ch 2: 'to overcome the inertia of decisional supranationalism' (63). Of course, this phrase harks back to J Weiler, 'The Transformation of Europe' (1991) 100(8) *Yale Law Journal* 2403.

[14] C Hodges, *European Regulation of Consumer Product Safety* (Oxford: Oxford University Press, 2005), 53.

[15] Schepel (n 13).

[16] The template for the New Approach can be traced back to the Low Voltage Directive, Council Directive 73/23 EEC. Egan (n 12), esp ch 6.

[17] Hodges (n 14) [citation omitted].

[18] *De facto*, this is largely the case. Producers are free to show compliance with essential requirements via other means, but in practice this is an expensive alternative.

[19] This is the case with regard to high-risk products, *ie* medical devices. Self-certification is permitted for certain less risky products. For a more detailed analysis, as well as the compromises this institutional design reflects, see Egan (n 12), ch 6.

Producers can then utilise any notification body on this list such that such a notification body may be based in another member state.[20] The member state should have an accreditation body in place that is charged with ensuring the notified bodies are competent.[21] In essence, 'the point is that the Community entrusts the task of ensuring free movement of the products covered by the Directive to private transnationalism'.[22] This is certainly true with respect to the establishment of standards. But an often overlooked and equally important dimension is that the role of controlling or monitoring conformity with standards is 'delegated' to private bodies, namely notification bodies at the pre-market stage. The NATS is a deliberate governance design, which reorganised the balance between governmental regulation and the use of private actors to advance public goods, that is, safety and reduced transaction costs. This was apt to blur the line between private and public because of the manner in which it integrated private actors into the governance design in relation to product standards.

At all events, these minimum standards constitute the requirements that allow for market access subject to certification of compliance with those standards. A comprehensive regulatory framework has emerged to enforce product safety in the EU.[23] The state in effect delegates 'upwards' to the EU to create the overall framework and, within this settlement, 'downwards' to notified bodies and manufacturers. This framework involves self-regulation *ex ante*, with manufacturers obliged to ensure compliance with the relevant minimum standards, certification requirements whereby private actors certify that a product is compliant (a monitoring function), and a restricted *ex post* market supervision role for public authorities (monitoring and public enforcement). The public authorities may withdraw a product from the market but only in

[20] JP Gallard, 'Legitimacy, Credibility and Responsibility of the (Big) European Third Party Certifiers', Working Paper, SASE Conference Chicago 2014, esp 3–4.

[21] Regulation (EC) of the European Parliament and Council setting out the requirements for accreditation and market surveillance relating to the marketing of products and repealing Council Regulation (CE) No 339/93, 9 July 2008, 765/2008.

[22] Schepel (n 13), 67.

[23] Schepel (n 13) treats this issue at ch 10, arguing for a greater role for a revised tort law in reviewing the standard-setting aspect: 'As regulatory law increasingly relies on voluntary standards, courts will cease deferring to regulatory decisions and take it upon themselves to scrutinise standards and the procedures that lead to their establishment. In this sense, tort law takes over the function of administrative law in the supervision of regulatory decision-making. And what courts look for in these instances cannot be very different from what the Restatement (Third) of Torts looks for in the determination of whether to have public law pre-empt tort actions: a deliberative process which is full, fair and thorough and reflected substantial expertise' (366). This is certainly relevant, but for our purposes what is more relevant is the addressees of liability where something goes wrong in regulation and who should be held responsible.

accordance with a strict procedure which requires that national authorities notify the commission. Therefore, what Hodges refers to as the hybrid role of notification bodies emerges: '[A] hybrid position of private commercial entities that are granted limited regulatory functions (for so long as they satisfy criteria) subject to scrutiny by competent authorities.'[24] The question often posed in legal doctrine and scholarship is whether these notification bodies can be considered to be performing a delegated public function in the general interest or whether they should be considered as exercising a purely private service and if the latter, whether private law should provide a remedy where their actions have clear third-party impacts. These questions are closely tied to the individual and organisational models of liability. A formal and individualistic (liability) approach focuses on the private nature of the contract between a producer and a notification body, but it is apt to mislead when the private status of the contract is itself at issue. An organisational (liability) approach, in contrast, focuses on how their activities might be conceptualised as a delegation of public authority and, therefore, whether they should be liable as 'emanations of the state' or whether the state should be liable *respondeat superior*. However, it is also misleading because there is an absence of risk creation[25] by notification bodies except in the most extenuated sense, and the state lacks control over the day-to-day activities of notification bodies. Additionally, aside from failures of notification bodies to regulate appropriately, a further question arises regarding how one conceptualises state liability due to the state's secondary position mostly aimed at ensuring compliance with safety requirements *ex post*. These issues can be problematised through the lens of the *PIP* scandal, of which the *Schmitt* judgment is a focal point.

2 *The PIP Imbroglio and* Schmitt: *Tort Law in the Spotlight*

(i) Background: Between Individual and Organisational Liability in National Law

The *PIP* imbroglio relates to a large number of claims that have been litigated or are pending before the courts of a number of jurisdictions.[26] The claimants

[24] Hodges (n 14), 219.

[25] The key, normative trigger of organisational liability as argued in Chapter 2. Conceptualised by Stapleton on the private side as 'moral enterprise liability', but *mutatis mutandis* organisational state liability. See J Stapleton, 'A New Theory of Strict Moral Enterprise Liability' in *Product Liability* (London: Butterworths, 1994), 185 *et seq*.

[26] The victims obtained recovery at first instance against TÜV before the Commercial Court in Toulon. This judgment was overturned on Appeal at Aix-en-Provence, but the Cour de Cassation reversed the Court of Appeal judgment in 2018. Arrêt n 610 du 10 octobre 2018 (15-

are women who obtained breast implants. The primary tortfeasor is *Poly Implant Prothèse* (PIP), a French manufacturer of silicone products. In 2000, following investigations of the Food and Drugs Administration (FDA) in the United States, it emerged that these implants were defective because the industrial silicone gel used in their production was 'sub-standard'. Subsequently, the silicone gel found to be defective was banned within the EU. PIP did not comply with the ban, but instead 'developed an elaborate scheme of deceit and continued to use sub-standard industrial silicone gel'.[27] Once a putative link was suggested between the defective silicone gel used and the harm caused to certain women due to silicone leakage, many women brought claims in respect of the cost of removing these implants. As a matter of causation, it was unclear the extent to which the defectiveness of the implants resulted in the bursting of the implants causing physical harm. In other words, although the product in question fell below the appropriate quality standard, the manufacturing process meant that it was unclear the extent and degree to which the relevant defective gel could be found in the products manufactured by PIP. Secondly, there is considerable scientific uncertainty as to the health risks posed by sub-standard breast implants. While it is true that the use of sub-standard silicone gel increases the chance of rupture, it is unclear whether this poses a long-term health risk to individuals. The main costs sought related to the cost of removal, the cost of the fitting of new implants and psychological injuries suffered because of the health scare involved.

The NATS appears to make market surveillance the 'task of the supervisory agencies'.[28] As a matter of fact, it was 2009 before the supervisory agency in France acted and 2010 before PIP products were withdrawn.[29] The manufacturer went into liquidation at this point, meaning that if the claimants were to

26.093) ECLI:FR:CCASS:2018:C100610, and remitted the matter to the Paris Court of Appeal, see www.courdecassation.fr/jurisprudence_2/premiere_chambre_civile_568/610_10_40402.html (accessed 5 July 2020). More recently, on 29 January 2019, before the Administrative Tribunal of Montreuil, state liability was accepted in principle. See http://montreuil.tribunal-administratif.fr/content/download/153531/1554476/version/1/file/1800068.pdf (accessed 5 July 2020). The dispute is still ongoing in France, and indeed in the United Kingdom and Germany. See https://pipaworld.com/en/category/news-en/ (accessed 5 July 2020). See also German *Bundesgerichthof* judgment of 27 February 2020 on notified body liability: www.bundesgerichtshof.de/SharedDocs/Termine/DE/Termine/VIIZR151.html (accessed 5 July 2020). Most recently, www.cours-appel.justice.fr/sites/default/files/2021-05/D%C3%A9cision%20Cour%20d%E2%80%99appel%20de%20Paris%20implants%20mammaires.pdf (accessed 19 June 2021), holding TÜV liable.

27 B Van Leeuwen, 'PIP Breast Implants, the EU's New Approach for Goods and Market Surveillance by Notified Bodies' (2014) 3 *European Journal of Risk Regulation* 1.

28 *Ibid*, 2.

29 *Ibid*.

recover at all,[30] recovery would have to be based on a claim against a so-called secondary tortfeasor.[31] The potential liability of the supervisory authority is left to one side for the moment, because the relevant legal actions were taken against the notification body. In this respect, circumstances are further complicated by the role and function of notification bodies whose task involves ensuring that appropriate standards as to quality are applied in practice. In the main, although not entirely, notification bodies are private bodies charged with an *ex ante* regulatory function which, in this case,[32] involved 'checking the quality management system and design dossier of the product – their certification is necessary to be able to place the products on the markets'.[33] Once a product is certified in this manner, the task of supervision falls primarily to the relevant public supervisory agency in the member state in question in conjunction with the commission.[34] Secondly, once certification is approved by the relevant body, the product in question is approved for distribution throughout the EU. However, what complicates matters is that the responsibility of the notification body does not end here, because the notification body is under a duty to ensure continued compliance with the quality standard in question. The notification body would appear, therefore, to perform certain functions equivalent to those of a public supervisory body. It is worth recalling that the relevant legal framework is the (old) Medical Devices Directive (Directive 93/42/EEC), which aims to ensure market access while balancing this requirement against health and safety concerns: 'It combines

30 One should recall that several parties were criminally prosecuted. The highest profile prosecution was that of its CEO, a Mr Jean-Claude Mas. See http://news.sky.com/story/pip-breast-implant-boss-jean-claude-mas-jailed10425136 (accessed 20 July 2016).

31 Accessing the funds of secondary tortfeasor's insurer, to be precise. An alternative claim could have been brought against the insurer with the aid of some ingenuity; HW Micklitz, N Reich & L Boucon, 'L'Action de la Victime Contra L'Assureur du Producteur' (2015) 1 *Revue Internationale de Droit Économique* 37. But, more recently, see Case C-581/18, *RB v TÜV Rheinland LGA Products GmbH and Allianz IARD SA* (2020) ECLI:EU:C:2020:453 rejecting this argumentation.

32 There are several options regarding certification. This is the so-called full quality assurance approach. It involves a management system review not requiring an inspection of the products themselves. But, as Gallard (n 20) notes it requires at least one member with past experience on the review team. This was not the case on the facts. Although unannounced inspections were not compulsory, per the Toulon court they would have uncovered the fraud.

33 *Ibid*, 3.

34 Article 10 of the Medical Devices Directive, Directive 93/42/EEC. This framework will be replaced by new regulations, namely Regulation (EU) 2017/745 and Regulation (EU) 2017/746. Regulation (EU) 2017/745 enters into force on 26 May 2021 and greatly increases the powers of notified bodies as well as the responsibility of the state to supervise notified bodies. On notified bodies, see Annex VII of Regulation (EU) 2017/745. This means, in effect, that their regulatory role is enhanced.

the goal to safeguard the freedom of trade and goods with the aim to ensure public health and safety of the products.'[35] The Medical Devices Directive falls under the NATS directives and, as such, combines *ex ante* self-regulation and *ex post* market surveillance by the relevant state authorities. Additionally, as has already been stated, pre-market certification by notified bodies forms an important part of the regulatory process and there is a requirement at paragraph 5.4 of Annex II for periodic post-market surveillance. Apart from the general aims of the directive, namely guaranteeing market access and a high level of protection of health and safety contained in the recitals, notified bodies are entrusted with certain specific tasks. Their tasks are pursuant to guidelines regarded as 'soft law' in the sense that they do not, ordinarily, give rise to legal obligations.[36] These tasks are specified in the Annex II of the Directive, particularly at section 3.3 which states:

> The notified body must audit the quality system to determine whether it meets the requirements referred to in Section 3.2. It must presume that quality systems which implement the relevant harmonized standards conform to these requirements.
>
> The assessment team must include *at least one number with past experience of assessments of the technology concerned*. The assessment procedure *must include an inspection on the manufacturer's premises* and, in duly substantiated cases, on the premises of the manufacturer's suppliers and/or subcontractors to inspect the manufacturing processes.
>
> (Emphasis added)

Additionally, sections 5.3 and 5.4 provide for post-market surveillance tasks: 'The notified body *must* periodically carry out appropriate inspections and assessments to make sure that the manufacturer applies the approved quality system and must supply the manufacturer with an assessment report' (emphasis added).

Finally, the notified body *may* pay unannounced visits to the manufacturer. At the time of such visits, the notified body may, where necessary, carry out or ask for tests in order to check that the quality system is working properly. It must provide the manufacturer with an inspection report and, if a test has been carried out, with a test report. However, in practice and within their discretion, TÜV Rheinland, the relevant notified body, made announced visits, and the compliance exercise was fulfilled by ensuring that certain

35 SM Singh, 'What Is the Best Way to Supervise the Quality of Medical Devices? Searching for a Balance between Ex-ante and Ex-post Regulation' (2013) 4 *European Journal of Risk Regulation* 465.

36 *Ibid*, 467.

paperwork was completed. The real question, therefore, was whether this was insufficient supervision and if it was, whether it should give rise to a legal duty which corresponded to a legal right of the claimant to seek compensation.[37]

It goes without saying, the primary tortfeasor is the manufacturer on classical liability principles because it is the manufacturer and its agents who acted improperly.[38] TÜV Rheinland alleged that the manufacturer had 'deceived' its inspectors.[39] When the dispute reached the German lower courts, the court defined the obligations of TÜV Rheinland narrowly under Annex II of the Medical Devices Directive. It was essentially a box-ticking exercise – nothing more, nothing less. TÜV was not obliged by EU law or contract to carry out unannounced on-site inspections. Second, the court focused on the private nature of the contract between TÜV and PIP. This rather formal and *individualistic* approach to liability in a contractual context (that is, privity of contract) meant that third parties could not derive rights from the relationship, because the claim could not be fitted within contracts having third-party effects or Article 823(2) BGB. Additionally, as a matter of law, the German lower court failed to hold TÜV liable because the claimant could not demonstrate that she had suffered any recognised specific harm. All the claimant could demonstrate was that there was an increased risk of rupture and this was insufficient to establish liability.[40]

However, the French lower court reached a contrary conclusion, focusing on the fact that TÜV Rheinland was exercising 'delegated public powers'. The exercise of these powers breached its obligations under the Medical Services Directive, and failure to carry out a more extensive (and unannounced) inspection despite being on notice since 2000 of the defective silicone gel, constituted a failure of control, surveillance and vigilance. Having established that TÜV could be held liable under the directive, the Toulon court more expansively interpreted the duties owing under the directive. The Toulon court used section 3.3 to establish a breach of duty towards the claimants as well as drawing on their post-market tasks detailed at section 5.3 and 5.4. The court focused, first, on the rather technical fact that the directive requires inspection to be carried out by a team consisting of at least one member with past experience, which did not occur, and, secondly, although it is not

37 This is, of course, not the only avenue which claimants might use to seek compensation, as Van Leeuwen (n 27) points out. However, for our purposes it is the theoretically important one.

38 And, of course, this approach was crystallised in the Product Liability Directive.

39 Van Leeuwen (n 27).

40 This traditional approach to causation of harm is somewhat at odds post-*Boston Scientific*, which focuses more expansively on the concept of legitimate consumer expectation regarding product defects.

compulsory under the directive, had TÜV conducted an unannounced inspection the fraud would have been uncovered. The court, in other words, found that the balance between precautions taken and the nature of the risk involved was insufficient or unreasonable. In other words, 'soft law' was turned into hard legal obligation against the notified body.[41] Ordinarily such guidelines are not binding on private parties and, as such, the first-instance judgment in Toulon created uncertainty. Singh clarifies: 'These guidelines are, however, not legally binding on those parties as the principle of sincere cooperation is not binding on private parties, only on Member States.'[42] That the breach was found, nonetheless, was enabled by the French courts viewing TÜV Rheinland as exercising a delegated public power.[43] Thus, in contrast to the German approach, which embodies a model of individual liability, the French approach is based on a concept of organisational liability.[44] The German lower court's judgment was appealed to the German Federal Court of Appeal (*Bundesgerichtshof*), which requested a preliminary reference. The referring court in effect asked whether the scope of national law (contracts having third-party effects or the case law arising from BGB Article 823(2)) ought to be reconsidered in light of EU law. This is the backdrop to the *Schmitt* judgment.

(ii) PIP before the CJEU: Neither Individual nor Organisational Liability

Both the opinion of the advocate-general and the CJEU's judgment in *Schmitt* will be examined.[45] AG Sharpston's reasoning, in short, develops the idea that notification bodies have a positive duty to be 'alert'. It is important to retrace the steps in her argument to fully grasp the significance of the CJEU's judgment, which largely follows her reasoning. In her opinion, AG Sharpston examines the role of notification bodies, which has developed

41 The consequences of this, in itself, are obviously intriguing beyond the context of the European Union.

42 Singh (n 35), 473.

43 Which, incidentally, seems to leave open the possibility of superior responsibility of the state, see Gallard (n 20), especially since the relevant state, here Germany, is meant to guarantee the competence of notified bodies. The potential liability of the French state is another question, which would focus on the ten-year gap between the action of the FDA and the implementation of a ban on PIP products. Again, see Micklitz, Reich & Boucon (n 31).

44 However, the judgment was overturned on appeal. See www.lemonde.fr/societe/article/2015/07/02/protheses-pip-le-certificateur-n-a-pas-commis-de-fauteselon-la-justice_4667137_3224.html. For a discussion of the first-instance judgment, see Van Leeuwen (n 27).

45 Advocate General's Opinion in Case C-219/15, *Schmitt v TÜV Rheinland LGA Products GmbH* (2016) ECLI:EU:C:2016:694; (2017) ECLI:EU:C:2017:128.

within the framework of Directive 93/42/EC.[46] She notes that within that context the directive aims not only to provide market access, but also a high level of protection for health and also safety.[47] Breast implants are categorised as class III products, meaning that they attract the most onerous compliance and surveillance obligations.[48] The AG appears early on to have dismissed a horizontal application argument,[49] but this does not dispose the claim because following *Marleasing*, the court may provide guidance as to how national law is to be construed considering EU law.[50] While Directive 85/374 imposes strict liability on producers, this does not preclude other forms of liability.[51] The core question to answer was whether a notified body owing to 'a culpable failure to comply with its obligations' may give rise to 'direct and unrestricted liability towards the patients concerned'.[52] Importantly in this respect, AG Sharpston notes at paragraph 33 that primary manufacturer responsibility does not preclude member state or notified body liability, stating: 'Plainly, however, that directive does not limit the obligations as to product safety to the manufacturer alone. It also 'imposes a number of duties on Member States', which she lists. Whereas the directive is 'silent' regarding notified bodies, because there is an express requirement of liability insurance vis-à-vis notified bodies, liability in some form must have been contemplated.[53] While liability is contemplated, it is for national courts to determine its contours subject to equivalence and effectiveness of EU law.[54] Pivotal is paragraph 39:

> Given the crucial role played by notified bodies . . . and bearing in mind, in particular, the high level of protection to patients and users that that directive aims to provide and the risks associated with the devices in relation to which they are required to carry out their examination, it seems to me entirely appropriate that those bodies should in principle be capable of bearing liability under national law to those patients and users for a culpable failure to fulfil their obligations thereunder, provided always that the principles of

46 Advocate General's Opinion in *Schmitt* (2016).

47 Para 26.

48 Directive 2003/12/EC.

49 Para 27, not the state nor an emanation of the state. But this is a formal rather than functional approach.

50 C-106/89, *Marleasing SA v La Comercial Internacional de Alimentación* SA [1991] 1 ECR 4135.

51 Para 32.

52 Para 28.

53 Para 35: 'The directive is silent as regards the imposition of liability on notified bodies, although the requirement under section 6 of Annex XI that they take out civil liability insurance makes it clear that liability for something is contemplated.'

54 Para 39.

equivalence and effectiveness are respected. That will be a matter for the national court to determine.

However, AG Sharpston makes significant inroads into national discretion because she proceeds to lay down a test. While observing that notified bodies are not to be equated with the state and that their powers are often discretionary, this does not mean the relationship between the notified body and the manufacturer is purely 'cooperative'.[55] Notified bodies have teeth and these include surveillance powers. While there is 'no general obligation to inspect devices, examine the manufacturer's business records or carry out unannounced inspections' per the directive, this does not mean that the notified body is without responsibility by simply adhering to the 'paper' method of compliance. At paragraph 54, AG Sharpston states:

> [A]s part of its general duty of diligence, a notified body is under *a duty to be alert* to the fact that either of those possibilities may arise in any given case. If, therefore, it is put on notice, whether as a result of information arising out of its own inspections and assessments or *otherwise*, it will be under a duty to act. (Emphasis added)

And at paragraph 57: 'The question will be: what would a notified body acting with all due care and diligence have done in the circumstances in question? The same applies to the question whether the notified body should have carried out unannounced inspections.'

Thus, notified bodies can be placed on notice or 'alert', and in those circumstances they may be held liable where there is a lack of due care and diligence in carrying out their duties, which is a question that turns on the facts. It is notable, in particular, that what is apparently a discretionary power to inspect per the directive may become a positive obligation when on notice. This is strong guidance as to outcome because it would be difficult given the facts to argue that TÜV was not on notice, because of the actions of the FDA and the French authorities.

The court largely followed AG Sharpston's opinion.[56] It accepts that the purpose of Directive 92/43 is both to harmonise law on patient safety and health, and to provide medical devices with a 'high level of protection'.[57] The court then reviews the directive's provisions, noting that it provides member states and notified bodies with surveillance powers. These powers are meant to

[55] Para 51.

[56] C-219/15, *Schmitt v TÜV Rheinland* (2017) (n 45). They avoid discussion of the extraordinary *ex tunc* aspect.

[57] Paras 4–5, respectively.

ensure that the manufacturer complies with safety requirements.[58] However, certain of these powers are discretionary. For example, recall that annex II section 5.4 provides that inspections *may* be unannounced and that during these inspections the notified body 'may where necessary, carry out or ask for tests in order to check that the quality system is working properly'. The argument of Ms Schmitt is essentially that had the notified body gone beyond a mere 'paper' inspection they would have uncovered the fraud by an inspection of delivery notes and invoices. From paragraph 38 onwards the court reasons that there is no general obligation on notified bodies to conduct unannounced inspections, to examine devices or the manufacturer's business records, because the directive envisages that discretion is conferred on notified bodies in the discharge of compliance duties. And yet:

> However, the obligations laid down in Article 16(6) of the directive and those set out in paragraph 41 above *would be a dead letter if the degree of discretion knew no limits*. The notified body would not be able to fulfil its function under the procedure relating to the EC declaration of conformity if it were free not to take any steps *in the face of evidence* indicating that a medical device might not comply with the requirements laid down in Directive 93/42.[59]

Thus, while there is no general obligation to go beyond a paper review, there is a general obligation to discharge their surveillance powers with due care and diligence in EU law.[60] The notified body 'in the face of evidence' of malpractice cannot simply attest to their discretionary powers.[61] Rehearsing AG Sharpston's terms, they must be 'alert'.[62] Whether the failure to exercise this discretionary power amounts to an absence of due care or diligence is, obviously, a question of fact.

The court turns then to examine whether the directive confers a subjective right on individuals. Unlike AG Sharpston, the court does not note the horizontal nature of the dispute squarely, but reaches the same substantive conclusion. The court notes that the directive aims not only to protect health

58 Annex II section 5(1): 'The aim of surveillance is to ensure that the manufacturer duly fulfils the obligations imposed by the approved quality system' (764 para 44; emphasis added).

59 Para 45.

60 Para 46.

61 Para 45.

62 Para 47: 'the Advocate General observed in point 54 of her Opinion, that a notified body is under a duty to be alert, with the result that, in the face of evidence indicating that a medical device may not comply with the requirements laid down in Directive 93/42, that body must take all steps necessary to ensure that it fulfils its obligations under Article 16(6) of the directive, as well as those set out in paragraph 41 above'.

'*stricto sensu*', but 'also the safety of persons and that it does not concern only patients and users of medical devices but, more generally, "third parties" or "other persons"'.[63] Thus, the directive's 'actual aim' 'is to protect the end users of medical devices'.[64] By this move, the court is placing tort law firmly in the mix. The court then identifies that while the primary responsible party for ensuring compliance under the directive is the manufacturer, this does not exclude the responsibility of member states or notified bodies.[65] However, retracing *Paul*, simply because a directive imposes surveillance obligations on certain bodies does not mean it is intended to confer rights on them.[66] And following *Paul*, because there is no 'express rule granting such a right' on the face of the directive, then 'it cannot be maintained that the purpose of the directive is to govern the conditions under which the end users of medical devices may be able to obtain compensation for culpable failure by those bodies to fulfil their obligations'.[67] Following AG Sharpston's reasoning, then, the issue is remitted to national courts for determination in accordance with the doctrines of equivalence and effectiveness.[68] While the court does not confer rights on individuals, this approach is highly suggestive that national law should do so.[69] The narrow approach to *Paul* is, however, to be regretted given the overall logic of the judgment. Nevertheless, the court's solution in the end will result in hybridisation of remedies by the manner in which it remitted the case to national courts. *Schmitt*'s significance should not be downplayed; the CJEU envisages that alongside manufactures and state supervisory bodies, a distinct tort liability of intermediary bodies has a basis in EU law.[70] In other words, it is clear from the CJEU analysis in *Schmitt* that TÜV is viewed as more than simply a private contractor operating on the market for compliance services, but discharges additionally important and legally relevant public functions. TÜV performs an important *ex ante* regulatory

63 Para 50.

64 *Ibid.*

65 Para 51. See paras 52–53 for the demarcation of the responsibilities of member states and notified bodies.

66 Para 55, citing *Peter Paul and Others v Bundesrepublik Deutschland* [2004] ECR I-09425.

67 Para 56.

68 Para 59.

69 It would have been helpful here to follow Reich's approach whereby he distinguishes *Paul* in a paper on horizontal liability, see N Reich, 'Rights without Duties? Reflections of the State Liability Law in the Multilevel Governance System of the Community: Is There a Need for a More Coherent Approach in European Private Law', EUI Working Paper Law 2009/10.

70 *Compare* M Rizzi, 'The Court as Pontius Pilate: Reflecting on Missed Opportunities in the PIP Decision' (2017) 1 *European Pharmaceutical Law Review* 42–48, for an excoriating criticism of the CJEU's reasoning effectively arguing that through this approach the court washes its hands of responsibility.

compliance and, indeed, *ex post* monitoring role. It is a 'regulatory intermediary' and, thus, a powerful actor for ensuring that market access should be accompanied by a 'high level of consumer protection'. In the absence of certification, the manufacturer's product cannot be affixed with a 'CE' certification, her 'European passport', and this certification includes an obligation of continued monitoring once a product is placed on the market. Notified bodies, therefore, exercise considerable regulatory power in the current framework, which raises the question as to why for the purposes of liability as a matter of EU law it should be treated differently from public bodies.[71] The CJEU sidestepped this question by using the *Marleasing* route inferring that national courts must impose liability on private parties for a culpable excess of discretion to conform with EU law. The CJEU did consider the question of whether a right is conferred, but following the *Paul* decision noted that where surveillance obligations are imposed on parties an individual right is not necessarily conferred, especially where a directive does not expressly grant such a right.[72] Had there been an express grant of a right, the next question would be whether the right conferred was capable of application vis-à-vis a private party. By contrast with *Paul*, in which the financial regulator is an 'emanation of the state', conferring a right vis-à-vis TÜV as a regulatory intermediary based on a directive amounts to *terra incognita* in EU law.[73] AG Sharpston seems more committed to an orthodox *Dori*[74] interpretation whereby directives cannot give rise to horizontal obligations *simpliciter*.[75] In substance, both solutions result in the matter being remitted to national tort law (in Germany, possibly contract law) for a solution in accordance with the principle of national procedural autonomy.[76]

Several points should be noted. First, the legal test developed mirrors *Francovich* state liability. In that context, as we will see, the court has developed a case law based on a number of conditions of liability, most

71 Van Leeuwen (n 27), noting the centrality of this question, its relation to the question of horizontal direct effect, the circumstances in which it might apply, and its justification.

72 Paras 55–56.

73 In a free movement of goods context, at least. But see *Fra.bo SpA v Deutsche Vereinigung des Gas- und Wasserfaches eV (DVGW)* (2012) ECLI:EU:C:2012:453 regarding a 'regulatory intermediary' in an art 34 claim.

74 *Paola Faccini Dori v Recreb Srl* [1994] ECR I-3325. See also Opinion of AG Van Gerven in Case C-128/92, *Banks I* [1994] ECR I-1209.

75 Opinion of AG Sharpston, para 27. 'It follows that there can be no question of the terms of that directive being directly enforceable against TÜV Rheinland, since the relationship between that body and Ms Schmitt is "horizontal" and not "vertical".'

76 See N Reich, 'Product Liability and Beyond: An Exercise in "Gap-Filling"' (2016) 3 *European Review of Private Law* 619, regarding what national law categories might be employed.

decisively the notion of 'sufficiently serious breach', which is otherwise termed as a 'manifest and grave' breach of discretion. This implies objective culpability for exceeding a discretion – albeit it is not clearly aligned with fault or negligence.[77] Thus, while the court consistent, with its earlier jurisprudence, does not imply rights from a directive vis-à-vis horizontal situations, national courts must apply a remarkably similar test. The CJEU in *Schmitt* appears to urge national courts to create the necessary *iuris vinculum* and even goes so far as to suggest the relevant standard. Second, it is obvious that by following the orthodox approach the court ends up with a hybridisation of remedies. This is inevitable because by using the *Marleasing* approach and thereby attempting to embed the remedy into national law, divergences will emerge throughout Europe.[78] Third, neither the AG's opinion nor the court's judgment make an *explicit* connection between the Charter, for example Article 35(2), and the directive. Instead they resolve the questions referred on a formal and textual interpretative approach. However, both AG Sharpston's opinion and the CJEU judgment have more than a touch of 'hidden constitutionalisation', because in effect the result is to buttress the *ex post* remedies based on a high level of consumer protection.[79] AG Sharpston and the court are clearly attempting to reconcile policies by reference to rights, but without clarifying their overarching normative framework.[80] Taking these factors into account, it is argued that in the long run such an under-theorisation fails to provide a sufficiently clear bedrock for the expansion of rights-remedies whereas, by contrast, as has been considered in *Boston Scientific*, the court creates a more developed and sophisticated understanding of the links between legitimate consumer expectation in the context of fundamental rights, and how this should be balanced against the competing norm of market access.[81] And, of

[77] *Ie* the criteria in C-46/93 and C-48/93, *Brasserie du Pêcheur v Germany* and *R (Factortame) v SS for Transport* (No 3) [1996] ECR I-1029.

[78] See, on member state divergences in *Francovich* state liability, R Condon & B Van Leeuwen, 'Bottom Up or Rock Bottom Harmonization? *Francovich* State Liability in National Courts' (2016) 35 *Yearbook of European Law* 1.

[79] Even if they failed to take the final step, and grant a right. On 'hidden constitutionalisation', see G Comandé, 'The Fifth Freedom: Aggregating Citizenship . . . around Private Law' in HW Micklitz (ed), *The Constitutionalization of European Private Law* (Oxford: Oxford University Press, 2014), 61.

[80] The *effet utile* of EU law, as is often the case, appears to be doing the heavy work, but it is not particularly transparent in the judgment how this is the case, save insofar as both AG Sharpston and the court indicate that the remedy in national law should be effective.

[81] Indeed, Reich noted this parallel, see N Reich, 'AGM-COSMET or: Who Is Protected by Safety Regulation?' (2008) 33(1) *European Law Review* 85.

course, from our perspective this has deeper 'horizontal' constitutional dimensions as chartering the boundaries of systems' discourses about acceptable levels of risk.[82]

Yet even though the 'tactical' approach in *Schmitt* is orthodox from an EU law perspective, the 'strategic' consequences of *Schmitt* are far-reaching. The court in effect has brought notification bodies within the scope of EU (tort) law. Second, within our frame of reference it impels us to rethink *Francovich* liability from a residual doctrine that has largely applied to non-implementation cases towards a more encompassing role with respect to misapplication situations.[83] Additionally, as well as the *Francovich*-like liability of notification bodies, both AG Sharpston and the CJEU envisage state liability in *Schmitt*. And the same type of argument, presumably, can be extended by analogy to the EU itself albeit not without greater difficulty.[84] In any event, the CJEU, albeit imperfectly, is reconstructing the *sociological* network of actors within an overall normative secondary *liability* regime that complements producer liability and encompasses notification bodies, state supervisors and, *ex hypothesi*, EU institutions. This is putting in place, in essence, a Teubnerian 'cupola' of responsibility.[85] The CJEU in effect took the step that the lower German courts were unwilling to take, namely to recognise the public functions of 'private' actors looking beyond the bilateral contract in question and glimpsing instead the wider network purpose of 'private' regulation.[86] However, unlike the French lower court, this does not rest on a 'delegation' of public powers and should not, therefore, be equated with organisational (state) liability.[87] Rather it rests on outlining an incipient

[82] Arbitrating *Sinnwelten* or 'spheres of meaning' and integration – not intended to mean horizontal rights in EU law. See P Kjaer, 'The Multiplicity of Normative Orders in World Society' in *Constitutionalism in the Global Realm* (Abingdon: Routledge, 2014), 41–59, esp 45–49.

[83] T Tridimas, *The General Principles of EU Law* 2nd ed (Oxford: Oxford University Press, 2006), ch 11, noting the distinction and the traditional trepidation of the CJEU to give guidance in non-application cases.

[84] Because here the question would focus on the failure to put in place an adequate regulatory framework. There is certain case law going in this direction in ECHR law, but not in EU law.

[85] G Teubner, 'The Invisible Cupola: From Causal to Collective Attribution in Ecological Liability' in G Teubner, L Farmer & Declan Murphy (eds), *Environmental Law and Ecological Responsibility: The Concept and Practice of Ecological Self-Organization* (Chichester: Wiley, 1994), 17.

[86] Chalmers (n 6). This gives so-called SSRs their due place within 'public' regulation. The former exclusion of SSRs from liability rested on what Chalmers refers to as too narrow a definition of the state or public power.

[87] The Toulon court emphasised delegation as the key trigger for liability, whereas the CJEU does not focus on this aspect. Their approach is more aligned to the functional exercise of powers of sanction and surveillance.

and distinct regime of secondary liability for *normatively secondary* tortfeasors. While *Boston Scientific* stands for strict-to-absolute primary (organisational) liability, *Schmitt* stands for culpability as an excess of discretion, thereby aligning the liability of notified bodies with the test for *Francovich* liability and the EU itself as secondary tortfeasor. It is at this point necessary to conceptualise these changes in the wider perspective of the last two chapters.

3 *Of Bits and Pieces: The Emergence of the* Cupola *of Responsibility and Its Theoretical Consequences*

In Chapter 3, it was argued that the rise of rights in CJEU legal reasoning, as a point of 're-entry' for different 'risk perspectives', impels compensation for risk exposure *simpliciter*. This is justified in terms of threats to important constitutionally protected interests.[88] These protected interests or simply rights stand as placeholders for more complex balancing of different sub-systems' understandings of risk.[89] It is a pity that CJEU did not follow this train of thought from *Boston Scientific* to *Schmitt* in a more overt manner.[90] Nevertheless, this rights-based reordering of *prima facie* policies reflects a deeper transformation. First, in *Boston Scientific* the idea that there are certain 'goods', such as human life or the environment on which a 'price' should not be placed and, as such, the concept of reasonable risk-taking is challenged by the idea that *potential* harms should be compensated.[91] It is argued that running an unreasonable risk, meaning a utilitarian calculus often formalised based on the Learned Hand test, is insufficient from this precautionary and rights-based perspective. If risk is thought of purely in cost–benefit terms, one might consider this a cognitivisation of the law ('economisation') by the economic

88 This seems the implicit message in the United Kingdom's 'asbestos' and more especially 'loss of chance' case law even if constitutional rights are never directly invoked (for obvious reasons). See S Deakin & Z Adams, *Markesinis & Deakin's Tort Law* (Oxford: Oxford University Press, 2019), ch 5; Deakin and Adams couch the discussion against underlying policy considerations as distinct from overtly constitutional terms.

89 In a very similar vein, see HW Micklitz, 'The Legal Subject, Social Class and Identity-Based Rights' in L Azoulai, S Barbou des Places & E Pataut (eds), *Constructing the Person in EU Law: Rights, Roles, Identities* (Portland, OR: Hart, 2016), 285.

90 Reich (n 76) draws this parallel.

91 Joined Cases C-503/13 and C-504/13, *Boston Scientific Medizintechnik v AOK Sachsen-Anhalt* (2015) ECLI:EU:C:2015:148, and of course, more recently the *Urgenda* saga in the context of environmental rights: www.urgenda.nl/wp-content/uploads/ENG-Dutch-Supreme-Court-Urgenda-v-Netherlands-20-12-2019.pdf (accessed 6 July 2020). Dutch Supreme Court relying on 'open norm' of art 162, Dutch Civil Code. Decommodification but through rights-based legal reasoning, rather than the more traditional route of 'command' by prohibition; see G Calabresi, 'Torts – The Law of the Mixed Society' (1977–78) 56 *Texas Law Review* 519.

system. However, by treating risk as a question of balancing norms via rights, cognitivisation is offset by its encasing in an overall normative framework that aims to develop counter-norms to out-and-out economic reasoning in law.[92] This 'reflexive' attitude towards risk, meaning a questioning of the concept of prevention, dovetails with the problem of discourse collisions.[93] From a private law perspective, it should be noted that this effectively downplays the role of 'direct' causation. *Boston Scientific* dramatically shows how in certain circumstances the requirement to prove specific harm is vitiated. In *Schmitt* there were doubts expressed by the German lower court on the same question. The influence of charter rights-based reasoning, the normative idea of a high level of consumer protection or consumer expectations, abstracts in the end from the individual of classical tort law – it is now *mandataire*. This is to be expected, it is submitted, once the shift is to the issue of discourse collision as the reflexivity of risks. Now, as Ewald correctly notes, in what I have referred to as the 'society of organisations', risk superseded fault as the main reason for attributing responsibility. However, until relatively recently the classical notion of cause remained important. Once a duty of care was admitted, the question turned to duty and standard of care, the latter determined according to running an unreasonable risk that *caused* harm to another.[94] The idea was that it is the organisation that 'causes' harm by setting in train an unreasonably risky activity and that should be liable when the activity results in harm to an individual. While this approach, certainly, looked beyond individual conduct to enterprise activities, the necessity of demonstrating cause and actual harm remained. In other words, liability for business risks still rested on a concept of moral responsibility even if it stretches the concept of agency beyond individuals to organisations.[95] However, today the evolution of causation, indeed, reflects a change in paradigm towards imposing liability for *enhancing a risk* alone.[96] Such an approach, which makes the enhancement of a risk the 'gist

92 Not without its critics, *eg* K Barker & J Steele, 'Drifting towards Proportionate Liability: Ethics and Pragmatics' (2015) 74(1) *Cambridge Law Journal* 49.

93 This is how Ewald frames the emerging 'precautionary paradigm'. See F Ewald (S Utz trans), 'The Return of Descartes Malicious Daemon: An Outline of the Philosophy of Precaution' in T Baker & J Simon (eds), *Embracing Risk: The Changing Culture of Insurance and Responsibility* (Chicago, IL: University of Chicago Press, 2002), 273; F Ewald, 'Philosophie Politique du Principe de Précaution' in F Ewald, C Gollier & N de Sadeleer (eds), *Le Principe de Précaution* 2nd ed (Paris: Presses Universitaires de France, 2008).

94 This is a simplification; often questions such as duty, cause in law or in fact, and standard of care become entangled.

95 And, thus, simultaneous achieved collective goals see Micklitz (n 89) on the dual nature of the legal subject in 'the social'.

96 Teubner (n 85). Howsoever framed in doctrine, *eg* Dutch example in *Urgenda*.

of negligence', as distinct from causing a harm, by necessary implication greatly expands the number of potential tortfeasors[97] as well as breaking down the distinction between acts and omissions. In this respect, *Boston Scientific* is indicative whereby liability was imposed for economic losses where specific harm was not proven. This is probabilistic causation, under conditions of uncertainty, forming part of a general shift towards liability without proof of specific harm. The harm in question is, in effect, the exposure (meaning enhancement) to a risk resulting in (economic or physical) losses. If enhancing a risk can justify the imposition of liability, then it applies potentially to multiple tortfeasors.[98] A strict application of the doctrine of causation is set aside in favour of balancing the rights of claimants against respondents, where this is sufficiently pressing, with those of the claimant coming out on top. Thus, instead of focusing on the question of causation, the courts instead invoke directly a balancing of rights, which in the circumstances allows for a relaxation of causal rules. 'Duties of care' are imposed built on rights-based reasoning that pins liability as turning on questions of culpable risk enhancement. In other words, it is, controversially, the risk itself that forms the basis of liability rather than the harm caused in both cases.[99] But while pointing to a massive increase in the potential addressees of liability, these profound legal changes do not bequeath a coherent normative model of liability.

It would certainly appear from *Schmitt* that responsibility for risk is not cognitively individualised (individual or organisation) but rather a collective phenomenon. Thus, while in *Boston Scientific* legitimate consumer expectations as rights underwrite the precautionary principle,[100] the use in *Schmitt* of a 'high level of consumer protection' to ground secondary liability thus reflects a more general shift towards a risk *society*.[101] Society is emphasised because risk

97 *Ibid*, Teubner pinpoints the practical effects: 'whenever the law loosens legal requirements for causation-in law it is necessarily creating constellations of collective liability. Individual actors are made responsible for deeds which other actors may have committed. Their responsibility is no longer exclusively connected to actions of their own that caused the damage, but is mediated by the overarching cupola that covers them and other actors. They become part of one and the same risk creating community' (432).

98 This has parallels with the treatment of asbestos-related injuries in UK courts. The obvious difference was that there the injured party died of cancer in the asbestos case law. However, the approach towards causation is quite similar. Deakin & Adams (n 88), 206–16.

99 Barker & Steele (n 92).

100 Albeit, one should recall that the CJEU judgment is fact-sensitive and not a once-and-for-all trade-off. The balance between discourses of risk is contingent, and embedded in a normative discourse.

101 U Beck (M Ritter trans), *Risk Society: Towards a New Modernity* (London: Sage Publications, 1992), esp ch 1.

is viewed not in individualised terms, but rather as a collective problem requiring management. Teubner refers to this in terms of a 'cupola' or 'risk community'; that is, the collective setting in which individual acts take place:

> Individual actors are made responsible for deeds which other actors may have committed. Their responsibility is no longer exclusively connected to actions of their own that caused the damage, but is mediated by the overarching cupola that covers them and other actors. They become part of one and the same risk creating community.[102]

Teubner argues that *all* actors should be *prima facie* liable because they belong to a common risk community. Risk communities are defined by their ability to use techniques of risk management to reduce the possibility of noisome consequences for third parties. However, once a risk community is cognitively identified, *legal* responsibility between the parties to the community requires normative demarcation. While risk is collective, a normative concept of liability is individualised as distinct from individualistic. *Normatively*, certain parties are primary tortfeasors, others fulfil more peripheral but nevertheless important roles. In other words, it is rather unproblematic that producers who place a defective product on the market should be liable for the injuries such products occasion. This is illustrated by the *Boston Scientific* judgment. Far more problematic is the liability of secondary actors not primarily responsible for injury in the sense of the normative concept of risk creation.[103] These actors are denoted by Stapleton as peripheral parties to the tort. Stapleton, notably, has provided convincing arguments as to why this approach is misguided.[104] In other words, it is misleading to think of state regulators or notification bodies as *respondeat superior* to producers or

[102] Teubner (n 85), 432, discussing the context of environmental liability, but the point is more generalisable.

[103] And it is a normative concept, see Chapter 2 for a discussion of '*causation industrielle*'. Outside the sphere of vertical integration or agency (subordination) it is a highly attenuated conceptualisation to say that the state or certification bodies are vertically vicariously liable for the acts of producers. Although Gallard (n 20) raises this possibility due to their duties under the relevant directive.

[104] See J Stapleton, 'Duty of Care: Peripheral Parties and Alternative Opportunities for Deterrence' (1995) 111 *Law Quarterly Review* 301. This is how we (re)interpret her argument. While Stapleton focuses on the individualistic and moral dimension to tort law, we suggest that what her analysis points to is an attempt to make the state liable on an organisational-type conceptualisation. For a rebuttal of her argument, see I Giesen, Regulating Regulators through Liability: The Case for Applying Normal Tort Rules to Supervisors' (2006) 2(1) *Utrecht Law Review* 8–31, at 19–21 (discussing some of the commonplace arguments against the liability of peripheral parties in the context of supervisors' liability).

certification bodies on any variant of a control test.[105] It does not make economic sense and nor is it fair to search for deep pockets.[106] Yet, while in governance networks the state or notified bodies cannot be considered a secondary actor able to *control* private parties, producers or manufacturers, this is not a sufficiently strong argument contra liability *per se*.[107] In a network, no organisation is really behind the tortfeasor – it is a collective and systemic failure of regulation.

Yet nor is it sufficient to simply impose a rule of proportionate liability once a risk community is identified. It fails, likewise, to sufficiently *normatively* distinguish between primary and secondary actors, merging them into one overall quasi-organisational structure.[108] Although proportionate liability *tout court* should be avoided, this alone should not blind us to the existence of a governance 'cupola' of which the NATS is indicative or, importantly, its *normative* significance. Indeed, *Schmitt* strongly indicates that primary (producer) liability does not exclude secondary liability. *Schmitt* outlines a normative concept of secondary responsibility as distinct from favouring the more *ad hoc* proportionate share solution.[109] In short, merging private actors and public regulators into a single corporate entity, whether based on an organisational model of liability or as an *ad hoc* solution is misplaced and misleading.[110] But *Schmitt* avoids such a combination by providing for an independent tortious

[105] *Ie* the route taken by the Commercial Court of Toulon via a delegation theory. That is, regarding the certification body, the private body is exercising a delegated public function. This logic, however, is strained and will be increasingly strained the more functional differentiation is embedded.

[106] The latter could, of course, be disputed. Although unless one views the state as insurer of all activities, with all the moral hazard implications, then it is not fair to impose such a burden on a secondary actor. Fairness, in the context of tort law, would require consistency with the logic of doing and suffering, rather than an unrestrained notion of distributive fairness. What doing and suffering means depends on a broader social epistemology, see Chapter 2.

[107] Giesen (n 104), elaborates on this point.

[108] This is our understanding of the controversial *Sindell* (n 9) 'market share liability'.

[109] *Ibid.* See J Coleman, *Risks and Wrongs* (New York: Cambridge University Press, 1992), ch 19.

[110] We may end up focusing on the wrong questions; *eg*, whether the state or the private actor is the right addressee of liability, problematised by Van Leeuwen. See B Van Leeuwen, 'An Illusion of Protection and an Assumption of Responsibility: The Possibility of Swedish State Liability after *Laval*' (2012) 14 *Cambridge Yearbook of European Legal Studies* 453, focuses on the question of whether the state is *really* behind a private regulatory regime and the consequence, according to that argument, that the state should be liable where it is. However, per our argument, this is an organisational perspective on liability, looking for the 'firm' or 'state' that is ultimately responsible and it is a way of searching for a solution that is not adapted to the network context.

basis of recovery outside of a concept of delegation or control.[111] What emerges is a type of 'horizontal vicarious liability', which will be referred to as *network liability*.[112] Teubner's concept of horizontal vicarious liability is useful insofar as it emphasises that the problem is one of developing rules of attribution and imputation for secondary tortfeasors.[113] More precisely, Teubner states:

> What we find in these constellations is an asymmetric collective responsibility, a kind of 'horizontal' vicarious liability. With 'vertical' vicarious liability in hierarchical organizations, employers are made responsible for the actions of their employees. Here [in horizontal vicarious liability] the law, by imputing causation where no causal link can actually be proven, makes on [*sic*] individual vicariously responsible 'horizontally', for wrongs that have been committed by some other members of a group of actors.[114]

However, Teubner's concept of horizontal vicarious liability *describes* the shift to a new type of 'vicarious liability' without *justifying* it.[115] To justify 'horizontal vicarious liability', a clear differentiation between primary and secondary actors is required that does not rest on organisational liability. *Schmitt-Francovich* liability points the way by creating a tort independent from primary liability or organisational liability based on the *normative* notion of a 'sufficiently serious breach' as a manifest failure to exercise discretion in the face of a patent risk. On the one hand, it recognises that there is a normative difference between creating a risk and enhancing a risk; on the other hand, it imputes responsibility to secondary network actors without imposing a regime of organisational liability. In this way, the incipient and innovative features of CJEU legal reasoning can be made explicit. The primary responsible actor for harms caused by product failures is the manufacturer; states or bodies fulfilling regulatory functions in their secondary role bear a (normatively) secondary responsibility by their contribution to the harm suffered in circumstances where its culpable inaction or negligent action

[111] The one hint at a type of proportional liability approach is the unusual *pro tunc* element in AG Sharpston's Opinion, which was not accepted by the CJEU.

[112] His terminology is unfortunate because the doctrine of vicarious liability, at least in the common law, is predominantly conceptualised as a servant's tort. In other words, it is a question of imputing the acts of others to a 'superior' demarcating the boundaries of organisational responsibility.

[113] Teubner (n 85)

[114] *Ibid*, 433.

[115] See G Teubner, *Networks as Connected Contracts* (Oxford: Hart, 2011), where Teubner builds convincing arguments for internal liability within a network 'firm', but merely outlines the problem of external network liability. See also Teubner (n 10), problematising 'reticular responsibility', but without developing a concept of responsibility.

enhances a risk of harm within an overall governance purpose. To reiterate, there are *two* torts – that of the primary tortfeasor and that of the secondary tortfeasor, independent but linked because of our conceptualisation of the problem as one of belonging to a risk management network. This of course focuses attention not on causation as such, but rather on demarcating the scope of the 'the duty of care', and the relevant standard.[116] This means a greater emphasis on positive duties to regulate analogous to positive obligations on states in ECHR law.[117] Once these positive obligations are accepted in principle, the question turns to developing a control test capable of reviewing the exercise of regulatory discretion considering the conflicting rights in question. This is the role of the normative concept of 'sufficiently serious breach', which is, in essence, liability for culpable inaction in the face of a patent risk. This admixture of public law (human or fundamental rights) positive obligations and a private law normative distinction between primary and secondary actors inaugurates a regime of liability for situations in which private actors, and indeed states, fulfil secondary roles in overall governance networks. Because what emerges from these considerations is a distinctive and principled form of liability, it will be referred to as network liability.

Table 4.1 details the evolution from an organisational to a network liability paradigm and summarises the argument from Chapter 3 and to this point in this chapter as the emergence of a new model of liability: network liability.

There are three remaining tasks to complete. The first is to focus more closely on the notion of 'sufficiently serious breach' as the threshold requirement for liability within an expanded and reimagined regime of *Francovich* state liability. The second is to make the case that instead of viewing individual liability, organisational liability and, now, network liability as competing regimes of liability, they should be viewed as component parts of an overall framework of network responsibility for a society of networks. The third and final task is to query whether this model of network responsibility can and should have a wider application outside simply the field of EU law and governance.

4 *Re-imagining* Francovich *State Liability*

Thus far, it has been argued that implicit in *Schmitt* is a clear *conceptual* link to *Francovich* state liability, and both should be considered as forms of

[116] See L Hoffmann, 'Causation' (2005) 121 *Law Quarterly Review* 592, not in line with who should pay but problematising inaction if based on partial discourses.

[117] See *O'Keeffe v Ireland*, [2014] ECHR 96.

TABLE 4.1. *The evolution of liability law towards network liability*

Different dimensions: from society of organisations to society of networks	Twentieth century	Twenty-first century
Knowledge base	Organisational	Network
Balancing	Positive integration of and through groups	Negative integration (compatibility) through networks
Legal reasoning	Policies	Rights
Addressee of liability	Individual tortfeasor as part of an organisation	Individual or organisational tortfeasor as part of a network
Normative 'gist of negligence'	Risk creation	Risk contribution or enhancement
Standard of care	Strict(er) liability	'Sufficiently serious breach'/ excess of discretion or culpable inaction

normative network liability for 'secondary' actors exercising 'public' functions in overall governance networks. This rendering of what is immanent in EU law is, of course, a reconstruction quasi-*de lege feranda*. For a genuinely European law of network liability to emerge from the bits and pieces of EU law, first, this implicit link between excess of discretion in *Schmitt* and in *Francovich* in the context of secondary regulatory actors would need to be explicitly acknowledged and, secondly, state liability law would need to be elevated from its adjunct status as a residual remedy where the *Defrenne (No 2)* criteria are not made out[118] to the position of a general remedy for breaches of rights – *ubi ius, ibi remedium* – in the architecture of EU law.[119] Once a

[118] Case C-43/75, *Defrenne v Sabena (No 2)* [1976] ECR 455, *ie* sufficiently precise and unconditional.

[119] There is considerable disagreement as to whether it should be conceptualised as a residual remedy, when the direct effect criteria are not obtaining, or a more encompassing remedy alongside other remedies, *eg* for 'residual remedy' see S Prechal, 'Member State Liability and Direct Effect: What's the Difference After All?' (2006) 17 *European Business Law Review* 299–316, at 300–3. The alternative perspective is to view it as an important, general and constitutional remedy, but which has been applied selectively ('selective deference') as a tool in a judicial dialogue. See T Tridimas, 'Liability for Breach of Community Law: Growing Up and Mellowing Down?' in D Fairgrieve, M Andenas & J Bell (eds), *Tort Liability of Public Authorities in Comparative Perspective* (London: BIICL, 2002), 149–81. It may, of course, be conceptualised as a general remedy, but one which requires claimants to first exhaust other remedies. In this direction, see D Leczykiewicz, 'Private Party Liability in EU Law: In Search

regime of primary rights is established, the question turns to how 'sufficiently serious breach' as culpable inaction should be understood in the context of the exercise of 'public' or 'private' administrative discretion. The final, equalising step – that is to say, the horizontal application of rights that *Schmitt* rejects – could be surpassed, but it need not be surpassed for the regime of network liability to take shape.[120]

Turning to *Francovich* state liability, it is evident that the key issue is its application in so-called misapplication case law in which national supervisors are afforded discretionary powers within an overall legislative framework.[121] There has been a marked reluctance to deem a right conferred outside the classical *Francovich* scenario of non-implementation or outside circumstances in which the relevant public body has directly contravened a clear line of CJEU case law.[122] When it comes, in other words, to exercising regulatory or supervisory discretion, the CJEU has taken a rather restrained approach to review by cutting short legal analysis at the first stage of the test, adopting a quasi-*schutznorm* interpretation of relevant legislation. This is evidenced in *Paul*, where the court, while noting the consumer protection objectives of relevant directives, stated that the directives were enacted in the general interest and did not intend to confer individual rights.[123] However, there is no reason in principle why the court should take from *Paul* a general rule[124]

of the General Regime' (2010) 12 *Cambridge Yearbook of European Legal Studies* 257–82, esp 260–65.

[120] The much-derided step of remitting the issue to national law in *Schmitt* does offend one's sense of symmetry in terms of 'public' and 'private' network liability in EU law. But, as was argued earlier, it does not mean that national law can avoid the issue of the liability of regulatory intermediaries, because the EU law-based liability requirement in *Schmitt* must be implemented, albeit based on national procedural autonomy. This appears to be the path that the *Cour d'Appel de Paris* followed recently, see the summary of the judgment here: www.cours-appel.justice.fr/sites/default/files/2021-05/D%C3%A9cision%20Cour%20d%E2%80%99appel%20de%20Paris%20implants%20mammaires.pdf (accessed 19 June 2021), holding TÜV liable. For a recent analysis of the variety of models of recovery this gives rise to in the context of *Köbler* liability, see Z Varga, *The Effectiveness of Köbler Liability in National Courts* (Oxford: Hart, 2020).

[121] I refer to mis-application case law. Perhaps, it would be more accurate to say situations where member states may have correctly implemented a directive, but where the directive has afforded discretionary powers, which requires the reconciliation of competing rights. This is long-winded, so the term 'mis-application' is used.

[122] Eg C-118/00, *Larsy II* [2001] ECLI:EU:C:2001:368 (Failure of national administration to apply clear ECJ case law).

[123] *Paul* (n 66), para 40ff.

[124] This is one way of interpreting *Paul, ie* as standing for a broader proposition, *eg Schmitt* (n 46). A distinct interpretation rests on interpreting it as a legislative and policy exclusion of private law liability in financial services depending on the wording of the relevant directives, and broader policy considerations. T Tridimas, 'Financial Regulation and Civil Liability in

that requires a modified *schutznorm* approach to misapplication case law,[125] and there is good reason why the issue of administrative discretion should be treated as part of a sufficiently serious breach analysis.[126] It is, indeed, inconsistent with the broader approach taken for non-implementation case law, which might be illustrated by reference to *Dillenkofer* in which the court, noting the different aims of the relevant directive concerning the general interests of the completion of the market and consumer protection took a very liberal and objective approach towards the identification of individual rights.[127] The effectiveness of EU law (*effet utile*) required that the individual right should be identified. This broad approach to the identification of individual rights has been followed in a number of more recent judgments,[128] and underscores the point that *Francovich* state liability does not rest on a subjective *schutznorm* theory.[129] Indeed, it is retraceable to *Brasserie* itself, in which, as Eilsmanberger notes, the court eschewed references of legislative intent.[130] The individual is, in other words, a *mandataire*: whether a right is

European Law' in O Cherednychenko & M Andenas (eds), *Financial Regulation and Civil Liability in European Law* (Cheltenham: Elgar, 2020), 47–72, at 70–71, noting the remote possibility of private law liability due to the wording of more recent directives.

125 N Reich, 'Horizontal Liability in EC Law: Hybridization of Remedies for Compensation in Case of Breaches of EC Rights' (2007) 44 *Common Market Law Review* 705–42, at 718, has referred to the approach in *Paul* as an 'objective schutznorm theory'.

126 Within the purview of EU law, the stakes are different from national law. While in national law, the state, and delegated public bodies, may exercise unfettered 'policy' discretion, based on separation of powers and sovereigntist arguments, in the EU law context, member states do not have an unfettered discretion. They enjoy a margin of discretion as to the means by which EU law policies might be achieved, but not the autonomy to define these policies. It seems appropriate, then, in the context of a review of this 'operational' discretion, that the 'sufficiently serious breach' criterion is the place where this discretion should be reviewed.

127 *Dillenkofer v Germany* (1996) ECLI:EU:C:1996:375. There must, of course, be some degree of 'ascertainability' of rights, but this may fall short of the direct effect criteria. *Compare* Prechal (n 119). But see H Hofmann & C Warin, 'Identifying Individual Rights in EU Law', Université du Luxembourg, Law Working Paper Series Paper 2017-004, 1–22, at 9, who argue that the individual must simply be 'concerned' 'in the compliance with the [relevant] obligation' retracing the argument to C-26/62, *Van Gend en Loos v Nederlandse Administratie der Belastingen* (1963) ECLI:EU:C:1963:1.

128 *Van Gend en Loos*, 6–8. Noting C-445/06, *Danske Slagterier* (2009) ECLI:EU:C:2009:178; T-217/11, *Staelen v Ombudsman* (2017) EU:T:2015:238.

129 *Compare* S Prechal, *Directives in EU Law* 2nd ed (Oxford: Oxford University Press, 2005), 284.

130 See T Eilsmanberger, 'The Relationship between Rights and Remedies in EC Law: In Search of the Missing Link' (2004) 41 *Common Market Law Review* 1199, draws out this conclusion: 'This reasoning is remarkable and revealing [*Brasserie*]. It should be remembered that in the case law referred to by the Court, the capacity of the cited two internal market provisions to create individual rights was derived solely from their sufficiently clear, precise and unconditional wording, and their resulting aptitude to be directly applied. The conclusion that rights created in this manner also satisfy the condition that the rule must be "intended" to

conferred is not *primarily* a question of whether the individual belongs to a protected class, but whether the effectiveness of EU law requires the grant of an individual right.[131] The individual is, perforce, functionally 'subjectifed' to serve the ends of EU law,[132] which may include the protection of public goods that extend beyond simply the completion of the internal market *qua* economic integration.[133] It is but a small step from the functional subjectification of the individual in EU law to the charter of fundamental rights, which elevates a number of 'non-relational' principles, among which are high levels of health, consumer and environmental protections.[134] These are non-justiciable so long as implementing measures have not been taken, but if taken, these principles can serve as aids to interpretation of relevant directives, *including* whether they confer individual rights: if a directive implements a charter principle, such as that of a high level of consumer protection, then the right to an effective remedy should influence the question as to whether a right has been conferred. Combining the effectiveness of EU law with the emphasis on the right to effective judicial protection in Article 47 of the charter, a virtuous circle can be created that buttresses and enhances

confer rights does, in my view, prove beyond doubt that the rights protected under the State liability doctrine are not to be determined by the concrete legislative purpose or protective scope (*Schutzzweck*) of the Community rule in question. The legislative intent to safeguard the interests of the injured party or to prevent the damage at issue from occurring is therefore neither a legal foundation of this type of liability nor a means to somehow restrict the scope of this remedy. This omission is surprising, as the protective scope of the infringed provision is taken into account in determining Community liability under Article 288 EC. The disregard of the protective scope of the injured provision also explains why no directions are given to determine legislative intent. It may also explain why the Court did not deem it necessary to specify that the rule in question conferred a right to the claimant in question but contented itself with concluding that it conferred rights to individuals in general' (1225–26).

[131] Prechal (n 129) succinctly describes this perspective without endorsing it: 'Where the ECJ says that rights are created for the benefit of the individual, it is not so much concerned with the protection of the interests of the individual as such, but rather uses or mobilizes the individuals for the enforcement of Community law' (180).

[132] M Rüffert, 'Rights and Remedies in European Community Law: A Comparative View' (1997) 34 *Common Market Law Review* 307.

[133] See C Warin, 'Individual Rights and Collective Interests in EU law: Three Approaches to a Still Volatile Relationship' (2019) 56 *Common Market Law Review* 463–88 (on the tension between functional subjectificaiton and the protection of collective interests). The objection as to *actio popularis* in AG-Hackl's Opinion in *Paul* does not make a good deal of sense in the context of the watchdog function given to individuals within the architecture of EU law extending back to *Van Gend en Loos*.

[134] These are Lock's terms. Lock adopts a Hohfeldian lens when analysing the difference between charter rights and principles. See T Lock, 'Rights and Principles in the EU Charter of Fundamental Rights' (2019) 56 *Common Market Law Review* 1201–26: 'the difference between rights and principles lies in the non-relational and non-intersubjective nature of the latter' (1203).

'individual' rights in EU law. In the terms that have been used in the preceding chapters, and perhaps very explicitly in EU law, given its peculiar features, these rights can and should be understood not only in their personalist dimension, but in their wider societal dimension as counterweights to out-and-out economic semantics. More explicitly, the charter as an aid to interpretation can empower the court to be more explicit that what is at issue is a balance of economic and fundamental rights in the name of effective judicial protection.[135] Therefore, this objective understanding of conferral of a right is, in the end, better equipped to mediate conflicting rationalities through the medium of rights.[136] In the language of the common law, the 'duty of care' should, on an appropriate reading of *Francovich*, be easily conferred, and what should take place is a merits-based assessment of whether a breach has occurred.

The sufficiently serious breach requirement is, then, the most important criterion because it provides a structural framework of analysis for problematising culpable inaction or inadequate action of normatively secondary actors in governance networks. The standard of sufficiently serious breach cannot be subjective or objective fault;[137] nor is it equivalent to intentional injury or gross negligence.[138] In certain circumstances, a mere breach of relevant law will constitute a sufficiently serious breach; in other circumstances, the standard approaches that of gross negligence.[139] The key to understanding the standard relates to the extent of discretion afforded to member states. Where the member state has a high degree of discretion as to the means through which it protects a given right, the standard approaches *faute lourde* or gross negligence. Where the state has a significantly reduced or no discretion (that is, an obligation of result), the standard approaches stricter liability.[140] In both cases, the fundamental question underlying the standard is the degree of culpability

135 Comandé (n 79) notes these patterns in citizenship case law: 'We can thereby note the Court's escalating tendency to relate rules and principles to the text of the Charter of the Fundamental Rights and additionally, its will to clearly express that when legislation makes explicit reference to the rights in the Charter, the validity of that legislation "must be assessed in the light of those provisions"'.

136 The court should be careful then not to overstate 'effective judicial protection' as concerned with *individual* rights. The precise relationship between effectiveness and rights protection is complex. A good attempt at giving this question analytical precision is Comandé (n 79). Eilsmanberger (n 130) notes a tension that runs through EU law in terms of the use of effectiveness.

137 *Brasserie* (n 77), paras 75–80.

138 *Ibid.*

139 Although mere breach is a sufficiently serious breach, the view in case law is not consistent.

140 It is not automatically 'sufficiently serious', see *Dillenkofer* (n 127).

involved, taking account of the discretion afforded. This is reflected in the relevant factors pronounced by the court, which:

> *include* the clarity and precision of the rule breached, the measure of discretion left by that rule to the national or Community authorities, whether the infringement and the damage caused was intentional or involuntary, whether any error of law was excusable or inexcusable, the fact that the position taken by a Community institution may have contributed towards the omission, and the adoption or retention of national measures or practices contrary to Community law.[141]

These factors are non-exhaustive, which further indicates that the standard is meant as a standard of review of objective culpability 'in the round'. Importantly, in the context of the supervisory discretion exercised by member states and public law bodies when applying EU law,[142] it is clear that so-called factual breaches fall within the scope of EU law. As Tison has argued, *Schmidberger* illustrates this point whereby the court examined the facts of the case, comparing them to *Commission v France* in detail to determine whether there was a breach of the treaty provisions on free movement of goods.[143] In the premises, the court found that the measures taken by Austria were legitimately justified. However, had they not been justified, this would be a matter that would have gone to the sufficiently serious nature of the breach and the court is willing to go quite far on occasion to examine its existence in factual terms.[144] The relevant question of discretion, then, would not be sovereign or unfettered public interest discretion, but so-called operational discretion when applying these policies. Giving a wider berth to the conferral of a right, such as consumer or health protection, the purported operational breaches would be reviewed in the light of the sufficiently serious breach criterion. In circumstances in which certain policies are advanced at the expense of others, as distinct from balanced – in other words, where certain policies are disregarded entirely – then a breach could be classified as sufficiently serious or manifest. Thus, the state could be held liable for culpable inaction in the face of a pressing right, which requires protection.

141 *Brasserie* (n 77), para 56 (emphasis added).

142 Case C-424/97, *Haim v Kassenzahnärztliche Vereinigung Nordrhein* (2000) ECLI:EU:C:2000:357, paras 27–28.

143 C-112/00, *Schmidberger v Republik Österreich* (2003) ECLI:EU:C:2003:333M. See Tison, 'Do not Attack the Watchdog! Banking Supervisor's Liability after Peter Paul', Financial Law Institute Working Paper Series 2005-02, 5, 20.

144 Eg Case C-5/94, *The Queen v Ministry of Agriculture, Fisheries and Food, ex parte: Hedley Lomas (Ireland) Ltd* (1996) ECR I-2553. See, generally, Tridimas (n 83), 513.

This is not, of course, a straightforward exercise because the balancing of rights against policies or, for example, the balancing of the rights of one group against the rights of others gives significant scope for legitimate choices. But the state has a significant margin of operational discretion, and while some of the *Brasserie* factors may be of limited usefulness, ultimately the question is one of culpability for gravely or manifestly exceeding the scope of their discretionary powers.[145] The standard amounts, in the context of non-application, to one of gross negligence or *faute lourde*, which distinguishes state liability from negligence or inadvertence, but falls short of misfeasance.[146] Therefore, a normative distinction is made between the liability of primary tortfeasors – which, depending on the context, is ordinary negligence or stricter liability – and the position of public gatekeepers in governance networks.[147] However, the important point is that the mere fact that rights require balancing is no good reason to exclude potential liability *tout court*. Applied in the context of administrative or operational discretion, then, *Francovich* state liability can form the basis of a proceduralised review of operational discretion where competing interests are in issue.[148] Ultimately, the degree of culpable risk enhancement attributable to secondary actors is put in issue against a backdrop of rights (or discourse) collisions. There is, to be sure, no clear way to determine these balances except by means of process-oriented case law, which scrutinises the (non-)exercise of discretion. The conceptual link to the liability of 'private' gatekeepers is clear insofar as they

145 C Harlow, 'Francovich and the Problem of the Disobedient State' (1996) 2 *European Law Journal* 199. Harlow captures this in terms of sanctioning the state, as opposed to vindicating the claimant's right to compensation. This tension between rights and obligations should be considered productively rather than as a structural weakness if one "re-imagines" the role of state liability here as concerned with the normative imputability of acts to secondary actors, and takes the view that individual rights in EU law are not primarily about vindicating corrective justice, but rather have a societal dimension.

146 See *Brasserie* (n 77), paras 75–80. Unless misfeasance is redefined or watered down. On the difference between misfeasance as subjective recklessness and gross negligence, see D Nolan, 'Varying the Standard of Care in Negligence' (2013) 72 *Cambridge Law Journal* 651.

147 Compare Giesen (n 104), 28–29, who argues for ordinary negligence. There is some merit to the argument that the standard of the reasonably prudent supervisor should hold good. However, the problem with this approach is it does not adequately take account of the *normatively* peripheral position of the 'secondary' actor.

148 As a type of justification through rationalisation, see F De Witte, 'Emancipation through Law' in Azoulai, Barbou de Places & Pataut (n 89), 15; C Joerges, 'The Europeanisation of Private Law as a Rationalization Process and as a Contest of Disciplines – An Analysis of the Directive on Unfair Terms in Consumer Contracts' (1995) 3 *European Review of Private Law* 175, at 180, on the importance of EU law for submitting national law, and administrative discretion, to a process of rationalisation, with sufficient serious breach, in our context, 'expos[ing] national legal systems to the constraints of explanation and justification' (180).

are also, per *Schmitt*, held liable for their culpable inaction in the face of a real and patent risk of harm.[149] Moreover, as the state must in EU law, their operational breaches are at issue, but unlike the state they do not necessarily have to weigh a plurality of interests.[150] Therefore, what amounts to a sufficiently serious breach may be weighted differently. Nonetheless, the fact that the threshold is culpable inaction in the face of a real and patent risk, and that they are being held liable, in effect, for disregarding an important right, and thereby enhancing a risk, suggests that the sufficiently serious breach criterion is appropriate in both cases.

The final step of the *Francovich* test is to demonstrate a (direct) causal link between the alleged breach of rights and the damage.[151] This has been the most underdeveloped aspect of the *Francovich* case law, with significant leeway given to member state courts to determine its contours. While it is certainly true that one can infer a liberal approach to causation from certain judgments such as *Francovich*[152] and *Cosmet*,[153] the leading cases which give guidance as to the issue of causation are *Brinkmann* and *Rechberger*, which do not deal directly with the issue of the liability of the state *qua* peripheral party. *Brinkmann* concerned the fact that the action of an administrative branch of government could have been said to have negated the breach of law by the legislature while *Rechberger* related to the non-implementation of a directive. In the latter respect, however, the CJEU held that the conduct of a private party could not negate state liability. It is, in other words, no excuse to say that the primary tortfeasor causes the tort where the state owes a duty to an individual and it is breached. However, the *Rechberger* case involved an *obligation de résultat*,[154] whereas a loss resulting from culpable inaction when exercising an operational discretion concerns an *obligation de moyens*. It is,

149 Recall that TÜV was not required to go fishing for defective products, but its duty was enhanced in the light of public knowledge.

150 Although, in certain cases, they may have to decide on the appropriate steps required when safeguarding the rights of individuals weighing the importance of individual rights protection against the context of their mandate both in public law and in contract.

151 *Brasserie* (n 77), and subsequent judgments, refer to 'direct' causal link. *Francovich* did not.

152 Although Mr Francovich ultimately lost his case on other grounds, see C-479/93, *Francovich v Italian Republic* (1995) ECLI:EU:C:1995:372.

153 Also Case C-265/95, *Commission v France* [1997] ECR I-6959 and *Schmidberger* (n 143) on factual breaches also contemplates, implicitly, a relaxed approach to causation where a private party is the primary tortfeasor.

154 C-140/97, *Rechberger v Republik Österreich* (1999) ECLI:EU:C:1999:306, para 74: 'Next, it should be pointed out that Article 7 of the Directive imposes an obligation of result, namely to guarantee package travellers the refund of money paid over and their repatriation in the event of the travel organiser's bankruptcy. Such a guarantee is specifically aimed at arming consumers against the consequences of the bankruptcy, whatever the causes of it may be.'

therefore, not feasible to extrapolate a more general rule on causation that distinguishes between state or public authorities' duties *per se* and private misconduct. The incomplete guidance given at EU level on causation encourages states then to fall back on their variegated domestic regimes of causation. Thus, as Anagnostaras states, writing in 2002 but still largely accurate: 'As the law stands at the moment, the community harmonisation that has been attained on the culpability standard is undermined by the application of the diverse national rules on matters of causation.'[155]

This is an unsatisfactory state of affairs *de lege lata* because it saps the state liability doctrine of its vigour. But *de lege ferenda*, if *Francovich* state liability is to be reimagined as a regime of gatekeepers' liability it is even more troublesome because at a conceptual level what is gained through a more expansive approach to rights, and a more vigorous approach to review, is undermined by causal orthodoxy. Anagnostaras argues, in particular, that the law is less than clear with regard to situations in which the tort in question is that of a private party, the relevant failure of the state being a failure to take positive steps to uphold treaty rights. Of course, there is some case law which indicates that in circumstances in which private actions create obstacles to the free movement of goods, the state may be held liable.[156] But beyond that context, guidance in EU law is scanty. This does not bode well for situations such as *Schmitt* in which the state and the notification body are peripheral parties and, as such, the lack of clarity on causation may result in the ground being used to circumvent the effectiveness and effective judicial protection rationale of the positive obligations conferred on the state. As Anagnostaras states clearly:

> The problem ... is that the original source of the damage continues to be the illegal activity of private parties. It is not thus at all clear whether the breach committed by the domestic authorities can be considered direct enough to establish the necessary causal link for the payment of compensation from the national treasury.[157]

In other words, more precision is required as to what level of 'directness' is needed and with regard to how it relates to the question of effective protection of individual rights. However, given the fact that what *Francovich* creates is, in effect, positive state duties equating a 'direct' causal link with a proximate cause (remoteness) requirement appears inapt, at least with regard to how

[155] G Anagnostaras, 'Not as Unproblematic as You Might Think: The Establishment of Causation in Governmental Liability Actions' (2002) *European Law Review* 663, 676.

[156] *Commission v France* (n 153).

[157] Anagnostaras (n 155), 669.

these concepts are traditionally understood in national law. The use of the word 'direct' causation, invoking an idea of immediacy, is apt to confuse national courts on this point.[158] The ECHR avoids the problem squarely by treating it as in the scope of positive state obligations. A *fortiori*, it cannot be that rights conferred on individuals, judged to be a sufficiently serious breach of EU law, can then be defeated by a restrictive approach to causation. This would restrict the *ubi ius, ibi remedium* principle by narrowing the rules of attribution. However, outside the narrow field of obligations of result, as I have argued, there is no clear case law on causation that demonstrates clearly that the state is to be held liable notwithstanding the misconduct of third parties. This is unfortunate because member state courts may fail to perceive the cupola of responsibility, its role in the achievement of effective rights protection in EU law, and continue to treat state liability according to an organisational model of liability looking for positive conduct or control.

The argument, *a contrario*, can be stated briefly. If a *prima facie* reallocation of rights and duties is made out, and the breach is considered sufficiently serious – a high threshold no doubt – then the question of causation ought to be developed on the basis of statistical increase of a risk rather than causation of specific harm. Did the acts or inactions of the state materially increase or contribute to the risk of harm to the plaintiff's rights such that it amounts to increased likelihood of harm. Alternatively, this can be dealt with as a sufficiently serious breach, which would be less radical, but would require some doctrinal adjustments. For example, once a sufficiently serious breach is made out, then there should be a rebuttable presumption of causation. These (casuistic) devices weigh in favour of the effectiveness of rights protection, the underlying logic. At the very least, failure to pronounce on the question of causation leaves matters vague and uncertain.[159]

Otherwise, it is difficult to see how the state might be held responsible in misapplication cases, where a factual error contributed to damage to the claimant. It is all too easy for national courts to manipulate this condition of liability to deny recovery on the basis that the act of the primary tortfeasor was a break in the chain of causation. The effectiveness of rights protection, considered paramount, would be comprised otherwise. This reasoning is somewhat similar to the approach taken by the ECHR in its positive

[158] *Ibid*. Anagnostaras refers to direct causation and proximity interchangeably. This is understandable, but confusing.

[159] Anagnostaras (n 155): 'it could be submitted that the state of legal uncertainty created by the absence of clear case law with regard to the causality factor may be possibly interpreted as a violation of the twin principles of effectiveness and effective judicial protection that the doctrine of governmental liability is based upon' (676).

obligations case law. A recent judgment that goes in this direction is *O'Keeffe v Ireland*. In that case, it was held that the seriousness of the right in question, the lack of state action (here, there was an inadequate protective framework for the individual's right) meant that there was a failure of a positive obligation. It did not matter that in Ireland, primary responsibility for education lay in the hands of the Catholic Church or that the teacher in question, the perpetrator, was not employed by the state and had committed a criminal act. What mattered was that the state had positive obligations to protect certain rights and, in the circumstances, it failed to give adequate priority to the right in question through its legislative framework. To say that inadequate steps were taken given the gravity of the risk is simply another way to say that inaction enhanced, or significantly contributed to, a risk. One might quibble as to the scope of these positive obligations, yet this is a question for sufficiently serious breach rather than causation. Rules regarding quantum can still reflect the secondary position of the tortfeasor, although whether proportionate liability or rules concerning joint and several liability are preferred is a controversy better solved at national level subject to the provisos of effectiveness and equivalence. Given the difficulties in this area in English asbestos case law, this should be given a wide deference.

Let's take stock. In this section, it has been argued that a clear conceptual link can be drawn between the liability of private gatekeepers and *Francovich* state liability, namely that both forms of liability are liability for peripheral parties performing public functions which fail to exercise discretion when important rights are in issue. In both cases, these can be characterised as sufficiently serious breaches where patent risks are disregarded or insufficiently taken into consideration. This failure to exercise discretion may lead to the enhancement of a risk of harm. But peripheral parties' enhancement of a risk of harm is not a normative concept. However, the notion of a sufficiently serious breach may, in the context of breach of discretion, be considered a European iteration of *faute lourde*, which also normatively distinguishes between the standard of care of primary and secondary actors. This conceptual link is, however, clouded by the fact that state liability law after a thunderous *entrée* has not been followed through to its logical conclusion.[160] I have provided a number of conceptual arguments, which would render the remedy serviceable to take on a role of liability of gatekeepers, which focus on upgrading its place in EU law by a way of a more liberal approach to rights conferral in the context of misapplication cases, a clearer interpretation of

160 What Tridimas (n 124) referred to recently as 'an outburst of remedial expediency' (50).

sufficiently serious breach and a downgrading of the causation requirement. Given that there is a clear conceptual link to the test in *Schmitt* for secondary private gatekeepers, there is no conceptual reason as to why the 'sufficiently serious breach' criterion could not be rendered serviceable there as a broader test for evaluating the acts or omissions of secondary tortfeasors. Of course, dogmatically and for now at least, the CJEU has not seen fit to make the parallel. While it would be desirable, in my view, to take this step, it is not conceptually necessary provided the duty to be alert and of diligence is interpreted in a similar way to a reconstituted sufficiently serious breach test.[161] Gatekeepers' liability, whether of formally public or private actors, when understood within an overall cupola of responsibility should be understood as a form of network liability.

5 *The Three-Track Liability Schemata: From Network Liability to Network Responsibility*

The argument throughout this book is that by coevolution with its knowledge base, tort law has developed different models of responsibility which cut across the public/private divide. While these models of responsibility can be reconstructed diachronically, first individualistic, then organisational, now network, from a conceptual perspective the models of responsibility once they have emerged in legal doctrine and practice should not be understood as historical artefacts.[162] Instead, they coexist as differentiated legal programmes, which courts can utilise among the variety of different tools at their disposal to frame and resolve particular and concrete problems.[163] New programmes emerge at

[161] There is a dogmatic route, Case C-171/11 *Fra.bo Spa v Deutsche Vereinigung des Gas- und Wasserfaches*, judgment of 31 December 2012, certification bodies with the scope of free movement of goods, although the analogy is inexact, read in conjunction with the functional definition of public power in *Foster* and following judgments treating certification bodies *as if* the state for the purposes of EU law. See, C-188/89, *Foster v British Gas plc* (1990) ECLI:EU:C:1990:313. See also HW Micklitz & R Van Gestel, 'European Integration through Standardization: How Judicial Review Is Breaking Down the Club House of Private Standardization Bodies' (2013) 50 *Common Market Law Review* 145, 146.

[162] I agree with G Brüggemeier, 'The Civilian Law of Delict: A Comparative and Historical Analysis' (2020) 7(4) *European Journal of Comparative Law* 339–83, who divides models of liability historically, but more importantly by reference to the problems that they attempt to solve, within a given social epistemology, and gives a prominent position to the organisation in his models of liability.

[163] As explained earlier, in Chapters 1 and 2, how the law 'perceives' a 'problem' is based on a complex co-evolution between knowledge base and legal programmes. It has no privileged access to 'reality', but must reconstruct 'reality' internally, which also impacts on how it characterises its problems. This is not a tort-specific issue, but characteristic of the legal system,

points of crisis both in terms of the social epistemology of the legal system (the problem of risk, then uncertainty against a background of diverse risk definitions)[164] and where the existing models of responsibility do not proffer (internally) normatively coherent and justifiable reasons to impose or restrict responsibility.[165] This places an evolutionary pressure on the legal system: either it develops new and normatively convincing models of responsibility or it loses its societal salience or relevance.[166] In this respect, it has been argued that EU law's fragmentary liability regime on normative (secondary) actors within overall governance networks provides the bedrock for a normatively convincing regime of responsibility of 'network liability' for actors beyond the state by distinguishing between the standard of care owed by these normatively peripheral actors fulfilling their 'network governance purpose', and the standard of care owed by primary tortfeasors within a governance

eg how criminal law channels personal culpability through rules of admissible evidence, and substantive criteria of criminal liability. This is how it works in practice, so to speak, where courts 'mediate' between models of responsibility. See *Barclays Bank v Various Claimants* [2020] UKSC 13 in which the court effectively set itself the task of determining the boundaries of the characteristic risks of the eponymous bank in a vicarious liability action. There, the question related to whether a doctor was an independent contractor or fell into the category 'akin to employment', which allows for recovery against firms outside the formal, legal boundaries of the firm. On the broader point regarding characteristic risks, and the difficulty encountered in determining their boundary, see G Keating, 'Products Liability As Enterprise Liability', USC Gould Legal Studies Research Papers Series No 16-38, 1–44, esp 7–9.

164 A 'rupture' or disruption. See KH Ladeur, 'The Evolution of General Administrative Law and the Emergence of Postmodern Administrative Law', Osgoode CLPE Research Paper 16/2011, 1–55, at 21: 'The exchange process between the law and the structured practical networks which generate and distribute societal experience is in constant flux. A distinction has to be made between the continuous flow of information which emerges from the permanent variation within societal knowledge basis, and the momentary suspension of normality by the rise of new factual paradigms which induce a kind of "break of symmetry" in the inter-relationship between technical normal knowledge and the feedback loops which have to be designed within the legal network of networks.'

165 See Chapter 2, discussing the problem of remote or indirect injury and the organisation. For a discussion, placing the problem in the context of 'the personal, spatial and temporal protective scope of liability' in organisational activity, see Brüggemeier (n 162), 356. In my terms, this should be considered as an evolution of legal doctrine that aims to solve the problem of organisational activity where the preceding model of liability based on individual, direct conduct could not adequately process the problems of mass accidents in an industrial society.

166 Of course, the law may muddle along applying pre-existing categories to new problems. But there is a 'cost' to path-dependent solutions, namely in terms of normative coherence and 'responsiveness'. The other side of over-socialisation of law is formalism, which *in extremis* can be characterised as verging on 'social self-closure', leading to problems of 'coordination with the system's environment'. In other words, the law's performance and coordinative role in systems theory terms is threatened. See G Teubner, 'After Legal Instrumentalism: Strategic Models of Post-Regulatory Law' in G Teubner (ed), *Dilemmas of Law in the Welfare State* (New York: De Gruyter, 1986), 299–321, at 309.

network, which goes beyond the public/private divide. A number of arguments have been made as to how the law *de lege lata* could be upgraded: first by explicitly linking the liability of 'private' peripheral parties to 'public' peripheral parties through the concept of a 'sufficiently serious breach' of discretion where an important 'right'[167] is at issue; secondly by elevating the position of state liability from the position of a residual regime to that of a general remedy in EU law. But the important point is not so much the contours of EU law as such, but the broader point that in effect the court is developing a test of liability for risk enhancement in circumstances in which the 'secondary' actor is a part of a network governance regime, but not the primary tortfeasor, which equates with a *faute lourde* standard.

The more conceptual point concerns how these models of responsibility fit together. Running through this chapter is the nagging sense that neither individual responsibility nor organisational responsibility seemed adequate; nor did normatively persuasive *comprehensive* models of liability for circumstances in which a peripheral party that neither creates a risk nor by whose individual conduct a harm occurs should be held legally responsible when a third party's rights are infringed.[168] The starting point here is to recognise a cupola of responsibility as legally significant in 'private' law. Where parties, whether primary tortfeasors (individuals or organisations) or secondary actors, are engaged in an overall network governance, then, the model of liability deployed should correspond to their position within the responsibility network.[169] This means, in effect, that individual responsibility and organisational

[167] In its personalist and societal sense. See Chapter 3.

[168] But here understood in terms of notions of protective scope, and also, more importantly, as I have argued, in terms of the societal dimension to liability. See Chapter 3.

[169] Network is not a legal concept, but it does not follow that the law cannot develop its *own* concept of network. All contracts are relational in the sociological sense, but not all relations (and contextual factors or 'implicit dimensions to contract' if one prefers) will result in a contract being deemed a 'relational contracts' in a legally significant way. This is because the law, internally, reconstructs its environment. For this reason, one might be sceptical of attempts to track commercial expectations, if this is an empirical thesis or, in a more sophisticated sense, an attempt to reconstruct 'immanent business norms' or an internal point of view of business persons on an input model. On this very point, in the context of relational contracts, see R Brownsword, 'After Investors: Interpretation, Expectation and the Implicit Dimension of the "New Contextualism' in D Campbell et al (eds), *Implicit Dimensions of Contract: Discrete, Relational, and Network Contracts* (Portland, OR: Hart, 2003), 103. Brownsword's argument is that the law cannot avoid taking a stand based on a (critical) morality. I disagree, and instead suggest that the differentiated morality should be internal to the law. See also, in this respect, judgments such as *Bhasin v Hrynew* (2014) SCC 71, which locate good faith as an organising principle of contract law. The most the law's cognitive 'awareness' of the presence of relations, beyond the adversarial model of classical contract law, can do, is exert pressure on contract law to internally differentiate. See, more broadly, G

responsibility are in the context of network governance downgraded from comprehensive regimes to the position of liability rules alongside network liability within a more encompassing and comprehensive regime or paradigm of network responsibility.[170] For individual conduct the classical rules of negligence apply, including its distinction between acts and omissions (*culpa levis*).[171] For organisational liability, the standard of care is stricter and liability is imposed for creating a risk.[172] For network liability, as has been argued, should be based on a heightened standard of care where the defendant has exceeded a discretion and thereby in a normatively significant way enhances a risk (*culpa lata*) by failing to advance the network purpose.[173] The important point is that these calibrated approaches are understood within an overall and comprehensive regime of network responsibility. This should be the *normative* frame of reference through which multi-actor regulatory (systemic) failures are approached within the law. In other words, governance failures by individuals, organisations and network gatekeepers are understood in network governance terms where there are multiple actors – public and private – all with specific responsibilities that contribute to an overall governance regime whether these actors are formally designated as public or private actors. This is meant to be a legally internal, normatively justifiable division of responsibility, which guards against ad hockery (for example, attempting to equate single organisations with the network without clear *legal* justification), and, at the same time, recognises the important strategic role played by gatekeepers in the definition and monitoring of acceptable risks with governance networks. These governance networks are the sites of meaning transfer between different social subsystems, and through the constitutionalisation of private law courts retain, and should retain, an important role in irritating different sub-systems of society by normatively regulating networks.[174] This reconceptualisation is contained in

Teubner, 'How the Law Thinks: Toward a Constructivist Epistemology of Law' (1989) 23(5) *Law & Society Review* 727–58.

170 Kuhn as a model that gives coherence to an interpretative practice.

171 This is largely responsibility for direct conduct, but rules of remoteness of course also apply.

172 This is largely recovery for organisational fault, or 'vertical vicarious liability' in Teubner's (n 85) terms. How strict it should be will depend on how important the right in issue is considered, but in terms of protective scope terms, and also based on risk discourse adjudication in the light of a discourse of constitutionalised rights.

173 *Ie Schmitt/Francovich* liability on our understanding.

174 See G Teubner, 'Legal Irritants: Good Faith in British Law or How Unifying Law Ends Up in New Differences' (1998) 61 *Modern Law Review* 11. Teubner focused on the effects of introducing an alien concept, namely good faith, into English law, and how it might provoke ('irritate') English legal culture. His message was clear – it will not result in an embrace of continental grand principles, but rather would be filtered through English law's own

TABLE 4.2. *The new model of societal responsibility*

Normative model: network responsibility				
Models of liability: twenty-first century	The trigger of liability	The conception of liability	Standard of care	Case illustration
Individual liability	Personal conduct: direct injury	Personalist/ individualistic	Fault	*AGM.Cosmet* (?)
Organisational liability	Risk creation: indirect injury	'Vertical vicarious liability'	Stricter liability	*Boston Scientific/ Sanofi*
Network liability (systemic risks)	Risk enhancement: indirect injury	'Horizontal vicarious liability'	Variable standard: sufficiently serious breach	*Schmitt/ Francovich*

Table 4.2, which is meant to represent an encompassing three-track liability model for network governance within EU law. The important point is that whether the liability rule is one of individual liability, organisational liability or network liability, the paradigmatic framing is in terms of network responsibility. It is paradigmatic because it contextualises models of liability within an overall frame of reference, which is the governance network. These different modalities of liability are, in other words, supplemental rather than rivalrous.

The crisis of legal models of responsibility should not, in other words, be met with a retreat of the legal system from the regulation of risks embodying a deferential attitude to 'public' schemes of regulation, which have emerged from hybrid regimes of network governance.[175] Tort law is an important legal institution because it is through tort disputes over the day-to-day operation of

conceptual and legal cultural notions. I think he was proved right. See *Yam Seng v ITC* [2013] 1 CLC 662 (implied terms). While I'm discussing intersystemic communication I adopt the term 'irritation' because it captures how the law, through developing rights-based liability rules to regulate networks, will inevitably send a signal to networks – the modern sites of meaning transfer – about how underrepresented systems might better be protected against the market leader, the economic system. This is meant, in other words, to provoke or irritate the internal dynamics of networks. Gatekeeper liability, or network liability, is meant to be a distinctive contribution that captures the missing legal link in network governance.

175 It is a bit of a stretch to refer to these schemes as public, in a traditional sense, since they cross the public/private divide by equipping private actors with law-making and enforcement capabilities beyond the state.

complex governance regimes that these regimes 'touch down', impacting directly on human and environmental interests. Therefore, tort law should undergo an *explicit* tertiary remodelling, which addresses the problems of discourse domination through a greater 'self-awareness' of the importance of legal rights[176] and can provide normatively convincing reasons for new forms of secondary liability. It has been argued that the bits and pieces of such a model of responsibility are implicit in EU law, but that they need to be pieced together. One could go further, of course, and argue that EU law should develop principles of individual liability alongside organisational liability, and its emergent concept of network liability.[177] But for present purposes the details of the EU liability regime are not critical; rather, what's crucial is that the model of network responsibility is emerging, and can be used productively as a frame of reference for network governance regimes. It is, therefore, relevant to turn now to contexts beyond EU liability law to test the utility of the ideal.

C BEYOND A RECONSTRUCTION OF EU 'STATE LIABILITY'? A MODEL FOR THE VALUE CHAIN?

1 *Between Individual and Organisational Liability in Tort*

There is a growing debate as to the appropriate regime of private law liability that should accompany the public law of value chains.[178] Within that debate, the main *problématique* concerns how liability of actors in supply chains should be conceptualised. Pursuant to soft law 'obligations',[179] so-called lead firms undertake through codes of conduct to monitor, build capacity and enforce human and environmental rights obligations in their value chains, which cuts across the public/private divide, and has been described as a 'system of self-contained autonomous systems of global law',[180] which relegates

[176] See Chapter 3.

[177] See C Sieburgh, 'The Attribution of Acts: Towards a Principled Assessment under EU and National Private Law' (2016) 3 *European Review of Private Law* 645.

[178] Eg V Ulfbeck et al, *Law and Responsible Supply Chain Management: Contract and Tort Interplay and Overlap* (Abingdon: Routledge, 2019), and special issue 2020(1) of the *European Review of Contract Law*.

[179] Eg UN Guiding Principles on Business and Human Rights; OECD Guidelines for Multinational Enterprises; ILO Tripartite Declaration of Principles Concerning Multinational Enterprises and Social Policy.

[180] LC Backer, 'Economic Globalization and the Rise of Efficient Systems of Global Private Lawmaking: Wal-Mart as Global Legislator' (2007) 39(4) *Connecticut Law Review* 1–46, at 4.

the state to the position of secondary actor.[181] It falls to national courts to interpret these commitments, and their legal characterisation and bindingness, when they 'touch down'[182] via various procedural gateways.[183] To date, national courts have channelled these disputes through the classical, individualistic or interpersonal model of responsibility in private law.

In the common law, where the case law on supply chains has witnessed significant recent developments,[184] it reveals an attempt to mediate between contract and tort law,[185] and between models of individual responsibility and organisational responsibility. From a contract law perspective, following an individualistic model of responsibility, the main problem concerns the enforceability of codes of conduct by third parties.[186] While the common law doctrinal analysis may be framed in several ways, most notably as an exception to the privity rule, or in terms of a unilateral contract, the logically antecedent question of whether a promise has been made at all tends to preoccupy the case law.[187] In other contexts, the legal enforceability of codes of conduct *per se* have caused difficulties,[188] and these difficulties are

[181] *Ibid*, 11: 'Within this system, the role of the state and other public bodies becomes secondary rather than primary. It becomes difficult to determine at the international level whether law is being sourced from consensus in private behavior or from legal norms developed through the deliberative political process' (11; citations omitted).

[182] R Wai, 'Transnational Liftoff and Juridical Touchdown: The Regulatory Function of Private International Law in an Era of Globalization' (2002) 40 *Columbia Journal of Transnational Law* 209–74.

[183] See *eg Vedanta v Lungowe* [2019] UKSC 20. But post-Brexit there is significant uncertainty as to whether these gateways will remain open, particularly since the United Kingdom has been denied entry to the Lugano Convention.

[184] This is fundamentally because of the legacy of British imperialism and the export of the common law to relevant countries, but more immediately because of various procedural and substantive gateways. The UK courts, for now at least, have taken over from the USA in terms of the leading jurisdiction. The USA has rowed back significantly in recent years, see most recently *Nestlé USA, Inc v Doe* 593 US (17 June 2021) in the context of the Alien Tort Statute, 1789.

[185] Some might argue that the *Vedanta*, para 53, judgment insofar as it contemplates circumstances in which published statements alone, without the exercise of control, may give rise to liability is a form of 'contort' reasoning. In other words, it contemplates through the tortious avenue of assumption of responsibility liability based on the meaning of statements from the point of view of the reasonable person, which might be viewed as a radical form of contextualism. See *eg* A Beckers, *Enforcing Corporate Social Responsibility Codes: On Global Self-Regulation and National Private Law* (Oxford: Hart, 2015), ch 7, using speech act theory to reconstruct these statements from the reasonable persons' perspective.

[186] Following ultimately from the basic presumption that contracts create rights *in personam*.

[187] There is very little case law on the issue. It might be more accurate to say, it dominates the academic discussion of what case law exists. See *eg* Beckers (n 185), ch 7.

[188] As general policy statements not indicating an intention to create legal relations or capable of amounting to a promise. In an employment law context, the relevant question is whether and

exacerbated where the individual attempting to rely on their putative commitments is a third party to the relevant contract. However, from the classical point of view, the most central problem for would-be claimants is demonstrating how what on their face appear to be discretionary powers – Company A *may* conduct audits and monitoring – become legal *necessities* with their breach entailing legal obligations towards suppliers' employees and other third parties. For example, in *Wal-mart v Doe*,[189] where the plaintiffs argued, among other things, that they were third-party beneficiaries to promises made between Wal-mart and its suppliers in a code of conduct, the court concluded on an analysis of the 'language and structure' of the agreement with its supplier that all Wal-mart did in the circumstances was reserve a unilateral right to inspect factories. While the language used stated that Wal-mart 'will undertake affirmative measures such as on-site inspection[s]' to monitor compliance, when placed against overall text of the agreement this was a power Wal-mart could exercise, but did not signal the undertaking of an obligation to do so. It follows as a matter of law and logic that a third-party beneficiary cannot assert rights greater than those of the promisee under the contract. This analysis is compounded where there is an explicit or implicit disclaimer of responsibility.[190] Additionally, on a classical analysis at least, reliance alone does not give rise to legal obligation.[191] In short, there is a gap between legal form and the role and function of value chain gatekeepers in contract law.[192]

to what extent codes of conduct have been incorporated into contracts of employment. In some jurisdictions, such as Ireland, a lot of this discussion is supervened by the horizontal application of constitutional rights to, for example, due process in an employment context. Seminal, *Glover v BLN* [1973] IR 388.

189 *Doe I v Wal-Mart Stores, Inc* 572 F3d 677 (2009).

190 Beckers (n 185), 246–47, deals with disclaimers stating, in effect, that these deny the legal effects of promises, but not the underlying promise which the promisor attempts to confine to a moral or social obligation. It is, however, difficult to see how a clearly expressed disclaimer cannot on orthodox principles but signal a lack of intention to create legal relations in the eyes of the reasonable promisee. Where there is a lack of clarity, then contextualist interpretation *may*, of course, result in legal obligation. However, even so, to whom is the promise made?

191 But see Restatement. (Second) of Contracts; in the United Kingdom, the promissory estoppel route to an implied contract appears blocked, see *Baird Textile Holdings Ltd v Marks & Spencer plc*, [2002] 1 All ER (Comm) 737 and in general the maxim that estoppel is a shield and not a sword holds good.

192 There are, of course, other potential contractual routes to recovery. However, none are particularly convincing based on an individualistic model of responsibility, *eg* unilateral promises require conduct or performance by the purported promisee, and not simply a diffuse promise, but the promise must represent an intention to undertake a legal obligation, *ie Carlill v Carbolic Smoke Ball* [1893] 1 QB 256. It is not inconceivable that the seriousness of an intention may be inferred from the circumstances, *eg* the statements made by a company, albeit unlikely. However, reliance remains difficult to demonstrate.

Claimants have in more recent years reframed their claims in tort law. This has resulted, at least at a preliminary stage, in some successes in high-profile UK Supreme Court case law.[193] The most important decision, *Vedanta v Lungowe*, in which the claimants, employees and local residents impacted by the mining activities of a subsidiary sued a parent company based on the tort of assumption of responsibility, the Supreme Court clarified that recovery against a parent company could, in principle, be based on control over a subsidiary or published statements that give rise to an objective and *personal* assumed responsibility.[194] Lord Briggs, first, clarified that the key legal question is that of establishing control over a subsidiary taking the case outside the ordinary degree of control that one might expect in a parent–subsidiary relationship. The manner in which a parent organises its relationship with a subsidiary is many and various and,[195] as such, attempting to 'shoehorn' the facts of a case into a legalistic straitjacket is misplaced.[196] Ultimately, a court is tasked with applying to the facts of the case a proximity analysis retraceable to *Dorset Yacht Club*.[197] Secondly, control over subsidiaries can take several forms. It must go beyond the 'opportunity'[198] to influence a subsidiary that arises from the ordinary parent–subsidiary relationship, and instead show that a parent has 'take[n] over, intervene[s] in, control[s], supervise[s] or advise[s] the management of the relevant operations (including land use) of the subsidiary'.[199] Additionally, while group-wide policies alone may be insufficient to show a duty of care, where those policies are defective and implemented 'as of course' by a subsidiary, resulting in harm to a third party, this may be enough to show requisite control.[200] Even where group-wide policies alone do not give rise to a

[193] It is unclear whether the Supreme Court's permissiveness at a preliminary stage will actually give rise to liability, but it may well act as an incentive to settle. The Supreme Court's approach relates to the inappropriateness of deciding novel cases on hypothetical facts, and goes back ultimately to *Barrett v Enfield DC* [2001] 2 AC 550, which, in turn, is a response to the ECHR's *Osman* judgment.

[194] *Vedanta* (n 181).

[195] *Ibid*, para 51.

[196] Para 51.

[197] Rejecting previous decisions which treated the case law as requiring an application of the *Caparo* test. It is also a subtle shift from *Hedley Byrne v Heller* [1964] AC 465, which emphasises conduct and reliance, like estoppel, as distinct from the tortious consequences of the position of control and supervision. The breakthrough case for this line of precedents is *Chandler v Cape Plc* [2012] EWCA Civ 525, para 80, which is very much a *Hedley Byrne*-inspired judgment in novel circumstances focusing on objective circumstances from which employee reliance could reasonably be inferred.

[198] *Vedanta* (n 183), para 49.

[199] *Ibid*.

[200] *Ibid*, para 52.

duty of care to third parties, they may do where they are not simply proclaimed, 'but active steps, by training, supervision and enforcement, to see that they are implemented by the relevant subsidiaries' occurs.[201] In the absence of active steps taken, there may be certain circumstances in which published statements which indicate that the parent is 'exercising that degree of supervision and control of its subsidiaries' may give rise to a duty of care.[202] Thus, control, actual or purported, with the latter coming close to form of 'contort', is enough to give rise to a duty of care in tort.[203] However, given its proximity framing, the judgment seems limited to the primary responsibility of parents which intervene in the activities of their subsidiaries within value chains,[204] and should not, perforce, extend to independent third parties.[205] In the latter context,[206] the degree of intervention required to reach the threshold of the relevant special relationship is likely to run up against the fact that control over upstream suppliers is normally indirect[207] and often outsourced.[208] It is true that certain lead firms put systems of training, supervision and periodic reporting in place, but normally these systems are light-touch,[209] discretionary and apply only to first-tier suppliers.[210] It is also unlikely that codes of conduct,

201 *Ibid*, para 53. This also seems like a proxy for control.

202 *Ibid*. This is close to the *Hedley Byrne* scenario. See also, more recently, *Okpabi v Shell* [2021] UKSC 3, which does not add much theoretically, but reaffirms and clarifies some points in *Vedanta*, *eg* para 147, that one must distinguish formal control from *de facto* management. The latter is what is required.

203 In the sense of a quasi-estoppel. There is of course significant disagreement as to whether assumption of responsibility belongs in contract, or tort, or is some third category unto itself. The predominating view is that it is an applied version of the neighbour principle, see A Robertson & J Wang, 'The Assumption of Responsibility' in K Barker et al (eds), *The Law of Misstatements: 50 Years on from Hedley Byrne v Heller* (Oxford: Hart, 2015), 49–82. But it has been argued that it is in fact a distinct category alongside contract and ordinary negligence. See D Nolan, 'Assumption of Responsibility: Four Questions' (2019) 72(1) *Current Legal Problems* 123–58.

204 Although see *Begum v Maran (UK) Ltd* [2021] EWCA Civ 326. There, Coulson LJ seemed to suggest that extending further towards the torts of third parties was possible at least, pursuant to the relevant test of strike-out, in the sense of being 'arguable' as distinct from 'fanciful'. In these circumstances, a fair, just and reasonable analysis would be required.

205 Compare *Begum*.

206 *Eg* the Rana Plaza disaster scenario. Even then problems of causation arise. In the Rana Plaza disaster, several retailers subcontracted from the same factory.

207 An additional difficulty for claimants is normally that published materials are scanty, and it is only disclosure at full trial that will reveal the relevant degree of control. However, even so, the network structure of supply chains, militates against relevant control.

208 To third-party auditors. The issue then becomes one of applying a *Hedley Byrne*-type analysis.

209 *Eg*, see *DAS v George Weston* [2018] ONCA 1053 (20 December 2018), where a basic audit only was conducted.

210 See *eg* Primark: '*Suppliers are also* responsible for ensuring that this Supplier Code of Conduct and all relevant laws and regulations are complied with within *their own supply chains*'

even inherently defective codes, that purport to extend to the supply chain as a whole are likely to reach the threshold of control given their abstraction when compared to internal group policies.[211] Additionally, codes of conduct and other published materials which indicate that lead firms ensure their products are ethically sourced in compliance with labour, environmental and human rights standards do not necessarily also indicate that they assume control over their first-tier suppliers.[212] They could instead indicate that they may terminate contracts with these suppliers, have put monitoring and supervision measures in place, but do not profess to exercising control over the suppliers directly. *A fortiori*, upstream second-tier suppliers.[213] This is not to say that there will be no circumstances in which a direct or personal duty of care will be assumed towards upstream tort victims[214] – it is as the courts have clarified a highly fact sensitive and objective inquiry[215] – but it does highlight that attempts to shoehorn recovery against suppliers into the personalist assumption of responsibility, as opposed to subsidiaries, where there is relevant third-party conduct, is unlikely to give rise to recovery in tort.[216] The fact that the test requires the assumption of responsibility towards a particular person or class of persons

(emphasis added). https://primark.a.bigcontent.io/v1/static/Primark_Code-of-Conduct_2019_English (accessed 6 July 2021).

[211] On this point, see *DAS* (n 209), at para 182.

[212] This would, of course, be a matter of the interpretation of these published materials. However, firms presumably would adjust for this 'liability risk' by explicitly declaring that they assume no legal duty over third parties.

[213] And, indeed, as several commentators have averred, this manner of framing the duty may create a perverse incentive to reduce human rights due diligence. See G Wagner, 'Tort Law and Human Rights' in M Saage-Maaß et al (eds), *Transnational Legal Activism in Global Value Chains* (Cham: Springer, 2021), 209–33, 226–27; M Kawakami, 'Pitfalls of Over-Legalization: When the Law Crowds Out and Spills Over' (2017) 24(1) *Indiana Journal of Global Legal Studies* 147–79, 161–66 (for examples of where this perverse incentive, or 'spill-over effects' in Kawakami's terms bore fruit).

[214] But it is highly unlikely for the reasons canvassed in *DAS* (n 209). It is also arguable here that this would involve an extension of legal principles rather than their application to novel facts, and would require an application of the rather indeterminate 'fair, just and reasonable' test. See *Robinson v CC of West Yorkshire Police* [2018] UKSC 4 per Lord Reed, at para 47.

[215] Assumption of responsibility is inferred from the circumstances, and not necessarily the subjective statements made by a party. In this sense, it comes close to contextualist analysis in contract. However, it also shares with contractual analysis the fact that explicit disclaimers may rebut the assumption. The presence of disclaiming language is not insurmountable either on interpretative grounds or based on statute, but it does make recovery difficult.

[216] J Smits, 'Enforcing Corporate Social Responsibility Codes under Private Law, or: On the Disciplining Power of Legal Doctrine', (2015) Maastricht European Private Law Institute Working Paper 2015/09, 8.

through control or through public statements purporting to exercise control indicates that, in the end, this extension of personal liability of parents where the acts or omissions of their subsidiaries are the direct cause of harm is a convoluted way around two inconvenient legal propositions. The first is the separate legal personality of subsidiaries and, in this respect, company law's firm rejection of 'single economic entity' theory;[217] the second is the fact that in tort law vicarious liability applies only for the acts of natural persons.[218] Therefore, the notion of assumed responsibility is walking a tightrope between individual responsibility and organisational responsibility by providing recovery based on exceptions to the ordinary rules of personal responsibility without directly invoking principles of organisational responsibility.[219] Ultimately, it is my view that it is a disguised and ingenious form of organisational fault, which aims at redressing judgment proofing within groups of companies whose separation is more imagined than real.[220] Because, therefore, it fits the model of organisational responsibility, namely liability for the characteristic risks of the *de facto* (vertically integrated) enterprise,[221] it is unsuited to problems of network governance within value chains that cannot easily be said to have the characteristics of a vertical disintegration of convenience,[222] and where

[217] See *Adams v Cape Industries* [1990] Ch 433, which rejected the 'single economic entity' notion in UK company law. *Compare* A Berle, 'The Theory of Enterprise Entity' (1947) 47 *Columbia Law Review* 343.

[218] For discussion, see J Morgan, 'Vicarious Liability for Group Companies: The Final Frontier of Vicarious Liability?' (2015) 31(4) *Professional Negligence* 276–99.

[219] Of course, one might argue, like J Goudkamp, 'Duties of Care between Actors in Supply Chains', Oxford Legal Studies Research Paper No 61/2017, that genuine principles of personal responsibility are being deployed post-*Chandler*, and this is certainly true. The problem in the context of network governance is that the hermeneutics of personal responsibility are not well-equipped to solve the problem.

[220] L LoPucki, 'The Death of Liability' (1996–97) 106(1) *Yale Law Journal* 2–92 (detailing the evasive strategies of firms). In other words, it is a motivated by a latent notion of quasi-*abus de droit*. This is the motivation behind all exceptions to separate legal personality, *ie* some element of morally culpable behaviour. *Compare* Goudkamp (n 219), who rejects this explanation. However, while I agree that the assumption of responsibility route is a genuinely tortious recovery, it follows the pattern of an 'escape' into tort where some special features take a case outside the ordinary rules of personal responsibility, and, one might add, separate legal personality. On the notion of 'escape' into tort, see B Markesinis, 'An Expanding Tort Law – The Price of a Rigid Contract Law' (1987) 103 *Law Quarterly Review* 354.

[221] This 'de facto' is a legal perception of reality coloured by its normative models of responsibility, and goes to the proper classification of responsibility, not a statement about reality 'out there'.

[222] One might distinguish between circumstances in which a third-party supplier's only customer is the lead firm or its subsidiary, in which case a *quasi*-organisational responsibility solution may be justified as a means to redress judgment proofing, and a situation in which the supplier has multiple customers. It is difficult in the latter scenario to plausibly conclude that the supplier should be equated with the lead firm, or that one is dealing with a 'network firm'. On the

multiple actors share in the overall governance of the network.[223] In simpler, common law terms, the necessary proximity between 'lead firms' and their suppliers cannot as a matter of course be made out.

For similar reasons, the idea of 'production liability' is misplaced as an overt alternative to the disguised organisational responsibility of lead firms. Ulfbeck and Salminen, in particular, have developed this idea by analogising between producers' liability and supply chain or production liability.[224] Producers' liability from the outset has conceived the distribution chain in organisational terms.[225] Looking behind legal form, common law courts and,[226] later, in a European context, the Product Liability Directive have attributed acts and omissions to producer-driven distribution chains.[227] Both Ulfbeck and Salminen argue by analogy that the model of product liability that has been developed in 'producer-driven' supply chains should be extended to 'buyer-driven' supply chains, which, like 'producer-driven' supply chains involve multiple parties in interdependent contractual relationships.[228] It is the supply chain *qua* organisation that creates and fails to control the risks of harms to employees and third parties just as it is the distribution chain which has created and failed to control product risks. From the point of view of imputation, in 'producer-driven' chains legal responsibility is then shouldered by producers as risk creators as the first-best solution for injured victims, and by other members of the supply chain, such as importers, distributors and retailers[229] that are implicated as actors *within* the supply chain, as a second-best

concept of network firm, see V Chassagnon, 'The Network Firm as a Single Real Entity: Beyond the Aggregate of Distinct Legal Entities' (2011) 45(1) *Journal of Economic Issues* 113–36; B Baudry & D Gindis, 'The V-Network Form: Economic Organization and the Theory of the Firm' (10 October 2005). https://ssrn.com/abstract=795244 or http://dx.doi.org/10.2139/ssrn.795244 (accessed 6 July 2021).

223 As Berle (n 215), 344, put it, the *de facto* corporation is viewed based on 'the underlying economic facts'.

224 See *eg* V Ulfbeck, 'Supply Chain Liability for Workers' Injuries – Lessons to be Learned from Products Liability?' (2018) 9(3) *Journal of European Tort Law* 269–88; J Salminen, 'From Product Liability to Production Liability: Modelling a Response to the Liability Deficit of Global Value Chains on Historical Transformations of Production' (2019) 23(4) *Competition & Change* 420–38.

225 See Chapter 2.

226 One could view manufacturer leapfrogging claims in this way, which then places a burden on manufacturers to use contract to reallocate losses along the chain.

227 Ulfbeck (n 224), citing G Gereffi and M Korzeniewicz (eds), *Commodity Chains and Global Capitalism* (Westport, CT: Praeger, 1994), who distinguishes 'production-driven' and 'buyer-driven' supply chains.

228 *Ibid*; Salminen (n 224).

229 Although the liability of retailers is not harmonised through the Product Liability Directive, see C-402/03, *Skov Æg v Bilka Lavprisvarehus A/S* (2006) ECLI:EU:C:2006:6.

solution.[230] In 'buyer-driven' chains, so the argument goes, the lead firm, given its position of control and supervision, should equally be held responsible for risks that materialise as harms. This appears to be an elegant and simple solution to the 'accountability gap'.[231]

However, the main difficulty with extending producer's liability to a new concept of 'production liability' is that, as Keating has argued, producers' liability has a definite normative justification. It rests on the *fairness* of holding enterprises strictly liable for the 'characteristic risks' *they* create through *their* activities.[232] According to an enterprise liability rationale, it is fairer that the actor who benefits from an activity should bear the (predictable and unavoidable) costs of accidents that arise in the course of those activities than to place these costs on the shoulders of innocent and isolated victims.[233] This holds true so long as the risks of activities can be said to have been created by the enterprise.[234] This is supported by two policy arguments; first, the producer is better placed to disperse the costs of accidents across society through insurance or self-insurance; secondly, the producer is best positioned to take precautions that minimise future accidents.[235] The combination of these

[230] The second-best solution, all things being equal, results in the efficient allocation of risk between actors on the supply-side through contract. And, of course, ultimately, losses are borne by 'society at large' by passing on losses through pricing, *etc.* But it also has a normative justification if it is assumed that the distribution chain should be responsible for the risks properly attributable to 'production'.

[231] D Hunter & N Bridgeman, 'Narrowing the Accountability Gap: Toward a New Foreign Investor Accountability Mechanism' (2008) 20(2) *Georgetown International Environmental Law Review* 187–236. Defining the 'accountability gap' as 'the policy space between the many international norms that apply to MNE activities and the lack of corresponding mechanisms to require adherence to those norms' (191). The norms referred to are both high-level public norms and norms emanating from private initiatives.

[232] See G Keating, 'Products Liability As Enterprise Liability', USC Gould Legal Studies Research Papers Series No 16-38, 1–44. It is not simply a case of responsibility for risks *simpliciter*, but a conception of liability that views enterprises as 'fundamental units of responsibility' (7); 'At the base is the idea that *enterprises, not individual actors, ought to be basic unit of legal responsibility*. Two premises are then attached to this foundation. The first is that *enterprises ought* to internalize the costs of the accidents that they cause without regard to their fault in precipitating that harm. The second is that enterprises ought to disperse the costs of their characteristic harms across all those who participate in the enterprise, ideally in proportion to the extent of their participation. The participants in an enterprise are ultimately answerable – collectively – for the harm that the enterprise does' (4–5; emphasis added).

[233] *Ibid*, 14. As Keating has perceptively pointed out, the normative justification should be separated from the non-causal or instrumental justification. *Compare* R Coase, 'The Problem of Social Cost' (1960) 3 *Journal of Law & Economics* 1–44.

[234] This justification goes all the way back to Saleilles' 'causalité industrielle'. R Saleilles, *Les Accidents du Travail et la Responsabilité Civile: (essai d'une théorie objective de la responsabilité délictuelle)* (Paris: Rousseau, 1897), 12.

[235] Keating (n 232), 16.

justifications is the trigger for consumer leapfrogging claims against producers. The distribution chain from retailer back to producer is considered *as if* a single organisation. This is no more plainly evidenced in the EU's Product Liability Directive, which while holding producers legally responsible for defective products gives,[236] at the same time, an artificial definition to producers, which is capable of encompassing all supply-side actors from importers to distributors.[237] However, it should be stressed that holding other actors apart from the producer strictly liable occurs *faute-de-mieux* when a producer cannot be readily identified. While for the purposes of attribution the distribution chain is treated as an 'organisation', when it comes to *imputation* the producer *stricto sensu* is the proper (normative) addressee of legal responsibility. In other words, while acts and omissions are attributed to the distribution chain *qua* 'organisation', this does not give rise to liability *in solidum*. Instead, the producer as risk creator is considered the primary tortfeasor and the liability regime is designed accordingly.[238] It is in the final analysis based on a moral argument regarding 'weak commutative justice' that justifies a special regime of liability for producers, which through *their activities* in the production process impose risks on third parties that materialise as harms.[239] Thus, as Keating rightly argues, the thorny legal issues surround defining the scope of characteristic risks of the enterprise or in other words the scope of the firm's own activities.

The problem of extending this strict enterprise liability by analogy with producers' liability to supply chains in order to create a form of 'production liability' is manifest. The lead firm is not the creator of the risk and therefore cannot be said to have caused the victims' injuries through their activities, which is the normative justification for legal responsibility. At most, the lead

[236] Council Directive 85/374, art 1.

[237] See art 3, Council Directive 85/374; the practical effect is that it turns it over to the private ordering of the supply-chain to allocate liability risk through contractual arrangements, and in the absence of contract, to let the loss lie with the suppliers rather than victims. Of course, retailers will be liable in contract or tort in national law and, as such, the EU regime supplements national law, albeit it displaces it within its scope of application; see *Skov Æg* (n 230).

[238] It is not liability based on failure to govern the distribution chain. The producer is not held liable for the acts or omissions of third parties; rather, *third parties* are held liable in contract or tort as second-best solution to producer liability or based on privity of contract. Instead, the defective product (and the risk) is created by the producer and the materialisation of the risk as a harm is the reason why the producer is held liable. Salminen (n 224), at 2, who views product liability as liability for 'inadequate governance', and at page 8 regarding liability for others.

[239] Enterprise liability applies to firms; however, the same logic can be seen in the development of the liability of public authorities. See Chapter 2.

firm's inaction in the face of third-party negligence enhances a pre-existing risk.[240] While it is true that the lead firm through contract and its code of conduct may be said to *de facto* influence working conditions in suppliers' factories either by creating the economic incentives that result in suppliers 'cutting corners', so to speak, or by failing to assiduously enforce its code of conduct, that is, its contract, this is not equivalent to the day-to-day exercise of control that a manufacturer has over its production design or processes such that the producer's acts or omissions can be said to have caused the relevant injury in the relevant sense.[241] In fact, applying the rule devised in 'producer-driven' supply chains to 'buyer-driven' supply chains inverts the logic of Product Liability Directive based, as it is, on moral enterprise liability.[242] In the 'buyer-driven' supply chain, the creator of the risk is the supplier, not the buyer. Making the buyer primarily responsible would be equivalent to making secondary actors such as importers and distributors – the second-best solution in EU producer liability – the primary addressees of liability. Whatever the economic justification for such a move,[243] it lacks a clear normative justification *in* enterprise liability.[244] In other words, unless one views the supplier as an agent of the lead firm, and even if one views the supply chain as an organisation, there is no good normative reason to hold the lead firm legally responsible for the acts of others.[245] It follows that the model of organisational responsibility is not an appropriate regime of tort liability for value chains, and individual responsibility has inherent limits.

240 Even this proposition, if one considers the problem on orthodox principles, is dubious. For a discussion, see J Phillips & SJ Lim, 'Their Brothers' Keeper: Global Buyers and the Legal Duty to Protect Suppliers' Employees' (2009) 61(2) *Rutgers Law Review* at 355–59.

241 See Keating (n 232), 14. Causation in the but-for sense is not what's in issue. Defining the zone of enterprise risk is what's relevant. This is a normative question about the imputation of 'characteristic risks' to enterprises.

242 See J Stapleton, 'A New Theory of Strict Moral Enterprise Liability' in *Product Liability* (London: Butterworths, 1994), 185, 191.

243 M Geistfeld, 'The Law and Economics of Tort Liability for Human Rights Violations in Global Supply Chains' (2019), NYU Law & Economics Research Paper Series Working Paper No 19-22, stating that it is efficient. However, as argued, the economic justification for enterprise liability is a secondary, or subsidiary, consideration. The primary justification is ensuring fairness in the distribution of the benefits and burdens of enterprise activities.

244 And perhaps in private law, more generally. *Compare* A Bagchi, 'Production Liability' (2019) 87 (6) *Fordham Law Review* 2501–38. For Bagchi, there is a good argument for moral responsibility in a public conception of justice, which *may* justify private law remedies, but it is not appropriate 'default' regime; rather, public regulation is preferred.

245 Normative, because it is less clear whether it is instrumentally justified to hold the lead firm liable. See Geistfeld (n 243), who argues it is instrumentally justified to do so.

2 *Beyond Individual and Organisational Responsibility in the Value Chain: Network Governance of the Supply Chain*

What then is the role and function of lead firms in value chains and how should this be reflected in a liability regime? Outside cases of vertical disintegration of convenience,[246] lead firms are normatively secondary actors or peripheral parties that share governance functions with a variety of public and private actors.[247] When a harm occurs to persons or to the environment through breaches of human, labour or environmental rights, there are multiple (putative) tortfeasors. Analytically, in tort, the primary tortfeasor is the supplier, which tolerates or condones breaches of worker or third-party rights. Secondary tortfeasors include the relevant state regulator, lead firms and third-party auditors. However, *de facto*, there are two potential addressees of liability, namely lead firms[248] and third-party certification organisations.[249] Neither lead firms nor third-party certification organisations create the risk of harm, except in a highly attenuated sense, nor do they through their conduct

[246] Where it may be possible to fit the case into individual liability or organisational liability *a la Vedanta*. Whether there is a genuine 'network firm' or whether disaggregation is a judgment proofing strategy causes similar classification issues that arise in vicarious liability actions. In vicarious liability actions, courts must decide whether the problem is better characterised as one of individual responsibility or organisational responsibility, and they do so through the distinction between employment and independent contractors with some fuzziness at the edges, *ie* relationships 'akin to employment'. Although the latter concept arose first in the context of relationship, which in certain respects surpassed the employment relationship in terms of 'relationality' – *ie* the relationship between monks and priests and their superiors – it will prospectively be applied to problems of the 'gig economy'. See *Hollis v Vabu Pty Ltd* [2001] HCA 44, and more recently *Barclays Bank v Various Claimants* [2020] UKSC 13, para 29. Similar issues arise in the context of defining the relationships that give rise to a non-delegable duty of care. The point is that in deciding between instances of vertical disintegration of convenience and true vertical disintegration, the task should not be beyond the wit of a court. Where the former holds, there is good reason to apply a model of organisational responsibility; in the latter case, a different model of responsibility is required. *Compare* Wagner (n 214), 209–33, 224–25, who cautions against organisational liability in the context of what I refer to as vertical disintegration of convenience because of the wide-reaching ramifications of disregarding the 'entity' theory through tort.

[247] It is important in this argument that one does not have to conceive of a 'network firm' as a real entity attracting 'network liability' in the Teubnerian (n 10) sense, as liability of the network, here. Instead, network liability in the context of network governance is liability for the exercise of public functions by private parties where those private parties are peripheral to the tort.

[248] A further complication arises where the same supplier contracts with several 'lead firms'.

[249] Not least because of weak state capture, and problems of access to justice in domestic settings. On weak state capture, see Backer (n 180), 26. On problems of access to justice, see *Vedanta* (n 183).

commit the tort.[250] At most, focusing on lead firms, through non-adherence to the codes of conduct that they promulgate, and which form part of their supply contracts, they can be said to enhance an (existing) risk of harm to third parties. These codes of conduct, in turn, reflect the operationalising of their 'public' responsibility[251] to respect the rights of third parties by exercising due diligence such that their value chains comply with human, labour and environmental rights.[252] In other words, endogenous constitutionalisation[253] through codes of conduct complements exogenous politico-legal constitutionalisation through soft law obligations in the form of the United Nations Guiding Principles (UNGP),[254] which are mandatory (but unenforceable) obligations of due diligence requiring, and affirming the responsibility of, lead firms to exercise 'public', regulatory and governance functions alongside their 'private' profit-seeking motivation.[255] In this sense, their codes of conduct cannot be conceived of simply as reputational devices,[256] but must be understood in a broader societal context of shared responsibility between 'private' gatekeepers and public bodies (that is, states).[257] In other words, lead firms partake in the public governance in the transnational space alongside governments, certification organisations and NGOs.[258] Given the public law

[250] Unless, of course, they do. See C Witting, 'Intra-Corporate Conspiracy: An Intriguing Prospect' (203) 72(1) *Cambridge Law Journal* 178–206.

[251] These norms did not arise quasi-spontaneously as bottom-up social norms, as some would have it, but arose from social pressure within a legal framework. However, this does not mean that the norm system is not quasi-autonomous in the sense of being normatively closed. Teubner would refer to this in terms of self-constitutionalisation. See *eg* G Teubner, 'Self-Constitutionalizing TNCs? On the Linkage of "Private" and "Public" Corporate Codes of Conduct' (2011) 18(2) *Indiana Journal of Global Legal Studies* 617–38.

[252] *Ibid*.

[253] *Ibid*, in Teubner's framing.

[254] Not only the UNGP, but it is the most important and influential international 'soft law' guidance.

[255] France.

[256] *Ie* cannot be viewed simply as private undertakings, or horatory statements with no legal effect.

[257] Backer (n 180). See more generally LC Backer, 'Multinational Corporations, Transnational Law: The United Nation's Norms on the Responsibility of Transnational Corporations as Harbinger of Corporate Responsibility in International Law' (2005) 37 *Columbia Human Rights Law Review* 101–92 (commenting on the more robust norms, which were watered down in the UDGP, but the underlying conceptual division of responsibility remains). Beckers (n 185), ch 7, examines this at the level of the speech act theory, *ie* how performative utterances create social expectations. However, aside from these possible effects, the more pressing issue is their functional role in governance, and private law's approach to recognising or not recognising this role as legally relevant.

[258] Increasingly, the obligation to have a code of conduct is viewed as obligatory also, and not simply at the election of firms. See France's duty of vigilance, *loi du 27 Mars 2017*. For commentary, see S Schiller (ed), *Le Devoir de Vigilance* (Paris: LexisNexis, 2019).

background, and more importantly their discharge of public functions, their private law contracts – including their undertakings to monitor and enforce the standards that these codes embody – should not be viewed solely through the lens of (classical) contract law. Instead, they form an emerging *ordre public* transnational,[259] 'fundamental principles of a (transnational) social order',[260] which are laid down generically and abstractly through 'public codes' and operationalised through 'private codes'.[261] But the more important point is that responsibility for the enforcement of public obligations falls to both public *and* private parties.[262] What is missing in this edification of 'responsibility to protect' is a private law remedial regime, which converts these soft obligations into hard legal rights and duties. Without this remedial avenue, public codes and private codes exist as two 'mutually closed normative networks'[263] or, in other words, a 'structural hole' exists between these two modes of communication, and the realisation of the letter and spirit of public codes left to 'private' ordering.[264]

Tort law is in a pole position to bridge this 'structural hole' given, as Van Dam states, the 'overlap' between human rights and the rights protected by tort law.[265] Indeed, tort law and human rights do not merely overlap, but rather private law precedes human and fundamental rights protection as an integral part of the constitution of civil society.[266] However, when the borders

[259] Teubner (n 251), 637 (transnational public policy).

[260] *Ibid*, 621.

[261] *Ibid*. Although Teubner would disagree with this characterisation because he does not view the public and private codes in a hierarchical relation, but instead sees them as interacting through an 'ultracycle': 'mutual perturbations . . . between closed networks' (634). This means, in effect, that they are simply weak impulses for the closed network of TNC constitutionalism and, at best, are perceived as moral suasion. This should not be underestimated, as Teubner perceives it as having effect on the cognitive expectations of TNC constitutionalism, but it assumes structural closure.

[262] See the division of responsibility in the UNGP, part II on corporate responsibility to respect human rights.

[263] *Ibid*, 633.

[264] Teubner, *ibid*, views the relationship as one of network closure. While both the 'public codes' and 'private codes' are legal communication, they are structurally closed. This, in my view, may be a true statement as it stands, but it is not analytically necessary. Bridging the gap between codes is not like bridging the gap between two distinct social sub-systems, *ie* unbridgeable without the dissolution of one of the two sub-systems, but rather more like bridging the gap between two legal orders, *ie* bridgeable through 'inter-textuality'. See H Collins, 'Utility and Rights in Common Law Reasoning: Rebalancing Private Law through Constitutionalizaton', LSE Law, Society and Economy Working Paper 6/2007, 16.

[265] For C Van Dam, 'Tort Law and Human Rights: Brothers in Arms on the Role of Tort Law in the Area of Business and Human Rights' (2011) 3 *Journal of European Tort Law* 221–54, 243.

[266] See F Rodl, 'Fundamental Rights, Private Law, and Societal Constitution: On the Logic of the So-Called Horizontal Effect' (2013) 20(2) *Indiana Journal of Global Legal Studies* 1015–34; and Chapter 3 more generally.

of civil society/state break down under conditions of globalisation a fusion of public and private law is required. In EU law, a hybrid model of public–private law of torts has emerged. This fusion of public rights and private remedies into a single, integrated regime of liability for network governance should apply beyond the context of EU law and act as a broader template of recovery in the society of networks. In the context of value chain liability, there should be a wide interpretation of tort's protected interests (duties of care: human rights) while, at the same time, normatively distinguishing the peripheral role played by secondary actors in networks. The duty of care should, in other words, be read in the light of the soft law (public) standards, but the liability regime should be adjusted for (private) the normatively peripheral role of lead firms and other gatekeepers.[267] Increasingly, mandatory codes of conduct[268] can inform how the breadth of obligations are operationalised, but do not delimit the scope of obligations.[269] This should be the case regardless of the direct enforceability of human rights against corporations. Human rights obligations allow for tort law to reflect on the scope of its protected interests,[270] its scheme of basic mandatory law in the private sphere.[271] Tort law, in other words, is an interpersonal law (internal dimension) with a societal dimension (external dimension), and the latter, should, in

[267] *Compare* Backer (n 257) raises concerns about this argument, which, it may be argued, involves the 'bottom up' (through contract or tort) adoption of international soft law without democratic scrutiny, and which radically alters the fundamentals of corporate law from a shareholder value to stakeholder approach. Additionally, he seems to argue that shifting at least some responsibility from states to TNCs may dilute state responsibility. This in my view at least, underestimates the constitutional nature of private law as well as the fact that it is commonplace in tort to adopt (international) standards of best practice through the standard of care, *eg* in product safety requirements.

[268] See, n 258 above on France. Also, EU legislation is in the offing: the European Parliament's new draft, EU Directive on Mandatory Human Rights, Environmental and Good Governance Due Diligence. www.europarl.europa.eu/doceo/document/TA-9-2021-0073_EN.pdf (accessed 9 July 2021), which contemplates both a mandatory due diligence standard and civil liability.

[269] Fitting the traditional tort law approach that custom may inform the law, but it does not determine the legal, normative standard. This traditional role of custom is very well explained in G Brüggemeier, *Common Principles of Tort Law: A Prestatement of Law* (London: BIICL, 2004), 66: '[determining the standard of due care] … is a normative question; not the empirical assessment of what is customary. Custom can be considered in determining this standard, but does not act as binding precedent for the standard of care.' However, for reasons of the peripheral position of lead firms, I would qualify this by reference to the standard of serious breach.

[270] In the sense in Chapter 3, *ie* a reflection mechanism in systems theory terms.

[271] The extent to which one can contract out of tort, as a background regime, is a matter of public policy. In these circumstances, the public policy arguments in favour of treating tort law as a default regime as distinct from a mandatory regime are not strong given the important rights in issue.

the context of mixed public–private governance, inform the development of its duties of care.

It should be apparent from our discussion until now that the model of network liability envisioned takes as its starting point that where important rights are at issue, that justifies the imposition of liability on those peripheral parties which in a normatively relevant way can be said to enhance a risk. However, because they are secondary or peripheral parties, this cannot be justified based on ordinary principles of negligence or through forms of stricter liability. Instead, network liability should be based on an objective, culpable breach of discretion, and the intensity of review of this discretion will vary according to the importance of the right in issue. In this scenario, the discretion available to lead firms when deciding on what due diligence requires should vary according to, *inter alia*, the clarity and precision of the *right* infringed, the excusable or inexcusable nature of the breach, and whether the breach was intentional or otherwise. Ultimately, however, the test should be one of whether the lead firm when discharging its 'public' governance function disregarded the interests of the right holder in circumstances in which there was a clear and patent risk of harm. These criteria approach a standard of *faute lourde* or gross negligence, which normatively distinguishes the position of secondary actors from those of primary tortfeasors in network governance. While the *ordre public transnational* is often implemented through contract, and is in this sense a voluntary undertaking, the protected rights are not voluntary but represent part of a transnational order of mandatory rights protection, which binds states and private parties fulfilling public functions in the transnational space. It is, then, a mandatory layer of basic protection irritating societal self-constitutionalisation processes.[272]

While there is no European-level tort law of value chain network liability,[273] the recent *Millieundefensie v Royal Dutch Shell Plc* judgment is illustrative in terms of both the assignment of rights and the relevant standard of care.[274] While the judgment concerns imminent 'serious and irreversible' environmental catastrophe,[275] the conceptual argument has wider salience. In *Millieundefensie*, a number of environmental NGOs brought a class action which sought an injunction against Royal Dutch Shell (RDS) obliging it to

[272] I see no great difference between this approach and the manner in which tort law has traditionally, *eg*, injected notions of informed consent into the health or medical discourse.

[273] Yet *cf* n 268.

[274] (2021) ECLI:NL:RBDHA:2021:5339 (Judgment of 26 May 2021).

[275] In Dutch law, the so-called *Kelderluik* criteria allow for recovery where damage is imminent and is a form of 'special precautionary' reasoning. On this point, see R Suryapratim & E Woerdman, 'Situating Urgenda v the Netherlands within Comparative Climate Change Litigation' (2016) 34 *Journal of Energy & Natural Resources Law* 165–89.

limit its group-wide emissions as well as the emissions attributable to its suppliers and end-users.[276] The basic argument was that the failure of RDS to put an adequate mitigation policy in place posed a serious risk to the rights of several thousand persons in the Wadden region,[277] and to the environment.

What is remarkable in the judgment is, first, how it read tort law in the light of (transnational) human rights guarantees (that is, indirect effect) in circumstances in which the 'private' party occupied the position of gatekeeper or regulatory intermediary,[278] and, secondly, how it distinguished between Shell's obligations with respect to its group activities and its regulatory role beyond its own activities. First, with respect to human rights obligations, these entered Dutch Tort Law through the open-textured reference to 'unwritten standard of care' in Dutch tort law,[279] which is a portal for public law rights to enter into the *interpretation* of private law duties. Although they cannot be directly invoked in a horizontal situation, the 'unwritten standard of care', like a good-faith provision, empowers Dutch courts to read tort law *in the light of* prevailing human rights law,[280] but also in the light of soft law instruments such as the UN Guiding Principles (UNGP) when determining the scope of *interpersonal* protection of Dutch tort law,[281] and ultimately the duties owed in a private law dispute. The UNGP envisages firms' 'individual responsibility'[282] in a wider and variegated sharing of responsibility[283] between states and businesses for the enforcement of CSR. This business 'individual responsibility' to respect human rights, including environmental rights, is considered mandatory reflecting '[t]he responsibility of business enterprises to respect

[276] Or at least no clear harm, see paras 2.3.7, and 2.3.9.

[277] This qualification was required for reasons of *locus standi* in Dutch law.

[278] This could be inferred from the size of RDS's operations and its environmental impact, which exceeded that of many nation-states, including the Netherlands.

[279] Book 6 Sect 163, Dutch Civil Code, art 6.123(2): 'As a tortious act is regarded a violation of someone else's right (entitlement) and an act or omission in violation of a duty imposed by law or of what according to unwritten law has to be regarded as proper social conduct, always as far as there was no justification for this behaviour.' http://dutchcivillaw.com/legislation/dcctitle6633.htm (accessed 27 June 2021).

[280] See also *Urgenda* in the context of state liability. In both cases, the Court used this path to 'read in' arts 2 & 8 of the ECHR into the private law dispute as well as the Human Rights Committee's interpretation of arts 6 & 17 of the ICCPR as including environmental rights protection as a facet of human rights.

[281] Which reflect 'current insights' alongside the OECD Guidelines for Multinational Enterprises, and the UN Global Compact principles.

[282] Para 4.4.52.

[283] States have positive obligations within their territory or jurisdiction, and must engage in policy balancing. However, this does not absolve businesses of their 'individual responsibility' or mean that they can simply wait for a legislative framework to be put in place, see para 4.4.13. In this sense, they must be proactive.

human rights, as formulated in the UNGP, is a *global standard of expected conduct* for all business enterprises wherever they operate'.[284] This applies whether the relevant business has a CSR policy or not,[285] and imposes an active duty on businesses, requiring instead that positive steps are taken to fulfil this obligation to respect.[286] While account may be taken for business size, where a company such as RDS has a 'policy-setting position' (that is, a gatekeeper) within a corporate group of some 1,100 subsidiaries, the obligation will be onerous.[287] This is a responsibility that extends to 'the company's entire value chain'.[288] Secondly, the court normatively distinguishes between the nature of the obligation owed by Shell and its subsidiaries, and by third parties.[289] Where the breach of rights at issue concerned one of Shell's 1,100 subsidiaries, over which it has 'far-reaching control and influence', the obligation is one of result.[290] This is, in other words, an organisational liability for the 'network firm' resting on its policy-setting position within the network firm.[291] Where the breach concerned a company (third-party supplier) or end-users not under the overall control of the Shell group, but instead is a third party, the obligation is an obligation of means.[292] In the latter circumstances, Shell would only be liable in tort in circumstances where Shell failed to exercise its 'best efforts' to reduce emissions.[293] In other words, with respect to the latter scenario, in the light of the 'serious (environmental) risk' Shell must take steps to mitigate the impact of impending environmental damage. How it may do so is within the discretion of RDS, but that it must do so through the formulation of appropriate corporate policy is not.[294] Moreover, the court will review the gap between its stated policies and their operationalisation. The

[284] Para 4.4.13 (emphasis added). See also para 4.4.14: 'It can be deduced from the UNGP and other soft law instruments that it is universally endorsed that companies must respect human rights.'

[285] Para 4.4.11. 'Due to the universally endorsed content of the UNGP, it is irrelevant whether or not RDS has committed itself to the UNGP, although RDS states on its website to support the UNGP.' *Ie* they represent an *ordre public* transnational.

[286] Para 4.4.15.

[287] Para 4.4.16.

[288] Para 4.4.17.

[289] Other suppliers outside the Shell Group, and consumers. The latter is referred to as Scope 3 emissions in the relevant literature.

[290] Para 4.4.23.

[291] See Chassagnon (n 222); Baudry & Gindis (n 222) on the concept of 'network firm'.

[292] The court does use the term 'control' here, but it is of a different nature to the control it exercises over its group. It may require divestment decisions as well as adjustments to the energy package it offers. It involves balancing discretion against the important rights at stake.

[293] Para 4.4.24.

[294] RDS argued that it had a plan in place, but the court decided it did not go far enough, at para 4.5.2: 'In the court's view, RDS' policy, policy intentions and ambitions for the Shell group

court side-steps the issue of causation, or perhaps more accurately redefines it in terms of responsibility. The fact that Shell cannot be wholly held responsible for potentially deleterious consequences for Dutch residents of the Wadden region 'does not absolve RDS of its individual partial responsibility to contribute to the fight against dangerous climate change according to its ability'.[295]

In other words, the court recognises the fact that RDS has a distinct responsibility extending to its entire value chain given the important rights in issue. The manner in which this responsibility is discharged is a matter for RDS, but it cannot simply disregard its obligation and sit back and adopt a wait-and-see attitude.[296] While a private party, it has an important public function. By calibrating the standard of care distinguishing between circumstances in which Shell bears an organisational liability ('network firm') from circumstances in which Shell owed a network liability ('network governance'), the Hague Court edged towards a concept of network responsibility where risks are the shared responsibility of public and 'private' actors. The court uses rights protection to bring both public and private actors within private law's scope of protection, and there are significant conceptual parallels between RDS's 'best efforts' obligation and the notion of culpable breach of discretion. The concept of a sufficiently serious breach, that can be calibrated towards simple breach, which approaches stricter liability, or towards gross negligence – depending on the importance of the right in issue, the factual circumstances, and the discretionary choices open – would assist in clarifying the nature of the 'best efforts' obligation. Rights reorder priorities and bring the network within the sphere of attribution (network responsibility); sufficiently serious breach forms a rule of imputation (network liability) for those secondary actors that regulate networks. In other words, the Hague court boldly bridges the structural hole between public and private codes. These principles should also apply to regulatory intermediaries such as auditors which fulfil similar gatekeeping roles (here, ensuring that compliance with standards are achieved) and these other regulatory intermediaries should not be able to escape liability by relying on classical principles of individual responsibility in contract or tort.[297] This much is evident from *Schmitt*, which brings regulatory intermediaries within the scope of

largely amount to rather intangible, undefined and nonbinding plans for the long-term (2050).' In other words, the court reviewed the exercise of discretion in the light of the rights at stake.

295 Para 4.4.37.

296 This approach is evident from Shell's website and is cited at para 2.5.11.

297 For an attempt to operationalise classic contract and tort law principles in German and English and extend them to certification bodies, see C Glinski & P Rott, 'The Role and Liability of Certification Organisations in Transnational Value Chains', CEVIA Working Paper Series, Issue 4/2019.

protection of EU law by close analogy with principles of state liability. But given their governance function in supply chains, these certification organisations should, in appropriate circumstances, and by analogy with lead firms, be held responsible for their culpable breaches of discretion.

D CONCLUSION

'Reticular irresponsibility' in governance networks should be redressed by an appropriate liability regime of network liability. The case law is plodding towards a regime of network responsibility, in bits and pieces, both inside EU law, where it is significantly developed towards a functional understanding of public activity and a relevant standard of care but could go further, and outside EU law, where it is advancing apace but without a clear standard of responsibility.[298] The task of this chapter was to bring these bits and pieces together into a coherent framework and outlook for the liability law of the twenty-first century. In this respect, it harkens back to Duguit, Josserand and Saleilles, who in a similar fashion recast the *code civil* to contemporary needs. In the society of networks, which is also a society of transnational hybrid governance, the walls between the public and private have caved in: structurally similar models of liability no longer should run in parallel, but instead are fused into a single regime of liability where private actors fulfil public functions.

[298] This is a pitfall of public international law standards, which are classically aimed at states, in terms of positive obligations of result, and do not have developed concepts of liability for means obligations.

Conclusion

In this book, it has been argued that tort law in the nation-state context has evolved two primary normative models of liability, namely individual responsibility and organisational liability. Whereas the former rests on subjective fault, albeit objectively defined (community standard of conduct) the latter rests on liability for typical and, therefore, foreseeable risks. Both forms of liability developed within the nation-state and apply with modifications to both private parties and the state. Both forms of liability additionally are second-order normative models of liability in an acentric society. A 'top-down' public law understanding of the law overestimates this significantly. By contrast, private law with its emphasis on private ordering and how the law tracks rather than determines 'the reasonable expectations of honest men' better reflects the relationship between legal system and society as a plurality of normative orders. In the society of individuals, will and fault reflect this acentricity and constitute its legal buttress. They are tied to the knowledge base of society via bridging concepts such as reasonableness. However, when the knowledge base of the society of individuals ruptured, caused by the rise of organisations, the law was reshaped in light of these organisational forms taking advantage of their capacity for planning and collective action. Reconciling groups, as placeholders for different functional discourses, was in the heyday of the nation-state the role of the state. In systems theory terminology, the state's role is that of mediator between different functional systems or different normative orders. The law was an important means of ensuring the positive integration society by mediating these different normative orders. In tort law terms, reasonableness turned from conduct to liability for typical risks, whether this meant internalisation within the firm or liability for the harmful effects of typical activities of the state. This involved the mediation of discourses, primarily between the political and economic systems. The organisational model of liability was considered both economically efficient and socially just. Beyond foreseeable harm, however, the law did not readily venture. At all events, it should be stressed that both models of liability, individual and organisational, exist concurrently and in tension in national law – as Lord Hoffmann states, the law of negligence attempts simultaneously to pursue different objectives.[1]

With the breaking of the frame of the nation-state, however, this diptych is disrupted. The centrality of the organisational form is replaced by the network. When in the form of governance networks,[2] they arise because territorial differentiation has been superseded by (global) functional differentiation and necessitating transnational institutional configurations. Regional and global governance networks represent an attempt to re-embed the economy into societal discourses or normative orders within, but importantly, beyond the stable frame of the state. They harness private actors, the state and transnational 'avant-garde' configurations such as the EU to this end. The New Approach may be considered as a paradigmatic example. First, it transforms the state's regulatory role, which has become more peripheral. Regulation is now achieved, first by private actors themselves, second by regulatory intermediaries, third by the state and finally by the EU in an overall regulatory architecture in which regulation is a shared endeavour. This reorganisation of regulatory power up to the EU level, 'down' to the private level reflects the decoupling of territorial differentiation and functional differentiation and, secondly, exposes the way in which the state is ever more peripheral to transnational private ordering. While the state in modernity always depended on its practical knowledge base, the breaking of the territorial frame deprives the state of its capacity for positive integration. Thinking of these trends in terms of delegation is misleading because it assumes that the state had at some point an exclusive capacity in law-making, rather than a role in terms of strategic intervention. The historical 'bottom-up' perspective has emerged most transparently at an EU level, where the pretence of exclusive state regulation is quite obviously mythical. The New Approach illustrates how the state's role is but one of several regulatory actors in network governance. What distinguishes the post-nation-state era from the state-centred one is

[1] L Hoffmann, 'Anthropomorphic Justice: The Reasonable Man and His Friends' (1995) 29 *Law Teacher* 127, 130.

[2] As distinct from the problem of liability rules for 'network firms' to which Teubner has given considerable attention albeit focusing on internal group liability primarily, and thus on contract.

that the state can no longer sit aloft society as the organisation *primus inter pares* ensuring the compatibility of different normative orders, because these normative orders have globalised in world society.

The changing role of the state in a society of networks gives rise to several consequences. It is no longer Hegelian in the sense of the primary unit of positive integration, but is now one institution (organisation) among several that pursue the public good. This means in effect that actors formerly considered 'private' transparently fulfil public roles. It also means that the role of the state is being redefined. The liberal state/society distinction, then, is no longer a plausible understanding of 'society', because the role of the state as the sole coordinator of society has been replaced by a more complex, de-territorialised institutional configuration.

The legal system has also broken the frame of the nation-state, but appears unable alone to fill the gap left by the decline of the state. The pre-eminence of the economic constitution in EU law can be understood in these terms. The economic system emerges as 'market leader'. The richer normative programming of the society of organisations in which the law pursued several aims simultaneously has been hollowed out. The vision tends to be primarily economic and the availability of rights are defined in its light. By redefining through double binary coding (otherwise, cognitivisation) other discourses in its light, the economic system tends to dominate society.

In legal terms, law's autonomy is threatened. The rather light-touch approach in terms of the duties incumbent on the state and notification bodies within the New Approach framework is indicative. The detailed analysis of *Paul* and *Cosmet* in Chapter 3 stand in for a broader point: the preference for market access over other concerns such as consumer protection is reflected in the regulatory culture of the New Approach. But who watches the watchdog? The economisation of law, EU and national, means that insufficient coordination of the different normative orders (*Sinnwelten*) of society occurs. Yet this dismal view of post-national law and society is an incomplete picture because the law, through increased reference to fundamental rights as a reflexive mechanism, provides a point of 're-entry' for other discourses into the law. This is well-illustrated and explicit in the legal reasoning of the court in *Boston Scientific*, and implicit in *PIP*.

Yet *Boston Scientific*, while constructing a better balance between market access and consumer protection, understood capaciously as not only protecting individuals but achieving a balance between normative orders – economic risk versus precautionary reasoning – within a framework of rights only goes part of the way to providing a regime of liability for a network society. The argument is that given that the existing models rest on either individual or organisational liability (*Boston Scientific*), they lack a convincing justification for providing liability for other actors in networks. This is because, normatively speaking, simply extending organisational liability to other actors in networks is unconvincing. Networks lack the hierarchical character of the firm or the welfare state. The point of Chapter 4 was to emphasise that the EU is developing a normative concept of secondary 'network' liability absent organisational control. This is individualised liability, which recognises that simply because the primary actor is at fault, this does not exclude liability against other regulatory actors. Indeed, in *PIP*, the court underlined this point clearly. While network is not a legal concept, this does not mean that functionally equivalent categories cannot be developed that 'model' the law's knowledge base, and that in legal theory the theorist should recognise network responsibility as the deeper concept of responsibility. I perceive *Boston Scientific* and *PIP* in these terms. These judgments are not simply a question of providing redress to the particular individuals harmed, but from our perspective are considered strategic public interventions to better balance economic functionalism and other underrepresented discourses in networks. Second, by providing for a nascent regime of primary and secondary liability, EU law is providing a blueprint for how liability ought to be distributed in a network. Collective risks are converted into normative categories of primary and secondary responsibility. Here, I think that while the approach of the CJEU is orthodox – there is no general liability for notified bodies – because of the conceptual closeness between culpable excess of discretion (*PIP*) and sufficiently serious breach in *Francovich* liability, one might trace an emergent regime of network liability. In a broader perspective, I see these developments in terms of EU law providing a means to police the guardians or gatekeepers of private transnationalism, ensuring that they remain on guard or 'alert' to the consequences of inaction for third parties, but also, at a deeper level, providing a baseline against discourse domination by a narrow and economic interpretation of acceptable levels of risk, which sidelines other discourses. To be fully developed, this requires a greater appreciation of what is at stake. Under the influence of the concept of precaution, tort law is being remoulded. Therefore – and this is the argument – there is a role for rights understood horizontally to re-normativise the law so that it maintains its distance from the economic system and is capable of setting boundaries on our market leader, the economic system. This is important if it is to continue to fulfil the role of providing normative counter-expectations and intermediating, in a secondary manner, between different discourses. And rights require remedies, otherwise they are 'dead letter'. The final pages of the book concerned the potential of such a model of network responsibility that extends out beyond EU law as a blueprint for seemingly intractable problems of network governance. This extension is both necessary and in the offing.

Index

abuse of rights, society of organisations and, 72
academic law, on society of organisations, 67
  in France, 69
  in Germany, 69
  in United States, 69
active risk takers, 69–71
administrative law. *See* global administrative law
Anns v Merton, 102–7
ascription in tort law. *See* normative ascription

bailment, in contract law, 44
Bazley v Curry, 96
Bernard v Attorney General for Jamaica, 96–97
Blyth v Birmingham Waterworks, 46–48
Boston Scientific judgment, 148–54, 174–78
bureaucracy. *See* public bureaucracy

causation
  of risk, 65
  in vicarious liability, 87
CEN. *See* European Committee for Standardisation
civil liability, 38–39
CJEU. *See* Court of Justice for European Union
Classical Legal Thought (CLT), 38
classical tort law
  misfeasance in, 16
  nonfeasance in, 16
CLT. *See* Classical Legal Thought
Code Civil, in France, subjective right and, 30–32
  society of individuals and, 31–32
cognitive rupture, 64–86
cognitivisation
  in EU law, 129–38
    debt-equity ratios as process of, 132
    for financial services regulation, 133–36
    for state liability, 132, 136
  Ladeur on, 9, 25
  of tort law, 2–3, 5–9, 11–12
    society of networks and, 25
coherentism, 33
common calling, in contract law, 44
common law
  continental approach to, 16
  in Germany, 38
  Holmes on, 6–7
  negligence and, 62
  New Approach to Technical Standards under, 198–99
  organisational liability under, 198–99
  social responsibility under, 80
  society of organisations and, 80
The Common Law (Holmes), 37
community standard of care, 50
commutative justice, 62, 73–74
consent. *See* informed consent
constitutional rights-remedies, 144–45
constitutionalisation
  in Germany, 141
  Ladeur on, 146–47
  of private law, 25–26, 31, 145
  re-constitutionalisation, 141
  re-programming of tort law through, 142–44
  from social justice perspective, 141
  society of organisations and, 143–44
  Systems Theory and, 141
  total, 141
  trans-constitutionalisation, 139–40
constitutions, in EU, 138–48

constitutions, in EU (cont.)
 classical private law and, 140–41
 eigenstructures and, 139
consumer protection law, 117
contract law, classical, 31
 coherentism and, 33
 default rules for, 116–17
 employment contracts, 32
 EU law and, 130
 in France, 31–33
 freedom of contract and, 31
 in Germany, 31–32
 liability in, 44
 nonfeasance in, 44
 recovery categories under, 44
 regulatory instrumentalism and, 33
 third-party claims in, 44
 will theory of, 32, 37–40
 Winterbottom v Wright, 41–45
Conway v George Wimpey & Co, 92–93
corporations, in United States, historical development of, 60
corrective justice, 21, 77, 79–81, 85
Court of Justice for European Union (CJEU)
 individual liability and, 27
 network liability and, 27–28
 New Approach to Technical Standards and, 26–27, 157–58, 166–74
 organisational liability and, 27
critical standard of care, 50
Crown Proceedings Act, England (1947), 59, 99

debt-equity ratios, 132
deterrence, 38–39
Dicey, A V, 105–6
discourse ethics, 15
distributive justice, society of organisations and, 58, 77–80
Donoghue v Stevenson, 75–81, 100–10
Durkheim, Emile, 7, 63
Dutton v Bognor Regis, 104–6
duty, as concept, society of organisations and, 73
duty of care, 75–81
 legal science and, 41–45
 from liberal legal orders, 61–62
 organisational liability and, 103
 standard of care compared to, 45
 state liability and, 103

EAL. *See* economic analysis of law
Earl v Lubbock, 44
East Suffolk v Kent, 100–2
economic analysis of law (EAL), systems theory and, 7
eigenstructures
 EU constitutions and, 139
 in Germany, 62
employment contracts, 32
 doctrine of vicarious liability, 52
England
 Crown Proceedings Act, 59, 99
 normative ascription of tort law, 57–59
  royal liability under, immunity from, 57–59
 organisational liability in, 65
  Anns v Merton, 102–7
  Dutton v Bognor Regis, 104–6
  East Suffolk v Kent, 100–2
  Home Office v Dorset Yacht Co Ltd, 102–4, 109
  state liability and, in English case law, 100–10
 Public Authorities Protection Act, 59
enterprise liability, 68
 moral basis of, 97
 social responsibility and, 82
enterprise risk liability, 91–98
Escola v Coca Cola Bottling Co, 90–91
ethics. *See* discourse ethics
EU. *See* European Union
EU law, 127–38
 cognitivisation in, 129–38
  debt-equity ratios as process of, 132
  for financial services regulation, 133–36
  for state liability, 132, 136
 contract law and, 130
 European Committee for Standardisation, 135–36
 Frankovich liability and, 136
 instrumentalist approach to, 131
 law of obligations and, 131
 legal reasoning in, 137–38
 national law and, 147–48
 New Approach to Technical Standards under, 183–85
  fragmentary liability regimes, 193–94
 Paul judgment, 132–35
 private law and, 130–31
 society of networks and, 24–26

structural coupling of, 129–30
European Committee for Standardisation (CEN), 135–36
European Union (EU). *See also* EU law
as network of networks, 139–40, 144
Europeanisation, of tort law, 5–6
experimentalism, 127

fault, 21
in France, 38, 40–41
in Germany, 38, 40–41
negligence and, 49–50
objective, 21
Pufendorf on, 41
society of organisations and, 72
social responsibility and, 81
standard of care and, 49–50
subjective, 21
in tort law, 34–35
in United Kingdom, 83
faute d'autrui (fault for things), 51
faute de service doctrine, 113–14
faute lourde doctrine, 113–14, 185–87, 191–92
feedback loops, in legal systems, 17, 19
financial services, regulation of, under EU law, 133–36
Forrester, Heinz Von, 116
fortuna concept
in France, in tort law, 48
negligence and, 47–48
fragmentary liability regimes, 193–94
frame of reference, for tort law, 2–3, 5–9
France
academic law in, 69
Code Civil
normative ascription of tort law and, 55–56
society of individuals and, 31–32
subjective right and, 30–32
contract law in, 31–33
fault in, as legal concept, 38, 40–41
faute d'autrui, 51
legal science in, 39
normative ascription of tort law in
Code Civil and, 55–56
faute d'autrui, 51
individual liability in, 56–57
public bureaucracy and, 54–57
state liability and, 56–57
organisational liability in, 65, 88
faute de service doctrine, 113–14
faute lourde doctrine, 113–14
social solidarity, 87–88
state liability and, 100, 110–14
society of organisations concept and, 69
tort law in, 40
fortuna concept in, 48
vicarious liability in, 95, 97–98
Francovich liability, 4, 26
EU law and, 136
freedom of contract, 31
French Revolution, social strata after
functional differentiation in, emergence of, 29–30
societal differentiation in, emergence of, 29–30
full quality assurance approach, to NATS, 163
fundamental rights, 142–43

Germany
academic law in, 69
constitutionalisation in, 141
contract law in, 31–32
doctrine of vicarious liability in, 53–54
eigenstructures in, 62
fault in, as legal concept, 38, 40–41
legal science in, 39–40
common law reform in, 38
as legal formalism, 38
social legislation in, 17–22
society of organisations concept in, 69
risk paradigms in, 66–68
tort law in, 40–41
doctrine of vicarious liability, 53–54
normative ascription of, 51
unlawfulness in, 41, 51
vicarious liability in, 97–98
global administrative law, 124–25
globalisation, of tort law, 5–6, 22–23
good faith, private law and, 145–46
governance networks. *See also* New Approach to Technical Standards
historical development of, 158–61
liability of, Court of Justice for European Union and, 27–28
gross negligence, 45–46
Grotius, Hugo, 38–39

Hirman v Westinghouse Elec. Co., 95
holism, 63
Holmes, Oliver Wendell, 37
on common law, 6–7

Home Office v Dorset Yacht Co Ltd, 102–4, 109
horizontal vicarious liability, 179–80
human rights, 143
hybrid negligence regimes, 74

individual liability
  Court of Justice for European Union and, 27
  New Approach to Technical Standards and, 161–74, 197–216
    under common law, 198–99
    Court of Justice for European Union judgments, 166–74
    Schmitt v TÜV Rheinland, 164–74, 182
    in tort law, 197–207
    value chains and, 208–16
  under normative ascription of tort law, in France, 56–57
  supply chain liability and, 208–16
individual responsibility, 3, 22
  normative ascription in tort law and, 86
individual rights, theory of, 6
inferences of negligence, 85
informed consent, 149
injuries, as capital, 21
institutional rights, 148–54
instrumentalism, EU law and, 131
insurance
  origins of, for maritime insurance, 48
  reparations under, 21
  in risk paradigms, 81
interdependence, 22
  society of organisations and, 63
    social responsibility and, 86
international soft law, 211

James, Fleming, 8
justice
  commutative, 62, 73–74
  distributive, 58, 77–80
  procedural, 34
  relational, 34
  of tort law, 7
justiciability, 143

Ladeur, KH
  on bridging concepts, 61–62
  on cognitivisation of law, 9, 25
  on constitutionalisation, 146–47
  on discourse ethics, criticism of, 15
  on negligence, 61–62
  on partial logics, 125
  on positive law, 35
  on society of networks, 23–28
    cognitivisation of law and, 25
    EU law and, 24–26
    private law and, constitutionalisation of, 25–26
    world society thesis, 24–25
  on society of organisations, 20, 22, 74
    knowledge base in society, 83
    tort liability and, 28
  on strict liability, 62
  on systems theory, 13–24
law. *See* legal systems
law of negligence, 8
law of obligations, EU law and, 131
Learned Hand test, 83–84
legal consciousness, 37
legal positivism, 35
legal reasoning
  in EU law, 137–38
  if/then structures of, 23
  neo-formalism in, 153
legal science, 37–41. *See also* fault
  development and origins of, 37
  duty of care, 41–45
  in France, 39
  in Germany, 39–40
    common law reform in, 38
    as legal formalism, 38
  legal consciousness and, 37
  stylistic foundations of, 40
legal systems, law and. *See also* common law; EU law
  acentric architecture of, 36–51
  Classical Legal Thought and, 38
  common law influences on, 39
  factual normality in, 16–17
  feedback loops in, 17, 19
  function of, 117
  modern normative remodelling of, 116–29
    for organizational liability, 120–23
    through organizational responsibility, 118–44
    in society of networks, 119–20
  natural law and, 36–37
  as observing system, 117
  overview of, 219–21
  reprogramming of, 36–51
  in systems theory, 16
Levy v Langridge, 42–45

liability. *See also* state liability; supply chain liability; tort liability; vicarious liability; *specific topics*
  civil, 38–39
  in contract law, 44
  enterprise, 68
    social responsibility and, 82
  Francovich liability, 4, 26
    EU law and, 136
    New Approach to Technical Standards and, 173, 180–92
  individual, 27
  Ladeur on, 62
  network liability, Court of Justice for European Union and, 27–28
  New Approach to Technical Standards and
    Francovich liability, 173, 180–92
    horizontal vicarious liability, 179–80
    legal models of liability, 157
    network liability, 179–80, 192–97
    vertical vicarious liability, 195
  normative model of, 64
  organisational, 27
  overview of, 219–21
liberal law, society of organisations and, 63–64
liberal legal order, 47
  duty of care from, 61–62
  standard of care from, 61–62
liberalism, 36
Luhmann, world society thesis, 24–25

MacPherson v Buick, 78, 88–90
maritime insurance, origins of, 48
Medical Devices Directive, 163–64
misfeasance, in classical tort law, 16

NATS. *See* New Approach to Technical Standards
negligence
  common law and, 62
  gross, 45–46
  hybrid regimes, 74
  inferences of, 85
  Ladeur on, 61–62
  as legal concept, 38
  ordinary, 45–46
  slight, 45–46
  standard of care and, 45–50
    Blyth v Birmingham Waterworks, 46–48
    fault and, 49–50
    fortuna concept and, 47–48
    providence and, 47
    Vaughan v Menlove, 46–47
neighbour principle, 78–79
neo-formalism, in legal reasoning, 153
network liability, Court of Justice for European Union and, 27–28
network responsibility, 4
  in tort law, 2–4
    individual responsibility, 3
    organisational responsibility, 3
New Approach to Technical Harmonisation, 128
New Approach to Technical Standards (NATS), 25, 123–24
  Boston Scientific judgment, 174–78
  Court of Justice for European Union and, 26–27, 157–58, 166–74
  under EU law, 183–85
    fragmentary liability regimes, 193–94
  faute lourde doctrine and, 185–87, 191–92
  historical development of, 158–97
    of network governance, 158–61
  individual liability and, 161–74, 197–216
    under common law, 198–99
    Court of Justice for European Union judgments, 166–74
    Schmitt v TÜV Rheinland, 164–74, 182
    in tort law, 197–207
    value chains and, 208–16
  liability, general, and
    Francovich liability, 173, 180–92
    horizontal vicarious, 179–80
    legal models of, 157
    network, 179–80, 192–97
    vertical vicarious, 195
  organisational liability and, 161–74, 197–216
    under common law, 198–99
    Court of Justice for European Union judgments, 166–74
    full quality assurance approach, 163
    under Medical Devices Directive, 163–64
    PIP judgment, 161–64
    in tort law, 197–207
    value chains and, 208–16
  Paul judgment, 182–83
  responsibility models, 192–97
    assumption of responsibility, 202–4
    crisis of, 196–97
    normative, for network responsibility, 196
  Restatement (Third) of Torts, 160
  self-regulatory regimes, 156

New Approach to Technical Standards (NATS) (cont.)
  state liability and, reconstruction of, 197–216
  theoretical approach to, 156–58
  under tort law
    organisational liability and, 197–207
    value chain models and, 210–16
  value chain models and, 197–216
    individual liability and, 208–16
    under international soft law, 211
    organisational liability and, 208–16
    tort law for, 210–16
nonfeasance
  in classical tort law, 16
  in contract law, 44
normative ascription, in tort law, 51–59
  applications of, 51
  bureaucracy and
    private, 51–54
    public, 54–59
  doctrine of vicarious liability, 51–54
    in employment context, 52
    in German law, 53–54
    justification of, 52–53
  in England, 57–59
    Crown Proceedings Act, 59
    Public Authorities Protection Act, 59
    royal liability in, immunity from, 57–59
  in France
    Code Civil and, 55–56
    faute d'autrui, 51
    individual liability in, 56–57
    public bureaucracy in, 54–57
    state liability in, 56–57
  in Germany, 51
    doctrine of vicarious liability, 53–54
  individual responsibility and, 86
  organisational responsibility and, 86
  Workmen's Compensation Acts, 54
normative model of liability, 64

objective fault, 21
O'Keefe v Ireland, 191
Oliphant, Ken, 65
ordinary negligence, 45–46
organisational liability, 87–114. *See also* state liability
  Court of Justice for European Union and, 27
  in England, 65
    Anns v Merton, 102–7
    Dutton v Bognor Regis, 104–6
    East Suffolk v Kent, 100–2
    Home Office v Dorset Yacht Co Ltd, 102–4, 109
    state liability and, in English case law, 100–10
  enterprise risk liability and, 91–98
  in France, 65, 88
    faute de service doctrine, 113–14
    faute lourde doctrine, 113–14
    social solidarity, 87–88
    state liability and, 100, 110–14
  New Approach to Technical Standards and, 161–74, 197–216
    under common law, 198–99
    Court of Justice for European Union judgments, 166–74
    full quality assurance approach, 163
    under Medical Devices Directive, 163–64
    PIP judgment, 161–64
    in tort law, 197–207
    value chains and, 208–16
  in normative remodelling of legal systems, 120–23
  product liability and, 88–91
    Escola v Coca Cola Bottling Co, 90–91
    MacPherson v Buick, 88–90
    res ipsa doctrine, 88–91
  supply chain liability and, 208–16
  vicarious liability and, 91–98
    as agent-centred, 92
    Conway v George Wimpey & Co, 92–93
    Rose v Plenty, 93
    Salmond test for, 92
organisational responsibility, 3, 22
  normative ascription in tort law and, 86
  in normative remodelling of legal systems, 120–23
outcome responsibility, 19

passive risk takers, 69–71
Paul judgment, 132–35, 182–83
personal rights, 148
PIP judgment, 161–64
pluralism, in tort law, 7–8
positive law, 35
post-national tort law, 219
precaution, 148–49
prevention, in risk paradigms, 65–67
private bureaucracy, in normative ascription of tort law, 51–54
private law

classical, EU constitutions and, 140–41
constitutionalisation of, 25–26, 31, 145
EU law and, 130–31
good faith and, 145–46
instrumental theory of, 7
justice of, 7
philosophical approaches to, 12
reasonableness and, 145–46
subjective rights in, 142
will theory in, 40
procedural justice, 34
product liability, 88–91
Escola v Coca Cola Bottling Co, 90–91
MacPherson v Buick, 88–90
res ipsa doctrine, 88–91
Product Liability Directive, 149–50, 204–7
providence, negligence and, 47
Public Authorities Protection Act, England (1893), 59
public bureaucracy
in normative ascription of tort law, 54–59
society of organisations and, 62–63
public law, society of organisations and, 69
public service-based theory, 86
Pufendorf, Samuel von, 41

reasonableness, private law and, 145–46
reciprocity theory, 6
re-constitutionalisation, 141
regulatory instrumentalism, 33
regulatory intermediaries, 170–71, 182, 213, 215–16, 218
relational justice, 7, 34
reparations, under insurance, 21
res ipsa doctrine, 88–91
responsibility. *See also* network responsibility; organisational responsibility; social responsibility; individual responsibility
assumption of, state liability and, 102
models of, 2–4
individual responsibility, 3, 22
organisational responsibility, 3, 22
New Approach to Technical Standards and, models for, 192–97
assumption of responsibility, 202–4
crisis of, 196–97
normative models, for network responsibility, 196
in society of organisations, 64–86
Restatement (Second) of Torts, 75
Restatement (Third) of Torts, 160
reticular irresponsibility, 125
rights
abuse of, 72
Boston Scientific judgment, 148–54
constitutional rights-remedies, 144–45
fundamental, 142–43
human, 143
institutional, 148–54
moral understanding of, 147–48
personal, 148
subjective
Code Civil and, 30–32
in private law, 142
theory of individual rights, 6
universal understanding of, 147–48
rights-balancing, 153–54
risk compensation theory, 70
risks
as concept, 49
society of organisations and, paradigms for, 65–74
for active risk takers, 69–71
causation of risk, 65
under German law, 66–68
insurance and, 81
for passive risk takers, 69–71
prevention in, 65–67
risk compensation theory, 70
security in, 66
standard of care and, 81–86
Rose v Plenty, 93
Rylands v Fletcher, 84

Salmond test, for vicarious liability, 92, 137
Schmitt v TÜV Rheinland, 164–74, 182
security, in risk paradigms, 66
self-constitutionalisation, society of organisations and, 143–44
slight negligence, 45–46
social interdependence, theory of, 7
interdependence, 22
society of organisations and, 63, 86
social legislation, 17–22, 59, 66, 68
social responsibility, society of organisations and, 77–86
under common law traditions, 80
Donoghue v Stevenson and, 75–81
duty of care and, 75–81
enterprise liability and, 82
fault and, 81
hybrid negligence regimes, 74

social responsibility, society of organisations and (cont.)
  interdependence and, 86
  MacPherson v Buick and, 78
  neighbour principle, 78–79
  in public service-based theory, 86
  Restatement (Second) of Torts, 75
  standard of care and, 81–86
society of networks
  as legal concept, 126
  in normative remodelling of legal systems, 120–23
  tort law and, 23–28
    cognitivisation of law and, 25
    EU law and, 24–26
    private law and, constitutionalisation of, 25–26
    world society thesis, 24–25
  tort liability and, 28
society of organisations, 20, 22. *See also* organisational liability; social responsibility
  abuse of rights and, 72
  academic law and, 67
    in France, 69
    in Germany, 69
    in United States, 69
  cognitive rupture and, 64–86
  commutative justice and, 62, 73–74
  conceptualisation of, 63
  constitutionalisation and, 143–44
  distributive justice and, 58, 77–80
  doctrine of vicarious liability, 64–65
  duty concept and, 73
  enterprise liability, 68
    social responsibility and, 82
  fault and, 72
    social responsibility and, 81
  historical context for, 61–64
  holism and, 63
  interdependence and, 63
    social responsibility and, 86
  Ladeur on, 74
    on knowledge base in, 83
  liberal law and, 63–64
  normative model of liability, 64
  public bureaucracy and, 62–63
  public law and, 69
  responsibility in, 64–86
  self-constitutionalisation and, 143–44
  societal transformation as influence on, 70
  standard of care and
    risk paradigms for, 81–86
    social responsibility and, 81–86
  tort liability and, 28, 68–74
soft law. *See* international soft law
standard of care, 45–51
  community, 50
  critical, 50
  duty of care compared to, 45
  elements of, 50
  from liberal legal order, 61–62
  negligence and, 45–50
    Blyth v Birmingham Waterworks, 46–48
    fault and, 49–50
    fortuna concept and, 47–48
    providence and, 47
    Vaughan v Menlove, 46–47
  society of organisations and
    risk paradigms in, 81–86
    social responsibility and, 81–86
state liability
  assumption of responsibility and, 102
  cognitivisation in EU law, 132, 136
  duty of care and, 103
  in England, in case law, 100–10
  under EU law, 132, 136
  in France
    normative ascription of tort law, 56–57
    organisational liability, 100, 110–14
  New Approach to Technical Standards and, 197–216
  organisational liability and, 98–114
    Anns v Merton, 102–7
    assumption of responsibility and, 102
    under Crown Proceedings Act, 99
    Donoghue v Stevenson, 100–10
    Dutton v Bognor Regis, 104–6
    duty of care and, 103
    East Suffolk v Kent, 100–2
    emergence of, 110–14
    in English case law, 100–10
    in France, 100, 110–14
    Home Office v Dorset Yacht Co Ltd, 102–4, 109
    social role of state, 112–13
    Yuen case, 107–8, 110
subjective fault, 21
subjective right
  Code Civil and, 30–32
    society of individuals and, 31–32
  in private law, 142

supply chain liability, 197–216
  individual liability and, 208–16
  under international soft law, 211
  organisational liability and, 208–16
  tort law for, 210–16
Systems Theory, 9–28
  communication systems, 11–12
    double contingency problems, 11
    individual paradigms, 14–23
    organisational paradigms, 14–23
  constitutionalisation and, 141
  economic analysis of law and, 7, 10
  as frame of reference, 9–14
    as analytical, 10
  Ladeur on, 13–24
    on individual paradigms, 14–23
    models of modernity in, 14–28
    on organisational paradigms, 14–23
  legal systems in, 16
  as observation of observations, 10
  for tort law, 1–2, 6
  Von Forrester and, 116

Technical Standards. *See* New Approach to Technical Standards
third-party claims, in contract law, 44
Tocqueville, Alexis de, 29
tort law, 217–18. *See also specific topics*
  classical
    misfeasance in, 16
    nonfeasance in, 16
  cognitivisation of, 2–3, 5–9, 11–12
  constitutionalisation and, re-programming through, 142–44
  Europeanisation of, 5–6
  fault in, 34–35
  frame of reference for, 2–3, 5–9
  functional complementarity of, 7
  functional equivalence of, 7
  globalisation of, 5–6, 22–23
  goals and purpose of, 8–9
  Grotius and, 38–39
  justice of, 7
  local knowledge in, 34–35
  models of responsibility in, 2–4
    individual responsibility, 3
    organisational responsibility, 3
  New Approach to Technical Standards under
    organisational liability and, 197–207
    value chain models and, 210–16
  pluralism in, 7–8
  post-national, 219
  Restatement (Second) of Torts, 75
  Restatement (Third) of Torts, 160
  society of networks and, 23–28
    cognitivisation of law and, 25
    EU law and, 24–26
    private law and, constitutionalisation of, 25–26
    world society thesis, 24–25
  supply chain liability under, tort law for, 210–16
  systems theory for, 1–2, 6
  theoretical approach to, 1–5
  will theory and, 18
tort liability, 4
  Francovich liability, 4
  models of, 28
  society of networks and, 28
  society of organisations and, 28
tort networks. *See* network responsibility; society of networks
tort theory. *See also* tort law; tort liability
  conceptualisation of, 1–5
total constitutionalisation, 141
trans-constitutionalisation, 139–40
Tuori, Kaarlo, 14–15

United Kingdom (UK). *See also* England
  fault in, 83
  social legislation in, 17–22
  Workmen's Compensation Acts, 54, 67–68
    enterprise liability and, 68
United States (US)
  academic law in, 69
  corporations in, historical development of, 60
  social legislation in, 17–22
  society of organisations concept in, 69
unlawfulness, in German law, 41, 51
US *See* United States

value chain models, liability in, 197–216
  individual liability, 208–16
  under international soft law, 211
  organisational liability and, 208–16
  tort law for, 210–16
Vaughan v Menlove, 46–47
vertical vicarious liability, 195
vicarious liability, 38
  causation in, 87

vicarious liability (cont.)
  doctrine of, 51–54
    in employment context, 52
    in German law, 53–54
    justification of, 52–53
    society of organisations and, 64–65
  expansion of, 93–94, 97
  historical development of, 95–98
    Bazley v Curry, 96
    Bernard v Attorney General for Jamaica, 96–97
    in France, 95, 97–98
    in Germany, 97–98
    Hirman v Westinghouse Elec. Co., 95
  horizontal, 179–80
  organisational liability and, 91–98
    as agent-centred, 92
    Conway v George Wimpey & Co, 92–93
    Rose v Plenty, 93
    Salmond test for, 92, 137
  vertical, 195
victim, as legal concept, 21

will theory
  of contract law, 32, 37–40
  in private law, 40
  tort law and, 18
Williams, Glanville, 87–88
Winterbottom v Wright, 41–45
Workmen's Compensation Acts, U.K. (1897), 54, 67–68
  enterprise liability and, 68
world society thesis, 24–25

Yuen case, 107–8, 110

For EU product safety concerns, contact us at Calle de José Abascal, 56–1°,
28003 Madrid, Spain or eugpsr@cambridge.org.

www.ingramcontent.com/pod-product-compliance
Ingram Content Group UK Ltd.
Pitfield, Milton Keynes, MK11 3LW, UK
UKHW022231220226
468302UK00017B/242
* 9 7 8 1 0 0 9 0 5 4 8 9 8 *